A
Geerhardus Vos
ANTHOLOGY

A
Geerhardus Vos
ANTHOLOGY

BIBLICAL AND THEOLOGICAL INSIGHTS
ALPHABETICALLY ARRANGED

EDITED BY

Danny E. Olinger

P&R
PUBLISHING
P.O. BOX 817 • PHILLIPSBURG • NEW JERSEY 08865-0817

Page design and typesetting by Lakeside Design Plus

Printed in the United States of America

Library of Congress Cataloging-in-Publication Data

Vos, Geerhardus, 1862–1949.
    A Geerhardus Vos anthology : biblical and theological insights alpha-
betically arranged / edited by Danny E. Olinger
        p. cm.
    Includes bibliographical references and index.
    ISBN 0-87552-618-7 (pbk.)
    1. Reformed Church—Doctrines—Miscellanea. I. Olinger, Danny E.,
1964– II. Title.

BX9422.3.V67 2005
230'.42—dc22

                                                            2004063198

Contents

List of Subjects

Preface

The idea for producing an anthology of the key biblical and theological insights of Geerhardus Vos came from reading J. Graham Miller's excellent book, *Calvin's Wisdom: An Anthology Arranged Alphabetically by a Grateful Reader*. To my surprise in reading the prologue of that book, I discovered that Miller and I share a common trait in reading our favorite theologians. We both had developed the habit of writing down the best of what we were reading on index cards. From his foundation of notes, Miller produced an anthology from the writings of John Calvin. I determined from the foundation that I had established to attempt the same type of anthology dealing with the works of the preeminent Reformed biblical theologian Geerhardus Vos.

Over a period of several years, then, I read and reread the works of Vos in English, taking notes and developing the anthology. During that time, James T. Dennison Jr. asked me to deliver a lecture on the writings of Vos at the inaugural Kerux Conference in 1999. The lecture was later published in *Kerux* and appears in edited form as the introduction to this anthology. It serves the dual purpose of introducing Vos to those who are not acquainted with his work and reinforcing his importance to those who are.

My own understanding of Vos's importance can be traced to the late Charles G. Dennison. In addition to sitting under Charlie's preaching and attending the Vos study group meetings he led on a monthly basis, I asked Charlie if he could teach me about redemptive history and biblical interpretation. For many years, then, Charlie graciously invited me into his home on Monday mornings where we would study Vos and the exegesis of biblical texts at his kitchen table. It was not only a wonderful experience for which I will always

xvi

be thankful, but also an education in reading and understanding Vos and biblical-theological exegesis. I would also like to extend my appreciation for the Vos study group that still meets regularly in Sewickley, Pennsylvania. The core members of that group, Lawrence Semel, Daniel Knox, Douglas Snyder, and Robert Broline have all helped me in understanding better the theological contributions of Vos. But, even more so, I have treasured their friendship, and rejoice continually in their Christ-centered ministries and service to the church.

In regard to the actual production of the book, the texts quoted from the respective works of Vos have for the most part been left in their original form. For the sake of consistency or clarity, slight adjustments have been made in capitalization, punctuation, spelling, and the format of Scripture references.

I am thankful for Barbara Lerch and Allan Fisher at P&R Publishing for their warm encouragement and support in moving toward publication. Jason Kirklin contributed greatly in checking the accuracy of the quotes. His enthusiasm and service were vital to the completion of the project. Westminster Seminary assistant librarian and archivist Grace Mullen, a dear friend and fellow lover of the writings of Vos, provided great assistance in sending to me certain documents. I am also grateful for the support of Richard B. Gaffin Jr., who read an early draft of a small portion of the work and encouraged me to move forward. I also wish to express gratitude to Yoshikazu Makita, Stewart Lauer, and the faculty of Kobe Reformed Theological Seminary for the opportunity to lecture on Vos's writings at the seminary in May 2001.

Finally, I am thankful to my wife, Diane, for her understanding, patience, and love. Calling upon her experience as editor of the *Ohio State Law Journal*, she graciously proofread and made invaluable suggestions in sharpening the readability of the material. And, last but not least, I am thankful for my children, Katharine, Daniel, Kristin, and David, and the constant joy they bring. They are truly a gift and blessing from the Lord.

Abbreviations

AC	Review of *Alexander Comrie*, by A. G. Honig
AL/*SW*	"The Alleged Legalism in Paul's Doctrine of Justification," in *SW*
AUP	Review of *Auferstehungshoffnung und Pneumagedanke bei Paulus*, by Kurt Diessner
BIP/*SW*	"The Biblical Importance of the Doctrine of Preterition," in *SW*
BT	*Biblical Theology: Old and New Testaments*
CDW/*GG*	"Christ's Deliberate Work," sermon in *Grace and Glory*
CEH	Review of *The Christology of the Epistle to the Hebrews, Including Its Relation to the Developing Christology of the Primitive Church*, by Harris L. MacNeill
CEV	*Charis, English Verses*
CFTBH/*SW*	"Christian Faith and the Truthfulness of Bible History," in *SW*
CH/*GG*	"The Christian's Hope," sermon in *Grace and Glory*
CT/*SW*	" 'Covenant' or 'Testament'?" in *SW*
DAU	Review of *Der alttestamentliche Unterbau des Reiches Gottes*, by Julius Boehmer
DB	Review of *Die Begriffe Geist und Leben bei Paulus in ihren Beziehungen zu einander*, by Emil Sokolowski
DBD	Review of *Der Begriff Diatheke im Neuen Testament*, by Johannes Behm

GP/*GG*	"The Gracious Provision," sermon in *Grace and Glory*
HED/*SW*	"Hebrews, the Epistle of the *Diathēkē*," in *SW*
HEL	Review of *Het eeuwige leven bij Paulus*, by Johan T. Ubbink
HM/*GG*	"Heavenly-Mindedness," sermon in *Grace and Glory*
HN/*ISBE*	"Heavens, New (and Earth, New)," in *ISBE*
HTR/*GG*	"Hungering and Thirsting after Righteousness," sermon in *Grace and Glory*
IBT/*SW*	"The Idea of Biblical Theology as a Science and as a Theological Discipline," in *SW*
IFP/*SW*	"The Idea of 'Fulfillment' of Prophecy in the Gospels," in *SW*
II	Review of *Israel's Ideal or Studies in Old Testament Theology*, by John Adams
JB/*SW*	"The Ministry of John the Baptist," in *SW*
JG/*SW*	Review of *Jesus and the Gospel: Christianity Justified in the Mind of Christ*, by J. Denney
JM	Review of *Joseph and Moses*, by Buchanan Blake
JP/*SW*	"Jeremiah's Plaint and Its Answer," in *SW*
JRL/*GG*	"The Joy of Resurrection Life," sermon in *Grace and Glory*
KC/*SW*	Review of *Kyrios Christos: Geschichte des Christusglaubens von den Anfängen des Christenthums bis Irenaeus*, by Wilhelm Bousset
KGC	*The Teaching of Jesus Concerning the Kingdom of God and the Church*
KOG/*SW*	"The Kingdom of God," in *SW*
LT	Review of *La Théologie de Saint Paul*, by F. Prat
MEM/*GG*	"The More Excellent Ministry," sermon in *Grace and Glory*

MGMA	Review of *The Messiah of the Gospels* and *The Messiah of the Apostles*, by Charles Augustus Briggs
MHRCEP	"The Modern Hypothesis and Recent Criticism of the Early Prophets," *Presbyterian and Reformed Review* 10
MOP	*The Mosaic Origin of the Pentateuchal Codes*
NABT	"The Nature and Aims of Biblical Theology," *Kerux*
NJ/*ISBE*	"Jerusalem, New," in *ISBE*
NST	"Notes on Systematic Theology," *Reformed Review*
OHGG/*GG*	"Our Holy and Gracious God," sermon in *Grace and Glory*
OLDR/*SW*	"Our Lord's Doctrine of the Resurrection," in *SW*
OM/*ISBE*	"Omnipotence," in *ISBE*
OMP/*ISBE*	"Omnipresence," in *ISBE*
OMS/*ISBE*	"Omniscience," in *ISBE*
PC/*SW*	"The Priesthood of Christ in the Epistle to the Hebrews," in *SW*
PCR/*SW*	"The Pauline Conception of Redemption," in *SW*
PDR	Review of *Paul's Doctrine of Redemption*, by Henry B. Carre
PE	*The Pauline Eschatology*
PEZ	Review of *Paulus en zijn brief aan de Romeinen*, by A. van Veldhuizen
PvBG	Review of *Prolegomena van Bijbelsche Godgeleerdheid*, by E. H. van Leeuwen
QHJ/*SW*	Review of *The Quest for the Historical Jesus: A Critical Study of Its Progress from Reimarus to Wrede*, by A. Schweitzer
R/*GG*	"Rabboni," sermon in *Grace and Glory*
RCEP	"The Modern Hypothesis and Recent Criticism of the Early Prophets," *Presbyterian and Reformed Review* 9

RES	Review of *The Religious Experience of Saint Paul*, by Percy Gardner
RIOT	Review of *The Religious Ideas of the Old Testament*, by H. Wheeler Robinson
RLT/*SW*	"The Range of the Logos Title in the Prologue to the Fourth Gospel," in *SW*
RR/*GG*	"Running the Race," sermon in *Grace and Glory*
SC/*SW*	"The Second Coming of Our Lord and the Millennium," in *SW*
SDFI/*SW*	"Some Doctrinal Features of the Early Prophecies of Isaiah," in *SW*
SDJ	*The Self-Disclosure of Jesus: The Modern Debate about the Messianic Consciousness*
SDL/*SW*	"The Scriptural Doctrine of the Love of God," in *SW*
SFS/*GG*	"Songs from the Soul," sermon in *Grace and Glory*
SIP/*SW*	"The Sacrificial Idea in Paul's Doctrine of the Atonement," in *SW*
SPC	Review of *St. Paul's Conception of the Last Things*, by H. A. A. Kennedy
SR/*GG*	"The Spiritual Resurrection of Believers," sermon in *Grace and Glory*
SSL/*GG*	"Seeking and Saving the Lost," sermon in *Grace and Glory*
SW	*Redemptive History and Biblical Interpretation: The Shorter Writings of Geerhardus Vos*
TCT	Review of *The Theology of Christ's Teaching*, by John M. King
TEC/*GG*	"The Eternal Christ," sermon in *Grace and Glory*
TEH	*The Teaching of the Epistle to the Hebrews*
TG	Review of *The Theology of the Gospels*, by James Moffatt

TOT	Review of *The Theology of the Old Testament*, by A. B. Davidson
TP/*SW*	"The Theology of Paul," in *SW*
TPCR/*SW*	"The Pauline Conception of Reconciliation," in *SW*
TT/*SW*	" 'True' and 'Truth' in the Johannine Writings," in *SW*
UMG/*SW*	"The Ubiquity of the Messiahship in the Gospels," in *SW*
WT/*GG*	"The Wonderful Tree," sermon in *Grace and Glory*

Introduction:
The Writings of Geerhardus Vos

Geerhardus Vos's first book, *The Mosaic Origin of the Pentateuchal Codes* (hereafter, *The Mosaic Origin*), was a thesis Vos prepared for a Hebrew fellowship while a student at Princeton Seminary.[1] It was so exceptional that his professors, particularly William Henry Green, thought it should be published, and it appeared in 1886.[2] In 1948 Vos, with the help of his son Johannes, produced his last book, *The Biblical Theology*.[3] In the sixty-two-year span between the publication of *The Mosaic Origin* in 1886 and *The Biblical Theology* in 1948, Vos put before Christendom an unmatched Reformed biblical-theological corpus. In this corpus made up of books, reviews, articles, sermons, and poems, Vos consistently labored to show that the diverse strands of biblical revelation from Genesis to Revelation are centered in Jesus Christ, his death and resurrection constituting the focal point of the Scriptures.[4]

This is not to say, however, that Vos's writings were greatly esteemed during his own lifetime. Upon Vos's death in 1949 the Trustee's Minutes in the *Princeton Student Bulletin* noted that Vos was one of the most learned and devout in Princeton's long line of teachers, and yet the same Trustee's Minutes mention that his published writings were the despair of his contemporaries.[5] All too often,

1. Geerhardus Vos, *The Mosaic Origin of the Pentateuchal Codes* (New York: A. C. Armstrong & Son, 1886), iii.

2. Richard B. Gaffin Jr., "Preface," in *Redemptive History and Biblical Interpretation: The Shorter Writings of Geerhardus Vos*, ed. Richard B. Gaffin Jr. (Phillipsburg, N.J.: P&R Publishing, 2001), ix.

3. Vos, *The Biblical Theology* (Grand Rapids: Eerdmans, 1985 reprint), vi.

4. Gaffin, "Preface," xvi.

5. *Princeton Seminary Bulletin* 43.3 (Winter 1950): 42.

liberals dismissed his writings while his conservative brethren did not understand them. The end result was that Vos's work was falling through the cracks, ignored and under- (if not un-) appreciated. One example of this is found with his seminal volume, *The Teaching of Jesus concerning the Kingdom of God and the Church* (hereafter, *The Kingdom of God*). Appearing in 1903 as the first major work from Vos during his stay at Princeton, the book went so unnoticed that Vos himself had to write the review that appeared in the *Princeton Theological Review*![6]

When recognition did come for Vos, it was often through the later work and testimony of his students. The very book which Vos had to review himself, *The Kingdom of God*, was brought to the attention of the Reformed world through the efforts of three of Vos's most well-known pupils, Ned B. Stonehouse, John Murray, and Cornelius Van Til. In reviewing Herman Ridderbos's *Coming of the Kingdom* in the pages of the *Westminster Theological Journal*, Stonehouse stated that what Ridderbos had done was indeed noteworthy, but that Vos had already presented the Lord's doctrine of the kingdom from the biblical-theological point of view. Stonehouse wrote, "It is refreshing . . . to receive a new reminder after fifty years [that] Vos's fundamental perspectives and conclusions are by no means outmoded."[7]

6. Geerhardus Vos, review of *The Teaching of Jesus concerning the Kingdom of God and the Church*, by Geerhardus Vos, *Princeton Theological Review* 2 (1904): 335–36.

7. Ned B. Stonehouse, review of *De Komst van het Koninkrijk*, by H. N. Ridderbos, *Westminster Theological Journal* 14 (1952): 160. Stonehouse followed in Vos's footsteps by teaching New Testament biblical theology at Westminster Seminary and always made known his indebtedness to his former mentor. In regard to Stonehouse's appreciation of Vos, there is a fascinating letter (June 7, 1962) in the Archives of the Orthodox Presbyterian Church that Stonehouse wrote in reply to a Dr. Snider of the Free Methodist Seminary of Japan. Snider had asked what five to ten books Stonehouse would recommend for Snider's own background study in teaching a course on New Testament theology. Stonehouse replied that there are almost an endless number of books in this general area, "but very few of them seem to me to be a biblical theology. Unless the authority of the Scripture is maintained, it seems to me that theology should not be described in this way. There is, however, one man who sought to develop a biblical theology on a thoroughly scriptural basis, and that is my old Professor Geerhardus Vos who taught at Princeton." Stonehouse then goes on

In the same year, Murray reviewed the reprinting of Vos's *Kingdom of God* for the *Westminster Theological Journal* and concluded by stating, "Vos provides us with a biblico-theological study which supplies us with the conceptions which must guide and govern our thinking if we are to be faithful to him who went preaching the kingdom of God."[8] And although not directly citing Vos's *Kingdom of God* by name, a decade and a half earlier Murray had defended Vos's kingdom views and exegetical ability in his review article of J. Oliver Buswell's *Unfulfilled Prophecies* in the *Presbyterian Guardian*. Murray wrote, "Dr. Buswell is guilty of pitiable distortion and misrepresentation of a scholar [Vos] who has done more than perhaps any other now living in the defense of the essential deity of the Lord, and that upon the basis of the most exact and penetrating exegesis and apologetic."[9]

Van Til also recognized his dependence upon the work of Vos. In Van Til's book *Christian Theistic Ethics* he argues that the kingdom of God is not realized by the righteousness of man, but by the righteousness of God, which is then given to man for his salvation. Van Til states that Vos beautifully works this out in his book *The Kingdom of God*.[10] Van Til also credits Vos for seeing the kingdom as a present and yet future reality: "The kingdom of God is a present

---

to list for Snider all of Vos's works, gives a brief description of each, and provides information on how to obtain them. Stonehouse mentions no other authors or works and concludes with the admonition, "if you do not know these books, you would find it advantageous to procure them for yourself."

8. John Murray, review of *The Teaching of Jesus concerning the Kingdom of God and the Church*, by Geerhardus Vos, *Westminster Theological Journal* 14 (1952): 231.

9. John Murray, "Dr. Buswell's Premillennialism," review of *Unfulfilled Prophecies*, by J. Oliver Buswell, *Presbyterian Guardian* 3 (Feb. 27, 1937): 207. Murray's high esteem for his former teacher is reflected in a personal letter written to J. Gresham Machen shortly following Murray's graduation from Princeton Seminary. Murray wrote, "It was with a certain amount of apprehension that I learned recently of the ill health of Dr. Vos. We can only hope that he will yet be spared for some time for further usefulness in the church of Christ. His praise is in all the church. Without question, through him as God's instrument, God's truth went into all the earth." Letter to Machen, April 2, 1928 (Archives of Westminster Theological Seminary).

10. Cornelius Van Til, *Christian Theistic Ethics* (Phillipsburg, N.J.: P&R Publishing, 1980), 78.

reality. We have entered into it. But it is also that for the realization of which we daily strive. Dr. Vos has made this two-fold aspect of the kingdom abundantly clear on the basis of the teaching of Jesus. It will not do to teach with modernism that the eschatological aspect of Jesus' teaching of the kingdom is not an important aspect."[11]

Like Stonehouse, Murray, and Van Til, other theologians have also recognized the value of Vos's theological insights. J. Gresham Machen, who believed that Vos had a better-developed "bump of reverence" than some other theological professors,[12] reportedly said, "If I knew half as much as Dr. Vos, I would be writing all the time. . . . Take for example that work of Dr. Vos on the Kingdom of God. Every sentence might well be the topic sentence of a paragraph."[13] Anthony Hoekema credited Vos for his balanced approach to biblical eschatology, which recognizes the full authority of the Scriptures and does full justice to the totality of biblical teaching.[14] H. Henry Meeter recalled that the classes he took from Vos "unearthed . . . some of the

11. Ibid., 90. So close was Van Til to Vos that in 1949 Van Til officiated at the burial service in Roaring Branch, Pennsylvania. According to Richard Gaffin, Van Til himself considered the solemn honor of conducting the service for his teacher and friend to be one of his most cherished memories. See Gaffin, "Geerhardus Vos and the Interpretation of Paul," in *Jerusalem and Athens*, ed. E. R. Geehan (Nutley, N.J.: P&R Publishing, 1971), 228.

12. Ned B. Stonehouse, *J. Gresham Machen* (South Holland, Ill.: Banner of Truth, 1987), 72.

13. Cited in H. Henry Meeter, "Professor Geerhardus Vos: March 14, 1862—August 13, 1949," *The Banner* 84 (Sept. 2, 1949): 1046. Vos's own appreciation for Machen is seen in a letter written to Machen's brother Arthur following J. Gresham's death. Vos wrote, "Dr. Machen for a short while was my pupil at Princeton Seminary. Afterwards for many years, we were associated as members of the faculty, and the time soon came that I learned more from him than had ever been my privilege to impart to him as a teacher. He was indeed a profound scholar, but what counts for more than that, a great man of God and a true defender of our Christian faith in its present-day form" (letter to Arthur Machen, January 5, 1937 [Archives of Westminster Theological Seminary]).

14. Anthony A. Hoekema, *The Bible and the Future* (Grand Rapids: Eerdmans, 1989), 301.

grandest thoughts of Holy Writ,"[15] and acknowledged his indebtedness to Vos in the writing of his doctrinal dissertation, "The Heavenly High Priesthood of Christ."[16] Meredith G. Kline viewed his own book *Kingdom Prologue* as a work that unfolds and develops the infrastructure found in Vos's *Biblical Theology*.[17] Edmund P. Clowney noted that the preacher who takes up Vos for the first time enters a rich new world.[18] Richard Gaffin considered Vos to be a theological genius with unparalleled biblical insight.[19] Sinclair Ferguson stated that Vos was "a scholar *par excellence*"[20] and that in Vos's sermons the sensitive and thoughtful reader "will be struck by the mountain peaks which Vos's mind and vocabulary seemed to be capable of scaling."[21] James T. Dennison Jr. declared that Vos's "presuppositions and panoramic insights into the programmatic or redemptive-historical nature of biblical revelation have justly earned him the title—Father of Reformed biblical theology."[22]

Given the complexity and breadth of Vos's literary output which has influenced not only the above-mentioned Reformed theologians,

15. Meeter, "Professor Geerhardus Vos," 1046. Meeter further wrote: "How often, as one sat in his classroom, one would experience something of the sentiments of the disciples of Emmaus: Did not our heart burn within us, while he talked to us in his lectures, and while he opened to us the Scriptures?"

16. Meeter, *The Heavenly High Priesthood of Christ* (Grand Rapids: Eerdmans-Sevensma, n.d.), 29. Meeter wrote, "I want to acknowledge my indebtedness to my former teacher, Professor Geerhardus Vos, Ph.D., D.D., of Princeton Theological Seminary, whose eminent class lectures on 'The Teachings of the Epistle to the Hebrews,' and whose articles on 'The Priesthood of Christ in the Epistle to the Hebrews,' [*Princeton Theological Review*, 1907] and on 'Hebrews, the Epistle of the Diathēkē,' [*Princeton Theological Review*, 1916] have been a very great help to me in the writing of this dissertation."

17. Meredith G. Kline, *Kingdom Prologue* (Meredith G. Kline, 1991), 5.

18. Edmund P. Clowney, *Preaching and Biblical Theology* (reprint; Phillipsburg, N.J.: Presbyterian and Reformed, 1979), 18.

19. Gaffin, "Preface," vii.

20. Sinclair Ferguson, "Introduction," in *Grace and Glory*, by Geerhardus Vos (Edinburgh: Banner of Truth, 1994), viii.

21. Ferguson, "Introduction," x–xi.

22. James T. Dennison Jr., "The Bible and the Second Coming," in *The Book of Books: Essays on the Scriptures in Honor of Johannes G. Vos*, ed. John H. White (Phillipsburg, N.J.: Presbyterian and Reformed, 1978), 57.

but also many others throughout Christendom, the task of reviewing his writings is an especially humbling endeavor. The reader should be warned that what follows is in no way the last word on Vos. Geerhardus Vos was a complex man, and his writings are no different. Gaffin, who assigns major portions of Vos for his students to read at Westminster Seminary, is fond of saying that every semester a student reading Vos for the first time comes up to him and asks when Vos is going to be translated into English.[23] It is my hope that this preliminary article not only will help those newly introduced to Vos to understand him better, but also will provide some fresh insights to those who have already profited from reading his many works. I will focus briefly on Vos's polemical writings, discuss some of his theological insights, and then consider select themes of his sermons.

Polemical Writings

During the first part of Vos's theological career, his writing style was highly polemical. In *The Mosaic Origin*, Vos wasted little time in establishing what he believed was the posture of liberal criticism. In the very first chapter of that book he argues, "Criticism on the part of our opponents has long since left its independent position, and become subservient to naturalistic tendencies. It manifests a spirit of enmity against the very material upon which it works."[24] The review of *The Mosaic Origin* which appeared in the 1886 edition of *Bibliotheca Sacra* picked up on Vos's distrust of modern critical methods. The reviewer commented, "There is at times something in the tone of the book which seems to indicate a misapprehension of the aims of biblical criticism . . . as if [the critics] were conspiring to overthrow the authority of Scripture and were unscrupulous as to the means which they used to establish their positions."[25]

The words of the reviewer regarding Vos's distrust of liberal criticism and its objectives would be proven correct over the years. Vos

23. Comments made during personal conversation with author, April 1, 1999.
24. Vos, *The Mosaic Origin*, 13.
25. Cited in John F. Jansen, "The Biblical Theology of Geerhardus Vos," *Princeton Seminary Bulletin* 66.2 (Summer 1974): 27–28.

believed that, despite its claims, modern criticism was neither scientific nor objective in dealing with the biblical text as it surrendered "to the most illegitimate subjective impulses."[26] Consequently, according to Vos, the fault with modern criticism and the critics who employ its methodology is that "from the very beginning, and ever increasingly as time goes on, they allow themselves to be guided in their literary criticism by viewpoints drawn from their historico-philosophical interpretation."[27] Vos understood one of the prejudices and failures of liberal theology to be, then, its forcing an alien element upon the biblical text with the liberal critic creating the conflict in the text instead of receiving it from the self-disclosure of God.[28] In Vos's words, "the half century of toil of the 'liberal' theology, instead of rehabilitating the historical Jesus, has only resulted in the construction of a far different figure."[29]

Another failure of criticism, according to Vos, is that in cherishing a most doctrinaire and tenacious belief in the inherent and endless perfectibility of human nature, it puts its faith not in God, but in man.[30]

And, as Vos argued, since faith in the last analysis can be glorified only through its object, modern criticism lacks the supreme glory of the faith of Christianity.[31] But, more than the weakness of such a faith commitment, Vos believed that modern criticism's hope in man revealed its underlying hostility to the Christianity of the Bible.

26. Vos, "The Ubiquity of the Messiahship in the Gospels," in *Redemptive History and Biblical Interpretation*, 335.

27. Vos, review of *Entwicklungsgeschichte des Reiches Gottes*, by H. J. Bestmann, *Presbyterian and Reformed Review* 12 (1901): 480.

28. Vos, *The Self-Disclosure of Jesus* (Grand Rapids: Eerdmans, 1954), 97. Vos commented, "The method we are criticizing is one of dogmatic appreciation rather than of historical investigation. It tells us what Jesus, from a certain standpoint, *ought* to have considered fundamental, and what he *might* have regarded as negligible; but it does not tell us what Jesus actually did assign or would have assigned to these respective categories had the question been put to him."

29. Ibid., 272.

30. Vos, "Eschatology of the Psalter," in *The Pauline Eschatology* (Phillipsburg, N.J.: Presbyterian and Reformed, 1986), 360.

31. Vos, "Eschatology of the Psalter," 360.

Whereas the biblical religion saw man, the creature, as being sub-servient to God, the Creator, the modern consciousness sought to make God subservient to man. If God existed, according to the modern religious spirit, he existed to serve man.[32] This was a main reason why Vos so relentlessly attacked liberal criticism—he believed it reversed the true nature of biblical religion by seeking to have God defer to man. In his sermon "Christ's Deliberate Work," Vos stated: "There is so much talk of service at the present day and it is so often deplorably noticeable that the idea people connect with this word is purely that of benevolence and helpfulness to man. If that is the meaning then the word is not fit to be the synonym of religion. The only true religious service is the one that puts foremost and guards foremost the supreme interest of God. That and nothing else is a true copy of the ministry of Jesus."[33]

For Vos, then, the true religion of the Bible stood opposite the false religion of criticism, and any attempt to combine the two was destructive. In his review of A. B. Davidson's *Theology of the Old Testament*, Vos lamented the fact that Davidson attempted to occupy an intermediate position between the modern view and the old view concerning the interpretation of the Old Testament. Vos stated that Davidson's position "does justice to neither the old nor the modern view and is, on account of its continual oscillation between the two, weaker than either of them."[34] Vos concluded, "Where the critical theories and any solid form of supernaturalism are combined, as is the case in Dr. Davidson's book, they eventually obscure and confuse each other."[35]

Vos did not believe that liberal Christianity and historic Christianity could exist side by side, nor did he believe that a compromise could be reached between the two. In his article "Christian Faith and

32. Vos, "The Alleged Legalism of the Pauline Doctrine of Justification," in *Redemptive History and Biblical Interpretation*, 399.

33. Vos, "Christ's Deliberate Work," in *Grace and Glory*, 255.

34. Vos, review of *The Theology of the Old Testament*, by A. B. Davidson, *Princeton Theological Review* 4 (1906): 116.

35. Ibid., 119.

the Truthfulness of Bible History," he wrote, "We, for our part, believe and we say it deliberately, that it were a thousand times better for the church to be torn and shaken for many years to come by the conflict with criticism than to buy a shameful peace at the stupendous doctrinal sacrifice which such a position involves."[36] In the *Pauline Eschatology* Vos addressed this issue again when he wrote concerning Paul's words in Ephesians 4:17–20: "Perhaps no more incisive criticism of the false modern slogan 'religion is not doctrine but life' than these verses from Ephesians can be conceived. What Paul says is not that perverted ideas concerning religion and Christ are unimportant and their correction negligible; what he maintains is that they are subversive to the true Christian religion, and ought to be resisted to the utmost."[37]

In his defense against the onslaught of liberal Christianity, Vos often wrote articles and reviews which dealt with the main issues of the day. For example, in 1896 on the heels of the trial of Charles Augustus Briggs, Vos severely criticized both Briggs's theological methodology and his view of Scripture.[38]

Another example of Vos's addressing the ecclesiastical situation can be seen in 1902 with his lecture "The Scriptural Doctrine of the Love of God," which opened the ninetieth session of Princeton Theological Seminary. He delivered this address in the context of the confessional crisis going on in the Presbyterian Church in the United States of America (hereafter, PCUSA) over the proposed revision to the Westminster Standards and the adding of the chapter "The Love of God and Missions." Vos argued that a failure to distinguish

36. Vos, "Christian Faith and the Truthfulness of Bible History," in *Redemptive History and Biblical Interpretation*, 468.

37. Vos, *Pauline Eschatology*, 311.

38. Vos, review of *The Messiah of the Gospels* and *The Messiah of the Apostles*, by Charles A. Briggs, *Presbyterian and Reformed Review* 7 (1896): 718–24. On p. 719 of the review, Vos remarked upon Briggs's rejection of historic Christianity: "Such wholesale condemnation of historic Christianity we have long been accustomed to from certain quarters where the contempt of so-called tradition is equaled by the lack of historic information, but in the case of a scholar and student of history like Dr. Briggs it is inexcusable."

between God's general benevolence and God's special love for his own would lessen the Calvinism of the Confession. Such a lessening Vos had no interest in: "the music of the [older orthodoxy] may not always please modern ears because it seems lacking in sweetness; but it ranged over a wider scale and made better harmonies than the popular strains of today."[39]

During the early and middle portions of his career, Vos labored vigorously to defend biblical Christianity. From 1890 to 1919, Vos contributed—by my count—108 reviews of books, many of which dealt with the pressing theological issues of the day.[40] After 1919, however, not one review appeared from his pen. There would be hints of his displeasure at the modern ecclesiastical scene, but such hints would come at the conclusion of articles or in chapters of his books. For instance, Vos did not make direct comment—as far as I can tell—concerning the proposed Plan of Union of 1918 which sought to combine multiple and diverse churches under a common preamble devoid of doctrinal distinctives.[41] Following the horrors of WWI, the mind-set of many wishing to adopt the Plan of Union was that doctrine divides and practice unites. Vos, however, argued at the conclusion of his 1920 article "The Eschatology of the Psalter" that the church would sign its own death-warrant as a distinct institution if it allowed itself to become subservient to the so-called concerns of the present time.[42]

As Vos matured and entered the final stage of his career at Princeton, he was still fighting, but in a different manner. Vos would turn in the 1920s to writing what Murray considered to be Vos's magnum opus,[43] *The Self-Disclosure of Jesus*. In this book Vos argued that the crucial question is whether Jesus believed and claimed that he was the Messiah, for "with its decision [on this issue] the Christian reli-

39. Vos, "The Scriptural Doctrine of the Love of God," in *Redemptive History and Biblical Interpretation*, 425.

40. James T. Dennison Jr., "A Bibliography of the Writings of Geerhardus Vos," in *Redemptive History and Biblical Interpretation*, 547–59.

41. Stonehouse, *Machen*, 304–14.

42. Vos, "Eschatology of the Psalter," 365.

43. Murray, "Dr. Buswell's Premillennialism," 207.

gion stands or falls."[44] Liberalism, especially that branch indebted to Tübingen, sought to eliminate the messianic self-consciousness.[45] Such modernistic efforts to eliminate the messianic self-consciousness cast doubt upon Christ's claim to be the object of faith, prayer, and worship,[46] and if Christ was mistaken, that is, if Christ did not fully understand himself, then a blow is struck to the heart of true religion which consists of the fellowship that takes place between God and man. Vos stated the matter plainly: "No one can take a Savior to his heart in that absolute, unqualified sense, which constitutes the glory of religious trust, if there persists in the background of his mind the thought that this Savior failed to understand himself."[47] However, Vos emphatically refuted the liberal contention that Jesus failed to understand himself. Commenting upon Matthew 11, Vos wrote, "Jesus' joy and thanksgiving do not relate to something taking place outside of himself, in regard to which he, although rejoicing in it, would after all be a mere spectator. Jesus thanks God because his own person is the pivot, the center, of the whole transaction."[48]

Theological Writings

There will be movement, then, for Vos in the way that he critiqued modern thought, but there will also be movement for Vos theologically. Charles Dennison maintained that Vos was working out of a classical grid in regard to theology early in his career, but that, as he matured as a biblical theologian, he in some ways—not in every way, but in some ways—left the classical grid behind.[49]

44. Vos, *Self-Disclosure*, 11.
45. Ransom Lewis Webster, "Geerhardus Vos (1862–1949): A Biographical Sketch," *Westminster Theological Journal* 40 (1978): 309.
46. Vos, "Modern Dislike of the Messianic Consciousness of Jesus," in *Redemptive History and Biblical Interpretation*, 331.
47. Vos, *Self-Disclosure*, 16.
48. Ibid., 147.
49. Comments made at the January 11, 1999 meeting of the "Vos Monday" study group. This is not to say that Vos lacked a covenantal, redemptive-historical hermeneutic in his younger days. Upon acceptance of the newly created chair of biblical theology at Princeton Seminary, Vos put forth basic principles to govern the

One example of the movement of Vos was his shift in seeing the biblical writers as theologians. In his inaugural lecture, "The Idea of Biblical Theology as a Science and as a Theological Discipline" (hereafter, "The Idea of Biblical Theology"), Vos stated, "As the heavens contain the material for astronomy and the crust of the earth for geology, so the mighty creation of the Word of God furnishes the material for theology in this scientific sense, but is no theology."[50] In the same paragraph he added, "that which the apostles teach is in no sense primarily to be viewed under the aspect of theology."[51] With these statements, Vos appeared at this early stage of his career to be in agreement with Abraham Kuyper that Scripture itself is not theology, but underlies it.[52]

Some four decades later in the *Pauline Eschatology*, however, Vos steadfastly maintained that Paul was engaged in a theological enterprise and that what he taught must be viewed under the aspect of theology. In the *Pauline Eschatology* Vos argued that if one is to gain insight into Paul, then one must comprehend "the apostle's construction of Christian truth."[53] Too often, however, the "Pauline system of truth" is not comprehended because "Paul's mind as a theological thinker was far more exacting" than the facile one-sidedness which weighs down many of his interpreters.[54]

---

work of the biblical theologian in his 1893 inaugural address, "The Idea of Biblical Theology as a Science and as a Theological Discipline." In this address, he presented what he believed the Bible to teach concerning the object and aim of theology, the relationship of revelation and redemption, the centrality of the covenant, and the nature of biblical theology. It is undeniable that the foundation for much of what Vos wrote is found in this lecture, but Dennison maintained that one errs in trying to understand Vos's contribution if it is seen as a finished product from the beginning. Dennison believed that, in analyzing the whole of Vos's theological corpus, we must take into consideration his internal and methodological development from working with the biblical text year after year.

50. Vos, "The Idea of Biblical Theology as a Science and as a Theological Discipline," in *Redemptive History and Biblical Interpretation*, 21.

51. Ibid.

52. Abraham Kuyper, *Encyclopedie der Heilige Godgeleerdheid* (Kampen: J. H. Kok, 1909), 3:167.

53. Vos, *Pauline Eschatology*, 148.

54. Ibid., 148–49.

In the *Biblical Theology*, Vos elaborated on the implications of the biblical writers engaging in theological activity. There he argued, "We know full well that we ourselves live just as much in the New Testament as did Peter and Paul and John."[55] Stressing the continuity that existed between himself and others as contemporary interpreters and the writers of the New Testament, Vos stood at a distance from his early Kuyper-like statement in the "The Idea of Biblical Theology" that the Word of God only furnishes the material for theology. Vos came to understand the roots of the theological enterprise to be in the text itself, and believers to be engaged in a common theological endeavor with the biblical writers.[56] In his article "Geerhardus Vos and the Interpretation of Paul," Gaffin elaborates upon what he believes is a crucial hermeneutical insight of Vos's in pointing out the continuity between the contemporary interpreter and the biblical writers. Gaffin writes, "The concept of theology is redemptive-historically conditioned. The essence of theology is interpretation of the history of redemption. Consequently, it is not only possible but necessary to speak of a theological continuity between Paul and his interpreters."[57]

Another key example of movement in Vos's views is found in comparing his earlier and later statements on justification. In 1903, when Vos wrote the article "The Alleged Legalism in Paul's Doctrine of Justification," Vos argued that the doctrine of justification stands central in Paul's teaching and is the entrance into understanding the apostle: "Paul's mind was to such an extent forensically oriented that he regarded the entire complex of subjective spiritual changes that take place in the believer and of subjective spiritual blessings enjoyed by the believer as the direct outcome of the forensic work of Christ applied in justification."[58]

However, by 1930 with the publication of *The Pauline Eschatology* Vos reversed direction on this point as he argued that eschatology is the key to penetrating Paul's thought. In this latter work Vos indi-

55. Vos, *Biblical Theology*, 303.
56. Vos, *Pauline Eschatology*, 44.
57. Gaffin, "Geerhardus Vos," 232.
58. Vos, "Alleged Legalism," 384.

14

cated that justification must be seen in light of the eschatological reality. Vos declared, "It [eschatology] no longer forms one item in the sum-total of revealed teaching, but draws within its circle as correlated and eschatologically-complexioned parts practically all of the fundamental tenets of Pauline Christianity. . . . It will appear throughout that to unfold the apostle's eschatology means to set forth his theology as a whole."[59] Vos also argued, "The eschatological strand is the most systematic in the entire fabric of the Pauline thought-world. For it now appears that the closely interwoven soteric tissue derives its pattern from the eschatological scheme, which bears all the marks of having the precedence in his mind."[60]

By placing the eschatological consideration first, something that Vos began to do with increasing consistency as he matured as a theologian, Vos blazed a comparatively new trail in Reformed theology. Traditional Reformed theology started from the standpoint of the *ordo salutis* and concluded that aspects of it, like justification by faith, were Paul's primary emphasis. Vos, in contrast to traditional Reformed theologians, understood the primary concern of Paul to be with the *historia salutis* as that history has attained to eschatological finality in the death, resurrection, and ascension of Christ.[61] Vos argued, "The question is not so much whether the doctrines of justification and possession of the Spirit and union with Christ carry with themselves an outlook of the future, but rather whether those acts and states to which these doctrines refer are not from the outset eschatological acts and states, or more strictly speaking, anticipations in this life of what had previously been regarded as reserved for the end."[62]

59. Vos, *Pauline Eschatology*, 11.

60. Ibid., 60.

61. According to Gaffin, ("Geerhardus Vos," 237), Vos and Herman Ridderbos are agreed in this understanding of the Pauline theology. In Gaffin's words, both view Paul's primary theological concern to be "with the *historia salutis* as that history has attained to its eschatological denouement in the death and especially the resurrection of Christ. Ridderbos expressed this belief deliberately and programmatically, while Vos expressed it implicitly, but also unmistakably."

62. Vos, review of *St. Paul's Conception of the Last Things*, by H. A. A. Kennedy, *Princeton Theological Review* 3 (1905): 485.

It is in this light that Vos represented a theological revolution at Princeton Seminary. Charles Hodge, representative of the Old Princeton theology, led with the *ordo salutis* in his theologizing.[63] William Dennison comments concerning the place of eschatology in Hodge's *Systematic Theology*, "Hodge's discussion of eschatology is an isolated deliberation of the 'state of the soul after death.' "[64] In contrast to Hodge, Vos pointed the church to a redemptive-historically conditioned methodology more in line with revelation itself. As Vos argued in support of a redemptive-historical or covenantally conditioned methodology, "God has not revealed himself in a school, but in the covenant; and the covenant as a communication of life is all-comprehensive, embracing all the conditions and interests of those contracting it."[65]

Vos, then, while working within the confines of the old system, continually pushed Princeton in a new direction theologically. Vos saw the Bible as leading with eschatology, he saw Jesus Christ leading with eschatology, and he believed that the Christian should lead with eschatology. In Scripture "the eschatological is an older strand in revelation than the soteric,"[66] and the historical was first before the theological,[67] and it should be the same for the Christian united to Christ and participating in the drama of redemption revealed through the Word of God.

Failure to grasp the primacy of eschatology to Vos leads to a failure to understand Vos fully. Foundational to Vos's hermeneutic is seeing Paul as arguing that Adam irrespective of sin had an eschatology, the hope of a higher future and communion with God. Before man needed to be saved from his sin, he had an eschatology in that he possessed a future hope.[68] As Vos argued in *Biblical Theology*, man was created per-

---

63. William Dennison, *Paul's Two-Age Construction and Apologetics* (Lanham, Md.: University Press of America, 1985), 88.

64. Ibid., 87.

65. Vos, "Idea of Biblical Theology," 10.

66. Vos, *Biblical Theology*, 140.

67. Vos, *Pauline Eschatology*, 41.

68. Vos, "The Eschatology of the New Testament," in *Redemptive History and Biblical Interpretation*, 49. In a private conversation with the author, June 24, 1991,

fectly good in a moral sense, yet he could rise to a still higher estate. The eschatological state is the goal of man irrespective of the fall into sin.[69] Vos stated the matter plainly in *The Pauline Eschatology*: "the eschatological process is intended not only to put man back at the point where he stood before the invasion of sin and death, but to carry him higher to a plane of life not attained before the probation nor, as far as we can see, attainable without it."[70] The attraction of heaven "is not something brought into the religious mind through sin."[71]

Vos believed, then, that the ultimate design of all of God's converse with man is to the end that God might make his abode with his people.[72] In the garden, even before the fall into sin, God came and he went—an acquaintance, if you will, of indirection that in the end is satisfying neither to God nor to man. Thus, as Vos wrote, "even if no tempter had existed,"[73] some type of probation for Adam would have been necessary to achieve the perfect communion which the tree of life symbolized. Adam, however, fell short, and unless God himself came to fulfill the demand of the covenant, the hope of that perfect communion with God would be lost.

What is lost with the first Adam's disobedience is realized with the coming of the second Adam. The fulfillment of the goal set before man from the beginning comes in the person and work of Jesus Christ. The coming age has begun to be present with the death and resurrection of Christ.[74] In particular, the resurrection of Jesus Christ

Charles Dennison maintained that the fundamental key to comprehending Vos's thought is understanding Vos's belief that the Bible teaches that before man needed salvation from sin, he had an eschatology, i.e., a future hope of communion with God on a higher plane. For Dennison's further comments on Vos, see "Geerhardus Vos and the Orthodox Presbyterian Church," in *History for a Pilgrim People: The Historical Writings of Charles G. Dennison*, ed. Danny E. Olinger and David K. Thompson (Willow Grove, Pa.: Committee for the Historian, 2002), 67–87.

69. Vos, *Biblical Theology*, 22.

70. Vos, *Pauline Eschatology*, 72.

71. Vos, "Heavenly-Mindedness," in *Grace and Glory*, 113.

72. Vos, *Biblical Theology*, 106.

73. Ibid., 33.

74. Vos, "The Eschatological Aspect of the Pauline Conception of the Spirit," in *Redemptive History and Biblical Interpretation*, 115.

not only serves to restore what has become the prey of decadence and death, but also achieves for man the goal of the pre-fall estate. The purpose of the resurrection is not to get man back to a pre-fall environment, but to place man in the eschatological goal of the pre-fall estate. Through the death and resurrection of Jesus Christ, the objective in view in revelation—uninterrupted personal intercourse between God and man—has been realized. As Vos commented, "To be a Christian is to live one's life not merely in obedience to God, nor merely in dependence on God, nor even merely for the sake of God; it is to stand in conscious, reciprocal fellowship with God, to be identified with him in thought and purpose and work, to receive from him and give back to him the ceaseless interplay of spiritual forces."[75]

Further, Vos argued that in Christian eschatology the Christ occupies center stage from the beginning to the end: "All developments, all transactions, all gifts, all experiences that make up the drama of the great world-change are related to him and derive their significance from him; he is the representative and exponent of the future life in its totality."[76] Consequently, according to Vos, the redemption Christ earns is graciously bestowed on those who are in relationship to him. Participation in the merits which flow from Christ's work is only through faith which effects a personal union with Christ. This faith, Vos argued, consists "not merely in the mental acceptance of [Christ's] sacrifice as a historic fact, but . . . mystically feeds upon him, the living sacrifice as he now exists in heaven."[77] For the one, then, whose life is hid with Christ in God, there is conformity to the life of the Savior. Vos commented, "Man's salvation appears to Paul not merely associated with Christ, but capable of description in terms of Christ."[78]

Being in covenantal relation with the risen Christ, the Christian, then, lives out of resurrection life earned by Christ and bestowed by

75. Vos, "Hebrews, the Epistle of the Diathēkē," in *Redemptive History and Biblical Interpretation*, 186.

76. Ibid., 197.

77. Vos, "The Gracious Provision," in *Grace and Glory*, 240.

78. Vos, "The Theology of Paul," in *Redemptive History and Biblical Interpretation*, 360.

grace, and that even as he prepares for resurrection life bodily in the new heavens and the new earth. Vos described this as the semi-eschatological nature of the Christian life, for the Christian, by the gracious gift of God, possesses the goal even as he moves toward it.[79] The kingdom of heaven has arrived, the blessings of the eschaton are a present possession for the believer, but yet the consummation of all things still awaits.[80]

Vos believed, therefore, that it is imperative for the believer living semi-eschatologically to keep in contact with the heavenly realm which has been ushered in by the death and resurrection of Christ: "The heavenly world is to the believer what the earth was to the giant in ancient mythology; so long as he remains in contact with it, an unintermittent stream of new spiritual power flows into his frame."[81] According to Vos, "The heaven in which the Christian by anticipation dwells is not the cosmological heaven; it is the thoroughly redemptive heaven, a heaven become what it is through the progressive upbuilding and enrichment pertaining to the age-long work of God in the sphere of redemption. As such it not only in principle beatifies but also still beckons onward the believer to its final consummation."[82]

As the Christian is beckoned onward to heaven, however, he is not to be indifferent to the natural environment in which he finds himself by the providence of God. What is incumbent on the Christian who finds himself in this present evil age is to gravitate toward the future life so that earthly concerns are subordinate and subservient to the heavenly realm.[83] In other words, "heavenly-mindedness can never give rise to neglect of the duties pertaining to the present life. It is the ordinance and will of God that not apart from, but on the

79. Vos, "Eschatological Aspect," 92. There Vos states, "Through the appearance of the Messiah, the great representative figure of the coming aeon, [the] new age has begun to enter into the actual existence of the believer. He has been translated into a state which, while falling short of the consummated life of eternity, yet may be truly characterized as semi-eschatological."

80. Vos, "Eschatology of the New Testament," in *Redemptive History and Biblical Interpretation*, 26.

81. Vos, "Running the Race," in *Grace and Glory*, 137.

82. Vos, *Pauline Eschatology*, 40.

83. Vos, "Running the Race," in *Grace and Glory*, 132.

basis of, and in contact with, the earthly sphere man shall work out his heavenly destiny."[84]

The agent for securing this heavenly dynamic, according to Vos, is the Spirit of God.[85] Christ is equipped by the Spirit for his mission; now, the Spirit equips the church for her mission. The Spirit is the epitome of the age to come. The Spirit is the communication of that life which pertains to the world to come. The distinctiveness of the Christian religion as it is lived by those who embrace it and the ethic derived from it is through the spiritual realm. The Spirit's proper realm is the future age, but from there he projects himself into the present, and becomes a prophecy of himself in his eschatological operations.[86]

Reading the Scriptures, then, in light of Christ's accomplishment, which means the dawning of the new age and outpouring of the Spirit upon the elect of God, Vos challenged his readers to see the Christian's heavenly citizenship in all of its fulness. As Vos stated in *The Pauline Eschatology*, the church is used to thinking and theologizing out of the present into the future, because its base of existence is in the present. However, the more biblical way to think and theologize and live is out of the future—a future which has become a reality with Christ's resurrection. Vos preached, then, that the Christian must bring the ultimate things which are now his to the forefront of his consciousness in order that in light of these things he might learn the better to understand the provisional and preparatory.[87] Consequently, Vos argued that the gauge of health in the Christian is the degree of his gravitation toward the future, eternal world.[88] The Christian possesses the goal in principle even as he moves toward it and is directed in his thinking by it.

Every task of Christian service is at the same time a means of grace from and an incentive to work for heaven.[89] The Christian's outlook is not bounded by the present life and the present world. The Chris-

---

84. Vos, "Heavenly-Mindedness," 113.
85. Vos, "Eschatological Aspect," 122.
86. Vos, *Pauline Eschatology*, 165.
87. Ibid., 42.
88. Vos, "Eschatology of the Psalter," 363.
89. Vos, "Heavenly-Mindedness," 119.

tian sees that which is and that which is to come in their true proportions and in their proper perspective. The center of gravity of the Christian's consciousness lies not in the present but in the future.[90] What Vos challenged his readers to see, then, was that the end conditions the present existence of the believer. "Eschatology posits an absolute goal at the end of the redemptive process corresponding to an absolute beginning of the world in creation: for then, no longer a segment but the whole sweep of history is drawn into one great perspective, and the mind impelled to view every part in relation to the whole."[91]

The disastrous result of not having the end condition one's thought and life can be seen in Israel who in her disobedience perceives that the land is her ultimate end. The hope of heaven evaporates for Israel, and she refuses to give up her life in this creation for her God. The Old Testament period was primarily a prospective period, a period in which Israel was reminded at every step that something higher and better was yet to appear with the coming visitation of God.[92] In her sin, however, Israel ceases to possess an eschatological vision which has God at the center of her hope. As Vos argued in "The Alleged Legalism," Israel replaces God as the center of expectation and no longer desires to be expendable for God and his glory. Consequently, "the Judaistic spirit made itself the end and God the means."[93] The Judaistic spirit gave itself the glory, and in making God the means, it made him into a passive God who must be subservient to Israel.

How easily not just unfaithful Israel, but also man in his sin enlists God as a means in the fight for creature-betterment, almost oblivious to the fact that the Lord is the King of glory for whose sake the whole world exists and the entire battle is waged.[94] Vos believed that the Bible teaches that the end of all existence does not rest in the creature, but in the Creator.[95] "God is the center of every hope worth

90. Vos, The Christian's Hope," in *Grace and Glory*, 142.
91. Vos, "Hebrews," 193.
92. Vos, "Running the Race," 130.
93. Vos, "Alleged Legalism," 391.
94. Vos, "The Wonderful Tree," in *Grace and Glory*, 17.
95. Vos, "Eschatology of the Psalter," 358.

cherishing for man, and to take God as source and end of all that exists and happens, and to hold such a view suffused with the warmth of genuine devotion . . . is by reason of its essence a veritable theological tree of life."[96]

The believer longs for heaven because it is the realm of closest embrace of God:

> Those who looked for the city that has foundations sought it for no other reason than that its maker and builder is God. It is because it is the city of God, the structure in which he has embodied his own perfection, in which his thoughts and purposes for his own stand objectified, that it forms a worthy object of the supreme religious quest of the believer. In it is God at every point, and those who dwell in it see him constantly. The measure of their desire for it becomes the measure of their love for God.[97]

Vos also declared, "A heaven that is not illumined by the light of God, and not a place for closest embrace of him, would be less than heaven."[98] In answering the objection of those who complain that glorifying God will at some point in heaven become redundant, Vos replied, "There clings an earth and time–savor to questioning what there will be to occupy one's self withal when arrived above. As if the Lord God himself would not be there with his inexhaustible fulness! In his presence there can be neither surfeit nor tedium."[99]

Vos also saw heavenly-mindedness at the heart of the biblical ethic: "The believer's whole ethico-religious existence, the sum-total of his Christian experience and progress, all that is distinctive of his life and conduct demands being viewed as a preparation for the crowning grace of the resurrection."[100] Through the work of Christ "the believer has been in principle snatched out of this present evil world and translated into the eternal kingdom of the Son of God's love."[101]

96. Vos, *Pauline Eschatology*, 61.
97. Vos, "Hebrews," 229.
98. Ibid., 122.
99. Vos, *Pauline Eschatology*, 316.
100. Ibid., 157.
101. Vos, "Hebrews," 197.

In regard, then, to ethical behavior, the believer must purge himself from all leaven as he finds the members of his body in the world even though in another sense he is already unleaven as he participates in the world to come.[102] Vos maintained that to be a Christian meant "to live not merely in obedience to God, nor merely in dependence on God, nor even merely for the sake of God; it is to stand in conscious, reciprocal fellowship with God, to be identified with him in thought, purpose and work, to receive from him and give back to him in the ceaseless interplay of spiritual forces."[103]

Sermons

We move finally to a more thorough consideration of Vos's sermons. Machen as a student at Princeton Seminary, upon hearing Vos preach his Easter sermon "Rabboni," told his mother that the sermon "rather surprised me . . . [for] Vos is usually rather too severely theological."[104] In the sermons, as we have already noted, the theological insights are there—the primacy of eschatology, the centrality of union with Christ, heavenly-mindedness and its relationship to Christian ethics—but in an arguably more palatable form.

I, for one, was never the same after reading the six sermons of the original 1922 edition of *Grace and Glory*. The centrality of Christ, the mutual fellowship between God and ourselves in the covenant, and our participation in eschatological blessings are what Vos preaches to us over and over again in his sermons. To read that, and to be directed by Vos back to the Scriptures themselves to see these blessed realities centered in the promised Messiah and fulfilled in his appearance for my salvation and participation in the age to come absolutely ruined me. The old way of theologizing with its inadvertent focus upon the self would not do. Clowney correctly comments that in Vos's sermons "we hear a scholar preaching to theological students . . . but with a burning tenderness and awesome realism that springs from

102. Vos, "The Sacrificial Idea in Paul's Doctrine of the Atonement," in *Redemptive History and Biblical Interpretation*, 381.
103. Vos, "Hebrews," 186.
104. Stonehouse, *Machen*, 72.

the grace and glory of God's revelation, the historical actualization of his eternal counsel of redemption."[105]

In Vos's sermons, he proclaimed in a variety of ways that God and his people have been joined in covenant fellowship through the work of Jesus Christ. Vos emphasized continually that in the covenant there is a mutual surrender of God and man. God condescends and gives himself to his people, and his people give themselves to their God. Vos believed that the essence of religion is a true communion between God and man, and in his sermonizing Vos often stressed communion with God as a present reality and future hope for the believer. For instance, in "The Wonderful Tree" Vos stated, "When Jehovah, entering into covenant with Israel says, 'I will be unto you a God, and ye shall be unto me a people,' this means infinitely more than the trite idea: henceforth you shall worship me and I will cultivate you. It is the mutual surrender of person to person."[106] In "The More Excellent Ministry" Vos declared, "The entire Christian life, root and stem and branch and blossom, is one continuous fellowship with Christ."[107] In "Songs from the Soul" Vos proclaimed, "The secret of the Lord . . . is the intimate converse between friend and friend as known from human life where there is no reserve, but thoughts and feelings of the heart are freely interchanged . . . the covenant being conceived not as a formal contract . . . but as a communion in which life touches life and intertwines with life so that the two become mutually assimilated."[108] In "The Christian's Hope" Vos said, "And the believer knows . . . that as long as he cannot fully possess God, God cannot fully possess him nor be completely glorified in him. This sentiment lies at the basis of all genuine God-born Christian hope."[109] In "Heavenly-Mindedness" Vos stated, "Traced to its ultimate root heavenly-mindedness is the thirst of the soul after God, the living God."[110]

105. Clowney, *Preaching*, 19.
106. Vos, "Wonderful Tree," 9–10.
107. Vos, "The More Excellent Ministry," in *Grace and Glory*, 94–95.
108. Vos, "Songs from the Soul," in *Grace and Glory*, 172–73.
109. Vos, "The Christian's Hope," 155.
110. Vos, "Heavenly-Mindedness," 113.

Vos impressed upon his readers, then, in a myriad of ways that the heart of religion is to be bound to the person of God in Jesus Christ. To be bound to Jesus Christ, and to live in light of that relationship, is what Vos typically drove toward in his sermons. In "The Spiritual Resurrection of Believers" Vos declared, "You must begin with [Christ] and end with him. If you are loved, it has been in him, as a member of his body. Therefore look to him! Only when he turns you away will you have the right to say that God has not loved you with an everlasting love, but not until then."[111]

Vos also fought against what he believed were the misguided attempts of some in Christendom to place the emphasis of the Christian life on anything other than communion with the living God. He declared in "Songs from the Soul," "I need not tell you that there is a tendency at the present day to make the religious life seek the surface, the periphery; to detach it more or less from its center which lies in the direct face-to-face communion of the soul with God."[112] The thirst that the Christian has for full fellowship with his God in an environment where there is no sin is the substance of the religion of the heart and drives the Christian in his service to his God in this world.[113] In "The Wonderful Tree" Vos stated quite forcefully, "Here lies the infallible test of what is truly religious in our so-called religion. Everything that lacks the unique reference to God, as its supreme owner and end, is automatically ruled out of that sphere."[114] "Religion," as Vos proclaimed in his sermon "Our Holy and Gracious God," "is love of God or a sense of dependence upon God but not entirely after the same manner as we cherish love for our fellow creatures or feel dependent on them in certain relations. Religion begins when we realize our dependence on the absolute, infinite being, the eternal, omnipresent, omnipotent, omniscient God."[115] In his sermons he sought consistently to demonstrate this belief that the entirety of man's existence is to be for his God—something that Vos

111. Vos, "The Spiritual Resurrection of Believers," in *Grace and Glory*, 230–31.
112. Vos, "Songs from the Soul," 179.
113. Vos, "The Joy of Resurrection Life," in *Grace and Glory*, 165–66.
114. Vos, "Wonderful Tree," 15.
115. Vos, "Our Holy and Gracious God," in *Grace and Glory*, 267–68.

believed was written over the entrance of the temple of Reformed theology.[116]

Interestingly, Vos often addressed preaching itself in the sermons he delivered. One possible reason for this might be that Vos had his audience in view, seminarians soon to be preachers themselves, as he proclaimed God's Word in the chapel at Princeton. Vos believed that there is a straightforwardness to preaching which is proportionate to the preacher's own trust in the absolute and inherent truthfulness of the gospel message.[117] The preacher must be convinced not only of the truthfulness of the gospel message, but also of the necessity of the supernatural work of God centered in Jesus Christ. Men preaching moral example do not preach Christ. Vos maintained that "to preach the risen Christ means to preach a gospel which claims to come with the demonstration of the Spirit and with power. It means to assume that this world is dead in trespasses and sins; and that no word of persuasion, no force of example, no release from the body, in fact nothing short of a new creation can give it life."[118] Vos cried out, "Oh the pity and shame of it, the Jesus that is being preached but too often is a Christ after the flesh, a religious genius, the product of evolution, powerless to save."[119] Vos then, admonished those who would be preachers:

> Whatever topic you preach on and whatever text you choose, there ought not to be in your whole repertoire a single sermon in which from beginning to end you do not convey to your hearers the impression that it is impossible for you to impart to them what you want other than as a correlate and consequence of the eternal salvation of their souls through the blood of Christ, because in your own conviction that alone is the remedy which you can honestly offer to a sinful world.[120]

116. Vos, "The Doctrine of the Covenant in Reformed Theology," in *Redemptive History and Biblical Interpretation*, 242.

117. Vos, "More Excellent Ministry," 100.

118. Vos, "Joy of Resurrection Life," 163.

119. Vos, "More Excellent Ministry," 102.

120. Vos, "Gracious Provision," 238. It must be noted that Vos himself does not always in a strict fashion follow his own advice. For example, while his sermon "The

Admittedly, what has been said examines only the top of the iceberg in attempting to analyze the writings of Vos. Much more could, and should be done, in seeking to understand the significance of Vos's contributions. For instance, Vos often directed his readers to see that there is a connectedness in the covenant between doctrine and life.[121] Doctrine is not isolated to articles of faith, but is a way of life in the covenant. What Vos saw as the biblical view of the active relationship between belief and duty cuts across the modern notion that "doctrine divides and practice unites." With biblical Christianity, doctrine and practice are united.

Another area of further study could be found in Charles Dennison's suggestion that Vos saw Jesus as a theologian. In one of his last presentations on Vos to the pastor's study group that meets monthly to discuss Vos's works, Dennison commented upon Vos's concluding chapter, "Recapitulation," in *The Kingdom of God*. He stated:

> This is no summary in the ordinary sense. . . . Vos must be seeing Jesus as theologian, who in the Synoptics, at least, sets forth the kingdom of God as the center point of his theology. This means that Vos, in some sense, is looking for the roots of theological method, not simply in the Scriptures as theological, but in Jesus as theologian.
>
> For Vos, Jesus' theological method rises first of all from the historical reality of God's interaction with this world. This historical reality involves the historical unity of God's Old Testament work and Jesus' labors recorded in the gospels. Jesus himself is conscious of this as he sets forth the kingdom as a great system of objective, supernatural facts and transactions, a system (or "world") which means this world's transformation or renewal.

Wonderful Tree" expresses deep truths concerning the covenant and the nature of biblical religion, it directly says little of Christ and his work.

121. See, for example, Vos's comments on the relationship of life and doctrine in his article "The Christian Faith and the Truthfulness of Bible History" and in his sermons "The Wonderful Tree" and "Songs from the Soul."

At the center of this other-worldly system is God and his glory together with the exalted position to which Jesus and his work have been elevated in the estimations of his church. Indispensable to Jesus' theology is his identity as Savior, a fact from which his church cannot separate itself and still be called the church. For Jesus to be Savior, in his theology of the kingdom, means the essential message of faith and repentance to those who would enter the kingdom. This message immediately draws the recipients of the kingdom message into the primacy of the spiritual and the ethical over the physical. The essence of the kingdom is understood in terms of salvation for another world, righteousness for that world, and blessedness intimately, in it.

In Jesus' theology, the kingdom captures the very essence of life itself; that life in this world finds its integration and end through the genuine religious devotion to God, a devotion that touches all forms and spheres of human experiences and expresses itself in complete sacrifice to the service of God, even as it did in Jesus himself.[122]

There is great profit in reading the writings of Geerhardus Vos, but, ultimately, I believe that it is safe to say that Vos would want us to read his writings in order that we might hunger more for the Word of God. For the believer living between the death and resurrection of Christ and his return, Vos argued that the Word remains what it has been from the beginning, "a signal of the presence of God and a vehicle of approach for the world of the supernatural."[123] Vos's passion was conformity to what he saw happening in the Scriptures— a Word-dominated life lived to the glory and enjoyment of the risen Christ. In his writings, he sought to point believers to the Scriptures that they might see their life there in the text and in their God, that God might receive the honor and glory, and they might be built up in the faith.

122. Manuscript of comments made to "Vos Monday" study group, September 21, 1998.
123. Vos, "Hebrews," 192.

The Anthology

Abraham

It is emphasized in the narrative that the patriarch's supreme blessedness consisted in the possession of God himself: "Fear not, Abraham, I am thy shield, thy exceeding great reward" (Gen. 15:1). For this treasure he could cheerfully renounce all other gifts. *BT*, 85.

Abraham throughout his history appears as the ideal friend of God, though only later revelation explicitly calls him so (2 Chron. 20:7; Isa. 41:8). SDL/*SW*, 430.

Faith was in Abraham's life the chief religious act and frame of mind. His whole life was a school of faith in which the divine training developed this grace from step to step. Even at the beginning there was a heavy demand on the patriarch's faith. He was called upon to leave his country, kindred, father's house. And God at first did not name the land of his destination. "The land that I will show thee" was its sole description. As Hebrews 11:8 tells us: "He went out, not knowing whither he went." The statement in Genesis 12:7, that God would give him that particular country, came as a surprise to him. *BT*, 83.

In connection with Abraham . . . the significant term "to know" is found for the first time, as descriptive of the loving condescension wherewith Jehovah chose him for a relation of special intimacy with himself. SDL/*SW*, 430.

In the biblical religion the subjective element is nowhere lacking; on the contrary, it enters into the fabric of practical Christianity with exceptional richness such as no pagan form of piety can rival. But it always keeps in the closest touch with what God has done in the objective sphere, outside the subjectivity of the believer. The most instructive example of this is found in the cultivation of Abraham's faith through the objective promises and their objective fulfillment on the part of Jehovah. *SDJ*, 21.

Absolutism

We must . . . take into account what may be called the *absolutism* of our Lord's way of thinking. He grasped things, not in their relative, but in their absolute, ideal aspect. To him, the thought of consummation was inseparable from the great realities handled in his teaching. The kingdom of God, in order to be truly the kingdom of God, is the *perfect* kingdom of God, in which the divine will shall be done on earth after no less absolute a fashion than it is done in heaven, and only at this acme of its realization does it fully deserve the name of God's kingdom. *SDJ*, 82.

Absolutism is characteristic of the eschatological frame of mind in general. In turn its occurrence in our Lord is one of the indications of his fundamentally eschatological outlook. Traces of its influence upon his way of speaking are found in connection with the messiahship no less than in conjunction with the kingdom. He sometimes refers to the eschatological crisis as *"the coming* of the kingdom of God," just as if no kingdom truly worthy of the name had previously existed: "For I say unto you I will not drink of the fruit of the vine, until the kingdom of God shall come" (Luke 22:18). Notice, he does not say, "until the kingdom shall be perfected," nor "until the eschatological form of the kingdom shall come," but simply *"until the kingdom of God shall come."* *SDJ*, 82.

Activism, Christian

The taunt of the masses, who feel themselves discriminated against in the treasures and comforts of this world, is that religion seeks to reconcile them to their spoiling of the present with the promise of an illusory or at best doubtful future. The temptation is strong to overcome this prejudice through giving greater prominence to the secular advantage connected with the Christian life and promoted by Christian activity. There is some warrant for this, for we are taught that godliness is profitable unto all things, having promise of the life that now is and of that which is to come. At the same time the danger should not be underestimated that out of this strategic concession to the demand of the age, may spring an actual compromise with the spirit that would secularize and terrestrialize Christianity as to its essence. EP, 363.

It is obvious that from the Christian standpoint no greater injury can be done to the true progress and healing of humanity in this present evil world than to make it promises and offer it remedies which have no vital connection with the hope of eternal life. For this hope alone can in the long run feed and keep flowing every stream of altruistic activity that deserves the name of religion. EP, 363.

Adam, First and Second

What we inherit in the second Adam is not restricted to what we lost in the first Adam: it is much rather the full realization of what the first Adam would have achieved for us had he remained unfallen and been confirmed in his state. DCRT/*SW*, 243.

Age, Coming

The eschatological point of view is, of course, originally historical and dramatic; a new world can come only with the new age and therefore lies at first in the future. But the coming age has begun to be present with the death and resurrection of Christ. EAP/*SW*, 115.

It is the Spirit of God who gives form and character to the eschatological life in the broadest and most pervasive sense, that the coming age is the age of the Spirit *par excellence*, so that all that enters into it, forms part of it, or takes place in it, must necessarily be baptized into the Pneuma as into an omnipresent element and thus itself become "spiritual" in its mode of existence and quality. EAP/*SW*, 122.

The reign in life promised to believers for the coming age is a dominion fulfilling itself through Jesus Christ (Rom. 5:17). *PE*, 309.

The writer [of Hebrews] in several instances affirms that believers are in actual contact with the world to come and its blessings. They are eschatological creatures. In 6:5 he states that they have tasted the powers *of the age to come*. In 9:11 and 10:1 he speaks of good things *to come*, and these good things to come are regarded as realized by the death of Christ. The writer affirms this not only in terms of time, but also in terms of place. The believers are situated where the eschatological world has its center. *TEH*, 50.

The age or world to come is the realm of redemption, the reign of the Spirit. HED/*SW*, 196.

Ages, Two

In NT eschatological teaching a general development in a well-defined direction is traceable. The starting-point is the historico-dramatic conception of the two successive ages. These two ages are distinguished as *houtos ho aiōn, ho nun aiōn, ho enestōs aiōn*, "this age," "the present age" . . . and *ho aiōn ekeinos, ho aiōn mellōn, ho aiōn erchomenos*," "that age," "the future age." ENT/*SW*, 28.

The contrast between these two ages is (especially with Paul) that between the evil and transitory, and the perfect and abiding. Thus to each age belongs its own characteristic order of things, and so the distinction passes over into that of two "worlds" in the sense of two systems. ENT/*SW*, 28.

What Paul gives in his distinction between the present world and the world to come and in the equation of Christianity with the latter is a religious philosophy of the history of the race in general. The present age and the present world stand for the reign of sin and evil, "the flesh," as Paul calls it; the age or world to come is the realm of redemption, the reign of the Spirit. HED/*SW*, 195–96.

▨ For Paul the present age is the *evil* age and the new age is the *perfect* age. Paul thus presents a bisection of universal history, with the resurrection of Christ as the dividing point. *TEH*, 52.

▨ In Hebrews . . . the old age is the Old Testament. Thus Hebrews presents not a bisection of universal history [as with Paul], but a bisection of the history of redemption, which results, therefore, in a philosophy of redemption and revelation. The writer of Hebrews does not regard the old *diathēkē* as something evil, but rather as *the world of shadows* (the Levitical world). . . . In Hebrews there is reflection not on the ethical contrast between this world and the world to come, but on the inadequate, preparatory character of the one as over against the perfect, final character of the other. *TEH*, 52.

▨ For if the Spirit be the Spirit of the αἰὼν μέλλων, then his most distinctive task must lie where the coming aeon is most sharply differentiated in principle from the present age. And this, as all the Pauline references to the two aeons go to prove, is the ethical quality of both. The αἰὼν ἐνεστώς is before all other things an αἰὼν πονηρός (Gal. 1:4). EAP/SW, 122.

All

▨ We read not only that Christ gave himself a ransom for all (1 Tim. 2:6), but also that God quickens all things (or keeps alive all things, 1 Tim. 6:13), that God will have all men to be saved and to come to the knowledge of the truth (1 Tim. 2:4), that the living God is the Savior of all men, especially of those that believe (1 Tim. 4:10), that in Christ the kindness (χρηστότης) and φιλανθρωπία of God our Savior toward men appeared (Titus 3:4). In the case of these passages the context clearly indicates that a reference of God's saving grace or Christ's saving work to all classes of men rather than to all men numerically considered, is meant to be affirmed. SDL/SW, 451.

▨ [commenting upon 1 Tim. 2] When the apostle first exhorts that supplications, prayers, intercessions, and giving of thanks be made for *all men*, then specializes this as including kings and all that are in authority, and finally assigns as the ground for this duty the fact that God will have *all men* to be saved, it is not only allowed but demanded by the principles of sound exegesis to interpret the second "all men" in the same sense as the first. SDL/*SW*, 451.

In the well-known passage of Romans (5:12–21), where a parallel is drawn between the first and second Adam and the spread of sin and righteousness in the world through the transgression of the one and the obedience of the other, Paul speaks of the operation not merely of the former principle, but also of the latter as extending to all. But if this were to be interpreted in a distributive sense, as applying to every man individually, then plainly not the loving desire of God to save all, but the actual salvation of all would be affirmed, for the apostle expressly declares that by the righteousness of the one the free gift has come upon all men unto justification of life. We are thus forced to assume that the "all" covers the totality of those who belong to the new human race which springs from the second Adam. SDL/*SW*, 449.

Already, Not Yet

Although in one sense the inheritance of this world lies yet in the future, yet in another sense it has already begun to be realized in principle and become ours in actual possession. The two spheres of the earthly and the heavenly life do not lie one above the other without touching at any point; heaven with its gifts and powers and joys descends into our earthly experience like the headlands of a great and marvelous continent projecting into the ocean. RR/*GG*, 137.

[commenting upon 1 Cor. 5:7] In one sense the Corinthians must still purge themselves from all leaven, in another sense they are already unleavened. The former applies to their subjective condition, the latter to their objective state. SIP/*SW*, 381.

Amos

The unlimited power of Jehovah is strongly emphasized by Amos, largely for the ethical purpose of magnifying the terror of the approaching judgment. *BT*, 238.

Amos is the preacher of justice and retribution *par excellence*. His mind is carried away by the unparalleled energy, one might almost say impetuosity, of the divine resentment against sin. Jehovah, according to Amos, executed righteousness, not from any lower motive, such as safeguarding the structure of society, or converting the sinner, but from the supreme motive of giving free sway to the infinite force of his ethical indignation. *BT*, 253.

[commenting upon the relationship between Amos and Isaiah] Both emphasize strongly the absoluteness and infinitude of the divine existence and activity. Amos, however, always does so with the definite, practical end in view of lending force by these descriptions to the one great burden of righteous judgment which all his energy is intent upon delivering. His interest is ethical, and he summons the divine omnipotence, omnipresence, and omniscience to give adequate expression to the force of his moral indignation. SDFI/*SW*, 277.

Amyraldianism

It was the great fault of the Amyraldian system that, on the one hand, it ascribed to the universal redemptive love which it assumed, the character of a purpose to save; and that, on the other hand, by doing so it made the special relation of God to the elect emerge at a secondary stage in the degree of redemption. This is not only destructive of the principle that the purpose of God cannot under any circumstances be frustrated; it also strikes at the root of the specifically religious significance of the doctrine of election. The love of God for his own thus becomes an afterthought and loses the better part of its value. SDL/*SW*, 456.

Angel of Jehovah

The Angel of Jehovah stands for the completeness and comprehensibility of Jehovah. Through this Angel the theophany is limited to redemption; for the visibility of appearance belongs to redemption. This procedure of linking Jehovah with one figure is practically equivalent to the later Messiah. The significance of the Messiah is to make God's work and significance concrete. Thus, the *malach-*

theophanies are real prophecies of the incarnation. The substantial reason is that the Messiah carries this principle to its logical conclusion, viz., that God is with us, Immanuel. *ESOT*, 86.

Angels

Throughout Scripture the angels are messengers, that is, carriers of information communicated to them, not of information arising out of their own natural endowment with knowledge. *SDJ*, 167.

Annihilation, against the Doctrine of

In support of the doctrine of conditional immortality it has been urged that other terms descriptive of the fate of the condemned, such as *apōleia*, "perdition," *phthora*, "corruption," *olethros*, "destruction," and *thanatos*, "death," point rather to a cessation of being. This, however, rests on an unscriptural interpretation of these terms, which everywhere in the OT and NT designate a state of existence with an undesirable content, never the pure negation of existence. ENT/*SW*, 53.

Perdition, corruption, destruction, death, are predicated in all such cases of the welfare or the ethical spiritual character of man, without implying the annihilation of his physical existence. ENT/*SW*, 53.

[commenting upon 2 Thess. 1:9] [Annihilation] is an extremely abstract idea, too philosophical, in fact, to find a natural place within the limits of the realistic biblical eschatology, least of all, it would seem, within this outburst of vehement indignation against the enemies of the gospel. Closely looked at [annihilation] is not a stronger but a weaker concept than that of protracted retribution to threaten with, so that, instead of contributing to the sharpness of the opposition intended, it would to a certain extent obliterate the latter. *PE*, 294.

Anointing

Through anointing, a unique relation with Jehovah is received. Such a person receives a unique sanctity and a supernatural influence owing to a close association with Jehovah. . . . Royal anointing involves: divine appointment; divine relation and reverence; divine Spirit. *ESOT*, 50.

Anthropomorphism

An anthropomorphism is never without an inner core of important truth, which only has to be translated into more theological language, where possible, to enrich our knowledge of God. *BT*, 255.

Antitype

To "type," the impression, corresponds "antitype," the counterimpression. *BT*, 145.

We say, as a rule, that the old covenant has the type, the new covenant the antitype. And this is scriptural; for the apostle Peter so conceives of it when he represents the water of the deluge as the type, the water of baptism as the antitype (1 Peter 3:21). And yet the author of Hebrews distinctly tells us (9:24) that the Old Testament tabernacle was the antitype, not the type. The explanation is very simple. It lies in this, that antitype means copy, that which is fashioned after the type, and the Old Testament tabernacle was copied, fashioned after the tabernacle in heaven. Likewise the author also finds it significant that Moses was shown a type, a model of the sanctuary on the Mount (8:5; cf. Ex. 25:40). And all the Old Testament things in general are in this sense called copies of the things in the heavens (9:23). HED/*SW*, 201.

Apostasy

The extension of Christianity on the periphery to the ends of the earth does not preclude a progressive apostasy within the bosom of Christianity itself. SC/*SW*, 420.

The idea of the Antichrist in general and that of the apostasy in particular ought to warn us . . . not to take for granted an uninterrupted progress of the cause of Christ through all ages on toward the end. As the reign of the truth will be gradually extended, so the power of evil will gather force toward the end. The making all things right and new in the world depends not on gradual amelioration but on the final interposition of God. *PE*, 134–35.

Assurance of Salvation

Assurance is exactly that element in which faith most clearly reveals its nature as the subjective counterpart of the scheme of grace. Only by throwing off his self-righteous doubts and fears, i.e., by allowing himself to be fully persuaded and assured, does a sinner fully appreciate the grace of God. *AC*, 334.

It is only in Christ Jesus that you can obtain certainty about the matter [of salvation]. Here, also, you must begin with him and end in him. If you are loved, it has been in him, as a member of his body. Therefore look to him! Only when he turns you away will you have the right to say that God has not loved you with an everlasting love, but not until then. SR/*GG*, 230–31.

It is of the essence of faith to crave assurance; hence it cannot come to rest until it has cast its anchor into the eternal. HM/*GG*, 117.

It is just as impossible that any one for whom Christ rose from the dead should fail to receive the righteousness of God as it is that God should undo the righteousness of Christ itself. Consequently, knowing ourselves one with Christ, we find in the resurrection the strongest possible assurance of pardon and peace. JRL/*GG*, 161–62.

[The Christian's] youth is like that of the heir who knows precisely what awaits him. No, more than this, the Christian has the assurance which no heir in temporal things can ever have. He knows with absolute certainty that the inheritance will not merely be kept for him, but that he will be kept for it. CH/*GG*, 143.

Atonement

The believer's faith, according to Paul, does not terminate upon the historical Christ but upon the Christ in glory. Nevertheless, in the glorified Christ the believer's faith grasps all the atoning significance of the cross, because the state of glory is the product and crown of the atonement. PC/*SW*, 158.

Atonement, Day of

The day of atonement . . . constituted . . . the culmination of the sacrificial system. HED/*SW*, 219.

Now it is altogether probable that the author of Hebrews looked upon the sacrifice of Christ on the cross as exactly corresponding to this act which by the hand of the high priest on the day of atonement took place in the court before the altar of burnt-offering. HED/*SW*, 220.

The author [of Hebrews] does not so much compare the ministry of Christ to the work of the Old Testament priests in general, but rather to the ministry performed by the high priest on the day of atonement. PC/*SW*, 159.

Attributes of God

In Isaiah 57:15, two aspects of the divine manifestation toward man are distinguished, the transcendental one, in virtue of which God dwells on high, and the condescending one, in virtue of which he bends down and dwells with the humble ones of his servants. This approaches in a broad way the well-known distinction between the incommunicable and communicable attributes. To the class of transcendental attributes belong omnipotence, omnipresence, eternity, omniscience, holiness. *BT*, 238.

Baptism, and the Flood

First Peter 3:20ff. compares the water of baptism with that of the flood. Both have an eschatological significance and are directed toward salvation. The water was an instrument of the world-judgment and separated godly and ungodly as it does in baptism. *ESOT*, 82.

Baptism, John's

John's baptism, belonging to the old covenant, shared with all the ceremonies of this dispensation the character of a type pointing forward to the fulfillment in Christ. As this does not hinder the fact that in another sense the Old Testament ceremonies were real means of grace, so it does not prove that John's baptism was a mere type. On the other hand, we need not go to the opposite extreme of placing it entirely on a line with Christian baptism, for the latter rests on the finished work of Christ. The true view is that John's baptism was a true sacrament of the old covenant and conveyed to all those who received it in faith the Old Testament manner and measure of grace. The difference was one of degree, not of substance. JB/*SW*, 301.

The suffering Servant of Jehovah was portrayed under the figure of a lamb, to indicate that, while in one sense identical with the wayward flock, he was yet in another respect different from them, because innocent himself and willing to bear in patience the punishment the others had deserved; so Jesus had come to the baptism of John, an Israelite of Israelites, identifying himself with the people of God, yet not because he needed this cleansing for his own individual sin, but because he vicariously took upon himself the penalty they had incurred. JB/*SW*, 302.

Bavinck, Herman

Dr. Bavinck ably vindicates the federal character of all true religion. *GD2/SW*, 492.

Beatitudes

At the beginning [of the Sermon on the Mount] stand the Beatitudes, engraven in golden script upon its portal, reminding us that we are not received by Jesus into a school of ethics but into a kingdom of redemption. It is blessedness that is promised here, and the word does not so much signify a state of mind, as that great realm of consummation and satisfaction which renders man's existence, once he has entered into it, serene and secure for evermore. HTR/*GG*, 28.

[In the Beatitudes, Jesus] links to the fundamental ethical and religious requirements the absolute eschatological promises: theirs is the kingdom of heaven; they shall see God; they shall be satisfied with righteousness. Viewed in this light, the Beatitudes are just as profoundly messianic as is the parable of the wise and foolish builders. *SDJ*, 63.

The state of mind here described [in the Beatitudes] is a receptive rather than a productive one. The hungering and thirsting stand on a line with the poor and the meek; they are conscious of not possessing the desired good in themselves and look to God for supplying it. When they are satisfied, this is due not to their own effort but to an act of God. *KGC*, 64–65.

Here those pronounced blessed are the poor in spirit, the mourners, the meek, and they that hunger and thirst after righteousness. It is in no wise to the self-satisfied mind that the Lord addresses himself; his call is not a call to exertion, not even to exertion in holiness. . . . It amounts to the declaration that the consciousness of having nothing, absolutely nothing, is the certain pledge of untold enrichment. So much is salvation a matter of giving on God's part that its best subjects are those in whom his grace of giving can have its perfect work. HTR/*GG*, 29.

The pure in heart shall see God, those that hunger and thirst after righteousness shall be completely satisfied with the same, the peacemakers shall be called the sons of God. These second clauses in the Beatitudes describe the essence of the final kingdom in which the reward will consist. *KGC*, 67.

[Jesus'] Beatitudes are the evangel, giving answer across the ages to the prophecies of old. It means that with comfort and riches and mercy and sonship and the vision of God, righteousness will be given in abundance to a destitute people. HTR/*GG*, 41.

Beauty

[Beauty], irreligiously esteemed, infringes upon the glory of Jehovah. To take any natural object or product of art, intended to reflect the divine beauty, so as to make it serve the magnifying of the creature is a species of godlessness. *BT*, 281.

Believer, Fundamental Duty of the

▦ The fundamental duty of the believer [is] to make his whole covenant-life a worship service of God. HED/*SW*, 223.

Berith

▦ [Jehovah] sought out Israel. Theologically speaking, we would say that the *berith* had its source in the divine election. *BT*, 260.

▦ A purely one-sided promise or ordinance or law becomes a *berith*, not by reason of its inherent conceptual or etymological meaning, but by reason of the religious sanction added. From this it will be understood that the outstanding characteristic of a *berith* is its unalterableness, its certainty, its eternal validity, and not (what would in certain cases be the very opposite) its voluntary, changeable nature. The *berith* as such is a "faithful *berith*," something not subject to abrogation. *BT*, 23–24.

▦ [commenting upon the Septuagint translators' understanding of *berith*] As the Greek distinguished διαθήκη from συνθήκη, so the Septuagint takes pains to distinguish between the *berith* from God to man, which is purely one-sided or at least one-sided in origin and the fixing of terms, and therefore to be rendered by διαθήκη, and the *berith* between man and man, which may be two-sided, and therefore can be rendered by συνθήκη CT/*SW*, 404.

▦ To charge the Old Testament, on account of its *berith*-conception, with the doctrine that God synergistically enters into contracts with man is a gross injustice. HED/*SW*, 167.

▦ The sense of "contract," "agreement" does not belong to the essence of the *berith*-conception at all. This does not mean that sometimes in the Old Testament the *berith* does not appear in the form of an "agreement" between parties and that this may not be an important feature theologically considered. It only means that even in such cases what constitutes the agreement a *berith* is not the two-sidedness but something else which equally well can appear where there is no compact at all. This essential element is the absolute confirmation of the arrangement by means of a religious sanction or ceremony; in other words, it is the introduction of the divine factor securing stability that gives to the *berith* its specific character. HED/*SW*, 167–68.

However bilateral the arrangement may be in its outcome, to God alone belongs the prerogative of initiating it and with him alone lies the right of determining its content. God never deliberates or bargains with man as to the terms of the *berith* he condescends to enter into. HED/*SW*, 168.

Bible

The Bible is not a dogmatic handbook but a historical book full of dramatic interest. *BT*, 17.

Bible as the Word of God, Belief in the

The Christian church is and always historically has been a church which believed in the Bible as an authoritative revelation, as well as a church trusting in Christ for salvation, because the former was recognized to be as much of her essence as the latter. *JG*/*SW*, 516.

Real communications came from God to man *ab extra*. . . . The offense at "dictation" frequently proceeds from an underestimate of God and an overestimate of man. If God condescends to give us a revelation, it is for him and not for us *a priori* to determine what forms it will assume. What we owe to the dignity of God is that we shall receive his speech at full divine value. *BT*, 12.

It is our duty to emphasize, especially as Reformed believers, that submission to the revealed truth is of the very essence of the Christian religion, being one of the fundamental aspects of that absolute dependence on and surrender to God in which true religion consists. *JG*/*SW*, 515.

Biblical Theology

Biblical theology, rightly defined, is nothing else than the exhibition of the organic process of supernatural revelation in its historic continuity and multiformity. IBT/*SW*, 15.

44

■ All our investigations as to the origin of the Scriptures, their collection into a canon, their original text, as well as the exegetical researches by which the contents of the biblical writings are inductively ascertained, ultimately serve the one purpose of teaching us what God has revealed concerning himself. None of these studies find their aim in themselves, but all have their value determined and their place assigned by the one central study to which they are leading up and in which they find their culminating point. This central study [is called] biblical theology. IBT/*SW*, 6.

■ Biblico-theological procedure . . . seeks faithfully to reproduce the structure and proportion of thought as it presented itself to the mind of the biblical writer himself. *LT*, 127.

■ The specific character of biblical theology lies in this, that it discusses both the form and contents of revelation from the point of view of the revealing activity of God himself. In other words, it deals with revelation in the active sense, as an act of God, and tries to understand and trace and describe this act, so far as this is possible to man and does not elude our finite observation. In biblical theology both the form and contents of revelation are considered as parts and products of a divine work. IBT/*SW*, 6–7.

■ Biblical theology must insist upon claiming for its object not the thoughts and reflections and speculations of man, but the oracles of God. Whosoever weakens or subjectivizes this fundamental idea of revelation, strikes a blow at the very heart of theology and supernatural Christianity, nay, of theism itself. Every type of biblical theology bent upon ignoring or minimizing this supreme, central idea, is a most dangerous product. IBT/*SW*, 19.

■ Many, in an altogether subjective manner, make the *religion* of Israel the object of Old Testament theology. . . . [This makes] biblical theology the description of the views and conceptions in which these acts were appropriated and interpreted. In either case biblical theology will have for its object something relative and human, and will be free to exhibit it as passing through the stages of a human and imperfect development. [This is a] serious error. *PvBG*, 143.

Back of the formation of the Scriptures as a whole, back of the writing of the single books of Scripture, lies the great process of the supernatural self-disclosure of God in history by word and act. Surely it cannot be superfluous to ascertain its laws, to observe its methods, to trace the mutual adjustment of its various stages, to watch the ripening of its purposes—in a word, to investigate its philosophy, so far as this is possible to the human mind. But this is precisely what biblical theology sets out to do. Whatever may be thought of the manner in which the task has been hitherto performed, the legitimacy of the undertaking will not be denied by any one who is a firm believer in the supernatural. NABT, 4.

The highest practical aim of biblical theology is that it grants us a new vision of the glory of God. As eternal, he lives above the sphere of history. . . . But, since for our salvation he has condescended to work and speak in the form of time, and thus to make his work and his speech partake of the peculiar glory that belongs to all organic growth, we must also seek to know him as the One that is, that was, and that is to come, in order that our theology may adequately perform its function of glorifying God in every mode of his self-revelation to us. NABT, 8.

On our estimate of the Scriptures, and more particularly on our estimate of their inspiration, the right of biblical theology to form a separate science depends. *PvBG*, 144.

Biblical Theology and Exegetical Theology

Biblical theology is that branch of exegetical theology which deals with the process of the self-revelation of God deposited in the Bible. *BT*, 5.

The two main requirements for biblico-theological study [are] the exegetical and historical spirit. *TCT*, 654.

Biblical Theology and Systematic Theology

The very name *biblical theology* is frequently vaunted so as to imply a protest against the alleged unbiblical character of dogmatics. I desire to state most emphatically here, that there is nothing in the nature and aims of biblical theology to justify such an implication. IBT/*SW*, 23.

Dogmatic theology is, when rightly cultivated, as truly a biblical and as truly an inductive science as its younger sister. And the latter needs a constructive principle for arranging her facts as well as does the former. The only difference is, that in the one case this constructive principle is systematic and logical, whereas in the other case it is purely historical. In other words, systematic theology endeavors to construct a circle, biblical theology seeks to reproduce a line. IBT/*SW*, 23.

The fact is that biblical theology just as much as systematic theology makes the material undergo a transformation. The sole difference is in the principle on which the transformation is conducted. In the case of biblical theology this is historical, in the case of systematic theology it is of a logical nature. *BT*, 14.

Dogmatics is the crown which grows out of all the work that biblical theology can accomplish. IBT/*SW*, 24.

Biblical Theology as a Theological Discipline

Biblical theology occupies a position between exegesis and systematic theology in the encyclopedia of theological disciplines. *BT*, v.

Biblical theology is a comparatively recent arrival in the theological family. In view of this, it can create little surprise that a wide divergence of opinion prevails in regard to the place she ought to occupy and the rights to be accorded to her, or even in regard to the question whether she can claim any rights or place at all. Many look upon the newcomer with suspicion, while others run into the opposite extreme of paying her such exclusive honor and attention as to treat her older sisters with unmerited coldness and neglect. NABT, 3.

Biblical Theology, Name

It cannot be denied that this name lies open to serious objection, although it may be impossible to displace it, now that it has become almost generally adopted. The appropriation of the adjective "biblical" would seem to call in question the biblical character of the other theological disciplines, which, from a Protestant point of view, would be tantamount to denying their right of existence altogether. . . . These difficulties can all be obviated by substituting for biblical theology the name "history of (special) revelation," which has actually been adopted by some writers. NABT, 8.

The term "biblical theology" is really unsatisfactory because of its liability to misconstruction. All truly Christian theology must be *biblical* theology—for apart from general revelation the Scriptures constitute the sole material with which the science of theology can deal. A more suitable name would be "history of special redemption," which precisely describes the subject matter of this discipline. Names, however, become fixed by long usage, and the term "biblical theology," in spite of its ambiguity, can hardly be abandoned now. *BT*, v.

Biblical Theology, Value of

The highest practical usefulness of the study of biblical theology is one belonging to it altogether apart from its usefulness for the student. Like unto all theology it finds its supreme end in the glory of God. This end it attains through giving us a new view of God as displaying a particular aspect of his nature in connection with his historical approach to and intercourse with man. *BT*, 18.

Biblical theology exhibits to the student of the Word the organic structure of the truth therein contained, and its organic growth as the result of revelation. It shows to him that in the Bible there is an organization finer, more complicated, more exquisite than even the texture of muscles and nerves and brain in the human body; that its various parts are interwoven and correlated in the most subtle manner, each sensitive to the impressions received from all the others, perfect in itself, and yet dependent upon the rest, while in them and through them all throbs as a unifying principle the Spirit of God's living truth. IBT/*SW*, 21–22.

Biblical theology in particular should derive its strength, not from any tacit or even outspoken opposition to the church doctrine, but should rather, in close alliance with the latter, attempt to show how the church, being guided by the Spirit, in its historical development of the truth has remained in closer contact with the Word than have the critical theories of the present day. *PvBG*, 143.

Boasting

Where then is boasting? It is excluded! All who with Paul's eye survey the plan of redemption from its ultimate origins in God's eternal choice to its final unfolding in a glorified soul, will not be able to do anything other than testify with Paul: "Free grace has saved me; for me Christ Jesus has become wisdom from God, righteousness, sanctification and complete redemption." SR/*GG*, 227–28.

Body, Psychical and Pneumatic

[commenting upon 1 Cor. 15:42–47] The body of creation, on the principle of prefiguration, pointed already forward to a higher body to be received in the second stage of the world-process: "if there exists a psychical body, there exists also a pneumatic body" (v. 44). ENT/*SW*, 49.

In 1 Corinthians 15:42–50 the apostle contrasts the two bodies which belong to the pre-eschatological and the eschatological state respectively. The former is characterized as ψυχικόν, the latter as πνευματικόν. Here, therefore, as regards the body, the eschatological state is the state in which the Pneuma rules, impressing upon the body its threefold characteristic of ἀφθαρσία, δόξα, δύναμις (vv. 42–43). And over against this, and preceding it, stands the "psychical" body characterized by φθορά, ἀτιμία, and ἀσθένεια. The proximate reference is to the body, and the contrast is between the body in the state of sin and the body in the resurrection-state. EAP/*SW*, 105–6.

The world of creation and the world to come are thus correlated, the one pointing forward to the other; on the principle of typology the first Adam prefigures the last Adam, the psychical body the pneumatic body (see Rom. 5:14). *PE*, 169.

[commenting upon 1 Cor. 15:42–49] The *psychical* body . . . precedes the *sōma Pneumatikon*. . . . The passage is unique even in the long register of the high mysteries of the faith with Paul, in that it contrasts not the body affected by sin, not the body as it came to exist as a result of the entrance of evil into the world, with the future body, but the primordial body of Adam ("the First Adam") and the body of the consummation. *PE*, 167.

Calvin, John

[Calvin's] theology was built on the basis of the Trinity. DCRT/*SW*, 236.

[Calvin] posited that God is everything and the creation nothing, and that the creature even in its highest interests, remains subordinated to God and is bound to serve him. That is why surrendering predestination means surrendering the doctrine of God's sovereignty, which in turn will lead to an incorrect interpretation of biblical doctrine at numerous points. NST, 145.

Calvinism

No higher commendation of Calvinism is conceivable than that it lends itself to being made the basis of a structure of truth so universally and comprehensively Christian in all its lines and proportions. *GD2/SW*, 485.

Canaan

The abode of Israel in Canaan typified the heavenly, perfected state of God's people. *BT*, 127.

Chiliasm (Premillennialism)

[Chiliasm] has to its credit the astounding readiness it evinces of taking the OT Scriptures in a realistic manner, with simple faith, not asking whether the fulfillment of these things is even logically conceivable, offering as its sole basis the conviction that to God all things are possible. This attitude is, of course, not attained except through a reckless abuse of the fundamental principles of OT exegesis, a perversion invading inevitably the precincts of NT exegesis likewise, heedless of the fact that already the OT itself points to the spiritualizing of most of the things in question. *PE*, 227.

[commenting upon the harm of the chiliastic position] The evil is not so much an evil in itself: it is a malformation or overrank outgrowth drawing to itself a surplusage of religious interest, at the expense of what is more essential and vital in the eschatological sphere. . . . In other words the subject of eschatology in its broad and tremendous significance has vanished from the field of vision; the delusion has been created that eschatology and chiliasm are interchangeable; the species has usurped the place of the genus, which is to be regretted. *PE*, 227–28.

The substance of the matter is that chiliasm divides the eschatological future following upon the parousia into two distinct stages, the one of a temporary, provisional, the other of an eternal, absolute character. The old traditional view of orthodox theology and the current interpretation of Paul know of no such dualism in the eschatological prospect; they make the eternal state, strictly so called, begin with the return of the Lord. *PE*, 228.

The Old Testament avails itself of earthly and eternal forms to convey heavenly and spiritual things. Sincere attachment to the Old Testament Scriptures and a profound conviction of their absolute veracity could and can still underlie a desire to see them in their whole extent literally fulfilled, and since the eternal world offers no scope for this, to create a sphere for such fulfillment in the millennial kingdom. Instead of casting upon such a state of mind the stigma of unspiritualness and narrow-mindedness, we should rather admire the faith-robustness which it unquestionably reveals. None the less, we believe such faith to be a misguided faith. It rests on a failure to apprehend the deeper spiritual import of the Old Testament forms of revelation and to follow the guidance offered us by the New Testament in this respect. SC/*SW*, 417.

Christh and Heaven

The ministry of the high priest under the old covenant belonged to the holy of holies, where he alone could officiate, and so the ministry of Christ belongs to heaven, where he alone can be a priest. PC/*SW*, 160.

According to the author [of the Epistle to the Hebrews], heaven and earth more or less intermingle for the Christian. The Christian already anticipates his heavenly state here on earth. But if this is true of believers, as a merely redemptive acquisition, how much more must it be true of Christ, who is himself directly *a heavenly person*? The act, therefore, was performed in the milieu of heaven, since Christ himself was a piece of heaven come down to earth. *TEH*, 114.

Christ and Righteousness

It should be remembered that the glory possessed by Christ in heaven is, to Paul, the emphatic, never-silent declaration of his absolute righteousness acquired during the state of humiliation. It sprang from his obedience and suffering and self-sacrifice in our stead. MEM/*GG*, 96.

Christ, Ascension of

Through his death plus his ascension [Christ] enters upon that uniquely fruitful state, from which by way of intercession and unlimited endowment with power the most universalizing effects will be made to extend in every direction. Herein lies the reason why both for his individual disciples and for the chosen organism of the world it is better that he should go than that he should remain (John 12:24, 32; 16:7). *SDJ*, 302.

Christel, Faithfulness of

[In Hebrews] the Savior is described as himself exercising faith, in fact as the one perfect, ideal believer. HM/*GG*, 104.

Faith [in the] sense of specific trust, through which a guilty sinner becomes just in the sight of God, our Lord could not exercise, because he was sinless. But the faith that is an assurance of things hoped for and a proving of things not seen had a large place in his experience. HM/*GG*, 104.

By very reason of the contrast between the higher world to which he belonged and this dark lower world of suffering and death to which he had surrendered himself it could not be otherwise than that faith, as a projection of his soul into the unseen and future, should have been the fundamental habit of the earthly life of his human nature. HM/*GG*, 104–5.

Jesus has not produced faith in us while himself living above the plane and beyond the need of faith; it is through his own perfect exercise of faith that he helps believers to follow in his footsteps. HED/*SW*, 213.

Christ, Human Nature of

The human nature of Jesus obtains its highest and final use in this . . . through it we are brought representatively into the presence of God: Christ entered into heaven to appear before the face of God for us (Heb. 9:24). HED/*SW*, 214.

Our Lord's whole human nature and all that entered into it of spiritual experience was not something existing for its own sake; it existed and operated for the sake of his messianic calling. *SDJ*, 103–4.

Most of the statements of the Epistle [to the Hebrews] . . . bring the necessity of the identification of Jesus with human nature and human experience into connection with the instrumental aspect of his priesthood. The possession of human nature was necessary for the great act of sacrifice which consisted in his death. PC/*SW*, 141.

Christt, Humanity and Divinity of

And as to the emphasis [in Hebrews] on the identification of Christ with human nature, this also is motivated not by any desire to tear down or offset the divine aspect, but arises purely from soteriological considerations, both the human and the divine natures being essential to the Savior's revealing and priestly function. *CEH*, 491.

As revealer, Christ's divine nature is emphasized (Heb. 1:3). But in the priesthood, the emphasis is on his human nature. If he had been an angel, he could not have been a priest. *TEH*, 95.

Everybody recognizes that, inasmuch as Jesus was a true man who exercised faith and prayed and gave glory to God, he *had* religion. But not all are willing to admit that, side by side with this, Jesus knew himself and the church from the beginning knew him in another aspect, in which he did not practice but *received* religion. *JG/SW*, 510.

Christ, Immortality of

The strongest affirmation in regard to the "immortality" of Christ is made by the writer to the Hebrews, who attributes to Christ a "ζωὴ ἀκατάλυτος," a life incapable of dissolution. The statement is made with specific reference to the priestly work of Christ which could not be suspended by his death even for a moment, since its very execution consisted in his death. *PE*, 313.

Christ, Work of

The whole saving work of Christ was, strictly speaking, an exemplification of the principle that life can come out of death. *DEI/SW*, 496.

The exalted Lord . . . in his exalted state sums up and carries in himself all the saving power which flows from his work in the flesh, from his death on the cross. PC/*SW*, 158.

Christian, Gauge of Health of

The gauge of health in the Christian is the degree of his gravitation to the future, eternal world. EP, 363.

Christian, Outlook of

The Christian is a man, according to Peter, who lives with his heavenly destiny ever in full view. His outlook is not bounded by the present life and the present world. He sees that which is and that which is to come in their true proportions and in their proper perspective. The center of gravity of his consciousness lies not in the present but in the future. Hope, not possession, is that which gives tone and color to his life. His is the frame of mind of the heir who knows himself entitled to large treasures upon which he will enter at a definite point of time, treasures which will enable him to become a man and develop his powers to their full capacity; and every one of whose thoughts therefore projects itself into the period when he shall have become of age and enjoy the fruition of his hope. CH/*GG*, 142.

The early Christians were not so one-sidedly occupied with "the historical Jesus" as certain groups of modern Christians are. Their preoccupation in daily intercourse and prayer was rather with Christ in heaven. *SDJ*, 121.

"If [nearing the end] we are such who have hope in Christ only in this life, we are of all men most pitiable." What else does this mean other than that the Christian's main thinking, feeling and striving revolve around the future state; and that, if this goal should prove to have no objective reality, the absoluteness with which the believer has staked everything in its attainment must make him appear in his delusion the most pitiable of all creatures? JRL/*GG*, 165.

Christian Life and the Spirit

The entire Christian life being to Paul a life of communion with Christ, it also becomes necessarily a life lived in and inspired by the Spirit in all its strata and activities. *BT*, 387.

The theocentric bent of Paul's mind makes for the conclusion that in the Christian life all must be from God and for God, and the Spirit of God would be the natural agent for securing this. EAP/*SW*, 122.

Christian Life, Pilgrim Nature of

The necessary consequence of this life of the Christian in hope is that he learns to consider the present earthly life as a journey, a pilgrimage, something necessary for the sake of the end but which does not have any independent value or attraction in itself. CH/*GG*, 146.

The Christian is a sojourner here and must live in the future because he knows full well that under the present conditions he can never attain to that full possession of God and his Savior for which in his best moments his heart and flesh cry out. CH/*GG*, 154.

Christian Life, Race to Be Run

The author [to the Hebrews] represents the Christian life as a race to be run [whose] whole character ought to be prospective; everything in it ought to be determined by the thought of the future. It is a race whose goal is the inheritance of the final kingdom of God. Just as one who is on the track running for a prize makes the attainment of this end his supreme—his only—concern, so the true believer obeys only the fundamental law of his Christian calling when he concentrates his mind and energy upon the future. RR/*GG*, 130.

Christian State, Semi-eschatological Nature of the

Paul looks upon the present Christian state as half-eschatological, because it is a state in the Spirit, the enjoyment of the firstfruits of the Spirit, the full possession of the Spirit constituting the life of heaven. SC/*SW*, 422.

Paul conceives of the present Christian state, ideally considered, as lived on so high a plane that nothing less nor lower than the absolute state of the eternal consummate kingdom appears worthy to be its sequel. *PE*, 235.

56

The Christian state is as truly part and foretaste of the things above as a portal forms part of the house. HM/*GG*, 111.

Christianity

The New Testament documents from the least to the most christological among them are at one in this, that they make the religion of the believer terminate in Christ. He is the object of faith and trust throughout in such a high sense that no distinction is drawn between God and him. This attitude is inherent in Christianity from the first. A different kind of Christianity has never existed. *JG/SW*, 511.

[Christianity] in its very essence is a religion of self-denial, cross-bearing and life-surrender. EC/*GG*, 187.

The latent existence of the verities and potencies of the Christian religion in the old dispensation is due to no other cause than that the Christian religion lived even at that time as redemptive truth and redemptive power in the heavenly world and from there created for itself an embryonic form of existence in the life of Israel. The writer of Hebrews would have subscribed to the belief that Christianity is as old as Abraham and as old as Moses, nay as old as Paradise, because it is heaven-born and not the child of earth. HED/*SW*, 199–200.

If Christianity is a worship, a service offered to God, then it must organize itself on a collective basis, for the worship of God cannot fulfill itself unless it proceeds from the congregation as a whole. HED/*SW*, 225.

For Paul [the] cognitive apprehension of Christianity derives its organic unity from the fact that it centers in God and in Christ. TP/*SW*, 357.

Christianity, Eschatological Character of

[Christianity] in its very origin bears an eschatological character. It means the appearance of the Messiah and the inauguration of his work; and from the OT point of view these form part of eschatology. ENT/*SW*, 25.

A so-called Christianity proving cold or hostile toward the interests of the life to come has ceased to be Christianity in the historic sense of the word. *PE*, 63.

In its origin and in the source from which in continuance its life is fed, Christianity is as little of this world as the future life is of this world. The conception of the Spirit proves that what Paul meant to do is precisely the opposite of what is imputed to him. Not to "transmute" the eschatological into a religion of time, but to raise the religion of time to the plane of eternity—such was the purport of his gospel. EAP/*SW*, 125.

Christianity, Factual Basis of

The difference between those who think they can do without the facts [of the Bible] and us who feel that we must have the facts [of the Bible], does not lie on the periphery of the Christian faith; it touches what to us is the center. It relates to nothing less than the claim of our holy religion to be a supernatural religion, and a religion which objectively saves from sin. It would be easy to show that a Christianity which can dispense with the facts of Bible history must, from the nature of the case, be a religion confined by the horizon of the present life and the present world, lacking that supernaturalistic eschatological outlook which is so characteristic of the biblical religion as a whole, and of historic Christianity as well. CFTBH/*SW*, 466.

To Paul the possession of objective religious truth as expressive of objective divine reality is of the very essence of religious experience. To call its possibility in doubt is to cut the nerve not merely of theology but of religion itself. *RES*, 320.

In the rush of modern religious activities, in the eagerness to make Christianity keep pace with the secular forces of life in their accelerated and intensified movement, there is a nervous desire to throw overboard everything that can be in any sense considered superfluous ballast to the craft of practical religion. Thus the whole theoretical side of faith has fallen into neglect, and this neglect involves, besides other things, the historical basis of facts. *CFTBH/SW*, 462.

58

Let us suppose for a moment that our religion aimed at nothing more than the disclosure of a system of truth for the spiritual enlightenment of mankind—that there were no sins to atone and no hearts to regenerate and no world to transform. In that case its connection with historical facts would have to be regarded as a purely incidental matter, established for the sake of a more vivid and effective presentation of the truth, and therefore separable from the essence of the truth itself. . . . It is plain, however, that both these conceptions of the function of Christianity, the intellectualistic as well as the moralizing, are tenable only from the standpoint of Pelagianism with its defective sense of sin. CFTBH/*SW*, 466–67.

Chronicles

In a certain sense Chronicles more than any OT book gives us the philosophy of OT history, and is the seat of the self-consciousness of the OT. *DTK*, 481.

Church

[The church] is the most blessed part of the present life. *BT*, 401–2.

The best proof for the church as an end in itself lies in the inclusion of the church in the eschatological world, for that world is not the world of things aimed at, but of things attained unto. *BT*, 402.

The church of Christ in all its complex service to the world can never forget that its primary concern is to call men into and prepare them for the life eternal. EP, 363.

The church actually has within herself the powers of the world to come. She is more than the immanent kingdom as it existed before Jesus' exaltation. She forms an intermediate link between the present life and the life of eternity. *KGC*, 84.

The Christian church binds up and heals the wounds of humanity, not in the sign of benevolence considered by itself, but in the sign of a compassion into which the love of God has put the tenderest tenderness of its touch. JP/*SW*, 297.

Reformed theology has certainly realized that the church has two sides, and that besides being the assembly of believers and the revelation of the body of Christ, she must also be the means by which new believers are added. But it has not separated these two sides; rather it has kept them in organic connection. Just because the promises of God have been given to the assembly of believers in its entirety, including their seed, this assembly is also a mother who conceives sons and daughters and is made to rejoice in her children by the Lord. DCRT/*SW*, 262–63.

Church, Eschatological Vision of the

It will have to be regarded as a serious spiritual fault in the New Testament believer if he ceases to give the future world that dominating influence over his entire life and thought which, as the goal of his Christian calling, it can properly claim. Whatever the difference in other respects, we are one with the whole church of God of every age, from the beginning of the history of redemption until now, in this fundamental trait—that we seek the absolute, the final, the perfect. RR/*GG*, 131.

The intensely eschatological atmosphere pervading the early church is explainable only on the basis that, with the appearance of the Messiah, the first act of the great drama of the End was believed to have been already staged. *SDJ*, 20.

[The church's] eschatology is its greatest religious glory, for in this the church expresses her faith in a future when all the accidents and externals of religion shall drop away, a great purging of the world-stage, which shall leave only the perfect and ripe fruitage of all God's intercourse with man from the beginning. The gospel of the life to come is the gospel of a church sure of herself and her own endless destiny. No other creed can bring it, and the Christian church can bring nothing less. In it lies the believer's own portion, and it is the only portion he should think it worthwhile to offer to a spiritually impoverished and starving world. It is moreover the portion which has the promise that all other things shall be added to it. EP, 365.

A religion that has ceased to set its face toward the celestial city is bound sooner or later to discard also all supernatural resources in its endeavor to transform this present world. The days are perhaps not far distant when we shall find ourselves confronted with a quasi-form of Christianity professing openly to place its dependence on and to work for the present life alone, a religion, to use the language of Hebrews, become profane and a fornicator like Esau, selling for a mess of earthly pottage its heavenly birthright. HM/*GG*, 119.

Church, Function of the

It is the special function of the church to speak unceasingly and unfalteringly for this one supreme aspect of the future world, to insist in season and out of season that in it God and the service of God are to the highest good and satisfaction of mankind, that without which all other desirable things will lose their value and abiding significance. EP, 358.

Church, Religious Orientation of the

For the church, to keep [her religious orientation] in mind is not to be indifferent to the lesser and secondary needs and distresses of mankind; it is in reality to obey the conviction that in no other way can her deep solicitude for the sinful world, and the resources she carries within herself for its healing, be successfully brought to bear upon it. There can be no doubt that the church owes the success with which in the past she has contributed to the progress of the world in civilization to her fidelity to this fundamental principle and the self-limitation it imposes upon her. EP, 358–59.

Circumcision

The ethical character of Old Testament religion is symbolized by circumcision. *BT*, 88.

For the doctrinal understanding of circumcision two facts are significant; first, it was instituted before the birth of Isaac; secondly, in the accompanying revelation only the second promise, relating to numerous posterity, is referred to. These two facts together show that circumcision has something to do with the process of propagation. Not in the sense that the act is in itself sinful, for there is no trace of this anywhere in the Old Testament. It is not the act but the product, that is, *human nature*, which is unclean, and stands in need of purification and qualification. *BT*, 90.

Circumcision teaches that physical descent from Abraham is not sufficient to make true Israelites. The uncleanness and disqualification of nature must be taken away. Dogmatically speaking, therefore, circumcision stands for justification and regeneration, plus sanctification (Rom. 4:9–12; Col. 2:11–13). *BT*, 90.

City of God

The highest thing that can be spoken about this city is that it is the city of our God, that he is in the midst of it. HM/*GG*, 122.

It is because it is the city of God, the structure in which [God] has embodied his own perfection, in which his thoughts and purposes for his own stand objectified, that it forms a worthy object of the supreme religious quest of the believer. In it is God at every point, and those who dwell in it see his face constantly. The measure of their desire for it becomes the measure of their love of God. HED/*SW*, 229.

Clean and Unclean

[commenting upon the ceremonial law and purification] We must avoid identifying cleanness with cleanliness, uncleanness with dirtiness. Sanitary significance the distinction does not have. It offers no excuse for identifying Christianity with hygiene. Positively, we may say that the conception has reference to the cult, that is, to the ritual approach to Jehovah in the sanctuary. We must not view it from the standpoint of inherent content or quality. "Clean" means qualified for the worship of Jehovah in the tabernacle, "unclean" the opposite. *BT*, 173.

Coming of the Messiah

To the Old Testament point of view and the point of view of Jesus himself, the coming of the Messiah signified consummation. *SDJ*, 20.

In the Old Testament only one coming of Christ is spoken of, and with this one coming the fulfillment of all the messianic predictions and promises is connected. SC/*SW*, 415.

[The] technical eschatological phrase "the coming of the Lord" . . . like an unbroken thread runs through both testaments. He comes, Jehovah comes, the Messiah comes, from Genesis to Revelation this is the import of the message in which ultimately the eschatological hope embodies itself. EP, 45.

The one expected coming of Christ is throughout associated with the absolute consummation of this world and not with the ushering in of a merely provisional order of affairs. SC/*SW*, 416.

Communion with Christ

[commenting upon John 20] Contact, communion with Christ had become to [Mary Magdalene] the vital breath of her spiritual life; to admit that the conditions rendering this possible had ceased to exist would have meant for her to deny salvation itself. R/*GG*, 70.

All . . . anti-soteric effort . . . can have only one practical result. It is bound to raise an insurmountable barrier between the historical Jesus and the refusers of his supreme gift. As he is entirely and at every moment intent upon thus imparting himself, every communion with him assumed to be operating on any other, nonsoteric basis, is only a pseudocommunion, impossible on psychological grounds alone, to say nothing of other reasons why it is unreal. *SDJ*, 28.

Communion with God

There is an inner sanctuary of communion, where all else disappears from sight, and the believer shut in with God gazes upon his loveliness, and appropriates him, as though outside of him nothing mattered or existed. WT/*GG*, 18.

If we may believe that this kingdom was to [Jesus] in part identical with the existence of certain spiritual states, such as righteousness and communion with God, then these receive with the kingdom the highest place in our Lord's estimation of values. *KGC*, 29.

In the ultimate analysis the Pauline conception of "life," as well as that of Jesus, is that of something dependent on communion with God. ENT/*SW*, 55.

[commenting upon Hebrews] We do not hesitate to say that in hardly any New Testament writing is the essential character of the Christian religion as consisting in face to face intercourse with God, mediated by Jesus Christ, so clearly realized and so pointedly brought out as in our epistle. The supremacy of the spiritual, when closely looked at, is only a result of drawing every religious state and act into the immediate presence of God, where nothing but the spiritual can abide. HED/*SW*, 186.

When declaring to Nathaniel, "Ye shall see the heavens opened and the angels of God ascending and descending upon the Son of Man" [John 1:51], [Jesus] implied that in his own life and ministry the idea of communion with God illustrated by Jacob's vision had received its supreme realization. *BT*, 97.

Man is said to have been made in the image of God, and obviously the underlying idea is that in his very constitution he is adapted and designed for communion with God. SDL/*SW*, 429.

Communion with God and the Covenant

[commenting upon Ps. 25:14] The covenant [is] conceived [here] not as a formal contract for the specific purpose, but as a communion in which life touches life and intertwines with life so that the two become mutually assimilated. Evidently the psalmists recognize in this private intercourse with God the highest function of religion—the only thing that will completely satisfy the child of God. SFS/*GG*, 173.

▓ The life of the people of God is essentially an intercourse with God, and this intercourse appears in [Heb. 9:14–15] as the very essence of the *diathēkē*. HED/*SW*, 183.

▓ [commenting upon Ps. 25:14] "The secret of the Lord is with them that fear him, and he will show them his covenant." The "secret" means the secret counsel, the *homilia* as one of the old translations has aptly rendered it. It is the intimate converse between friend and friend as known from human life where there is no reserve, but the thoughts and feelings of the heart are freely interchanged. SFS/*GG*, 172–73.

▓ The psalmists are convinced that God himself desires to enter upon close fellowship with man; that . . . he is in his very nature a covenant God. SFS/*GG*, 176.

▓ "I shall be to them a God and they shall be to me a people," and "All shall know me from the least to the greatest." According to this the covenant means that God gives himself to man and man gives himself to God for that full measure of mutual acquaintance and enjoyment of which each side to the relation is capable. HED/*SW*, 186.

▓ [God] himself being *aiōnios*, there can be no thorough, no adequate reception of him into our finite consciousness, unless there be some assurance of the unceasingness of our communion with him. He is not a God of the dead but of the living. All temporal, partial experience of God inevitably leaves a sense of dissatisfaction behind. *PE*, 293.

▓ For if we had the tongues of angels and the gift of prophecy, and all knowledge and all faith, and if our hands were ceaselessly busy with removing mountains of evil from the world, nevertheless if the features of the face of God remained strange to us, and we had no experience of the divine embrace and benedictions, it would profit us nothing. Nor would it profit God. His desire for us, no less than our need of him, can be satisfied in no other way than in a thorough spiritual penetration and possession. JP/*SW*, 291–92.

Communion with God, Eschatological Goal of Man

▓ The ultimate design of all God's converse with man is, that he may make his abode with his people. *BT*, 106.

▓ The fellowship with God which stands as the goal inevitably assumes the form of a service, a worship of God by man. It is covenant-communion exercised in a sanctuary, where God alone is supreme and where he sets upon everything that enters the stamp of his own majesty and dominion. HED/*SW*, 223–24.

▓ [The] convergence upon and final arrival of life at the center of satisfaction in God, while inextricably interwoven with the fundamental texture of religion, receives with Paul an additional and intensified force from its connection with the life of the exalted Christ, and thus the deepest mystical verity in soteriology and Christology is found to join itself to the eschatological prospect. *PE*, 309.

▓ The highest gift that can be bestowed on the pure in heart is that in the final kingdom they shall have the beatific vision of God face-to-face. *KGC*, 74–75.

Communion with God, Old Testament Fear of Loss of at Death

▓ We find that with the psalmists the chief cause of solicitude and perplexity is the problem of their future relation to Jehovah. Will there be in these strange shadowy regions remembrance of Jehovah, experience of his goodness, praise of his glory? "What profit is there in my blood, when I go down to the pit; shall the dust praise thee, shall it declare thy truth?" What they most feared was not death as such, nor that they might lose themselves in death, but that they might lose contact with Jehovah. EP, 346.

▓ Did you ever observe what is the thought that seems to have most acutely distressed and perplexed the writers of some of the Psalms when they tried in vain to pierce the veil of mystery enveloping to them the future world? It was the fear that in these strange regions there might be no remembrance of God, no knowledge of his goodness, no praise of his glory. We may be assured that when a religious want is projected into the world to come in this way, so that the fear of its not being satisfied proves stronger than the fear of death in itself, we may be sure that there it has been recognized as the supreme, the essential thing in religion. SFS/*GG*, 179.

[commenting upon Ps. 89:46–49] Here the bitterness of death is measured by the danger that it may sweep out of reach the vision of Jehovah and the enjoyment of his glorious reign at the end. To lose touch with him in Sheol would be painful, to miss him at his final epiphany intolerable; it would be the supreme tragedy of religion. EP, 346.

Communion with God, Subservient to Glorifying God

The believer does not merely desire to have intercourse with God, but specifically to make this intercourse subservient to glorifying God. Hence on the one hand the high place which the direct worship of God holds in the exercise of the religious function, on the other hand the consistent effort to organize the whole of life on the principle of a comprehensive service of God, the religious impulse imparting to every human activity and achievement that spirit by which they are made to redound to the honoring of God's name. HED/*SW*, 232.

Confession, and Scripture

One of the gravest symptoms of the revision movement in the Presbyterian Church today consists in the absence of serious appeal to scriptural authority for the changes of confessional statement that are advocated. From the attitude assumed by man, one would be led to think that no longer the infallible Word of God, but public sentiment, the so-called Christian consciousness, has become the recognized rule of faith among us. BIP/*SW*, 412.

Consummate State

In general Paul conceives of the final state after a highly theocentric fashion (1 Cor. 15:28); it is the state of immediate vision of and perfect communion with God and Christ; the future life alone can bring the perfected sonship. ENT/*SW*, 55.

The scene of the consummate state is the new heaven and new earth, which are called into being by the eschatological palingenesia "regeneration." ENT/*SW*, 55.

An annihilation of the substance of the present world is not taught (see the comparison of the future world-conflagration with the deluge in 2 Peter 3:6). The central abode of the redeemed will be in heaven, although the renewed earth will remain accessible to them and a part of the inheritance. ENT/*SW*, 55.

Contrition

True contrition . . . is the specifically religious response to [the] moral perceptions whereby the sinner abhors his unholiness not from any selfish motive but from the standpoint of God; from the profound conviction that it is a slight upon his purity and infringes on the supremacy of his glory. Spiritual penitence is God-centered. OHGG/*GG*, 272.

Genuine contrition acknowledges the propriety that sin, the sinner and everything defiled by sin should be swept away, and Jehovah of Hosts be exalted in judgment and God the Holy One be sanctified in righteousness. OHGG/*GG*, 272.

Conversion

To be converted is to die with Christ and to rise with him. MEM/*GG*, 94.

Covenant

The covenant expresses the very heart of God's purpose. MEM/*GG*, 86.

68

■ Those who dwell together in the holy companionship of the covenant grow like each other. WT/*GG*, 21.

■ In the covenant the servant is, as it were, made part of the wonder-world of salvation itself. MEM/*GG*, 87.

■ God has not revealed himself in a school, but in a covenant; and the covenant as a communion of life is all-comprehensive, embracing the conditions and interests of those contracting it. IBT/*SW*, 10.

■ When Jehovah entering into covenant with Israel says, "I will be unto you a God, and ye shall be unto me a people," this means infinitely more than the trite idea: henceforth you shall worship me and I will cultivate you. It is the mutual surrender of person to person. Jehovah throws in his lot with Israel, no less truly than Israel's lot is bound up with Jehovah. WT/*GG*, 9–10.

■ To have God and to be owned by God in the profound covenant sense would be impossible and result in doing violence to the nature of God and man alike, if the character of man could not be made to fit into the nature and will of God. The basis of all religion is that man must exist in the image of God. WT/*GG*, 22.

■ A close and unique bond exists between Jehovah and Israel. This is so self-understood as not to need explicit affirmation. Indirectly its existence is expressed through the references to its origin. Jehovah chose Israel, they are his people; he married her, they are like a vineyard which he cultivates for the sake of its fruit. A technical term for it is *berith*, usually rendered by "covenant." *BT*, 256.

■ The covenant is an all-comprehensive communion of life, in which every self-disclosure is made subservient to a practical end. NABT, 5.

■ The covenant-idea is an eminently historical idea, most intimately associated with the gradual unfolding of God's self-disclosure to his people. This reaches even back of the regime of redemption and characterizes God's dealings with man in the state of rectitude. HED/*SW*, 192.

In [the] gospel of Paradise we already discern the essential features of a covenant-relation, though the formal notion of a covenant does not attach to it. IBT/*SW*, 11.

To be in covenant with God—what finer and what more adequate definition of the perfect religious life could be conceived than this? HED/*SW*, 186.

Covenant and Ministry

To have such a covenant ministry means to be identified with God in the most intimate manner, for the covenant expresses the very heart of God's purpose. It means to be initiated into the holiest mysteries of redemption, for in the covenant these are transacted. It means to be enrolled on the list of the great historic servants of God, for in the organism of the covenant these are united and salute each other across the ages. It means to become a channel through which supernatural currents flow. In the covenant the servant is, as it were, made part of the wonder-world of salvation itself. MEM/*GG*, 86–87.

Covenant and Priesthood

The priesthood fulfills itself in being near and bringing near to God, and the purpose of the covenant is precisely the same. Both look to communion with God. HED/*SW*, 220–21.

Jesus is the surety of an intrinsically better covenant, thus once more confirming the rule that the excellence of the covenant is in exact proportion to the excellence of the priesthood. The synonymous terms "surety" and "mediator" also mark the interdependence of the priesthood and the covenant, for it is precisely as priest that Jesus becomes the surety, the sponsor of the new covenant: because he is an oath-appointed priest, he is a better surety. Through the manner of his priesthood he renders the effectuation of the covenant assured. HED/*SW*, 222.

Among the eternal possessions to which believers have come in the heavenly Jerusalem the author here assigns the highest place to Jesus and that in his capacity of mediator of the new covenant. Both the covenant and the priesthood retain in the eternal world their abiding significance. In the eternal priest the covenant has become eternalized. For this reason the blood with which Jesus was brought back from the dead, that is, the expiation which in his endless resurrection-life he makes available, is called the blood of an everlasting covenant (Heb. 13:20), and in virtue of it Jesus never ceases to be the great Shepherd of the sheep of the Israel of God. HED/*SW*, 222.

Covenant and Priesthood and Revelation

[Priesthood and revelation] represent two mutually complementary movements, each beginning at the point opposite that from which the other proceeds, and having for their common destination the realization of fellowship between God and man. In revelation God makes his approach to man; through the priesthood man makes his approach to God; where both reach their ideal perfection, there the ideal covenant is given. The covenant movement must necessarily flow through these two channels. HED/*SW*, 226–27.

Covenant and Service

The reality of the covenant is placed in this, that Jehovah is a God to Israel and Israel is to Jehovah a people (Heb. 8:8–12). Believers are in virtue of the covenant "a household of God" (Heb. 3:6). Their life is essentially a $\lambda\alpha\tau\rho\epsilon\iota\alpha$, a religious service, and this $\lambda\alpha\tau\rho\epsilon\iota\alpha$ is nothing else but the outward manifestation of the covenant (Heb. 9:14). PC/*SW*, 137.

Covenant and the Sovereignty of God

Scripture always so represents it that the *berith* [covenant] in its origin and in the determination of its content is not two-sided but based on the sovereignty of God. In our opinion the whole richness of the idea in a religious point of view can be appreciated only by making the sovereign and the condescending aspects of it illuminate and accentuate each other. That the sovereign majestic procedure issues in condescension and fellowship of life . . . this is that religious treasure which the covenant-idea carries in itself. *DBD*, 516–17.

The preposition σύν in συνθήκη expresses the coequality and coefficiency of the persons concerned in the *berith*. Such a coequality and coefficiency cannot exist between God and man; even where God most condescendingly enters upon a relation of true friendship with man, it is still out of place to conceive of this as a treaty in the ordinary sense. God cannot forgo the right of sovereignly framing and imposing the arrangement that shall control the religious intercourse between himself and man, and that he exercises this right is admirably expressed by the preposition διά in διαθήκη. HED/*SW*, 172.

Covenant, New

What Moses stood for was glorious but lacked permanence. The day was bound to come when its splendor would vanish. On the other hand the new covenant is final and abiding. The times cannot outgrow, the developments of history cannot age it; it carries within itself the pledge of eternity. MEM/*GG*, 89.

What is possessed by the new covenant is not the glory of God as such, but the glory of God in the face of Jesus Christ. MEM/*GG*, 94.

[Jeremiah] contrasts the new covenant of the future with the old Mosaic covenant in this respect, that in the latter the law was not written upon the heart; in his opinion, therefore, the internal disposition to obey was lacking both before and after the making of the covenant (Jer. 31:33). SDL/*SW*, 436.

The [new covenant] embodies the consummation of all the work of God for His people; it is the ocean into which all the rivers of history roll their waters from the beginning of the world. HED/*SW*, 194.

In regard to the second covenant and the age to come there is complete identification; those who are under the one are in principle in the other; Christians do taste the powers of the age to come and have arrived at the eschatological Mount Zion, the heavenly

Jerusalem, the city of the living God. The revelation of the new covenant is not only better comparatively speaking; it is final and eternal because delivered in a Son, than whom God could send no higher revealer. HED/*SW*, 194.

Covenant of Works

Ever since the goal set by the covenant of works came within his ken, man carries with him in all his converse with this world the sense of belonging to another. HM/*GG*, 113.

Had there been no sin in the world, even then [Paul] would not have been able to conceive of an ideal religious relation between God and man, without a solid substructure of a forensic nature rendering the whole religious process subordinate to the revealed moral excellence of God. It is to the credit of Reformed theology that it has appreciated this deeper motive of the Pauline doctrine and has given it formal recognition in its conception of the covenant of works. AL/*SW*, 397–98.

Our conclusion is therefore that this freedom in Adam's case is something quite unique. It is connected with the covenant of works. This covenant, instead of being excluded by Adam's holiness, was really related to it inasmuch as this holiness was changeable and not an unchangeable holiness. NST, 94, 98.

Insofar as the covenant of works posited for mankind an absolute goal and unchangeable future, the eschatological may be even said to have preceded the soteric religion. EP, 325.

Covenant, Old

The prophetic looking-forward dispensation of the old covenant reaches its close in John. *KGC*, 34.

The same world of heavenly spiritual realities, which has now come to light in the person and work of Christ, already existed during the course of the old covenant, and in a provisional typical way through revelation reflected itself in and through redemption projected itself into the religious experience of the ancient people of God, so that they in their own partial manner and measure had access to and communion with and enjoyment of the higher world, which has now been let down and thrown open to our full knowledge and possession. HED/*SW*, 199.

Covenant Theology

At present there is general agreement that the doctrine of the covenants is a peculiarly Reformed doctrine. It emerged in Reformed theology where it was assured of a permanent place and in a way that has also remained confined within these bounds. DCRT/*SW*, 234.

Creation and Christ

[commenting upon John 1:3] That the Evangelist not merely intends to ascribe to Christ a part in the creation of all things in general, but specifically means to represent him as performing that part in the capacity of Logos, follows from the preposition employed. The statement is not πάντα ὑπ᾽ αὐτοῦ ἐγένετο but πάντα δι᾽ αὐτοῦ ἐγένετο. For the general thought that Christ participated in the creation of all things the former would have been the natural expression; for conveying the specific idea that his role was the role played by the divine word in Genesis, the construction with διά was the one peculiarly fitted. RLT/*SW*, 62–63.

Creation State and Eschatological State

It is worth observation that the distinction between the two strands that enter into the Pauline doctrine of the work of the Spirit is clearly marked by the twofold antithesis σαρκικός—πνευματικός and ψυχικός—πνευματικός. The psychic man is the natural man as such. The sarkic man is the sinful natural man. It is certainly significant that in 1 Corinthians 15:45–50,where Paul puts over against each other the creation state and the eschatological state of pneumatic life, he does not characterize the former as sarkic but as psychic. *KC/SW*, 541–42.

▨ First Corinthians 15:45–49 [is] the one passage in which Paul goes back of the fact of sin to find the determining basis for the relatively inferior state of man, as compared with his eschatological destiny, in the mode of his creation. But the technical term for this is not here "sarkikos," it is "psychikos"; the idea of sin does not enter. *PE*, 34.

Creationism and Traducianism

▨ The anti-federalist needs traducianism to maintain his position. The federalist is by no means thus dependent upon creationism. While traducianism has been frequently exploited to controvert the federalistic view, this has always been done at the expense of logic. Federalism *as such* can with equal case be combined with the traducianistic and creationistic theory. Still, it remains possible that the immanent tendency of every doctrinal development to advance its position beyond the range of possible attack has influenced the Reformed in this point. For, although traducianism can be held consistently with federalism, creationism may have appeared preferable insofar as it positively requires the federalistic principle in order to explain the connection between Adam's fall and the sinfulness of his descendants. *GD2/SW*, 493.

Creator/Creature Distinction

▨ Isaiah knows of no gradations to fill up the distance between the Creator and the creature: it is an infinite distance which nothing can fill up, however exalted. The seraphim, though themselves belonging to a higher world, worship in Jehovah's temple and cover their faces and their feet with the same profound sense of their own insignificance as the earth-born prophet. Each time Isaiah proclaims the absolute greatness of God there follows without fail as an echo the confession of the absolute littleness of every creature. OHGG/*GG*, 266.

▨ As Jehovah has the only title to divinity, so he is the only absolute agent. Man has a breath in his nostrils, is dependent on an extraneous source of life (Isa. 2:22), is therefore weak and perishable, whilst Jehovah is spirit moved from and by himself, inexhaustible in power. SDFI/*SW*, 278.

Scripture teaches that all creaturely life is derived from God and is nourished only in fellowship with him. SR/*GG*, 216.

Creature, Exists for God's Sake

A deep impression of the divine majesty colors all intercourse with him. For him are all things and through him are all things. The creature exists for his sake. He is the living God into whose hands it is fearful to fall, for those who disobey him a consuming fire. HED/*SW*, 231.

Creeds

[commenting upon James Denney's proposal for the Presbyterian Church to adopt a one-sentence creed in place of the Westminster Standards] Dr. Denney overlooks that this unity which he would produce by his simplified confession needs no longer to be created, because it already exists in the invisible church, in which all Protestants believe. It rests on a bond deeper and closer than any confession can make. But what is superfluous from the point of view of the invisible church becomes wholly inadequate from the point of view of the visible church. No visible church organization can lead a normal healthy existence on such a basis. Even in the apostolic age there was a large background of authoritative doctrine behind the practical faith in Christ. Nor is it desirable that the visible church should divest herself of the right to formulate and proclaim her belief in the form of a creed. *JG/SW*, 515.

It is our duty to emphasize, especially as Reformed believers, that submission to the revealed truth is of the very essence of the Christian religion, being one of the fundamental aspects of that absolute dependence on and surrender to God in which true religion consists. Because we wish to be more fully religious, religious in our intellect as well as in our will, we desire a creed, in order that our acceptance of the truth may be articulate. *JG/SW*, 515.

Because the Christian church is and always historically has been a church which believed in the Bible as an authoritative revelation, as well as a church trusting in Christ for salvation, because the former was recognized to be as much of her essence as the latter, therefore she has from early times felt in duty bound to act as a professing, creed-making church. Where this belief in the Bible is in principle abandoned, or in the same degree that it is weakened and represented as immaterial, a lack of interest in and finally intolerance of creed must of necessity result. *JG/SW*, 516.

Criticism

It is a mistake to conceive of the critical process as the simple operation of drawing logical inferences from given facts. If this were so, the only thing to do would be to dispute either the reality of the facts or the correctness of the conclusions. But the critical process is in reality a much more subtle and complicated matter. *DMOV*, 107.

[Criticism] on the part of our opponents has long since left its independent position, and become subservient to naturalistic tendencies. It manifests a spirit of enmity against the very material upon which it works. *MOP*, 13.

Criticism and Revelation

Revelation is on principle inseparable from a background of historic facts, with which to bring man's life into vital contact is indeed the main reason for its existence. He who has once clearly perceived this will not even for a moment consider the possibility that his faith and such criticism as destroys the supernatural facts can peacefully dwell together in the same mind. To him the facts are become the very bread of life. Though you tell him a thousand times that the value of the biblical narratives for moral and religious instruction remains precisely the same, whether the facts occurred or not, it will not satisfy him, because he knows full well that all moral instruction and religious impressions combined cannot save his soul. In his thirst for redemption from sin he will not rest in anything short of an authentic record of how God wrought wonders in history for the salvation of his people. CFTBH/*SW*, 467.

The critics, it is true, disorganize the Scriptures and reject the harmony wherewith they offer themselves to us. But we should remember that they reconstruct the dissected parts into an artificial organism to which a certain grandeur cannot be denied. The defenders of the biblical view will always be weak unless they succeed in outlining with ever-growing clearness and placing over against this artificial structure the living organism of revelation as contained in the historical Scriptures. *DMOV*, 109.

So far as we can see, the only honest thing is to acknowledge that the modern critical attitude, when it evaporates the historicity of the ancient narratives, is fundamentally different from the attitude in which the biblical authors recorded them. . . . To the inspired writers these histories had a specific historico-religious value apart from all the lessons they might teach in virtue of their moral or religious content. They were of supreme importance because they spoke of acts objectively done by God and experiences had by man, on which the whole structure of Israel's religious relation to God was built. *JM*, 471.

[A] quasi-historical Christ can be recovered from the Synoptics only by a process of persistent denial of their accuracy and trustworthiness as historical witnesses, by frequent repudiation of what they do say and by as frequent substitution for it of something they do not want to say. It is this unprincipled treatment of the Gospel narrative, more than anything else, that has fostered the skeptical attitude of the modern mind and brought it to a point where it is almost compelled in deference to its regard for honesty and frankness to face the question, whether there is any confidence to be placed in the narrative at all, whether Jesus is actually a historical person. *DGJ*, 489–90.

We venture to say that the dissection of the Law and the Prophets, absurd though it be in itself, has had the indirect beneficial result of making us more intimately acquainted with the minutest peculiarities of the Word of God than we could have been, had not the necessity of defense, that was laid upon it, compelled Christian scholarship to scrutinize and rescrutinize the content of Holy Writ, so that not one jot or one tittle escaped investigation. Modern criticism has at least preserved or cured the church from one fault—the fault of indolence in research with regard to the facts of God's revealed truth. CFTBH/*SW*, 460.

There is no other way of showing [the extent that critical theories disorganize the Bible] than by placing over against the critical theories the organic history of revelation, as the Bible itself constructs it. As soon as this is done, everybody will be able to see at a glance that the two are mutually subversive. This very thing biblical theology endeavors to do. It thus meets the critical assaults, not in a negative way by defending point after point of the citadel, whereby no total effect is produced and the critics are always permitted to reply that they attack merely the outworks, not the central position of the faith; but in the most positive manner, by setting forth what the principle of revelation involves according to the Bible, and how one part of it stands or falls together with all the others. IBT/*SW*, 22.

Criticism, Conflict with

We, for our part, believe, and we say it deliberately, that it were a thousand times better for the church to be torn and shaken for many years to come by the conflict with criticism than to buy a shameful peace at the stupendous doctrinal sacrifice which such a position involves. CFTBH/*SW*, 468.

Cross

The sacrifice on the cross was one of the events in which the eternal enters into the temporal, as the headlands of a continent . . . project into the ocean. PC/*SW*, 160.

Jesus accepted the cross out of a motive of love for God even more than, and before, he accepted it because of his love for man. His submission to the cross was a supreme act of religious devotion. *SDJ*, 280.

[commenting upon Gal. 6:14–15] The cross is here represented as effecting an absolute separation between two worlds, so as to have cut loose the apostle from the world to which he at first belonged, and having transplanted him into another. And this separation was so radical that the two parts between whom it took place were afterwards equally unable to have community of interests one with the other: the world was no less crucified to Paul than Paul was to the world. *PE*, 48.

Though [Christ's] whole life in the flesh was sin-bearing from beginning to end, yet it was specifically in the cross that the condemnatory power of the law was concentrated on Christ. There it was made manifest that he had become sin for us, the curse incarnate. JRL/*GG*, 160.

[The cross] serves to furnish an example of the self-sacrificing service which constitutes the law of life for the disciple in the kingdom of God. CDW/*GG*, 244.

So long as regard was had to what man would get out of the messiahship, the cross could not but appear preposterous. But Jesus sought the cross from the love of God. *SDJ*, 61.

[Jesus] is the impersonation of the God who pronounces the judgment and of the God who sovereignly takes it away, the one who bears our curse, and, while bearing it, speaks peace to our souls. For this reason he came to the cross, so that he might be able to act for God in this solemn, anticipated judgment through which every sinner passes. SSL/*GG*, 62.

Cross and Resurrection

The crucifixion and resurrection of Christ were acts not exclusively intended to reveal something to man, but primarily intended to serve some definite purpose in reference to God. IBT/*SW*, 9.

David's Son and David's Lord

The Messiah must be God's Son in order to be capable of the things predicated of him in the Psalm [110]. Here, then, the divine sonship of Jesus is represented as the basis of that higher character of messiahship which expressed his own ideal: because he is the Son of God, he rules the world to come. Nor do we think it straining the words too much if we find in Jesus' statement [Luke 20:41–44] the implication that the messianic sovereignty must cover the world to come because only as an inhabitant of the world to come could David be subject to it. *SDJ*, 165–66.

The antithesis between "David's Son" and "David's Lord" has for its background the distinction between this world and the world to come. *SDJ*, 166.

Day of Jehovah

With Amos the day of Jehovah is a day of punishment of the wicked; it is darkness and not light, very darkness and no brightness in it (5:20). The sweeping away of evil is the supreme interest of this prophet of righteousness; hence he depicts the scene from its subjective and human side. SDFI/*SW*, 283.

Isaiah immediately shows the theological bent of his spirit in seizing upon the day of judgment as the occasion for a supreme self-manifestation of Jehovah. Punishment for him becomes revelation, theophany, together with the unmasking of what is falsely deified. Thus the day of Jehovah will be in the full sense what its name entitles it to be, a day in which he is the central figure, attracting by his glorious appearance the attention of all (see 5:16). SDFI/*SW*, 283.

Day of the Lord

"Light" belongs to the day as its characteristic, the opposite of the darkness that pertains to the night. Hence "the day of the Lord" can be visualized as a day of deliverance, joy and blessedness. *PE*, 81.

Death

[Death] is a word that looms large in the Pauline epistles. By no one perhaps has the terribleness of death been so intensely realized as by the apostle. Death appears to him personified as a great enemy, a hugh spectre, casting its dreadful shadow over human existence, something that is impossible to become reconciled to, more horrible than any other shape or form to be encountered in the spiritual world. JRL/*GG*, 159.

▨ Paul abhors and hates death because it is the wages, the penalty of sin. Whatever else it might be, to him it appeared first of all a minister of condemnation, the personified, incarnate sentence of God against sin. JRL/*GG*, 160.

▨ Death is the exponent of sin. Its sentence and penalty is one with which the criminality of sin ineffaceably stamps the sinner. The sting of death is sin, and the power of sin is the law, and the law is nothing else than God himself personally confronting the transgressor and rendering judgment: "the soul that sinneth it shall die." JRL/*GG*, 160.

▨ [Death] can be defined as being cut off from the source of life. . . . In temporal death it is the body that is cut off from the source of its life, that is, the soul. . . . In spiritual death it is cut off from the fountainhead of its life, the living God. SR/*GG*, 217.

▨ [commenting upon Gen. 3] An allusion to the connection of death with the separation from God is found in v. 23: "God sent him forth to till the ground from whence he was taken." "Tilling the ground from whence he was taken" contains an unmistakable reminder of v. 19. In other words: expulsion from the garden (i.e. from God's presence) means expulsion to death. The root of death is in having been sent forth from God. *BT*, 40.

Death of Jesus Christ

▨ Christ died, the just for the unjust, that he might bring us near unto God. The death of Jesus negatively takes away the disqualifications and positively bestows the qualifications necessary for the worship-service of God in the heavenly sanctuary. *SDJ*, 300–301.

▨ [commenting upon 1 Cor. 5:7] The death of Christ is here represented as a Passover sacrifice for two reasons: (1) Because it is the source of objective freedom from the impurity of the guilt of sin; (2) Because it is the source of subjective purity. SIP/*SW*, 381.

■ He who suffers and dies does a great thing, but he who suffers and dies for another by putting himself in the place of the other as a sin-bearer, and submitting vicariously to the punishment due to the other, does a far greater thing. Jesus has done the greater—the greatest—thing, and this is what lends supreme force to his example. *SDJ*, 282.

■ [Jesus'] death appeared to him not so much *inevitable* as *indispensable*. He does not say to Peter that the circumstances require his death; what he does say is that the interests of God demand his death. ... The implication plainly is that in the cross Jesus renders a positive service to God; for him to die is an act of obedience, whereas to withdraw would be a wrong committed against God. *SDJ*, 280.

■ That the Gospels regard the death of our Lord as the very core and climax of his life on earth appears most clearly from their structure, which makes the narrative gravitate toward the end. *SDJ*, 273.

■ [commenting upon Mark 10:45] What [Jesus] says carries the knowledge of his death and of the saving purpose of his death back into the initial act of his appearance upon earth: his coming was with this end and none other in view. CDW/*GG*, 245.

■ In dying, as in all else [Jesus] did, he hallowed God's name. Not in the frame of mind of a martyr, but in the fulness of his messianic purpose did he set his face toward Jerusalem there to make his decease. *SDJ*, 61.

■ His death is that act whereby the promise of the great eschatological cleansing from sin will be fulfilled, and a new and holy Israel be made ready for God. *SDJ*, 61.

■ [commenting upon Eph. 5:1–2] Christ gave himself up in death for us. This act was the highest manifestation of his love toward us and is therefore held up as an example for the imitation of believers in their conduct toward one another. SIP/*SW*, 381–82.

▓ [Christ's] death on earth . . . is not only the indispensable presupposition of the ministry in glory, but the ministry in glory is a perpetuated, eternalized proclamation of what the death of Christ meant. Expressed in priestly terminology, this reads that Jesus through his blood has entered into the heavenly sanctuary, that there he makes his blood purify. PC/*SW*, 158.

Decalogue

▓ The Decalogue strikingly illustrates the redemptive structure of the theocracy as a whole. It is introduced by the summing up of what Jehovah has done for Israel in delivering them from the house of bondage. *BT*, 129.

▓ It joins together the beginning and the end of the entire theocratic movement, the redeeming act of God, and the resultant state of holiness and conformity to the nature and will of God into which the theocracy is designed to issue. At the same time it gives these elements in a form that is adjusted to the practical needs and limitations of the people. Like the theocracy in general it hovers above the life of the people as an ideal never realizable, nor realizable at the then existing stage; and at the same time it descends into and condescends to the abnormalities of Israel. *BT*, 129–30.

▓ The most striking feature of the Decalogue is its specifically religious character. It is not an ethical code in and by itself, resting, as it were, on the bare imperative of God. The preamble brings the affection to Jehovah, in view of what he has done redemptively for the people, to bear through a responsive affection upon their conduct. If we may apply the term "Christian" thus retrospectively to the Decalogue, we should say, what it contains is not general but Christian ethics. Ethics is represented as the redemptive product; something else, lying behind, as the source. *BT*, 132.

Decalogue, Reformed vs. Roman Catholic and Lutheran Division

The Reformed [Church considers] the preamble as standing outside of the circle of ten. The first word then applies to the prohibition of worshipping other gods, the second to the prohibition of images, and so on to the end in the manner familiar to us. . . . The Roman Catholic and Lutheran churches count as one what we reckon as the first and second words. Inasmuch as the number ten is required, this compels the dividing up of what we call the tenth commandment into the ninth ("thou shalt not covet thy neighbor's house") and the tenth ("thou shalt not covet thy neighbor's wife," etc.). *BT*, 133.

Decree of God

The recognition of the wisdom of God's decree, when combined with its universality, must lead to the conclusion that everything in the world is ruled by thought and possesses ideal significance. Blind, purposeless being, without any thought at all, does not exist. The counsel of God contains a perspicuous plan of the entire world of reality. NST, 37.

God's decree is one and it is directed toward one supreme goal: the glorification of his name, i.e., of himself. The principal goal, however, toward which God's decree is directed is the glorification of God himself in his rational creatures, angels and men. The proof for this lies in God's simplicity and his aseity. God's decree is universal; it comprises all things. NST, 58.

God's decree concerns the means as well as the ends that must be reached. For that reason it is absurd to abstain from the means with the thought that God's counsel will come to pass anyhow. Not as if the latter would not be true, but man deceives himself if he thinks that his aversion and his unwill[ingness] to use the means have no relation with the final outcome. On the contrary that unwill[ingness] is in many cases the means which God uses to prevent a certain result from taking place. NST, 76.

God is sure in everything he decrees, and all things, as concerns their certainty, derive that certainty only from God's decree. NST, 135.

Delight, to Jehovah

That which is represented as yielding delight to Jehovah is the surrender of man's life in consecration of obedience. *BT*, 169.

Deuteronomy

[Deuteronomy] stands on the dividing line between the legal and the prophetic types of revelation. While embodying a real law code, it at the same time approaches the character of prophecy in that it goes back from the single concrete commandments of Jehovah to certain general, spiritual principles, and varies the categorical imperative of the other codes with the winning note of persuasion and exhortation. SDL/*SW*, 430.

Disciple

The true disciple does not seek to be made better for his own glory but in the interest and for the glory of God. He feels with Paul that he must apprehend, because he was apprehended for that very purpose. HTR/*GG*, 39.

The disciple must seek first the kingdom of the heavenly Father and his righteousness, in distinction from the pagan frame of mind which seeks after the things of the world. KOG/*SW*, 312.

Diversity of the Biblical Witness

For, God having chosen to reveal the truth through human instruments, it follows that these instruments must be both numerous and of varied adaptation to the common end. Individual coloring, therefore, and a peculiar manner of representation are not only not detrimental to a full statement of the truth, but directly subservient to it. IBT/*SW*, 14.

The divine objectivity and the human individuality here do not collide, nor exclude each other, because the man . . . with his whole character, his gifts, and his training, is subsumed under the divine plan. The human is but the glass through which the divine light is reflected, and all the sides and angles into which the glass has been cut serve no other purpose than to distribute to us the truth in all the riches of its prismatic colors. IBT/*SW*, 14.

Dogmatics

Dogmatics is the crown which grows out of all the work that biblical theology can accomplish. IBT/*SW*, 24.

[commenting upon Bavinck's *Gereformeerde Dogmatiek*, vol. 1] His work is free from what has harmed dogmatics in the past, perhaps, more than anything else: the inordinate desire to furnish a definite, precise answer to all minute and abstruse questions. *GD1*/*SW*, 357.

[commenting upon Bavinck's *Gereformeerde Dogmatiek*, vol. 2] The very opening words of the volume show that Dr. Bavinck is profoundly impressed with the inherent limitations of every scientific discussion of the nature and attributes of God. "Mystery," he says, "is the life-element of Dogmatics." *GD2*/*SW*, 486.

Dogmatic theology is, when rightly cultivated, as truly a biblical and as truly an inductive science as its younger sister. IBT/*SW*, 23.

Dogmatics and Eschatology

In dogmatics the chapter devoted to eschatology is ordinarily given the last place. The sequence in the actual process predetermines the scientific arrangement. The developments at the end are naturally viewed in the light of a consummation of the redemptive acts and experiences dealt with in soteriology. The interest attaching to them, if not wholly, yet most frequently, arises from the desire to see "perfected" what has been begun, a desire fully justified both from a theoretical and a practical point of view. At bottom, of course, the desire springs and gathers momentum from the habitual consciousness of the Christian state as an unfinished state with which the protracted abode of the church in this world, and our own life under preliminary conditions have familiarized but not satisfied us. This provisional state of affairs has been crystalized in a theological system with its own laws of perspective. We think and theologize out of the present into the future, because our base of existence is in the present. Whether this is as it ought to be need not be here considered; it certainly is a matter-of-fact state of mind. *PE*, 42.

Dona Supernaturalia

[commenting upon Bavinck's refutation of the Romanist doctrine of *dona supernaturalia*] The Romanist doctrine of the *dona supernaturalia* is shown to have two roots, one in the neo-Platonist idea of a mystical deification as the true destiny of man, the other in the Pelagian principle of the meritoriousness of good works. If man is to earn the *status gloriae* which is supernatural, he can do so only by employment of a principle likewise intrinsically supernatural, the *gratia infusa* or *gratia gratum faciens*. The Reformed doctrine of the covenant of works differs from this in that according to it eternal life was not to be earned by Adam *ex condigno*, but *ex pacto* . . . not by supernatural, but by natural means. Virtually Rome eliminates all grace, for there is no reason to call the *donum superadditum* grace, in any other sense than life, intellect, wisdom, power were grace to Adam. *GD2/SW*, 492.

Easter

It seems a pity that in the more prominent associations of our Easter observance so little place has been left to it. The Pauline remembrance of the supreme fact, so significant for redemption from sin, and the modern-Christian celebration of the feast have gradually become two quite different things. Who at the present time thinks of Easter as intended and adapted to fill the soul with a new jubilant assurance of the forgiveness of sin as the guarantee of the inheritance of eternal life? *PE*, 153.

Ecstatic Speech

It is plain on the surface of the biblical data that ecstasy in the Philonic or Montanist sense had no place in prophetism. The biblical prophets coming out of the visionary state have a distinct remembrance of the things seen and heard. Biblical prophecy is not a process in which God dislodges the mind of man. *BT*, 226.

Edom

Until the destruction of Jerusalem the prophets speak of Edom as the representative of the enemies of God's people. *MOP*, 198.

Effectual Calling

Zacchaeus, who perhaps had never before encountered the Savior, who would have hardly ventured to approach Jesus, at a single word is transformed into a disciple of the Lord. He knows the voice of the Shepherd immediately, makes haste to come down and receives him with joy. This is that wonderful effectual calling by name, which takes place wherever a sinner is saved, and which, while it may not always take place with such suddenness and under such striking circumstances as happened here, yet is in substance everywhere equally supernatural and immediate. SSL/*GG*, 53.

El-Shaddai

This name . . . designates the divine power as standing in the service of his covenant-relation to the patriarchs, as transcending nature and overpowering it in the interests of redemption. OM/*ISBE*, 2188.

If [*El* and *Elohim*] signify God's relation to nature, and *Jehovah* is his redemptive name, then *El-Shaddai* may be said to express how God uses nature for supernature. *BT*, 82.

Election

The Scriptures do not leave room for the opinion that at any point, either in the eternal decree or in its historical unfolding, God's love for those intended to become his people has been undifferentiated from his love for wider groups of humanity. Every formula which would efface or even tend to obscure this fundamental distinction ought to be at the outset rejected as unbiblical. SDL/*SW*, 456.

▨ The ultimate root of every believer's relation to God lies in the most intimate and individual act of election, an act wherein the love of God consciously chooses and sets up over against itself a human spirit to be bound to God in the bonds of everlasting friendship. Election and the covenants answer to each other as the root and the fruitage of the highest type of religion. HED/*SW*, 232.

▨ God's purpose with us in presenting this teaching in his Word has never been that we should sit down and attempt, by brooding, to find out whether we, too, are numbered among those who from eternity are loved in Christ Jesus. That is a hopeless task! It is like arithmetic without numbers. SR/*GG*, 230.

▨ The Scriptures do not assert that election and preterition are arbitrary decrees to the mind of God. All they insist upon is that the motives underlying them are inscrutable to us, and have nothing whatever to do with the worthiness or unworthiness of man. SDL/*SW*, 444.

▨ The idea of election . . . designates an act whereby God chooses for himself, or unto holiness, with the definite purpose that those chosen shall stand in a relationship of the closest appurtenance and most intimate love to himself. SDL/*SW*, 454.

▨ Election is intended to bring out the *gratuitous* character of grace. With regard to the objective part of the work of redemption there is scarcely any need of stressing this. That man himself has made no contribution toward accomplishing the atonement is obvious in itself. But no sooner does the redeeming work enter into the subjectivity of man than the obviousness ceases, although the reality of the principle is not, of course, in the least abated. The semblance easily results, that in receiving and working out the subjective benefits of grace for his transformation, the individual man has to some extent been the decisive factor. And to affirm this, to however small a degree, would be to detract in the same proportion from the monergism of the divine grace and from the glory of God. *BT*, 94.

Elizabeth

Elizabeth means "God is my Oath"; i.e. the one object of my religious devotion. *CEV*, 1.

Enjoyment of God

We see . . . how thoroughly this life, which constitutes man's blessed possession of the kingdom, is dominated by the thought of communion with God, as its chief source of enjoyment. *KGC*, 76.

The eschatological state is before all else a state in which the enjoyment of Jehovah, the beatific vision of his face, the pleasures at his right hand, the perpetual dwelling with him in his sanctuary, form the supreme good. EP, 349.

The possession of Jehovah himself by his people will be of all the delights of the world to come the chief and most satisfying, the paradise within the paradise of God. WT/*GG*, 3.

Eschatological Consciousness

[commenting upon the early church] They could not help correlating more closely than we are accustomed to do their present beliefs and experiences with the final, eternal issues of the history of redemption, and interpreting the former in the light of the latter. To an extent we can hardly appreciate theoretically, far less reproduce in our mode of feeling, they were conscious of standing at the turning point of the ages, of living in the very presence of the world to come. EAP/*SW*, 91.

The believer should not be indifferent to the natural environment in which the providence of God has placed him; but he should not have his portion in the present life in the same sense as the children of the world have it. He must gravitate toward the future life and must make every contact into which he comes with earthly concerns subordinated and subservient to this. RR/*GG*, 132.

Jesus being consciously the Messiah, his whole manner of thinking and feeling could not be otherwise than steeped in [an eschatological] atmosphere. It was an atmosphere in which the currents of air from this world and those from the world to come constantly intermingled, with the stronger breeze steadily blowing toward the future. Only for those to whom this state of mind is a religiously congenial state can there be more than a passing, superficial acquaintance with Jesus. *SDJ*, 21.

Eschatological, Semi-

In principle, but in principle only, the coming age has already arrived. This conception is similar to that presented by Christ in his statements that the kingdom has come, and still must come. This may be called a semi-eschatological state of mind. *TEH*, 53.

What Paul considered essential for the present (in Ephesians particularly emphasized) semi-eschatological life on earth he regarded as in the highest degree normative for the heavenly life in the fully-attained state of eternity. *PE*, 311.

Through the appearance of the Messiah, as the great representative figure of the coming aeon, [the] new age has begun to enter into the actual experience of the believer. He has been translated into a state which, while falling short of the consummated life of eternity, yet may be truly characterized as semi-eschatological. *EAP/SW*, 92.

The passages in which the entrance upon the Christian state is represented as a being raised with Christ come here under consideration. As shown before, they are semi-eschatological in import; they take for granted that in principle the believer has been translated into the higher world of the new aeon. Still for this very reason they establish a real, a vital relationship between what is enjoyed already, and what will be received at the end, for it is characteristic of the principle to lead on unto the final fulfillment. *PE*, 157.

Living . . . in a world of semi-futurities there is every reason to expect that the thought of the earliest Christians should have moved backwards from the anticipated attainment in its fulness to the present partial experiences and interpreted these in terms of the former.

Just as natural as it appears to us to regard eschatology the crown of soteriology, it must have felt to them to scan the endowments and enjoyments already in their possession as veritable precursors of the inheritance outstanding. *PE*, 43–44.

Eschatology

Eschatology is simply the crowning of redemption. *BT*, 366.

The Messiah is the introducer and beginner of the eschatological world. *PE*, 289.

The eschatological point of view is, of course, originally historical and dramatic; a new world can come only with the new age and therefore lies at first in the future. EAP/*SW*, 115.

The peculiar feature of eschatology is that it brings something *new*. It brings the eternal side of the promises of God. *TEH*, 21.

[Eschatology] is "the doctrine of the last things." It deals with the teaching or belief that the world-movement, religiously considered, tends toward a definite final goal, beyond which a new order of affairs will be established, frequently with the further implication that this new order of affairs will not be subject to any further change, but will partake of the static character of the eternal. *PE*, 1.

Eschatology and Christ

In Christian eschatology the Christ occupies from beginning to end the center of the stage. All developments, all transactions, all gifts, all experiences that make up the drama of the great world-change are related to him and derive their significance from him; he is the representative and exponent of the future life in its totality. "To be forever with the Lord" is the succinct expression of what the eschatological hope means to a Christian. HED/*SW*, 197.

Eschatology and History

[commenting upon Paul's eschatological structure] For in it the world process is viewed as a unit. The end is placed in the light of the beginning, and all intermediate developments are construed with reference to the purpose *a quo* and the terminus *ad quem*. Eschatology, in other words, even that of the most primitive kind, yields *ipso facto* a philosophy of history, be it of the most rudimentary sort. And every philosophy of history bears in itself the seed of a theology. To this must be added that the Pauline outline of history possessed in the messianic concept a centralizing factor of extraordinary potency, an element whereby the antitheses above named were dissolved into an exceptionally harmonious synthesis. *PE*, 61.

All eschatological interpretation of history, when united to a strong religious mentality, cannot but produce the finest practical theological fruitage. To take God as source and end of all that exists and happens, and to hold such a view suffused with the warmth of genuine devotion, stands not only related to theology as the fruit stands to the tree: it is by reason of its essence a veritable theological tree of life. *PE*, 61.

Eschatology and Soteriology

The New Testament writers [make] the future the interpreter of the present, eschatology the norm and example of soteriological experience. EAP/*SW*, 92.

[commenting upon the Sabbath] The Sabbath brings [the] principle of the eschatological structure of history to bear upon the mind of man after a symbolical and a typical fashion. . . . Man is reminded in this way that life is not an aimless existence, that a goal lies beyond. This was true before, and apart from, redemption. The eschatological is an older strand in revelation than the soteric. *BT*, 140.

Insofar as the covenant of works posited for mankind an absolute goal and unchangeable future, the eschatological may be even said to have preceded the soteric religion. EP, 325.

The Spirit's eschatological functions are simply the prolongation of his work in the soteriological sphere. *PE*, 160.

   The NT doctrine of salvation has grown up to a large extent in the closest interaction with its eschatological teaching. The present experience was interpreted in light of the future. ENT/*SW*, 26.

   [Paul] is not content with giving a soteriological construction, as in the contrast between the disobedience of Adam and the obedience of Christ (Rom. 5:12–20), though this is in itself one of the boldest and grandest contrasts ever drawn; but, recognizing that Christ accomplishes far more than the restoration of what Adam ever lost, he places the two over against each other in 1 Corinthians 15:45–49 as the representatives of two successive stages in the carrying out of God's sublime purpose for humanity, in such a way that the state of rectitude and the state of glory are by a sudden flash of light seen in their mutual relation, detached as it were for a moment from the soteriological process intervening. TP/*SW*, 359.

   The time when God gathers his fruit is the joyous vintage-feast of all high religion. The value of a work lies in its ultimate product. Consequently, where religion entwines itself around a progressive work of God, such as redemption, its general responsiveness becomes prospective, cumulative, climacteric; it gravitates with all its inherent weight toward the end. A redemptive religion without eschatological interest would be a contradiction in terms. The orthodox interpretation of Scripture has always recognized this. To it redemption and eschatology are co-eval in biblical history. EP, 324–25.

   The question is not so much whether the doctrines of justification and possession of the Spirit and union with Christ carry with themselves an outlook into the future, but rather whether those acts and states to which these doctrines refer are not from the outset eschatological acts and states, or, more strictly speaking, anticipations in this life of what had previously been regarded as reserved for the end. Only by realizing the extent to which this is true can we appreciate the profound eschatological interest that pervades all Paul's teaching. *SPC*, 485.

The eschatological strand is the most systematic in the entire fabric of the Pauline thought-world. For it now appears that the closely interwoven soteric tissue derives its pattern from the eschatological scheme, which bears all the marks of having had precedence in his mind. *PE*, 60.

Just as natural as it appears to us to regard eschatology the crown of soteriology, it must have felt to [the early church] to scan the endowments and enjoyments already in their possession as veritable precursors of the inheritance outstanding. *PE*, 43–44.

Eschatology, Centrality of

The eschatological interest of early believers was no mere fringe of their religious experience, but the very heart of its inspiration. It expressed and embodied the profound supernaturalism and soteriological character of the NT faith. ENT/*SW*, 26.

[The] eschatological outlook is what holds the religion of the Prophets and the religion of Jesus and the religion of Paul together, despite all apparent variations in particulars. And it is the one supreme criterion of what constitutes, historically speaking, a Christian. It is the mother-soil out of which the tree of the whole redemptive organism has sprung. *SDJ*, 21–22.

[contrasting the eschatological mindset of early Christians with the non-eschatological mindset of present Christians] To the early Christians a different orientation had been given, and that not merely as a matter of practical religious outlook, but likewise through the teaching of Revelation. The ultimate things were brought forward in their consciousness, in order that in the light of these they might learn the better to understand the provisional and the preparatory. For the ultimate is in a very important sense the normative, that to which every preceding stage will have to conform itself to prove the genuineness of its Christian character. *PE*, 42.

So long as the consciousness of redemption contents itself with living in the present moment, or ranges over a limited outlook backwards and forwards, the theological impulse may remain dormant and no desire need be felt to bring order and system into the wealth of the divine acts and disclosures as one after the other they enter into the cognition or experience of man. But the matter becomes entirely different when eschatology posits an absolute goal at the end of the redemptive process corresponding to an absolute beginning of the world in creation: for then, no longer a segment but the whole sweep of history is drawn into one great perspective, and the mind is impelled to view every part in relation to the whole. To do this means to construct a primitive theological system. Thus eschatology becomes the mother of theology and that first of all theology in the form of a philosophy of redemptive history. HED/*SW*, 193.

Eschatology, Contrasted to Evolution

Evolution means constant transformation, in the present case constant spiritual growth, but without any crisis or catastrophe. Eschatology, on the other hand, means a break in the process of development, suspension of the continuity, a sovereign termination of the historical process by the intervention of God. OLDR/*SW*, 317.

Eschatology, Jewish

Because it was felt that the earthly and the heavenly, the sensual and the spiritual, the temporal and the eternal, the political and the transcendental, the national and the cosmical would not combine, and yet neither of the two could safely be abandoned, the incongruous elements were mechanically forced together in the scheme of two successive kingdoms, during the former of which the urgent claims of Israel pertaining to this world would receive at least a transient satisfaction, whilst in the latter the higher and broader hopes would find their everlasting embodiment. Under this scheme the Messiah and his work inevitably became associated with the provisional temporal order of affairs and ceased to be of significance for the final state. EAP/*SW*, 91–92.

[commenting upon Israel] Ignorance as to the end would easily produce ignorance or imperfect understanding with reference to the whole order of things under which the people were living. MEM/*GG*, 91.

Eschatology, Modern Attack upon

The eschatological frame of mind is a hopeless anachronism to the modern consciousness. EAP/*SW*, 94.

If you have ever moved for a time in circles where the Christian faith has ceased to exist, where the belief in immortality has practically vanished, where people live consciously and professedly for this world only (and do not even attempt to break down the bars that shut them in), then you will have felt how sadly life was degraded, how pitifully brought down to the animal stage, even though it had all the advantages of worldly refinement and culture, simply because [the] element of hope had been taken out of it. CH/*GG*, 145.

With the rise of Rationalism, eschatology was bound to drift into troubled waters. Eschatology is preeminently historical, and Rationalism is from its cradle devoid of historic sense. It despises tradition; the past it ignores and the future it barely tolerates with a supercilious conceit of self. Moreover Rationalism is bent upon and enamored of the inward. To it the essence and value of all religion lie in purely-subjective ethico-religious experiences. Now in the eschatological process from the nature of the case, the forces of propulsion must come from *ab extra*. *PE*, preface.

The practical spirit of the age demands concentration of the religious energy upon the needs and issues of the present moment and of the tangible world, whilst eschatology invites an expenditure of spiritual power on transcendental realities both unseen and remote. OLDR/*SW*, 317.

The difference between the modern apathy in eschatological matters and the interest this subject possessed to the mind of Jesus is due not to an external change of age and environment, but to a difference in the very tone and spirit of religion itself. OLDR/*SW*, 319.

▪ [commenting on reasons for the decline of the eschatological consciousness] Various causes have contributed toward this state of neglect into which eschatology has fallen. Among them we may mention the extensive application of the principle of evolution to the history of God's kingdom, the preeminently practical bent of modern Christianity, the spread of a one-sided moralizing conception of the Christian religion, and, perhaps more than anything else, the general anti-supernaturalism by which present-day theological thinking is colored. OLDR/*SW*, 317.

▪ [Eschatology] has become the large mountain of offense lying across the pathway of modern unbelief. That part of it which we call messiahship was already a piece broken from that rock in the days of Jesus. The double offense was one at bottom. Neither will be tolerated in modern religious thought. And the results will inevitably be the same. Paul divorced from his eschatology becomes unfit for his apostleship; Jesus divested of his messiahship can no longer serve us as a Savior. *PE*, preface.

Eschatology, New Testament

▪ Everything after Christ's ascension, including the present life of believers, belongs to *those days*, that is, to the eschatological period. *TEH*, 53.

▪ The NT, by spiritualizing the entire messianic circle of ideas, becomes keenly alive to its affinity to the content of the highest eternal hope, and consequently tends to identify the two, to find the age to come anticipated in the present. ENT/*SW*, 26.

▪ Even though [the NT] regards the present work of Christ as preliminary to the consummate order of things, it does not separate the two in essence or quality, it does not exclude the Messiah from a supreme place in the coming world, and does not expect a temporal messianic kingdom in the future as distinguished from Christ's present spiritual reign, and as preceding the state of eternity. ENT/*SW*, 27.

Broadly speaking, the development of NT eschatology consists in this, that the two ages are increasingly recognized as answering to two spheres of being which coexist from of old, so that the coming of the new age assumes the character of a revelation and extension of the supernal order of things, rather than of its first entrance into existence. Inasmuch as the coming world stood for the perfect and eternal and in the realm of heaven such a perfect, eternal order of things already existed, the reflection inevitably arose that these two were in some sense identical. ENT/*SW*, 28.

The appearance and eschatologizing of the post-resurrection state of the Messiah changes all . . . anxious, half-querulous questioning into an enthusiastic hope. *PE*, 35.

So far as the authoritative teaching of the New Testament books is concerned, it consistently emphasizes the thought that what believers seek in the world to come is the perfection of their religious relation to God. HED/*SW*, 230.

It is a recognized principle in New Testament teaching that in one aspect the eschatological order of things is identical with the heavenly order of things. EAP/*SW*, 97.

Eschatology, Pagan

The pagan eschatological beliefs have a mythical or astronomic basis; they bear no definite relation to any scheme of historical progress, and, with the exception of Parsism, know of no absolute final crisis, beyond which no further change is contemplated. These two defects are closely connected. Because the ideas have their origin with the present world-process, they cannot lead to anything beyond it. The world-cycle runs its course, obeys its stars, absolves its round, and then the end links on to a new beginning, ushering in a repetition of the same sequence. The golden age is bound to return, but it will be no more enduring than it was before. EP, 334.

Eschatology, Pauline

For with Paul, as elsewhere in Scripture, eschatology is supernaturalism in the *n*th degree. *PE*, 62.

Paul looked upon the Christian state as something belonging to a totally different order of affairs from the state of nature, and the eschatological contrast was to him the only category which could adequately convey this difference. EAP/*SW*, 118.

The theocentric bent of Paul's mind makes for the conclusion that in the Christian life all must be from God and for God, and the Spirit of God would be the natural agent for securing this. EAP/*SW*, 122.

[Paul] views the resurrection of Christ as the beginning of the general resurrection of the saints. The general resurrection of the saints being an eschatological event, indeed constituting together with the judgment the main content of the eschatological program, it follows that to Paul in this one point at least the eschatological course of events had already been set in motion, an integral piece of "the last things" has become an accomplished fact. EAP/*SW*, 92–93.

Paul . . . teaches that through the cross of Christ the believer has been in principle snatched out of this present evil world and translated into the eternal kingdom of the Son of God's love. The resurrection of Christ is to the apostle the first act in the general resurrection that will introduce the final kingdom of God. Christians have in effect passed over from the age that is into the age to come. Their commonwealth is above, where they sit with Christ in heavenly places, and all that is necessary in the future is that they shall undergo the last change which will make them, in body as well as in soul, redeemed, supernatural, eschatological creatures. HED/*SW*, 197.

To unfold the apostle's eschatology means to set forth his theology as a whole. Through a conceptual retroversion the end will be seen to give birth to the beginning in the emergence of truth. *PE*, 11.

For to Paul the chief actor in this drama [of redemption] *had come* upon the scene; the Messiah had been made present, and could not but be looked upon as henceforth the dominating figure in all further developments. And Christ was to Paul so close, so all-comprehensive and all-pervasive, that nothing could remain peripheral wherein he occupied the central place. We hope . . . to show that, as a matter of fact, not only the Christology but also the soteriology of the apostle's teaching is so closely interwoven with the eschatology, that, were the question put, which of the strands is more central, which more peripheral, the eschatology would have as good a claim to the central place as the others. *PE*, 26–28.

Although Paul exhibited in all his labors for the gospel the most intense zeal, and an outpouring of apparently exhaustless energy, yet, when it comes to the point of eschatology, there is to all this a sort of counterpoise, owing to which the apostle never loses the desire of finding rest in the unnamable, unfathomable depths of a mystic satisfaction in God and Christ, such as craved no further out-venturing into realms beyond. All Paul's labor was a most strenuous endeavor to bring the restlessly-temporal to where it would lose itself in the forever-undisturbable aionion. There is no passage in the Epistles indicative of an opposite trend or desire. *PE*, 315–16.

[The] great eschatological transactions have already begun to take place, and . . . believers have already attained to at least partial enjoyment of eschatological privileges. . . . With Paul there has been a prelude to the last judgment and resurrection in the death and resurrection of Christ, and the life in the Spirit is the firstfruits of the heavenly state to come. ENT/*SW*, 26.

Eschatology, Practicality of

The aionion-concept . . . belongs to the acme of religion, serving to express its absoluteness. Eschatology ceases to be an abstract speculation for those who have learned, and in principle experienced this: it becomes the profoundest and most practical of all thought-complexes because they, like Paul, live and move and have their redemptively-religious treasures in God. *PE*, 293–94.

Eternal

[Eternal] is that which belongs to the heavenly world and partakes of its nature and power. PC/*SW*, 153.

Eternal Life

It is obvious that from the Christian standpoint no greater injury can be done to the true progress and healing of humanity in this present evil world than to make it promises and offer it remedies which have no vital connection with the hope of eternal life. EP, 363–64.

Eternal State

To conceive of Paul as focusing his mind on any phase of relative consummation, and as tying up to this the term "parousia," inevitably would involve his relegating the eternal things to a rank of secondary importance. It would have meant a repetition, or perhaps a continuation, of the Judaistic scheme of thought. *PE*, 76.

The main character of the state following the resurrection and judgment is described by the adjective "*aiōnios*." *PE*, 288.

The Christian train of thought [concerning the eternal state] is the reversal of that of the Old Testament: the eternal is not so much a prolongation of the temporal, but the temporal rather an anticipation of the eternal. EP, 363.

[commenting upon the final judgment] The eschatological process . . . on its evil no less than on its favorable side, issues into a state that is literally eternal. *PE*, 296.

The coming of the Christ had fixed [the New Testament writers'] attention upon the eternal world in all its absoluteness and fulness, and with this in mind they interpreted everything that through the Christ happened for them and in them. EAP/*SW*, 92.

Eternity

It is the prerogative of God, the Eternal One, to work for eternity. MEM/*GG*, 90.

Eternity is the form of the divine existence, that in which Jehovah dwells, the atmosphere that surrounds him. OHGG/*GG*, 265.

It is in Hebrews for the first time that conscious reflection is observed and positive emphasis placed upon the primordial, constant, stable existence of the higher world, antedating and overarching and outlasting all temporal developments, a world of the αἰώνιον, not subject to change and harboring the supreme realities. Hebrews recognizes, with Paul, that the finale of the great drama of redemption in the death and ascension of Christ has put its impress upon the things above. The heavenly sanctuary was cleansed; through Christ's sacrifice the spirits of just men were made perfect; he carried with his new life the supreme form of the rest of God into the sabbath that had been celebrated above from the beginning. Still the main stress is laid on the other side, on the fact that in reality all along the world to come had preexisted in its heavenly form. The chronological relation is reversed; that which in course of historical development appeared the last was in a deeper and truer sense the first. Broadly speaking, the Christian things are not a new product of time; they are rather the descent into time of the essence of eternity. HED/*SW*, 198–99.

Eternity is not pregnant with other eternities. We do not hear of further sowing nor further reaping in the fields of the blessed. It is useless to carry the spirit of time into the heart of eternity. There clings an earth and time–savor to this questioning what there will be to occupy one's self withal when arrived above. As if the Lord God himself would not be there with his inexhaustible fulness! *PE*, 316.

Because the New Testament times brought the final realization of the divine counsel of redemption as to its objective and central facts . . . the deepest depths of eternity are opened up to the eye of apostle and seer. IBT/*SW*, 13.

Eternity, Essential to Christianity

[commenting upon a this-world-only Christianity] A God who treated the fugitive generations of the race as so many passing acquaintances, content to see them afloat in and float out of the luminous circle of his own immortal life, could not continue to evoke the worship of his creatures. Pagan cult he might receive, but Christian service not. Men would become, and in a far more tragic sense than the psalmist meant it, strangers and sojourners with him. The Psalter bears eloquent witness to the truth that a hope of indefinite perpetuation for the collective body is not enough. It requires the assurance of the eternity of religion in the individual soul to secure the permanence of religion as such. EP, 364–65.

Ethics

Our Lord speaks not only as authoritative but as sovereign in the sphere of ethics. We feel that his authority in the world of teaching rests on his sovereignty in the world of things. He did not come to propound a new system of ethics as a thinker of moral genius, but to summon into being a new realm of moral and religious realities, even the kingdom of God. He stands and speaks out of the midst of a great redemptive movement of which he himself is the central and controlling factor. UMG/*SW*, 341–42.

The messianic consciousness underlies all the high idealism of our Lord's ethics and alone renders it historically intelligible. UMG/*SW*, 342.

It cannot be too much emphasized that "holiness" is in the Pauline vocabulary never ethical perfection as such and without regard to its terminus in God. No construction of the idea losing this out of sight is from the apostle's viewpoint a thoroughly Christianized idea. Whatever fruit it may cultivate, it can never produce the highest, which is in this case the only true religious fruitage, its subserviency to the glory of God who is the absolute end of all ethical striving. *PE*, 310.

[Ethics] are not, however, represented as independent of religion, much less as the sole content of religion; but they are the product of religion. Genesis 17:1 contains the classic expression of this: "I am El-Shaddai; walk before me, then thou shalt be blameless." The "walking before Jehovah" pictures the constant presence of Jehovah as walking behind Abraham, and supervising him. The thought of the divine approval furnishes the motive for obedience. Also the force of El-Shaddai must be noticed. What shapes Abraham's conduct is not the general thought of God as moral ruler, but specifically the thought of El-Shaddai, who fills his life with miraculous grace. Thus morality is put on a redemptive basis and inspired by the principle of faith. *BT*, 88.

Too much is often made of the purely autonomous movement of ethics, eliminating as unworthy the unexplained, unmotivated demand of God. To do the good and reject the evil from a reasoned insight into their respective natures is a noble thing, but it is a still nobler thing to do so out of regard for the nature of God, and the noblest thing of all is the ethical strength, which, when required, will act from personal attachment to God, without for the moment enquiring into these more abstruse reasons. The pure delight in obedience adds to the ethical value of a choice. *BT*, 32.

To Jesus the question of right and wrong was not a purely moral, but in the deepest sense a religious question. His teaching on righteousness means the subsumption of ethics under religion. *KGC*, 64.

[Jesus] did not come as a thinker to propound a new system of ethics; he came to summon into being a new kingdom of moral realities. He stands in and speaks out of the midst of a great redemptive movement in which he himself is the central and controlling factor. *SDJ*, 62.

[commenting upon Matt. 5:6] What renders [righteousness] desirable is the vision of it as associated with God. In its ultimate analysis it is the passion for God himself. Here is the cry of the psalmist: "Whom have I in heaven but thee, and there is none upon earth that I desire besides thee," translated into terms of ethics. HTR/*GG*, 36.

Where the norm of righteousness is a deified law rather than a personal lawgiver, and where the supreme motive for obedience is a self-interested one, there inevitably the faults above enumerated [formalism, casuistry, self-righteousness, hypocrisy, etc.] must make their appearance. *KGC*, 61.

■ [If] the controlling motive is self-centered, the escape from transgression will form a more serious concern than the positive fulfillment of what the spirit of the law demands. *KGC*, 61.

Ethics and Eschatology

■ The believer's whole ethico-religious existence, the sum-total of his Christian experience and progress, all that is distinctive of his life and conduct demands being viewed as a preparation for the crowning grace of the resurrection. *PE*, 157.

■ [It cannot] be claimed that the ethical teaching of Jesus, simply because it is not in each instance correlated with the eschatological hope, is for that reason internally detached from or indifferent to such hope. The two had their higher unity in Jesus' insistence upon the glory of God as the supreme end of his mission. Precisely because he was an ethical teacher in the service of God, and an eschatological enthusiast for the sake of God, these two motives could not clash in his mind. Had he been an eschatologist for the sake of eschatology, as Schweitzer and others make him out, the case would have been different. *TG*, 112.

■ The question whether intense eschatological interest and due regard for the duties of the present hour can go together, has in principle received its answer. The two things were compatible in Jesus' mind because both alike drew their life-sap from his absolute absorption in the love of God. The cosmical movements of the great eschatological drama and the little private experiences and concerns of the individual soul, the prayer in the closet, the alms in secret, met together in that they both subserved the glory of God. *SDJ*, 65.

■ The spirit of the age is not overfriendly to eschatology, and on the other hand is inclined to ethicize in every direction. Will it still continue to bow before Jesus as the supreme teacher of ethics after having been told that righteousness did not form a constituent element of his crowning religious conception? *DR*, 303.

Ethics, Failure of Jewish

▓ The characteristic faults of the Jewish ethics were formalism, casuistry, an inclination to emphasize the prohibition rather than the commandment, and, worst of all, self-righteousness and hypocrisy. *KGC*, 60.

▓ [commenting upon the twofold source behind Jewish ethical failure] On the one hand, Judaism had virtually become a worship of the law as such. The dead letter of the law had taken the place of the living God. . . . On the other hand, the Jewish law-observance was self-centered, because it was chiefly intended to be the instrument for securing the blessedness of the coming age. *KGC*, 60–61.

▓ Where the moral life is thus concentrated on the outward conduct, where the conscience does not search and judge itself in the presence of the personal God, who knows the heart, there the sins of self-righteousness and hypocrisy find a fertile soil for development. *KGC*, 61.

Evangelism

▓ We shall never succeed in impressing men, untouched by grace, with the riches and glory of religion, until we learn from Jesus to hold up to them the mirror of their sin and destitution. SSL/*GG*, 60.

Exodus

▓ The same act which made Jehovah Israel's Father likewise made him Israel's King, viz., the redemption from Egypt. KOG/*SW*, 314.

▓ The Hebrews were delivered not merely from outside foreign bondage, they were likewise rescued from inward spiritual degradation and sin. *BT*, 111.

Externalism, Religious

▓ [commenting upon religious externalism being the problem addressed in the Epistle to the Hebrews] As they took exception to the humiliation, so they took exception to the exaltation of the Savior, not of course as such, but because it involved his absence, invisibleness, the unostentatious character of his ministry in a remote sphere. On earth the Messiah's glory was veiled by his lowliness, in heaven it is withdrawn from sight through his exaltation. But the disposition which finds fault with both is in each case in principle the same: it is the desire to see, to have near, to touch, in a word, religious externalism. PC/*SW*, 131.

Fact, Relationship to Faith

To join in the outcry against dogma and fact means to lower the ideal of what the Christian consciousness ought normally to be to the level of the spiritual depression of our own day and generation. How much better that we should all strive to raise our drooping faith and to re-enrich our depleted experience up to the standard of those blessed periods in the life of the church, when the belief in the Bible history and religion of the heart went hand in hand and kept equal pace, when people were ready to lay down their lives for facts and doctrines, because facts and doctrines formed the daily spiritual nourishment of their souls. CFTBH/*SW*, 471.

What does Christ mean for us? For what do we need him? If we have learned to know ourselves as guilty sinners, destitute of all hope and life in ourselves, and if we have experienced that from him came to us pardon, peace and strength, will it not sound like mockery in our ears if somebody tells us that it does not matter whether Jesus rose from the dead on the third day? It is of the very essence of saving faith that it clamors for facts, facts to show that the heavens have opened, that the tide of sinful nature has been reversed, the guilt of sin expiated, the reign of death destroyed and life and immortality brought to light. R/*GG*, 71.

It is plain at a glance that the faith of the apostles and the faith of the apostolic church revolved around the great redemptive facts in which they found the interpretation of the inner meaning of the Savior's life. To the earliest Christian consciousness doctrine and fact were wedded from the outset. Facts, like the incarnation, the atonement, the resurrection, the ascension, the future coming of Christ, were believed not merely in virtue of their miraculous character, as so many grounds of faith; they belonged to the very essence of the object of faith, constituted that in which faith laid hold of God. CFTBH/*SW*, 469.

The source of danger does not lie in the facts or doctrines as such, but in the religious apathy and superficiality of our own minds, which seem no longer capable of responding to the wealth of spiritual forces stored up in the world of redemption. There is not a fact in which the Bible summons us to believe that is not the exponent of some great principle adapted to stir the depths of our religious life. CFTBH/*SW*, 471.

Faith

[Faith] is the great spiritualizing principle, for faith is the state of mind that keeps us in touch with the higher world. *TEH*, 22.

Religious belief exists not in its last analysis on what we can prove to be so, but on the fact of God having declared it to be so. Behind the belief, the assent, therefore, there lies an antecedent trust distinguishable from the subsequent trust. And this reliance upon the word of God is an eminently religious act. Hence it is inaccurate to say that belief is merely the prerequisite of faith and not an element of faith itself. *BT*, 84.

In the biblical religion the subjective element is nowhere lacking; on the contrary, it enters into the fabric of practical Christianity with exceptional richness such as no pagan form of piety can rival. But it always keeps in the closest touch with what God has done in the objective sphere, outside the subjectivity of the believer. The most instructive example of this is found in the cultivation of Abraham's faith through the objective promises and their objective fulfillment on the part of Jehovah. *SDJ*, 21.

According to Romans 4:20, the innermost essence of faith is that it gives glory to God. AL/*SW*, 398.

110

To the vision of faith that which Jehovah will do at the end, his conclusive, consummate action, must surpass everything in importance. Faith will sing its supreme song when face to face, either in anticipation or reality, with the supreme act of God. EP, 324.

[Faith] annihilates the distance of time as much as of space [and] deals with heaven as it exists. HM/*GG*, 115.

Faith and Christ

In the matter of justification, Paul directs the gaze of faith not merely to the cross retrospectively, but likewise upward to the glorified existence of Christ in heaven, wherein all the merit of the cross is laid up and made available forever. *PE*, 154.

The believer's faith, according to Paul, does not terminate upon the historical Christ but upon the Christ in glory. Nevertheless, in the glorified Christ the believer's faith grasps all the atoning significance of the cross, because the state of glory is the product and crown of the atonement. PC/*SW*, 158.

There can be no participation in the merits which flow from Christ's atoning death except through such a faith as effects a personal union with him; a faith consisting not merely in the mental acceptance of his sacrifice as a historic fact, but a faith which mystically feeds upon him, the living sacrifice as he now exists in heaven. GP/*GG*, 240.

Jesus Christ goes with his church through all the changes and vicissitudes of time, the same yesterday, today and forever. He is always accessible, under every condition reliable and therefore the one proper object of faith, the only safe source of confidence because in him alone is that eternal certainty which faith needs to rest upon if it is to be faith at all. TEC/*GG*, 202.

Faith and Desire for More Faith

Faith and a desire for more faith frequently go hand in hand. The reason is that through faith we lay hold of God, and in grasping the infinite object, the utter inadequacy of each single act of appropriation immediately reveals itself in the very act. It is the same in the Gospel: "Lord, I believe; help thou mine unbelief" [Mark 9:24]. *BT*, 83.

Faith and Knowledge

[Faith] presupposes knowledge, because it needs a mental complex, person or things, to be occupied about. . . . In fact knowledge is so interwoven with faith that the question arises, whether it be sufficient to call it a prerequisite, and not rather an ingredient of faith. *BT*, 388.

Faith, Justifying

In Romans and Galatians faith is in the main trust in the grace of God, the instrument of justification, the channel through which the vital influences flowing from Christ are received by the believer. HM/*GG*, 103.

[In Romans and Galatians] Christ is the object of faith, the One toward whom the sinner's trust is directed. HM/*GG*, 104.

Faith Recognizes Salvation as a Divine Work

[Faith] is the practical (not purely reasoning) recognition on the part of man that the saving work of the kingdom is exclusively a divine work. *BT*, 388.

Faith must be the work of God in man, because only so can it be in harmony with itself as the recognition that we owe everything to God's working for us and in us. *KGC*, 99.

Broadly speaking, faith bears a two-fold significance in scriptural teaching and experience: it is, firstly, dependence on the supernatural power and grace of God; and secondly, the state or act of projection into a higher, spiritual world. *BT*, 83.

Faith is nothing else than that act whereby man lays hold of, appropriates for himself the endless power of God. *KGC*, 96.

112

All genuine saving faith is as profoundly conscious of its utter dependence on God for deliverance from sin as the recipients of our Lord's miraculous cures were convinced that God alone could heal their bodies from disease. *KGC*, 97.

Faith, "the assurance of things hoped for, the proving of things not seen"

The author of the Epistle to the Hebrews defines faith as "the assurance of things hoped for, the proving of things not seen," and thus makes it directly refer to the historical developments of redemption, as well as to the invisible realities of the supernatural world. CFTBH/*SW*, 470.

[commenting upon Heb. 11] Though faith is the organ of perception of the unseen and future realities and takes in with its vision a comprehensive realm of objects, there is in this circle which it sweeps a center, a focus; the things not seen and the things hoped for have a true unity, and this unity lies in God. No greater mistake could be made than to imagine that the faith illustrated in this chapter is no more than the innate human faculty to believe in things that cannot be perceived by the senses. HED/*SW*, 227.

[Faith] is the organ for apprehension of unseen and future realities, giving access to and contact with another world. It is the hand stretched out through the vast distances of space and time, whereby the Christian draws to himself the things far beyond, so that they become actual to him. HM/*GG*, 104.

It is a faith through which, like Moses, the Christian can endure seeing him who is invisible, which chooses rather to share ill-treatment with a people that belongs to God, than to inherit the treasures of Egypt. It is the responsive act on the believer's part to the act of covenant-committal on the part of God. Religion consummates itself in a mutual avowal, the people bearing God's reproach and offering up a sacrifice of praise to him continually, even the fruit of lips that make confession to his name, and God not being ashamed to be called their God and preparing them a city. HED/*SW*, 230.

■ [commenting on Heb. 11] The obedience, the self-sacrifice, the patience, the fortitude, the exercise of all these in the profound Christian sense would have been impossible, if the saints had not had through faith their eye firmly fixed on the unseen and promised world. HM/*GG*, 106.

■ [commenting on Heb. 11] Through faith the powers of the higher world were placed at the disposal of those whom this world threatened to overwhelm, and so the miracle resulted that from weakness they were made strong. HM/*GG*, 107.

■ [commenting on Heb. 11] Faith is here but another name for other-worldliness or heavenly-mindedness. HM/*GG*, 108.

"Fear of Jehovah"

■ "The fear of Jehovah" remains throughout the Old Testament the generic name for religion. *BT*, 86.

Feasts, Old Testament

■ The Old Testament feasts had, among other important features, this one peculiarity, that they brought to the remembrance of Israel the great underlying facts and principles of their covenant-relation to Jehovah. They invited the pious Israelite at stated seasons to collect his thoughts and fix them upon those things which were fundamental in his religious life. GP/*GG*, 233.

■ The Passover was pre-eminently a historical feast. It pointed back to the deliverance of the people from Egypt, a deliverance through sacrifice, a deliverance from the slaying angel, a deliverance in which manifestly the grace of God alone had made a distinction between them and their persecutors. Each time this feast was celebrated in the families of Israel, it proclaimed anew that redemption through blood, and by grace and sovereign choice was the great fact which lay at the basis of their historic existence; the source from which everything that Israel was and had or could ever hope to be and have ultimately flowed. GP/*GG*, 234.

The feast of tabernacles reminded [Israel] of their dwelling in tents in the wilderness, and of the wonderful guidance and deliverance through which they had been enabled to overcome the perils of their journey and enter upon the possession of the promised land. GP/*GG*, 233.

The feast of weeks, by requiring [Israel] to bring the first loaves of bread prepared from the new harvest to the sanctuary of Jehovah, reminded them that all the fruits of the land, all of the blessings of their life, were on the one hand the free gift of God, on the other hand designed to be consecrated to God. GP/*GG*, 233.

Fellowship with Christ

The entire Christian life, root and stem and branch and blossom, is one continuous fellowship with Christ. MEM/*GG*, 94–95.

Fellowship with God

To be a Christian is to live one's life not merely in obedience to God, nor merely in dependence on God, nor even merely for the sake of God; it is to stand in conscious, reciprocal fellowship with God, to be identified with him in thought and purpose and work, to receive from him and give back to him in the ceaseless interplay of spiritual forces. It is this direct confrontation of the religious mind with God which finds in the covenant-idea its perfect expression. HED/*SW*, 186.

God everywhere reserves to himself and exercises the right of independently fixing the terms of the relation between himself and man. That is an essential principle from a religious point of view. But the opposite principle, that Jehovah condescends to enter into covenant with man, is no less important; it enshrines all the wealth and glory of the biblical religion as a religion of conscious fellowship and mutual devotion between God and his people. CT/*SW*, 405.

God . . . has appointed as the eschatological goal of religious fellowship with himself, among other things, the prize of an incorruption such as is equivalent to eternal life (Rom. 2:7). *PE*, 293.

Figurative

It is true, our Lord speaks of the future blessedness in terms of eating and drinking, lying at table, celebrating a banquet, inheriting the earth. But it should be remembered that already in the Old Testament such descriptions are often meant figuratively, that in some cases where Jesus employs them the figurative character is written on their very face, and that we have at least one explicit declaration of his, which denies the continuance in the future kingdom of the sensual enjoyments of this present life (Mark 12:25). KOG/*SW*, 308.

By saying . . . that Jesus speaks in "figurative" terms, we take the word "figurative" in that specific sense which it receives from the principle of parallelism between the heavenly and the earthly spheres. What he says about the forms of eternal life is not arbitrarily chosen, but taken from things which in their very nature are a copy of the higher world. Thus they give a real revelation concerning that world and yet do not lie open to the charge of expressing a sensualistic conception of the eschatological kingdom. KOG/*SW*, 308–9.

Firstfruits

Peter looked upon the risen Christ as the beginning, the firstfruits of that new world of God in which the believer's hope is anchored. Jesus did not rise as he had been before, but transformed, glorified, eternalized, the possessor and author of a transcendent heavenly life at one and the same time, the revealer, the sample and the pledge of the future realization of the true kingdom of God. CH/*GG*, 150.

Flesh

Paul . . . characterizes *sinful human nature* by the name *sarx*. *PE*, 299.

While the σάρξ chiefly appears as a power or principle in the subjective experience of man, yet this is by no means the only aspect under which Paul regards it. It is an organism, an order of things beyond the individual man, even beyond human nature. It is something that is not inherently evil; the evil predicates are joined to it by means of a synthetic judgment. Still further, it has its affiliations and ramifications in the external, physical, natural (as opposed to super-natural) constitution of things. Now if σάρξ was originally the char-acteristic designation of the first world-order, as *Pneuma* is that of the second, all these features could be easily accounted for without having recourse to Hellenistic-dualistic explanations. From its asso-ciation with the entire present aeon, the σάρξ could derive its per-vasive, comprehensive significance, in virtue of which a man can be ἐν σαρκί as he can be ἐν πνεύματι; like the aeon it lends a uniform complexion to all existing things. It would also derive from this its partial coincidence with the somatic, because the whole first aeon moves on the external, provisional, physical plane. EAP/*SW*, 123.

▨ [Flesh] expresses the weakness and impotence of the creature over against God (Isa 2:22; 31:3). OM/*ISBE*, 2189.

▨ It is not true that the σάρξ [flesh] in its technical sense represents the original natural condition of man. Insofar as it is synonymous with sin it is not the product of creation. Paul nowhere affirms it to be so, and to charge this monstrous doctrine to him even by impli-cation, for the sole reason that he does not explicitly repudiate it, or says in so many words that the σάρξ was produced in man through sin, is hardly fair. *KC/SW*, 541.

▨ [commenting upon the Epistle to the Hebrews] As to the substance or content of the two dispensations, the author makes use of the con-trast between flesh (*sarx*) and spirit (*pneuma*). The old covenant is spoken of as *sarkikos* and *sarkinos*. . . . The use of the term *sarx* here is quite distinct from that found in Paul's writings. The author of Hebrews says that the entire Old Testament is *sarx*. Paul, on the other hand, protests that the law is spiritual (*pneumatikos*, Rom. 7:14) and the commandment is holy, righteous and good. Paul used *sarx* with an ethical connotation of evil. But in Hebrews the term means sim-ply *material* or *external*. Paul was also familiar with this same con-trast, to be sure, but he expresses the contrast in other terms. He speaks of the Old Testament, for example, as "weak and beggarly ele-ments," in contrast to the New Testament. *TEH*, 63.

Fool

Folly, in the most advanced sense of a systematically conceived and applied theory of life opposed to that of wisdom, is equivalent to practical atheism. The fool . . . is he who has said in his heart, "There is no God"; by which, not a theoretical denial of the divine existence, but a practical negation of God's moral government is meant (Ps. 14:1; 53:1; 39:8; Isa. 9:17). FOOL/*DB*, 44.

Of the natural foolishness belonging to the heathen mind, the only remedy for which lies in the wisdom supplied by revelation, we read in Romans 2:20, Titus 3:3. . . . Inasmuch, however, as the Gentile mind sustains a radically wrong relation to the moral world, it fails to see this marvelous adaptation and decries the gospel as foolishness. Even the converted Gentile is under temptation to justify its reasonableness from the worldly point of view by such a presentation as will materially alter its character. Hence the sharp antithesis (1 Cor. 1:21–25; 2:14; 3:18–23; 4:10), the wisdom of the world is foolishness to God, the foolishness of Christ crucified is the wisdom of God. FOOL/*DB*, 44.

Foreknowledge

The word "foreknowledge" is employed where the deepest source of the act of election comes under consideration . . . for this word, "foreknowledge," expresses nothing else than that God by an act of condescension draws a person into the circle of his special notice and interest. SDL/*SW*, 454.

When saying, in the well-known passage of Romans (8:29), that those whom God foreknew he also predestinated to be conformed to the image of his Son, the apostle means to ascribe by this to the foreknowledge an intensity of love, such as in predetermining the destiny of believers made God seize upon the highest conceivable ideal of power and glory and blessedness, the image of God's Son— i.e., the mediatorial glory of the exalted Christ. SDL/*SW*, 454.

Forensic

In our opinion Paul consciously and consistently subordinated the mystical aspect of the relation to Christ to the forensic one. Paul's mind was to such an extent forensically oriented that he regarded the entire complex of subjective spiritual blessings enjoyed by the believer as the direct outcome of the forensic work of Christ applied in justification. The mystical is based on the forensic, not the forensic on the mystical. AL/*SW*, 384.

Foreordination

The elect form one body. In a body the members must be fitted together and be destined for one another. If this body of Christ originated accidentally through a free choice of the will of individual people, there would not be any guarantee that the body would become proportionate. God must determine beforehand how many shall belong to it, who they are going to be, and when they will be fitted in. Foreordination is nothing else than God's determination concerning these things. NST, 145.

Forerunner

The ἀρχηγὸς τῆς ζωῆς in Peter's speech, Acts 3:15, is not merely the Ruler of life, but the one who first entered into life for his own person and now dispenses life unto others. PC/*SW*, 133.

[commenting upon Heb. 6:20] The author calls Jesus πρόδρομος, "forerunner," because as the first he has entered into that which is within the veil, and through that act of first entrance with his own blood has made it possible for us now to project our hope as an anchor of the soul into the same holy place and hereafter to follow him in person. HED/*SW*, 213.

Freedom

[Jesus] came to minister to men so as to place them in a state of freedom. CDW/*GG*, 250.

Freedom of God

In our making of a decision a free choice is involved. With us this freedom is always relative, and as creatures we are bound by many things, whereas God's freedom in the making of his decree is absolutely boundless, being subject to no other rule than that of his glorious virtues which form his very essence. NST, 18.

Freedom of the Will, against Pelagian Conception of

Decisions are guided by motivations. A Pelagian freedom of the will, which is supposed to be entirely groundless, does not exist, not even for God. Its implication would not be perfection but imperfection. Absolute arbitrariness is an imperfection. God's decree is, therefore, perfectly free and at the same time it is ruled by wise motives. No grounds from without determine him in the making of his decree but grounds derived from himself. These grounds do not, therefore, force him, but they indicate the direction of his own perfect will. NST, 19.

The Pelagian concept of the free will . . . amounts to a self-determination without causation. NST, 94.

Regardless whether we deal with Adam or with fallen man, if man has a free will as the Pelagian teaches, he is outside the decree of God. It is important to maintain that even Adam was not free in the Pelagian sense. NST, 114.

Fulness of Time

The sending forth of Christ marks to [Paul] the πλήρωμα τοῦ χρόνου (Gal. 4:4), a phrase which certainly means more than that the time was ripe for the introduction of Christ into the world: the fulness of the time means the end of that aeon and the commencement of another world-period. EAP/SW, 93.

The very scheme of the two successive worlds renders it unthinkable that at any arbitrary chosen point the world to come should supersede the world that is. The phrase πλήρωμα τοῦ χρόνου (Gal.

120

4:4), implies an orderly unrolling of the preceding stages of world-history toward a fixed end. *PE*, 83.

"Fulness" in not meant here in the first instance as "ripeness"; it signifies the completion of what was "time" and the succession of it by what is different from time through the mission of the Messiah into the world. For the Messiah is the introducer and beginner of the eschatological world. *PE*, 289.

Garden

The tree of life stands in the midst of the garden. The garden is "the garden of God," not in the first instance an abode for man as such, but specifically a place of reception of man into fellowship with God in God's own dwelling-place. The God-centered character of religion finds its first, but already fundamental, expression in this arrangement (see Gen. 2:8; Ezek. 28:13, 16). *BT*, 27–28.

God, Centrality of

How easily the mind falls into the habit of merely enlisting God as an ally in the fight for creature-betterment, almost oblivious to the fact that he is the King of glory for whose sake the whole world exists and the entire battle is waged! WT/*GG*, 16–17.

The end of existence for all things lies in God. EP, 357–58.

[God] is the center of every hope worth cherishing for man. EP, 359.

To take God as source and end of all that exists and happens, and to hold such a view suffused with the warmth of genuine devotion, stands not only related to theology as the fruit stands to the tree: it is by reason of its essence a veritable theological tree of life. *PE*, 61.

God is the center of attraction in the kingdom of glory; so that to lose touch with God inevitably means to stop in the midst of the race toward heaven. RR/*GG*, 133.

There are found in the Gospels many apparently extreme sayings in regard to giving up all human interests and ties even of the most sacred nature, nay, life itself, for the sake of a single-minded devotion to God. Such statements . . . are qualified in their range of obligation by Jesus himself. Our Lord says: if thy hand, thy foot, thine eye offend thee, cut it off, pluck it out; it is only when these natural things become occasions for failing in the whole-souled devotion to God, that their absolute renouncement is demanded. From this, however, it follows that an abstract rule of universal surrender of such things cannot be laid down. It is the inner pseudo-religious attachment to something outside of God that must be given up in the interest of the true religion. *BT*, 398.

God, Glory of

In [Rom. 5:2] the glory of God is projected into the future and represented as an eschatological inheritance, the means of its apprehension being hope. *PE*, 313.

What could be more adapted to warm our hearts than the constant thought of God's eternal excellence and glory? OHGG/*GG*, 274.

[commenting upon Isa. 57:15] [There] is the note of blessed self-surrender wherein the prophet, at first almost overwhelmed by the sense of the divine majesty, regains his mental poise and recognizes as the only possible, the only satisfying purpose of created existence, the glory of God. OHGG/*GG*, 264.

Some questioning has arisen concerning the precise force of the genitive in the phrase "the glory of God." Grammatically considered this could mean "the glory possessed by God." Parallel constructions are: "the life of God," "the peace of God," "the righteousness of God"; the peculiar feature of which is that they are pregnant constructions, in which the triple ideas of "original in God," "reflected from God" and "communicated in an ectypical sense to man" meet. The underlying principle is in each case that the inherent excellence of God is reproduced and brought to revelation in his beatified creatures. No stronger witness than this to the God-centered character of the eternal world can be conceived. *PE*, 313–14.

God, His Love for His People

God appears putting himself at the service of man, and that with the absolute generosity born of supreme love. This relation into which it pleases God to receive Israel with himself has in it a sublime abandon; it knows neither restraint nor reserve. WT/*GG*, 4–5.

God, King of Israel

In the Old Testament God is frequently represented as the King of the universe not only, but also as the King of Israel in a special, redemptive sense. He became so at the time of the deliverance from Egypt and the organization of Israel on the basis of the covenant (Ex. 19:4–6; cf. Deut. 33:4–5). KOG/*SW*, 304.

God, Loving Him for His Own Sake

Let each one examine himself whether to any extent he is caught in the whirl of this centrifugal movement. The question, though searching, is an extremely simple one: Do we love God for his own sake, and find in this love the inspiration of service, or do we patronize him as an influential partner under whose auspices we can better conduct our manifold activities in the service of the world? WT/*GG*, 16–17.

God, Possession of

The possession of Jehovah himself by his people will be of all the delights of the world to come the chief and most satisfying, the paradise within the paradise of God. WT/*GG*, 3.

[commenting upon Gen. 15] It is emphasized in the narrative that [Abraham's] supreme blessedness consisted in the possession of God himself: "Fear not, Abraham, I am thy shield, thy exceeding great reward" [Gen. 15:1]. For this treasure he could cheerfully renounce all other gifts. *BT*, 85.

God, Seeking after

In Matthew 6:33 the seeking after the kingdom is opposed to the seeking after earthly things, because it is at the bottom the seeking after God himself. *KGC*, 51.

Gospel, Purpose of

The gospel serves no other purpose than to bring men face to face with the glory of Christ. It is nothing else but a tale of Christ, a Christ in words, the exact counterpart of Christ's person and work in their glorious state. MEM/*GG*, 95.

Grace

[commenting upon the modern hypothesis that Jehovah does not and cannot deal with Israel according to grace, but rather exclusively according to works] With the elimination of the idea of grace the conception of faith must undergo considerable modification. RCEP, 615.

[commenting upon the exodus] The deliverance from Egypt was a signal demonstration of the sovereign grace of God. The Egyptians were judged with respect to their idolatry, and the Israelites were rescued and spared, in spite of having become associated with their oppressors in idolatrous practices. It is plain that the principle of sovereign grace alone will account for such facts. This is called "putting difference between Israelites and Egyptians" (Ex. 8:23; 11:7). In harmony with this it is repeatedly stated in the Pentateuch, that the source of Israel's privilege lies exclusively in free divine grace, not in any good qualities possessed by the people from themselves (Deut. 7:7; 9:4–6). *BT*, 113–14.

The king is according to oriental conceptions the source of grace and the fountain of blessing for all his subjects. Hence not infrequently salvation is described in our Lord's parables under the figure of a feast or banquet, prepared by the king. KOG/*SW*, 314.

Grace knows no jealousy except for the honor of God. SSL/*GG*, 63.

To estimate truly the riches of grace one must have passed through the abjectness and poverty and despair of sin. JP/*SW*, 295.

[commenting upon Rom. 9] The phrase "the elective purpose of God" is explained in the following words: "not of works but of him that calleth." This is equivalent to: "not of works but of grace," the idea of "calling" being with Paul an exponent of divine monergism. Revelation of the doctrine of election, therefore, serves the revelation of the doctrine of grace. God calls attention to his sovereign discrimination between man and man, to place the proper emphasis upon the truth, that his grace alone is the source of all spiritual good to be found in man. *BT*, 95.

[commenting upon Luke 19:10] Being told, therefore, that it was the "Son of man," who came to seek and to save, our first thought surely should be of that unspeakable grace of our Lord, who, being rich as God alone can be rich, yet for our sake became poor as sinful man only can be poor, that by his poverty we might be made rich. SSL/*GG*, 49.

Heart

Whatever may be the nicer distinction between spirit and heart in the scriptural usage, both terms are at one in this; that they denote those central seats of man's inner life in which the reality, mode and condition of his own existence reveal themselves to him. OHGG/*GG*, 262.

Why are evil and good with such insistency pushed back into the region of the heart? The reason is none other than that in the heart man confronts God. HTR/*GG*, 33.

There is neither quietness nor repose for the believer's heart except on the bosom of eternity. There and there alone is shelter from the relentless pursuit of change. HM/*GG*, 117–18.

A Jew lives in you and me and in every human heart by nature. If we ever were tempted to think ourselves able to fulfill the law of God, was it not perhaps for this reason—that the sense of God's absolute claim upon us and knowledge of us had become dim to our conscience? HTR/*GG*, 32.

Heaven

[commenting upon Matthew's usage of the phrase "kingdom of heaven"] Heaven stands for God not as a mere conventional substitute, but adds a new element to the conception expressed by the latter. Heaven is the center of all supernatural influence that is brought to bear upon the lower world. To say that a work is done by God leaves the mode of its accomplishment undetermined; to say that it is done from heaven is the strongest possible affirmation of its strictly supernatural origin. Heaven means God in a special mode of activity. KOG/*SW*, 306.

Especially in the later epistles, but also to some extent already in the earlier ones, the Christian state is represented as a belonging to and participation in the sphere of heaven and the heavenly order of things. The principle is, of course, implied in everything taught about communion with the heavenly Christ. EAP/*SW*, 114–15.

Heaven, so to speak, has received time and history into itself, no less than time has received unchangeableness and eternity into itself. Herein lies the inner significance of the repatriation of Christ into heaven, carrying thither with himself all the historical time-matured fruit of his earthly stage of work, and now from there guiding with impartial solicitude the two lines of terrestrial and celestial development of his church. *PE*, 40.

And heaven above all else partakes of the character of eternity. It is the realm of the unchangeable. HM/*GG*, 117.

There clings an earth and time–savor to [the] questioning what there will be to occupy one's self withal when arrived above. As if the Lord God himself would not be there with his inexhaustible fulness! In his presence there can be neither surfeit nor tedium. *PE*, 316.

A heaven that was not illumined by the light of God, and not a place for closest embrace of him, would be less than heaven. HM/*GG*, 122.

Heaven is the primordial, earth the secondary creation. In heaven are the supreme realities; what surrounds us here below is a copy and shadow of the celestial things. HM/*GG*, 113.

126

The word "heaven" . . . draws man's thought upwards to the place where God reveals his glory in perfection. *KGC*, 25.

The heavenly world does not appear desirable as simply a second improved edition of this life; that would be nothing else than earthly-mindedness projected into the future. The very opposite takes place: heaven spiritualizes in advance our present walk with God. HM/*GG*, 121.

The heavenly world is to the believer what the earth was to the giant in ancient mythology; so long as he remains in contact with it, an unintermittent stream of new spiritual power flows into his frame. RR/*GG*, 137.

By the pneumatic as a synonym of the heavenly Paul does not mean heaven or the spiritual in the abstract, but heaven and the spiritual as they have become in result of the process of redemption. EAP/*SW*, 116.

Heaven and Jesus

[Commenting upon the Epistle to the Hebrews] Christ belongs throughout the epistle to the heavenly world in which everything bears the character of the unchangeable, the abiding. TEC/*GG*, 204.

What else enabled [Christ] to endure the cross and despise the shame, but that in faith undimmed he had his eye constantly fixed upon the joy that was set before him and in uninterrupted intercourse with the world of heaven received daily strength sufficient for the running of his race? RR/*GG*, 137–38.

[commenting upon John 14:6] In 14:6 "I am the way, the truth and the life," the co-ordination of "truth" and "life" with each other and the connection of these two with "the way (to heaven)" certainly suggests that Jesus is the truth in a more substantial personal sense than that he brings the truth, and that this truth which he is has special connection with the heavenly world. *DBDW*, 671.

Heaven and the Spirit

Christ has through his resurrection carried the center of [the] new world into heaven, where he reigns and whence he extends its influence and boundaries. The two coexisting worlds therefore broadly coincide with the spheres of heaven and earth. If now the higher, heavenly world to which the Christian belongs is that of the Spirit, it must always be remembered that it has become this in virtue of the progress of the eschatological drama and will become more so in the same degree that this drama hastens on to its final denouement. EAP/*SW*, 115–16.

The heavenly life, regarded as a reward for the believer, will essentially consist in *pneuma*, which, of course, extends to its bodily form. EAP/*SW*, 102.

Heaven, as the Goal

Heaven is in the consciousness of Jesus the goal toward which every aspiration of the disciple in the kingdom ought to tend (see Matt. 6:19–21). KOG/*SW*, 306.

The ideal destiny of God's people has always been to be received of him to the most consummate fellowship [in the heavenly habitation of God]. *BT*, 154.

Heaven, as the Pattern

Heaven . . . as the abode of God, in relation to earth [is] the ideal pattern to which all things here below ought to conform. In this sense to say that a thing is "of heaven" means not only that it is "of God" in general, but in that specific sense in which the heavenly realities agree with God's nature (see Matt. 6:10). KOG/*SW*, 306.

Inasmuch as the Christian life on earth anticipates the conditions of the world to come, it likewise must needs bear the impress of the eternal molds into which it will be cast hereafter. HED/*SW*, 225.

128

Heaven, Attraction of

The attraction of heaven is in part the attraction of freedom from sin. . . . Still the principle remains in force, that the desirability of heaven should never possess exclusively or mainly negative significance. It is not something first brought into the religious mind through sin. HM/*GG*, 112–13.

Heaven, Citizenship in

The Christian has his πολιτεία in heaven, not upon earth, and therefore should not mind earthy things (Phil. 3:19–20). Being raised with Christ, he must seek and set his mind upon things that are above, not upon the things that are upon the earth (Col. 3:1–2). EAP/*SW*, 115.

In the new covenant the heavenly eternal world projects itself into [the] lower sphere. Even of believers it is true that they have now come to the heavenly city and stand in real connection through faith with the congregation above. If this applies to believers in general, how much more will it apply to Jesus, who not merely is the captain and finisher of faith, but who also, in virtue of his divine nature, continued to be part of the celestial order of things wherever he might abide in space. HED/*SW*, 220.

The Christian has only his members upon earth, which are to be mortified; himself, and as a whole, he belongs to the high mountainland above (Col. 3:5). *PE*, 41.

[In Heb. 12:22] the author states that Christians have come to Mount Zion, the city of the living God, the heavenly Jerusalem. We miss the writer's meaning of this if we regard this as a mere metaphor. Christians are really in vital connection with the heavenly world. It projects into their lives as a headland projects out into the ocean. *TEH*, 51.

In Philippians 3:20 Paul states, "We have our commonwealth in heaven." Christians therefore are colonists, living in the dispersion in this present world. The same idea is set forth still more strongly in Ephesians 2:6, "made us to sit with him in the heavenly places," and also in Galatians 1:4, "that he might deliver us out of this present evil world." The Christian therefore is a peculiar chronological phenomenon. *TEH*, 51.

The Christian is blessed in Christ with every spiritual blessing "in the heavenly regions" (Eph. 1:3), a way of expression clearly indicating the christological basis of the transfer of the believer's domicile and possessions to heaven. *PE*, 39.

In the Epistle to the Philippians the Christians' "πολιτεία" ("commonwealth" or "citizenship") is said to be in heaven for the reason of Christ's being there. *PE*, 39.

The heaven in which the Christian by anticipation dwells is not the cosmical heaven; it is a thoroughly redemptive heaven, a heaven become what it is through the progressive upbuilding and enrichment pertaining to the age-long work of God in the sphere of redemption. *PE*, 40.

Heavenly-Mindedness

[The] whole representation of the Christian state as centrally and potentially anchored in heaven is not the abrogation, it is the most intense and the most practical assertion of the other-worldly tenor of the believer's life. *PE*, 39.

Practically speaking, the higher sphere is that whither all religious tending and striving must be directed. *BT*, 355.

Those who looked for the city that has foundations sought it for no other reason than that its maker and builder is God. It is because it is the city of God, the structure in which he has embodied his own perfection, in which his thoughts and purposes for his own stand objectified, that it forms a worthy object of the supreme religious quest of the believer. In it is God at every point, and those who dwell in it see his face constantly. The measure of their desire for it becomes the measure of their love for God. HED/*SW*, 229.

130

The believer should not be indifferent to the natural environment in which the providence of God has placed him; but he should not have his portion in the present life in the same sense as the children of the world have it. He must gravitate toward the future life and must make every contact into which he comes with earthly concerns subordinated and subservient to this. RR/*GG*, 132.

The writer [of the Book of Hebrews] ascribes [to the patriarchs] a degree of acquaintance with the idea of a heavenly life. His meaning is not that, unknown to themselves, they symbolized through their mode of living the principle of destination for heaven. On the contrary, we are expressly told that they confessed, that they made it manifest, that they looked for, that they desired. There existed with them an intelligent and outspoken apprehension of the celestial world. HM/*GG*, 110.

Because the relation between the two spheres [heaven and earth] is positive, and not negative, not mutually repulsive, heavenly-mindedness can never give rise to neglect of the duties pertaining to the present life. It is the ordinance and will of God, that not apart from, but on the basis of, and in contact with, the earthly sphere man shall work out his heavenly destiny. HM/*GG*, 113.

Our modern Christian life so often lacks the poise and stability of the eternal. Religion has come so overmuch to occupy itself with the things of time that it catches the spirit of time. Its purposes turn fickle and unsteady; its methods become superficial and ephemeral; it alters its course so constantly; it borrows so readily from sources beneath itself, that it undermines its own prestige in matters pertaining to the eternal world. Where lies the remedy? It would be useless to seek it in withdrawal from the struggles of this present world. The true corrective lies in this, that we must learn again to carry a heaven-fed and heaven-centered spirit into our walk and work below. HM/*GG*, 119.

Every task should be at the same time a means of grace from and an incentive to work for heaven. HM/*GG*, 119.

Traced to its ultimate root heavenly-mindedness is the thirst of the soul after God, the living God. The patriarchs looked not for some city in general, but for a city whose builder and maker was God. HM/*GG*, 122.

Hebrews (Epistle to)

There is nothing in the New Testament which teaches so emphatically the absolute indispensableness of the divine nature of Christ for the work of redemption as the Epistle to the Hebrews. TEC/*GG*, 205.

The Epistle to the Hebrews deals mainly with the two great offices of Christ as Revealer and as Priest. It is clear that the author consciously coordinates the two. In the opening verses, which serve as a prelude to the entire epistle, we have side by side: "God spake in a Son" and "Having made purification of sins he sat down on the right hand of the majesty on high." But especially 3:1 is interesting from this point of view. Here the Savior is called "apostle and high priest of our confession." The article, put only once, binds the two conceptions most closely together: he is apostle and high priest in one, and his chief value for the believer consists in his being the two jointly; hence he forms as such the content of the confession, and the readers are exhorted carefully "to consider" him in this twofold capacity. PC/*SW*, 126.

In Hebrews the christological element is not the dominant element: it is shaped by the soteriological element rather than that it shapes the latter. To understand the document fully it would be necessary to bring out how such a Christology was bound to arise out of such a general milieu of teaching. *CEH*, 490.

The outstanding feature of the Epistle to the Hebrews is its connection with the Old Testament and the prominence of the Old Testament in it. *TEH*, 11.

The writer begins at once with a piece of Christology touching upon two of Christ's offices, namely his priesthood and his kingship. Therefore we may conclude that the trouble with the original read-

132

ers was in part, at least, christological. What their particular christological trouble was appears in the second chapter, namely, that
Christ did not appear to them externally as they had expected. And
they even found something objectionable in Christ's humiliation and
sufferings. Therefore from 2:5 on, the reasonableness and necessity
of Christ's humiliation are set forth. *TEH*, 20.

The author describes the believers as the household of God, and
this household is declared to be *one*, in both the old and the new
diathēkē (Heb. 3:2–6). This has also an eschatological outlook, in the
conception of *the city to come*. Note the description of the great eschatological assembly in Hebrews 12:22. Thus it is affirmed of believers that they have not only joined in worship, but that they have been
incorporated into the worshipping community. *TEH*, 45.

Hebrews is the epistle of the cultus, and the Christian life it portrays is a cultus in the noblest sense of the word. At a time when the
man-ward functions of religion are in the ascendant, especially when
the word "service" is being almost monopolized for the Christian
activities that aim at the promotion of the well-being of man, it can
do no harm to let ourselves be reminded by the writer of this epistle
that there is such a thing as a service to God that is not rendered by
indirection, but is as exclusively and directly appropriated to him as
the gift that is laid upon the altar, an alabaster-vase of ointment whose
very preciousness consists in this, that it cannot even be sold and the
proceeds given to the poor. HED/*SW*, 224.

Hebrews (Epistle to) and the Covenant

In revelation God makes his approach to man; through the priesthood man makes his approach to God; where both reach their ideal
perfection, there the ideal covenant is given. The covenant movement must necessarily flow through these two channels. And, since
Hebrews makes the covenant-idea central, by far the larger part of
what it has to teach concerning the interplay of religion between God
and man attaches itself to these two conceptions. HED/*SW*, 227.

Now the covenant is conceived of in the epistle in a twofold way. On the one hand it is an instrumental institution, a means to an ulterior end, which end is variously described as salvation, rest, inheritance, arrival in the heavenly country or the city with the foundations, receiving of the unshakable kingdom. On the other hand it also appears as constituting in itself the ideal of religion realized, the perfect covenant being the consummate approach and nearness to God. As such it is the highest category of religion itself. PC/*SW*, 137.

To a mind thus spiritually oriented the interpretation of religion in terms of the covenant was bound to offer a special attraction. For it is precisely in religion as a covenant-religion that everything is reduced to ultimate, spiritual, conscious values. The new covenant is the ideal covenant because in it the will and law of God are internalized, put on the heart and written upon the mind. Here its nature as a covenant can first freely and perfectly unfold itself. HED/*SW*, 185.

Heirship

For heirship, again, is nothing else but messianic possession of all things. *SDJ*, 163.

Heresy

It is a well-known fact that all heresy begins with a partial truth. SDL/*SW*, 426.

Historical Jesus, Quest for

As to the motive from which the whole movement sprang, we are told that it "did not take its rise from a purely historical interest; it turned to the Jesus of history, as an ally in the struggle against the tyranny of dogma." "Hate as well as love can write a life of Jesus and the greatest of them are written with hate." By "hate" in this connection is meant not hate of the person of Jesus, but hate of the supernatural nimbus with which he appears surrounded in the faith of the church. And this defect in the initial motive has proved a veritable *vitium origins* in the entire after-history of the movement. *QHJ*/*SW*, 517–18.

134

■ Because the so-called "historical Jesus" was at the outset enlisted as an ally in the great theological strife of the age, he had forever after to put on the armor and wear the colors of the party that had enlisted him and to share in its successive evolutions and transformations. He had to become all things to all: to the vulgar rationalists a rationalist, to the liberals a liberal, to the mediating theologians, a mediating type of mind and character. *QHJ/SW*, 518.

■ Historical study has become a powerful instrument in the service of the antisupernaturalistic spirit of the modern age. Professing to be strictly neutral and to seek nothing but the truth, it has in point of fact directed its assault along the whole line against the outstanding miraculous events of sacred history. It has rewritten this history so as to make the supernatural elements disappear from its record. It has called into question the historicity of one after the other of the great redemptive acts of God. CFTBH/*SW*, 461.

History

■ The goal of God's work in history . . . is none other than the finished heaven. HM/*GG*, 115.

■ Jesus knew himself as at once the goal of history and the servant of history. *KGC*, 15.

■ History we need, and that not only in the form of the tale of a certain perfect ethical and religious experience, which has somewhere come to the surface on the endless stream of phenomena, but such a history as shall involve the opening of the heavens, the coming down of God, the introduction of miraculous regenerative forces into humanity, the enactment of a veritable drama of redemption between the supernatural and the natural world. CFTBH/*SW*, 467.

■ God's saving deeds mark the critical epochs of history, and as such, have continued to shape its course for centuries after their occurrence. IBT/*SW*, 9.

■ It is not enough to know that history moves toward a goal; the great question, without the solution of which the thinking mind cannot rest satisfied, concerns the element of identity in the flux of development. What is the stable, the constant substance that underlies the ceaseless, never-resting change? To what extent and where and in what form is the goal that beckons at the end present at the beginning? HED/*SW*, 196.

History and Eschatology

[commenting upon the Psalter] The Psalter is wide awake to the significance of history as leading up to the eschatological act of God. It knows that it deals with a God who spake and speaks and shall speak, who wrought and works and shall work, who came and is coming and is about to come. EP, 335.

History and Revelation

Besides making use of words, God has also employed acts to reveal great principles of truth. . . . We refer . . . to those great, supernatural, history-making acts of which we have examples in the redemption of the covenant-people from Egypt, or in the crucifixion and resurrection of Christ. In these cases the history itself forms a part of revelation. There is a self-disclosure of God in such acts. They would speak even if left to speak for themselves. IBT/*SW*, 9.

Chronology is the frame of history; and Israel's history is nothing but the record of God's revelation, its beginning, progress and fulfillment. Separated from the world, that it might be holy unto God, with Israel everything becomes subservient to this high calling. Hence its history is not shaped by accident or chance, or according to earthly purposes: it does not run its course independent of God's intentions with regard to his people, but flows from beginning to end in the channels of his revealing grace. *MOP*, 53.

[commenting on the historicity of the patriarchs] The historicity of the patriarchs can never be, to us, a matter of small importance. The religion of the Old Testament being a factual religion, it is untrue that these figures retain the same usefulness, through the lessons that can be drawn from their stories, as actual history would possess. This prejudges the answer to the fundamental question, what religion is for. If, on the Pelagian principle, it serves no other purpose than to teach religious and moral lessons from example, then the historicity is no longer of material importance. We can learn the same lessons from legendary or mythical figures. But, if according to the Bible they are real actors in the drama of redemption, the actual beginning of the people of God, the first embodiment of objective religion; if Abraham was the father of the faithful, the nucleus of the church; then the denial of their historicity makes them useless from our point of view. *BT*, 67.

■ According to our view, the historical books were written with the very purpose of making past history a mirror and warning for the future Israel. According to the critics, all tendency toward instruction is of later date. In other words, we claim that the self-conscious, revealing God was in history from the beginning, and caused history to be written as such; the critics refuse to recognize any history as genuine except as it presents itself under the fascinating disguise of a legend or myth. All deeper conception of history is excluded. This amounts, of course, to a denial of the supernatural element in its course. *MOP*, 215.

History, Writing of

■ The true principle of history writing, that which makes history more than a chronicling of events, because it discovers a plan and posits a goal, was thus grasped, not first by the Greek historians, but by the prophets of Israel. *BT*, 190.

History of Redemption, Centrality of Christ in

■ Everything temporal and provisional, especially if it does not know itself as such, is apt to wear a veil. It often lacks the faculty of discriminating between what is higher and lower in its composition. Things that are ends and things that are mere means to an end are not always clearly separated. Every preparatory stage in the history of redemption can fully understand itself only in the light of that which fulfills it. The veil of the old covenant is lifted only in Christ.

The Christian standpoint alone furnishes the necessary perspective for apprehending its place and function in the organism of the whole. MEM/*GG*, 91–92.

Holiness

The reaction upon the revelation of Jehovah's ethical holiness is a consciousness of sin. But this consciousness of sin carries in itself a profound realization of the majesty of God. It contemplates the holiness not as "purity" simply. It were better to define it as "majestic purity" or "ethical sublimity." *BT*, 248.

Side by side with holiness in God himself, holiness is predicated of certain things that are more or less closely related to him. The temple is holy, heaven is called holy, the sabbath is holy, the mountain of Jehovah is holy. *BT*, 248.

If Jehovah is unapproachably majestic, then it becomes important to draw a circle of holiness around him, which shall bar out the "profane." On our view the holiness predicated of God is the primary, original conception, the holiness of the other things is derivatory. The divine holiness radiates, as it were, in every direction, and creates a light inaccessible. *BT*, 248.

While we are accustomed to speak of holiness in terms of intensity, the prophet [Isaiah] speaks of it in terms of dimension. By it as much as by his eternity Jehovah is exalted above all finite being. Holiness in God has a peculiar divine glory distinguishing it from created holiness in angels or man. Even apart from the consciousness of sin, its revelation is so majestic as to fill the soul with awe. OHGG/*GG*, 269.

In Jehovah's holiness his divinity as it were concentrates itself. It involves not merely that his nature is stainless, empirically free from sin, but means that he is exalted above the possibility of sin—in him, as the absolutely good, evil cannot enter. (If owing to this the sinless seraphim hide themselves while proclaiming him holy, how should sinful man endure?) OHGG/*GG*, 269.

138

Holiness was the ever-recurring condition of God's dwelling amongst [the Israelites] . . . the one great demand, which the ritual was both to symbolize and to effect. *MOP*, 67.

Isaiah . . . represents the divine holiness as a devouring fire (1:25, 31; 5:24–25; 9:19; 29:6). It is true, this figure here associates itself for Isaiah with the thought of Jehovah's dwelling among Israel on Zion, and assumes the specific form that those who reside in the center of the theocracy are most exposed to the consuming power of his ethical nature. MHRCEP, 80.

Holiness and Judgment

The unique character of the divine holiness appears in Isaiah's preaching of judgment. Being not merely holy but majestic in holiness, Jehovah upholds and asserts his ethical glory for the punishment of sin. Isaiah has felt most keenly that God would not be God, would not respect his own divinity, did he not avenge evil. Because he is the absolutely good, because his name, the essence of his being, is holy; therefore in him holiness is attended with the sovereign right to vindicate its own supremacy. Nowhere else are we taught so clearly as in Isaiah that the vindicating justice of God is only the intensity of his holiness translated into action. OHGG/*GG*, 270–71.

Hope

The Christian *is* saved "upon the basis of hope" . . . for hope and the things upon which it terminates constitute the supreme goal of salvation (Rom. 8:24). *PE*, 30.

It is obvious that from the Christian standpoint no greater injury can be done to the true progress and healing of humanity in this present evil world than to make it promises and offer it remedies which have no vital connection with the hope of eternal life. For this hope alone can in the long run feed and keep flowing every stream of altruistic activity that deserves the name of religion. EP, 364.

And of ancient paganism Paul [sums] up the whole sad story in the double statement that it was without hope and without God in the world (Eph. 2:12), an exile from what is the noblest birthright of humanity. Now if this is so, how imperative becomes the duty of every true believer in the present age to cultivate the grace of hope; to make himself remember and to make others feel, not so much by direct affirmation but rather by the tone of life, that the future belongs to us and that we belong to the future; that we are children of the world to come and that even now we allow that world to mold and rule and transform us in our thoughts, desires and feelings. CH/*GG*, 145.

■ The pre-Christian pagan state is characterized by the absence of God and of hope, and these two are not meant as two simply coordinated items of religious destitution; the second arises from the first and the implication is that foremost among the benefits of religion (that is of "having God") is to have hope (Eph. 2:12; 1 Thess. 4:13). *PE*, 30.

■ The essence of what Christians are consists in this—that they have a hope. They are born again for that. When they were made new creatures, it was that they might have a new hope. CH/*GG*, 140.

■ The Christian is a man, according to Peter, who lives with his heavenly destiny ever in full view. His outlook is not bounded by the present life and the present world. He sees that which is and that which is to come in their true proportions and in their proper perspective. The center of gravity of his consciousness lies not in the present but in the future. Hope, not possession, is that which gives tone and color to his life. CH/*GG*, 142.

■ [Hope] is in [the Christian] a vitalizing power. It lives by the things that are not as though they were already, and makes the future supply strength for the present. HM/*GG*, 116.

■ [commenting upon Peter] Through the resurrection of Christ his hope has been made to terminate directly upon the heavenly inheritance in all its compass. It was a birth into a state of consciousness that knew itself infinitely rich in heavenly places in Christ. CH/*GG*, 151.

140

A living hope is a hope which is not dead material in the mind of the believer, but an active force in his life—something that makes its influence felt and carries him along, that sustains and inspires him. The hope of the Christian can do this because it relates to something that is not purely future, but already exists in the present because it is a hope in an inheritance, the most real of all realities. CH/*GG*, 153.

And the believer knows, moreover, that as long as he cannot fully possess God, God cannot fully possess him nor be completely glorified in him. This sentiment lies at the basis of all genuine God-born Christian hope. CH/*GG*, 154.

[Hope] annihilates the distance of time as much as of space. If faith deals with heaven as it exists, hope seizes upon it as it will be at the end. Hope attaches itself to promises; it sees and greets from afar. HM/*GG*, 115.

[Hope] does not contemplate purely provisional and earthly developments, does not come to rest in the happenings of intermediate ages, but relates to the end. In one unbroken flight it soars to the goal of God's work in history, which is none other than the finished heaven. HM/*GG*, 115.

The Christian can hope perfectly. He is the only one who can hope perfectly for that which is to be brought to him. For him not to have his face set forward and upward would be an anomaly, sickliness, decadence. To have it set upward and forward is life and health and strength. The air of the world to come is the vital atmosphere which he delights to breathe and outside of which he feels depressed and languid. CH/*GG*, 143.

Hosea

The prophet works out everything belonging to the union of Jehovah with Israel on the basis of the marriage between the two. It is incapable of proof that in his day every marriage was *per se* a species of *berith*. Still, this does not exclude the possibility of Hosea's having made the equation. *BT*, 258.

▨ The state of mind which the people ought to cultivate, by reason of their union with Jehovah, is described by Amos, Isaiah and Micah on the whole from an ethical, by Hosea from an affectional point of view. When Amos, Isaiah and Micah say: not sacrifices but righteousness, Hosea says: not sacrifices but the knowledge of Jehovah. All the demands made of the people are summed up in this one thing, that there should be the knowledge of God among them, and that not as a theoretical perception of what is Jehovah's nature, but as a practical acquaintance, the intimacy of love. It is that which corresponds on Israel's part to the knowledge of Jehovah from which the whole marriage sprang (13:4–5); this knowledge is intended to make Israel like unto Jehovah, it has a character-forming influence. *BT*, 261.

▨ Hosea has become instrumental in imparting an individualizing direction to the teaching about [the *berith*]. His emotional temperament was a potent factor to this effect. From its emotional side, more than in any other aspect, religion is a personal, individual matter. Even where Hosea speaks of the people collectively, the impulse toward this is so strong as to make him personify and individualize Israel. Several of such passages the individual believer may appropriate even now almost without change (2:7, 16, 23; 6:1–3; 8:2; 14:2, 4, 8). *BT*, 262–63.

▨ Hosea dwells upon the sin which Israel as a unit has committed against Jehovah. Sin is to Hosea want of conformity to the ideal of marriage-affection and loyalty. His indictment of Israel reads: "There is no truth (i.e. faithfulness), no lovingkindness, no knowledge of God in the land" (4:1). . . . Not merely that the people transgress the laws of Jehovah, but their considering them "a strange thing" constitutes the wickedness of their conduct; they disavow that special claim on their obedience which God has as their marriage-Lord (8:12). *BT*, 276.

House of God

▨ "Whom have I in heaven, but thee? And there is none upon the earth that I desire beside thee: though my flesh and my heart shall fail, God is the strength of my heart and my portion forever" (Ps. 73:25–26). This and nothing else underlies all the passages in which the psalmists speak of their love for the house of God or deplore their compelled absence from it. Their attachment to the house of God is at bottom an attachment to the person of God himself. SFS/*GG*, 178.

Another name for the body of believers is "the house of God." . . . In this name, "house of God," the principle of organic continuity of grace is implied. HED/*SW*, 226.

Humiliation, Christ's

Christ's humiliation was necessary for his own sake, namely for his glorification. We see him crowned with glory and honor, *because* of sufferings and death. *TEH*, 20.

He existed as Messiah in a state of humiliation. After that had been passed through, a state of exaltation would follow, in which these various things now offered to him as temptations would become perfectly normal and allowable. What was not inherently sinful became so in his case, because of the law of humiliation and service under which his life had for the present been put. The animus of the temptation, from Satan's point of view, consisted in the attempt to move him out of this spirit and attitude of service and humiliation, so as to yield to the natural desire for his messianic glory without an interval of suffering. *BT*, 335.

Humility

Now the humble spirit and the contrite heart are nothing else than that specific attitude of self-consciousness which is sensitive and responsive to the loftiness, holiness, the eternal glory and divinity of God. OHGG/*GG*, 262.

Hunger and Thirst

To hunger and thirst after a thing means the recognition that without that thing there can be no life. It involves that in this one desire and its satisfaction the whole meaning of life is centered, that the whole energy of life is directed toward it, that the goal of life is identified with it. To the sense of this fundamental spiritual craving all other things are obliterated. As to the hungry and thirsty gold and silver become worthless, so to the disciple in whom this desire has awakened, the wealth of the universe, were he offered it, would have no attraction. HTR/*GG*, 36.

The beginning of hungering and thirsting after righteousness lies in the birth of conviction of sin. HTR/*GG*, 37.

Hyssop

Hyssop figures everywhere as an instrument of purification. *BT*, 120.

Idolatry

Because idols are the caricature of divinity, idolatry is the caricature of religion. SDFI/*SW*, 278.

Those who come to Baal-Peor and consecrate themselves to the shameful thing become abominable like that which they love. The principle laid down applies to all idolatry, open or disguised; whatever man substitutes for the living God as an object of his supreme devotion not only turns into his master, but ends with becoming a superimposed character fashioning him irresistibly into likeness with itself. There is no worshipper but bears the image of his god. WT/*GG*, 22.

Anything that is cherished and cultivated apart from God (in such a sense that we cannot carry it with us in the Godward movement of our life) becomes necessarily a hindrance, a profanation, and at last a source of idolatry. WT/*GG*, 15.

Idols

The idols are to the prophet's view the opposite of all Jehovah stands for. As Jehovah is the Holy One, so the idols contract, as it were, a sort of positive unholiness; they are to be defiled, to be dishonored (Isa. 30:22). *BT*, 280.

Immortality

"Immortality" can designate, in eschatological language, that state of man in which he has been made immune to death, because immune to sin. Man was not, in virtue of creation, immortal in this highest sense: this is a result of redemption accompanied by eschatological treatment. Such "immortality" is the possession, first of all of God, who has it by nature (see 1 Tim. 6:16); next of the glorified human nature of Christ, who has it in virtue of his resurrection; next of the regenerate, here already in principle (John 11:26], and, of course, in their heavenly state. *BT*, 39.

Incarnation

We need God incarnate for redemptive reasons. The whole incarnation, with all that pertains to it, is one great sacrament of redemption. *BT*, 75.

The joint-sonship of Christ with believers does not follow from the incarnation, it produces the incarnation: because those with whom he was spiritually identified, those whom he resembled in sonship, partook of flesh and blood, he carried his solidarity with them to the point of the assumption of their nature. HED/*SW*, 206.

All the separate lines along which through the ages revelation was carried, have converged and met at a single point. The seed of the woman and the angel of Jehovah are become one in the incarnate Word. IBT/*SW*, 13.

[Jesus] was born for this purpose, and this purpose only, to seek and save the lost. . . . He was made incarnate for the work of salvation. SSL/*GG*, 46–47.

Individualism

Religion as centered in the heart cannot but incline toward individualism, for the heart with its hidden feelings is the most incapable of duplication of all the factors that enter into it. WT/*GG*, 19.

Infralapsarianism and Supralapsarianism

Undoubtedly the old way of tabulating the order of the decrees fostered the misapprehension that creation and sin subserve the glory of God only indirectly, in so far as they furnish the theater for the display of his mercy and righteousness. This was a hypersoteriological one-sidedness. The decrees in reference to both have also their direct relation to the glory of God, and are therefore to be represented also as coordinated with those of election and reprobation as means to this end. *GD2/SW*, 490.

It can hardly be called a merit of infralapsarianism that it insisted upon the coordination of the decrees with reference to the glory of God. Its motive in doing so was not so much a positive desire to vindicate an element of truth which supralapsarianism had neglected, but the merely negative one of escaping from what seemed to it the excessive harshness of the supralapsarian position. In other words, while supralapsarianism may have been partial and one-sided, infralapsarianism was agnostic in its tendency. Even that element of truth which it seemed specially called upon to maintain, the glory of God as directly subserved by creation, it has done no more to develop than has the opposing theory. *GD2/SW*, 490.

Inheritance and Hope

[Peter] describes the hope to which the Christian has been born again as a living hope. This is only another way of saying that the inheritance unto which he has been born again is a living inheritance; an inheritance that moves and sways, that strengthens and inspires us not merely subjectively through our knowledge of it, but objectively through the spiritual power that proceeds from it. CH/*GG*, 152.

Inheritance and Resurrection

[commenting upon 1 Peter 1:3–5] Through the resurrection of Christ [Peter's] hope has been made to terminate directly upon the heavenly inheritance in all its compass. It was a birth into a state of consciousness that knew itself infinitely rich in heavenly places in Christ. CH/*GG*, 151.

Interpretation and Typology

We must not infer from our comparatively easy reading of the types that Israelites of old felt the same ease in interpreting them. It is unhistorical to carry back into the Old Testament mind our developed doctrinal consciousness of these matters. The failure to understand, however, does not detract from the objective significance these types had in the intent of God. But it also is possible to commit the opposite error, that of perpetuating the Old Testament typical form of religion through importing it into the New Testament. This the Romish Church does on a large scale. And in doing so, instead of lifting the substance of the types to a higher plane, it simply reproduces and repeats. This is destructive of the whole typical relation. *BT*, 148.

Interpretation, Literalistic

[commenting upon the chiliastic interpretation of 1 Thess. 4] We have here before us a striking example of the possibility of over-stressing the literalness of the language and imagery used, and yet, while thus seeming to do justice to the writer's speech, missing in reality the deeper and finer qualities and objectives of his true conception. The literalistic may appear to our human vision nearer the real, and yet, owing to our pardonable craving for the concrete, be more subjective than the spiritualized. *PE*, 142.

Interpretation, Principles of

Everything temporal and provisional, especially if it does not know itself as such, is apt to wear a veil. It often lacks the faculty of discriminating between what is higher and lower in its composition. Things that are ends and things that are mere means to an end are not always clearly separated. Every preparatory stage in the history of redemption can fully understand itself only in the light of what fulfills it. The veil of the old covenant is lifted only in Christ. The Christian standpoint alone furnishes the necessary perspective for apprehending its place and function in the organism of the whole. MEM/*GG*, 91–92.

■ Let us beware of incurring the charge of making Jesus fit the times, instead of fitting the times to his teaching. There are still other times than ours for the instruction and inspiration and encouragement of which his figure must remain intact. *SDJ*, 64.

■ Taken in a broad sense, the New Testament regards itself as the perfect and true realization of the prophetic program, and that not in spite of but precisely in virtue of its spiritual complexion. It nowhere voices the feeling that scant justice has been done to the Old Testament, because its forecasts have come true in spiritual form, but on the contrary glories in this as a realization far exceeding all that could be asked for or conceived. It were to discredit this whole trend of progress in the direction of spirituality, and to ignore the right of revelation to explain itself, if one sought on the basis of the Old Testament alone to decide which elements of prophecy require literal fulfillment and accordingly postulate a millennium, and which items have found their sufficient realization in the spiritual developments of the new covenant. SC/*SW*, 417.

Intoxication

■ [commenting upon the Book of Isaiah] Isaiah speaks once and again of the sin of intoxication (Isa. 5:11–12, 22; 22:2, 13; 28:1, 3, 7). Especially the last of these passages is extremely realistic in its picture of the drunken revels of the priests and prophets. The prophet does not, of course, condemn the use of wine as such. On the contrary, some of his noblest figures are derived from it (Isa. 1:22; 5; 16:8–10; 18:5; 25:6). But intoxication is irreligious and degrading, because it darkens the perception of the divine spiritual realities in man, and so renders him brutish. The drunkards at Jerusalem "err through wine and through strong drink go astray; they err in vision, they stumble in judgment" (Isa. 28:7). *BT*, 280.

148

Inward Man

▥ [commenting upon 2 Cor. 4:16–17] "The inward man" does not signify here a composite human person, consisting of the *Pneuma* plus a new body. It stands for the Spirit as distinguished from the present fleshly body. *PE*, 204.

Isaac

▥ It ought to be remembered that Isaac was surrendered to God not merely as an object of paternal affection, but as the exponent and instrument and pledge of the fulfillment of all the promises, which thus appeared to perish with his death. *BT*, 84.

▥ Isaac's life forms a sharp contrast to that of Abraham. The contrast, strange to say, arises from the similarity. Abraham's history teems with originality; in Isaac's there is repetition of these originalities on almost every page. In the protracted barrenness of his wife, in his exposure to danger in Gerar, in the treatment received from Abimelech, in the differentiation of character between his two sons—in all this the similarity is too striking to be regarded as accidental. *BT*, 90–91.

Isaiah

▥ The first outstanding feature of Isaiah's prophecy [is] what may be called its theophanic character. In every message he has to proclaim, in every interpretation of nature and history he is sent to make, we see rising up before us this same divine presence which rose up before the prophet in the temple. Self-manifestation of Jehovah is the fundamental aspect of every utterance or discourse. SDFI/*SW*, 274.

▥ Other prophets may make us see with greater distinctness some single work or purpose of Jehovah; there is none who gives us a more real sense of how the one Jehovah reveals himself in the entire unfolding of his counsel and all his works. SDFI/*SW*, 274.

▥ Isaiah is the most theological of all the prophets; not of course in the scientific meaning of that term, but in the more simple and practical sense. His God is to him the one supreme reality from whom all other things derive their significance and to subserve whose end their history is shaped. His mind is filled to overflowing with the thought of God. The whole secret of the wide extent of his vision lies in this elevation of his standpoint. OHGG/*GG*, 259–60.

It would be difficult to find in the history of the church of God the record of a life more entirely consumed on the altar of service than that of Isaiah. But like everything else in this life, the cry "Send me!" was a cry uttered under the constraint of the vision of Jehovah's glory. OHGG/*GG*, 275.

The idea of God obtains in the prophecies of Isaiah a peculiar ascendancy and pervasiveness. God becomes the one supreme reality from whom everything else derives its significance. The thought of Jehovah expands until it fills all the recesses of creation, and there is no place left for any other being except as a medium for reflecting the divine glory. SDFI/*SW*, 275.

[Isaiah's] whole point of view is theocentric, emphasizing that Israel lives for the sake of Jehovah. *BT*, 259.

The controlling, unifying, productive principle of Isaiah's teaching lies in the complete subordination of every other thought to that of the divine glory. This is the secret of the prophet's power. SDFI/*SW*, 286.

Isaiah and Paul

Isaiah is an Old Testament Paul and Paul a New Testament Isaiah. For both, there is the same deep impression of the infinite majesty and absolute sovereignty of Jehovah; the same intense realization of the awfulness of the divine justice and the inexorable nature of its claims; the unworthiness, the helplessness of sinful man; the same insistence upon the exclusive activity of God in the work of saving his people; the same prominence of the idea of faith as the only thing whereby man can appropriate the blessings of salvation; the same abounding truth in the marvelous condescension and overflowing grace of God; the same unlimited and unlimitable faith in the world-embracing character of the divine purpose. OHGG/*GG*, 260

Paul seems to have felt something of the congeniality of Isaiah's mind to his own. He quotes from him often and with that fine spiritual insight which penetrates beyond the surface meaning of a passage into the innermost mind of the author and divines the subtle shade of his momentary thought and feeling. "Isaiah is very bold" (Rom. 10:20), he exclaims with evident appreciation of a noble trait exemplified to a high degree in his own character. OHGG/*GG*, 260–61.

Israel and the New Israel

There is an exact correspondence in this respect between the large movement of redemption, taken as a whole, and the enactment of its principles on a smaller scale within the history of Israel. As the second Adam is greater than the first, and the paradise of the future fairer than that of the past, so the new-born Israel to the prophet's vision is a nobler figure and exists under far more favorable conditions than the empirical Israel of before. WT/*GG*, 7.

Israel and the New Testament Church

If Israel be not the people of God, then the entire Old Testament promise becomes void, and the gospel, which professes to be the fulfillment of this promise, a structure without foundation. *DEI*/*SW*, 494–95.

Israel, God's Gracious Favor toward

[Jeremiah] declares that the Mosaic generation was disobedient from the beginning (Jer. 11:7–8). Isaiah says Israel was called a transgressor from the womb (Isa. 48:8). Nor do Amos and Hosea judge differently (Amos 5:25–26; Hos. 9:10; 11:1–2). All these prophets know of no other explanation for the favor once shown to Israel, and to be shown to her again, than the sovereign love of God. SDL/*SW*, 436.

Israel, Unbelieving

The one great adultery consists in this: that Israel does not know, and does not care to know Jehovah. WT/*GG*, 23.

Jesus' conflict with Israel was the direct result of the fact that in the name and for the sake of God he proceeded to charge the people with sin, declaring them unfit for entrance upon the eschatological inheritance, and summoning them to repentance. *SDJ*, 60.

Although the religious atmosphere in [Jesus'] day was surcharged with the notions of law-keeping and merit and retribution, there was lacking the vivid consciousness of God as a perpetual witness and interested participant in every moral transaction. The automaton of the law had taken the place of the living God. Well might our Lord quote the words of the prophet Isaiah: "This people honoreth me with their lips, but their heart is far from me" [29:13]. HTR/*GG*, 32.

[commenting upon the Book of Hosea] Israel ought to love Jehovah supremely for his own sake, and should seek the external blessings only because in them his love expresses itself. As it is, the very opposite takes place: the people care only for the gifts and are indifferent to the Giver. *BT*, 277.

[Isaiah's condemnation of unbelieving Israel] Deep-rooted unbelief made them scorn the prophet's counsel to seek their strength in quietness and confidence, instead of which they chose to rely on their own petty diplomacy. This underlying conceit of being better masters of the situation than Jehovah, more powerful than he to control the forces of history and guide them to the goal of Judah's deliverance, this, as the figure of the potter and the clay already intimates, constitutes for Isaiah the supreme folly of their line of action. RCEP, 631.

Jacob

The main principle embodied in the history of Jacob-Israel is that of subjective transformation of life, with a renewed stress on the productive activity of the divine factor. This must be kept in mind in order to read the history aright. Of the characters of the three patriarchs, that of Jacob is least represented as an ideal one. Its reprehensible features are rather strongly brought out. This is done in order to show that divine grace is not the reward for, but the source of noble traits. Grace overcoming human sin and transforming human nature is the keynote of the revelation here. *BT*, 93.

Jehovah

The thought of Jehovah's exaltation so absolute as to efface all relative distinctions in human greatness is quite familiar to the Old Testament. Having no rival and being no rival, it is his divine prerogative to take account of the weak and poor as much as of the strong and honorable. "For Jehovah your God, He is God of gods and Lord of lords, the great God, the mighty and the terrible, which regardeth not persons nor taketh reward. He doth execute the judgment of the fatherless and widow and loveth the stranger in giving him food and raiment" (Deut. 10:17–18). OHGG/*GG*, 258.

[commenting upon Isa. 57:15] The thought trembles on the verge of the paradoxical: Jehovah the high and lofty one, inhabiting eternity, dwelling in the high and holy place, declares his willingness to abide with the contrite and humble. That Jehovah should dwell with individual man at all is in itself a conception sufficiently startling on the basis of the Old Testament. OHGG/*GG*, 261.

[commenting upon Ex. 3] The name Jehovah signifies primarily that in all God does for his people, he is from-within-determined, not moved upon by outside influences. *BT*, 119.

Jehovah, Possession of

The possession of Jehovah himself by his people will be of all the delights of the world to come the chief and most satisfying, the paradise within the paradise of God. WT/*GG*, 3.

Jeremiah

His was a retiring, peace-loving disposition, which from the very beginning protested against the Lord's call to enter upon this public office: "Ah Lord Jehovah, behold I know not how to speak, for I am a child" (1:6). An almost idyllic, pastoral nature, he would have far preferred to lead the quiet priestly life, a shepherd among tranquil sheep. JP/*SW*, 289.

Jeremiah's personal experience proved a typical forecast of Israel's future enjoyment of God. Through all the distress and terror of his ministry he had learned to know God with a new incomparable knowledge. Even that former sense of discord and protest in which the right always appeared on God's side, had only served to lay bare the ultimate rock where his soul was anchored with unbreakable chains to Jehovah. . . . Here lies the birthplace of that heroism of religion by which some were enabled momentarily to rise above self-interest and self-safety in the simple satisfaction of having and knowing God himself. JP/*SW*, 295–96.

Jerusalem, New

[commenting upon Rev. 21 and 22] The picture is drawn from a twofold point of view: the new Jerusalem is a restoration of Paradise (Rev. 21:6; 22:1, 2, 14); it is also the ideal of the theocracy realized (Rev. 21:3, 12, 14, 22). The latter viewpoint explains the peculiar representation that the city descends "out of heaven from God" (Rev. 21:2, 10), which characterizes it as, on the one hand, a product of God's supernatural workmanship, and as, on the other hand, the culmination of the historic process of redemption. In other NT passages, where the theocratic point of view is less prominent, the anti-typical Jerusalem appears as having its seat in heaven instead of, as here, coming down from heaven to earth (cf. Gal. 4:26; Heb. 11:10; 12:22). NJ/*ISBE*, 1622.

Jesus

[Jesus] did not come to propound a new system of ethics as a thinker or a moral genius, but to summon into being a new realm of moral and religious realities, even the kingdom of God. He stands and speaks out of the midst of a great redemptive movement of which he himself is the central and controlling factor. UMG/*SW*, 341–42.

[Jesus is] the supernaturalism of heaven incarnate. *SDJ*, 24.

154

[Jesus] regarded the whole Old Testament movement as a divinely directed and inspired movement, as having arrived at its goal in himself, so that he himself in his historic appearance and work being taken away, the Old Testament would lose its purpose and significance. This none other could say. He was the confirmation and consummation of the Old Testament in his own person, and this yielded the one substratum of his interpretation of himself in the world of religion. *BT*, 358.

To Paul Jesus is the One from heaven, the second Adam, the prototype of the heavenly image believers are to receive in the resurrection. *SDJ*, 24.

[commenting upon Isa. 42] In accord with this prophetic utterance, Jesus desires to perform his miracles in as unostentatious a manner as possible. This sprang not merely from the ethical principle of humility, but equally from the soteric purpose of bringing his miracles into harmony with the law of humiliation imposed upon his earthly life. *SDJ*, 71.

[Jesus] was born for this purpose and this purpose only, to seek and to save the lost. SSL/*GG*, 46.

Our Lord's life was a human life which derived its meaning from beginning to end from his vocation as a Savior. SSL/*GG*, 47.

There are not two figures of Jesus in the Gospels, the one clothed with the mantle of royalty, the other bent upon the pursuit of purely humanitarian tasks; these two are one and the same. They have their common principle in the requirements imposed and the equipment conferred by his messianic anointing. *SDJ*, 115.

What [Jesus] endured in the race of his earthly life became the legal ground on which God based the bestowal upon him of all the glory and blessedness of his exalted state. RR/*GG*, 135.

Jesus and Paul

[commenting upon Veldhuizen's *Paulus*] We could wish that the relation between Paul and Jesus had been somewhat more definitely formulated than is done on p. 18, where Paul is said to have coined the gold furnished by Jesus. The figure is striking, but it fails to express the fundamental fact, so much in need of emphasis, that the relation between the two is not on the whole that between two successive teachers, but that between the interpreted and the interpreter, between the author of redemption and the apostle of redemption. *PEZ*, 181.

Jesus and Religion

Everybody recognizes that, inasmuch as Jesus was a true man who exercised faith and prayed and gave glory to God, he *had* religion. But not all are willing to admit that, side by side with this, Jesus knew himself and the church from the beginning knew him in another aspect, in which he did not practice but *received* religion. *JG/SW*, 510.

Jesus, Eschatologist

Jesus was a consistent eschatologist in the very core of his religion; he had grasped eschatology as something without which religion ceases to exist. *SDJ*, 35.

Jesus [was] an eschatologist for the sake of God. Our Lord's interest in eschatology was religiously oriented in the deepest and most ideal sense of the word. *SDJ*, 21.

[against Schweitzer's view of the eschatological Jesus] It failed to distinguish between eschatology as a theological obsession, and eschatology as the finest flower of religion cultivated for the glory of God. The latter, not the former, eschatology surely was for Jesus. And in him it was as deep as his religion itself. *SDJ*, 36.

Jesus, Messianic Self-Consciousness of

Jesus' self-consciousness is the focal point in which all rays of religious contemplation of Jesus and communion with Jesus meet, and whence they derive their reflection. *SDJ*, 14.

▓ [commenting upon Matt. 11:27–30] Jesus' joy and thanksgiving do not relate to something taking place outside of himself, in regard to which he, although rejoicing in it, would after all be a mere spectator. Jesus thanks God because his own person is the pivot, the center, of the whole transaction. The glory of the gospel dispensation with its sovereignty and wisdom is focused in his own person: "All things were delivered unto me by my Father." *SDJ*, 147.

Jewish Legalism, Condemnation of

▓ The apostle's polemic against the Jewish legalism proceeds along two distinct lines of attack. In the first place, it is rejected because utterly impracticable and futile, because it has never led and can never lead to the end for which the Jewish mind pursues it. In the second place, not satisfied with this practical dismissal of it, Paul condemns it on the fundamental ground of its irreligious character and tendency. AL/*SW*, 388.

▓ The Judaistic dependence on works was questionable not merely because it rested on a great untruth, but even more because it subverted the normal relation between God and man. AL/*SW*, 391.

▓ The Judaistic spirit made itself the end and God the means, gave to itself the glory and to God the part of subserving the interests of this human glory by his moral government; . . . it led the creature to regard itself as the active and God as the merely passive factor in the determination of eternal destiny. AL/*SW*, 391.

▓ It is this profoundly sinful, specifically Jewish καυχᾶσθαι [pride, boasting], against which the religious spirit of Paul rises in protest, and which makes him so uncompromising in his repudiation of the legal system. Inspired by such motives, it becomes to him the absolute antithesis to the very idea of religion. AL/*SW*, 391.

▓ Our Lord was confronted with the abnormal spectacle of a religious system which claimed to be the product of special soteriological revelation, and in which, nevertheless, God has been so far removed from man as to be no longer the object of trust and love. In

Judaism everything had been put on the basis of commercial inter-course with the Almighty. Over against this it was necessary before all else to awaken the religious consciousness to the recognition of the fact that God is personally interested in man; that instead of merely exploiting man in his service, he lovingly gives himself to man, and desires to be met in the spirit of trust and affection. SDL/*SW*, 441.

Job

Here lies the birthplace of that heroism of religion by which some were enabled momentarily to rise above self-interest and self-safety in the simple satisfaction of having and knowing God himself. Here lies the explanation of the outcry of Job, "Though he slay me, yet will I hope in him" (13:15). JP/*SW*, 295–96.

John, Gospel of

The Fourth [Gospel's] primary purpose is theological. According to [John 20:30–31] the author was guided in his selection of mate-rial by the desire to convince his readers that Jesus is the Christ, the Son of God, and that, believing, they might have life through his name. The salvation is here, as elsewhere, lifted to the high plane of receiving through faith the revelation of Jesus as divine into one's self. It is a revelation which not merely informs but which, through supernaturally informing, saves. *SDJ*, 299.

[commenting upon John 1:1–18] The unique feature of the pro-logue consists in this, that it views the cosmical function of the pre-existent Christ as a revealing function and places it in direct conti-nuity with his revealing work in the sphere of redemption. Not that the Messiah has a share in the creation of the world or in providence, but that in mediating both he acts as the revealing Logos of God—this is the valuable information which the prologue supplies. RLT/*SW*, 90.

It is the method of the Fourth Gospel to resolve the Savior's task into the several aspects of what he is by his eternal nature or his his-torical equipment. Life, light, truth, grace—such concepts as these in the case of Jesus practically cease to be abstractions, and rather pass over into concrete personal names. *SDJ*, 255.

It is precisely in John that the theological principle of the duplex structure and stratification of the universe is explicitly enunciated. The great contrasts governing the teaching here . . . are expressed in the terms "earth" (opp. "heaven"); the "world" (opp. "not this world"); "the earthly things" (opp. "the heavenly things"); "the things beneath" (opp. "the things above"). Between these fundamental contrasts the relation prevails that in order of thought and pre-eminence the heavenly things precede. *BT*, 355.

[In John] unbelief is shown to spring from a radically wrong attitude of man's nature toward God. *BT*, 391.

The Fourth Gospel eternalizes the present state of the believer and emphasizes the identity rather than the difference between the life now possessed and the life to be inherited hereafter. *EAP/SW*, 95.

The Gospel of John contains revelations contemporaneous with those of the Synoptists, so that chronologically we can distribute its material over the pages of Matthew, Mark, and Luke. Nevertheless, taken as a whole and in its unity, the Gospel of John represents a fuller and wider self-revelation of Christ than the Synoptists; and not only so, but it also represents a type of revelation which presupposes the facts and teachings of the other Gospels, and is, in point of order, subsequent to them. *IBT/SW*, 14.

The "supernaturalism" of Jesus' gospel and of his person, as determining that of the gospel, finds most pointed expression in John. One might call it the anti-evolutionistic document in the Scriptures, *par excellence*, so far as ethics and religion are concerned (John 8:23). *BT*, 355.

Instead of things being naturalized and made less other-worldly in the Fourth Gospel, it would be more correct to say that the eschatological-supernatural appears in John in its highest potency, inas-

much as, turned backward, it draws the entire *ante mortem* life of
the believer into the sphere of its transforming influence. *SDJ*, 24.

John, Gospel of, and Jesus

The signs of Jesus in the Fourth Gospel were recorded in order
that the readers might "believe that Jesus is the Christ, the Son of
God" (John 20:31). This is, therefore, pre-eminently the Gospel of
the Savior's sonship. *SDJ*, 195.

[John's] mind was so post-resurrection-centered as to lead him
to lay stress, in his treatment of the earthly life of Jesus, on precisely
those aspects of it that prefigured the glorified state. *SDJ*, 121.

Here the person of Jesus as the Son of God stands in the foreground, and the whole compass of his work is represented as given
in and resulting from his person. Salvation according to the discourses
preserved in this Gospel is made up of those primal elements into
which the being of Christ can be resolved, such as light, life, grace,
truth. What the Savior does is the outcome of what he is. *KGC*, 10.

In the Fourth Gospel . . . Jesus gives clearly [the understanding]
that the physical acts are intended to point to corresponding spiritual acts. The healing of the blind, the raising of the dead find their
counterpart in what he does for the souls of sinners. *KGC*, 56.

John, Gospel of, and the Logos

If Christ as Logos has a wider task than that of imparting light
and knowledge, if he fulfills his Logos-nature in the production of
life, then the Gospel can be truly a Logos-Gospel. . . . The new-
creation of all things in the sphere of redemption becomes, on this
wider and more correct view, as truly a part of the Logos-function
as the communication of supernatural knowledge. *RLT/SW*, 66.

The peculiar teaching in the body of the Gospel [of John] has not
been deduced from the Logos-idea, and yet can as a matter of fact
be deduced from it, because the Logos-idea is to the mind of the
Evangelist simply the most appropriate conception into which he

160

has gathered up the teaching of Jesus concerning himself in the discourses. RLT/*SW*, 72.

John the Baptist

John's forerunning of Jesus was to all intents a forerunning of the entire Old Testament with reference to the Christ. And this applied not by any means to externals only; the real substance of the Old Testament was recapitulated in John. If we distinguish the two elements of law and prophecy, both were plainly summed up in the message: "Repent, for the kingdom of heaven is at hand." *BT*, 315.

The culmination of Old Testament prophecy is in him, and this position entitles him to be called "greatest of them born of women." *BT*, 313.

Through him the kingdom had passed out of the sphere of pure futurity belonging to it under the Old Testament; it had become something actual engaging the thoughts and swaying the emotions of men. To have effected this was the great act of John, that which made him "more than a prophet." *BT*, 313.

He was not so much a revealer of new truth as a recapitulator of the old. At the point where the old covenant is about to pass over into the new, John once more sums up in his ministry the entire message of all preceding revelation and thus becomes the connecting link between it and the fulfillment which was to follow. JB/*SW*, 299.

Almost every feature in the Baptist's appearance bears witness to the intimate connection between him and the old covenant. He led the life of a Nazirite, one of the Old Testament forms of consecration to Jehovah's service (Luke 1:15). His desert surroundings were symbolic of the dead, barren, unspiritual state of Israel (Hos. 2:14–15; Isa. 40:1–4); his approach to asceticism in the matter of fasting points in the same direction (Matt. 11:10). JB/*SW*, 299.

We have the express declaration of our Lord which places John outside the limits of the kingdom of heaven, i.e., outside of the New

Testament realization of this kingdom historically inaugurated by Jesus himself. Our Lord did not mean that John was not a believer in the Old Testament sense, but simply that officially and personally he did not share in the far greater privileges of the new covenant; he that is lesser in the kingdom of heaven, i.e., occupies a relatively lower place than John under the Old Testament, is nevertheless absolutely greater than John, because the kingdom itself is far superior to the typical stage of the theocracy (Matt. 11:11). JB/*SW*, 300.

As John's ministry summed up in itself the substance of all Old Testament truth, so his ministry in its turn was summed up in his baptism. JB/*SW*, 301.

We shall not be able to appreciate, however, the real greatness of John until we realize that his effacement was of the nature of a self-effacement, willingly nay joyfully made by him, in order that he might serve by it his Lord. If nothing else, then this will show that John, while standing officially outside of the kingdom, had understood and assimilated the great principle on which the kingdom is built, that of self-denial and service. JB/*SW*, 303.

Judaism

The Old Testament and Judaism are not to be identified. The latter our Lord not seldom found fault with; that he did so with the former remains to be proved. *BT*, 364.

Judaism was a religion of law. So the kingdom came to mean a more perfect enforcement of the legalistic principle than could be attained in the present state. *BT*, 374.

The Jewish ethic suffered from two fundamental defects: its tendency toward deism and its infection by self-centeredness. *BT*, 395.

Judaism and the Law

[In Judaism] the law was not obeyed with the idea of the supervision of God in mind; the service of the law had taken the place of the service of the living God (Gal. 2:18–21). *BT*, 395.

■ [In] the Judaistic law-practice [the] main concern was not to attain the positive end of the law, but rather to avoid negatively the disasters feared from non-observance; the system degenerated into a system of avoidance. *BT*, 396.

Judaizers

■ [Paul's] main contention with the Judaizers was that they insisted upon interpreting the patriarchal period on the basis of the Mosaic period. *BT*, 79.

Judgment

■ The judgment is, of course, the inevitable summing up of a world-process that has fallen subject to the moral abnormalcy of sin. *PE*, 72.

■ Being not merely holy but majestic in holiness, Jehovah upholds and asserts his ethical glory for the punishment of sin. Isaiah has felt most keenly that God would not be God, would not respect his own divinity, did he not avenge evil. OHGG/*GG*, 271.

■ Nowhere else are we taught so clearly as in Isaiah that the vindicating justice of God is only the intensity of his holiness translated into action. OHGG/*GG*, 271.

■ Judging is in the Orient a regal function, the king being lawgiver and law-executor in one. *PE*, 284.

■ It is God from whom all righteousness and judgment issue, and to whom all the, to men un-disentanglible, threads of conduct, be it inward or outward, are clear, who as his divine right executes this conclusive judicial act and thus receives this part of the glory that must accrue to him from all that has ever happened in the world. *PE*, 285.

Judgment and Resurrection

■ The two overtowering final events in the drama of eschatology are the resurrection and the judgment. As we shall presently see they are the points where the rivers of history issue into the ocean. *PE*, 72.

The general resurrection of the saints [is] an eschatological event, indeed constituting together with the judgment the main content of the eschatological program. EAP/SW, 93.

Resurrection and judgment are the two correlated acts of the final consummation of things. They are like twin-woes in the travail by which the age to come is brought to birth. *PE*, 261.

In the resurrection there is already wrapped up a judging-process, at least for believers: the raising act in their case, together with the attending change, plainly involves a pronouncement of vindication. *PE*, 260.

[Judgment] places the seal on what the believer has received in the resurrection. *PE*, 261.

Judgment, Blessing Precedes in the New Testament

This also affords the explanation of John's somewhat impatient enquiry in regard to the messianic authentication of Jesus. In it the Old Testament once more, as it were, voices its impatience about the tarrying of the Messiah. But as there, so here, the impatience centered on one particular point, the slowness of God's procedure in destroying the wicked. John had been specifically appointed to proclaim the judgment-aspect of the coming crisis. Hence a certain disappointment at the procedure of Jesus [but] it was not Jesus' task for the present to judge, at least not in that way. The judgment would come at a subsequent stage. *BT*, 313–14.

Justification

Justification is, of course, to Paul the basis on which the whole Christian state rests, and in so far eminently concerns the present, and yet in its finality and comprehensiveness, covering not merely time but likewise eternity, it presents remarkable analogies to the absolute vindication expected at the end. EAP/SW, 93.

164

■ Through justification we are even in this life filled with the fulness of [Jesus'] merit, and appear to God as spotless and blameless as though sin had never touched us. HTR/*GG*, 43.

■ What Paul calls justification, Jesus calls entrance into the kingdom or becoming a son of God. *BT*, 394.

■ Paul's mind was to such an extent forensically oriented that he regarded the entire complex of subjective spiritual changes that take place in the believer and of subjective spiritual blessings enjoyed by the believer as the direct outcome of the forensic work of Christ applied in justification. AL/*SW*, 384.

Justification and Eschatology

■ Here lies precisely the point where eschatology and justification intersect. By making both the negative element of the forgiveness of sin and the positive element of bestowal of the benefits of salvation unqualified, the apostle made the act of justification to all intents, so far as the believer is concerned, a last judgment anticipated. If the act dealt with present and past sins only, leaving the future product in uncertainty, it could not be regarded as possessing such absoluteness, and the comparison with the last judgment would break down at the decisive point. *PE*, 55.

Justification and Resurrection

■ In the justification of Christ lie the certainty and the root of the Christian's resurrection. For the supreme fruit of Christ's justification, on the basis of passive and active obedience, is nothing else but the Spirit, and in turn the Spirit bears in himself the efficacious principle of all transformation to come, the resurrection with its entire compass included. Resurrection thus comes out of justification, and justification comes, after a manner most carefully to be defined, out of the resurrection; not, be it noted, out of the spiritual resurrection of the believer himself, but out of the resurrection of Christ. On the basis of merit this is so. Christ's resurrection was the *de facto* declaration of God in regard to his being just. *PE*, 151.

Justification and Sanctification

Justification and sanctification are not the same, and an endless amount of harm has been done by the short-sighted attempt to identify them. But neither are these two independent one of the other; the one sets the goal and fixes the direction, the other follows. *PE*, 149.

In our opinion the true reason why justification entails sanctification must not be sought on the subjective side, in faith, but on the objective side, in the *modus operandi* of the atonement. Because Paul views the ethical bondage of man under sin as a result of his condemnation by the law, therefore the removal of this condemnation, the canceling of the guilt, *ipso facto*, also sets him ethically free; more strictly speaking, enables God forensically to free him in the ethical sphere. *DB*, 318.

Keys of the Kingdom

[commenting upon Matt. 16] The keys spoken of are in all probability not the keys of the outer door, but the keys pertaining to the entire house, the keys not of the gate-keeper, but of the house-steward, and therefore symbolize the administration of the affairs of the house in general; see Isaiah 22:22; Revelation 3:7. *KGC*, 81.

Kindness

"Chesed" is the loyal, tender attachment practiced in daily intercourse by reason of some original, more ultimate union preceding it. If the primordial love did not lie back of it, Jehovah's kindness could never be an assured possession of Israel. *JP/SW*, 297.

King

To the ancient Shemitic consciousness the king is *ipso facto* the lawgiver and the executor of the law (see Ps. 72; Isa. 33:22). Far more also than we can imagine, the king is the center of political life, for whose sake the state and the subjects exist. *BT*, 393.

Kingdom of God

■ [The] perfect kingdom of God [is that] toward which all the streams of human history roll their waters as toward their final goal. TP/*SW*, 359.

■ The kingdom of God, in order to be truly the kingdom of God, is the *perfect* kingdom of God, in which the divine will shall be done on earth after no less absolute a fashion than it is done in heaven, and only at this acme of its realization does it fully deserve the name of God's kingdom. *SDJ*, 82.

■ We are accustomed to finding in Jesus' teaching the idea of a present spiritual kingdom, realized, in the invisible, internal sphere, through his ministry on earth. We assume that he regarded the kingdom as in principle already present, although he regarded the eschatological consummation as still future. *SDJ*, 80.

■ The doctrine of the kingdom stands for the principle that the Christian religion is not a mere matter of subjective ideas or experiences, but is related to a great system of objective, supernatural facts and transactions. *KGC*, 102.

Kingdom of God, and Christ

■ It touches, through the kingship of Christ, the very acme and perfection of the biblical religion. *BT*, 185–86.

Kingdom of God, and Redemption

■ Jesus everywhere proclaims the gospel he summons men to accept as a gospel of the kingdom of God. And the kingdom of God, what else is it but a new world of supernatural realities supplanting this natural world of sin? If the Ritschlians do not clearly perceive this, it is due to their unhistorical, essentially modern interpretation of the kingdom as an ethical organization of mankind and nothing more. CFTBH/*SW*, 470.

Kingdom of God, and Religion

The kingdom is a conception which must of necessity remain unintelligible and unacceptable to every view of the world and of religion which magnifies man at the expense of God. *KGC*, 52.

The kingdom of God was to Jesus the supreme religious ideal. Consequently, whatever is made to fall outside of this can no longer lay claim to absolute importance. *DR*, 303.

The kingdom-idea is the clearest expression of the principle that in the sphere of objective reality, as well as in the sphere of human consciousness, everything is *subservient to the glory of God*. In this respect the kingdom is the most profoundly *religious* of all biblical conceptions. *KGC*, 102.

The thought of the kingdom of God implies the subjection of the entire range of human life in all its forms and spheres to the ends of religion. The kingdom reminds us of *the absoluteness, the pervasiveness, the unrestricted dominion*, which of right belong to all true religion. It proclaims that religion, and religion alone, can act as *the supreme unifying, centralizing factor* in the life of man, as that which binds all together and perfects all by leading it to its final goal in the service of God. *KGC*, 103.

Kingdom of God, and Righteousness

The kingdom (kingship) of God is identified with righteousness. They are concurrent, or mutually in-existent, because the doing of righteousness amounts to the practical recognition and furtherance of his kingship. *BT*, 393.

The coming order of things, the new kingdom of God, brings with itself, chief of all blessings, a perfect righteousness, as truly and absolutely the gift of God to man as is the entire kingdom. What is true of the kingdom, that no human merit can deserve, no human effort call it into being, applies with equal force to the righteousness that forms its center. It is God's creation, not man's. HTR/*GG*, 41.

Kingdom of God, and the Church

▓ Every view which would keep the kingdom and the church separate as two entirely distinct spheres is not in harmony with the trend of our Lord's teaching. The church is a form which the kingdom assumes in result of the new stage upon which the messiahship of Jesus enters with his death and resurrection. *KGC*, 85–86.

▓ In its church form the kingdom already assumes the character of an organized community, standing midway between the invisible spiritual kingdom forces as such and the perfectly organized eschatological consummation. KOG/*SW*, 316.

▓ The kingdom as the church bears the features of a community of men. It appears as a house. This character belonged to the Old Testament church for which that of Jesus is substituted; it also finds expression in the very name *ecclesia*, which designates the assembly of free citizens called together to deliberate and take action in matters pertaining to the commonwealth. *KGC*, 82.

▓ That form which the kingdom assumes in the church shows it to be inseparably associated *with the person and work of Jesus himself.* The religion of the kingdom is a religion in which there is not only a place but in which the central place is for the Savior. The church form of the kingdom rightly bears the name of *Christianity*, because in it on Christ everything depends. *KGC*, 103.

▓ Toward the close of his ministry our Lord opened up the prospect of a new form of development upon which in result of his death and glorification the spiritual kingdom would enter. This is the church (see Matt. 16:18–19). KOG/*SW*, 315.

Kingdom of God, and the Messiah

▓ [Jesus] distinguished two forms of messianic activity, one on earth in humility, one from the throne of glory, and corresponding to this two forms of the kingdom, one invisible now, one visible at the end; and, thus understood, the two-sidedness of the messianic consciousness affords a striking parallel to the two-sidedness of his kingdom-conception. *KGC*, 38.

It is agreed on all hands that Jesus made the kingdom of God and the messiahship the great pivotal points of his world-view. *SDJ*, 80–81.

The kingdom was and was not yet; even so the Messiah was and was not yet. As the future coming of the kingdom, so frequently affirmed, was not meant to deny the very real existence of a present phase of the same, so neither did the prospective contemplation of the messiahship exclude every mode of present realization in its case. *SDJ*, 81.

Kingdom of God, as Preliminary

The difference between this Jewish representation and Jesus' idea of the preliminary kingdom lies in this, that according to the Jewish view the kingdom is always there, it being only a question whether man will take it upon himself, whereas according to Jesus, who thought less of human efforts, but had a deeper insight into the sinfulness of man and a higher conception of what the true reign of God involves, even this partial kingdom must first come through an act of God before man can be invited to receive it. *KGC*, 31.

Kingdom of God, as Treasure

On account of the blessedness involved, the kingdom appears under the figure of a treasure or a precious pearl, in each case it being explicitly stated that the finder sold all he had in order to possess himself of the coveted object, which means, of course, that it was more precious than all other values combined. *BT*, 399.

The inestimable value of the kingdom from man's point of view finds clearest expression in the parable of the treasure of the field and the pearl of great price. In both cases it is emphasized that the finder sells all his possessions in order to secure this one transcendent good (cf. Matt. 19:12; Mark 9:43–47; Luke 18:29). *KGC*, 71.

Kingdom of God, Blessings of

To the kingdom belong all the gifts of grace—the forgiveness of sins, the reception into sonship, the enjoyment of the love of God, the bestowal of life—in short, the entire content of the idea of salvation in its widest range. Especially the state of communion with God and of blessedness into which redemption issues is for this reason identified with the kingdom. KOG/SW, 315.

Negatively, the kingdom includes the deliverance from all evil. Foremost among the blessings pertaining to this side stands the forgiveness of sins. *KGC*, 72.

Positively there corresponds to this the gift of righteousness, which cannot but carry with itself a sense of the highest spiritual delight and satisfaction for those who obtain it. *KGC*, 72.

Kingdom of God, Centered in God and His Glory

Not the thought of man's welfare, but that of the glory of God was supreme in our Lord's teaching concerning the kingdom. While emphasizing this, we must not forget, however, that to him this thought was inseparably connected with the idea of the greatest conceivable blessedness for man. That God should reign was in his view so much the only natural, normal state of things, that he could not conceive of any true happiness apart from it, nor of it without a concomitant state of happiness for those who give to God the first and highest place. *KGC*, 70.

To [Jesus] the kingdom exists there, where not merely God is supreme, for that is true at all times and under all circumstances, but where God supernaturally carries through his supremacy against all opposing powers and brings man to the willing recognition of the same. It is a state of things in which everything converges and tends toward God as the highest good. *KGC*, 50.

[The kingdom is] centered in God himself; it can be represented by our Lord as the supreme object of human pursuit. This would plainly be impossible if the idea of the kingdom was conceived on any lower plane, for in that case some other object would be interposed between God and man as the absolute end of man's religious aspiration. [The] kingdom of God means the ideal of religion in this highest sense realized. *KGC*, 51.

Because the kingdom is thus centered in God himself and in his glory, it can be represented by our Lord as the highest object after which men are to strive. KOG/*SW*, 311.

God is the center of attraction in the kingdom of glory; so that to lose touch with God inevitably means to stop in the midst of the race toward heaven. RR/*GG*, 133.

Kingdom of God, Coming of

[Jesus] sometimes refers to the eschatological crisis as *"the coming of* the kingdom of God," just as if no kingdom truly worthy of the name had previously existed: "For I say unto you I will not drink of the fruit of the vine, until the kingdom of God shall come" (Luke 22:16–18). Notice, he does not say, "until the kingdom shall be perfected," nor "until the eschatological form of the kingdom shall come," but simply *"until the kingdom of God shall come." SDJ*, 82.

[commenting upon the Sermon on the Mount] Our Lord's meaning obviously is that the coming order of things, the new kingdom of God, brings with itself, chief of all blessings, a perfect righteousness, as truly and absolutely the gift of God to man as is the entire kingdom. HTR/*GG*, 41.

The organic kingdom comes in the internal, invisible sphere, so that its realization is a hidden process; the eschatological kingdom comes in the external, visible sphere, so that its realization will be a manifest act observable by all. KOG/*SW*, 309–10.

Kingdom of God, Eschatological

The eschatological kingdom will, according to [Jesus], have its own external environment, and its own external forms of life. Only, these are to be of a higher order than those which belong to the

172

earthly state of existence, in consequence of which great differences prevail between the two. KOG/*SW*, 308.

Although the eschatological kingdom differs from the present kingdom largely in the fact that it will receive an external, visible embodiment, yet this does not hinder that even in it the core is constituted by those spiritual realities and relations which make the present kingdom. Still it will have its outward form as the doctrine of the resurrection and the regenerated earth plainly show. ENT/*SW*, 54.

The eschatological coming of the kingdom does more than merely make externally manifest what internally was already there before. The entire language which Jesus employs in regard to it presupposes that it will bring blessings transcending those of the present stage of the kingdom. All imperfections will be done away with, all enemies vanquished, the wheat and the tares will no longer be permitted to intermingle, the full satisfaction with righteousness and the beatific vision of God will be enjoyed. KOG/*SW*, 310.

On the whole the gospel eschatology is kingdom eschatology. It deals with the large collective events which shall usher in the final perfect state of the kingdom. OLDR/*SW*, 320–21.

Kingdom of God, Jesus' Doctrine of

Jesus' doctrine of the kingdom as both inward and outward, coming first in the heart of man and afterwards in the external world, upholds *the primacy of the spiritual and ethical* over the physical. The invisible world of the inner religious life, the righteousness of the disposition, the sonship of God are in it made supreme, the essence of the kingdom, the ultimate realities to which everything else is subordinate. *KGC*, 103.

Kingdom of God, Jesus' Usage of the Term

Jesus never speaks of the kingdom of God as previously existing. To him the kingdom is throughout something new, now first to be realized. *KGC*, 15.

The true explanation is undoubtedly to be found in the absolute, ideal character our Lord ascribed to the order of things associated with the name of the kingdom. To his mind it involved such altogether new forces and such unparalleled blessings, that all relative and provisional forms previously assumed by the work of God on earth seemed by comparison unworthy of the name. Thus, while he would not have denied that the Old Testament institutions represented a real kingdom of God, the high sense with which he had invested the term made it unnatural for him to apply it to these. *KGC*, 16–17.

It is true, our Lord always emphasizes that the heart and essence of the kingdom may be possessed in the present life. But it is plain that he could not have spoken so absolutely of the eschatological crisis as *the coming of the kingdom,* had not the thought been in his mind that, after all, only the end of the world can bring the full and adequate possession of even those spiritual blessings in which the kernel of the kingdom consists. KOG/*SW*, 310.

Kingdom of God, Mystery of

This mystery, this new truth, we may find in the revelation that the kingdom is realized gradually, imperceptibly, spiritually, for in comparison with the Jewish exclusively eschatological expectations this was so novel and startling a thought that it might be fitly called a mystery. KOG/*SW*, 307.

Kingdom of God, Old Testament Conception of

In the Old Testament [the kingdom] designates the rule of God established through creation and extending through providence over the universe. . . . Besides this . . . there is a specifically-redemptive Kingdom, usually called "the theocracy." *BT*, 372–73.

[commenting upon Ex. 19:6] It speaks of a present kingdom from the Old Testament point of view. Still, the Old Testament likewise speaks of the kingdom as a futurity. It may seem strange that what one has, one should still look forward to, and that not as a matter of relative improvement, but as a matter of absolutely new creation. *BT*, 373.

Kingdom of God, Present Reality of

[In Luke 11:20] Jesus affirms that the driving out of the demons by the Spirit signifies the coming of the kingdom. The underlying principle is that in the world of spirits there is no neutral territory; where the demons depart, the divine Spirit enters. . . . The passage, therefore, teaches a present kingdom. *BT*, 382.

[commenting upon Matt. 6:33] The kingdom itself appears as a possession obtainable in this life. For food and clothing are here represented as something to be added not to the seeking of the kingdom but to the kingdom itself, and it goes without saying, that this is applicable only to the kingdom in its present state of existence. *KGC*, 35.

A present kingdom necessarily carries with itself a present enjoyment of life. *KGC*, 75.

Kingdom of God, Relationship between Present and Final

The present kingdom comes gradually, the final kingdom catastrophically. *BT*, 384.

The present kingdom comes largely in the internal, invisible sphere, the final kingdom in the form of a world-wide visible manifestation. *BT*, 384.

The present kingdom up to the eschatological point remains subject to imperfections; the final kingdom will be without all imperfections. *BT*, 384.

Kingdom of God, Spiritual Nature of

What our Lord did was to give to [the] Jewish mode of representation an infinitely higher content, while formally retaining it. He lifted it out of the political sphere into the spiritual. The conquests to which he refers are those over Satan and the demons, over sin and evil. It is kingdom against kingdom, but both of these opposing kingdoms belong to a higher world than that to which Rome and her empire belong. *KGC*, 53.

The question naturally arises, how can this identification of the kingdom with the effects of a power working largely in the physical sphere be reconciled with the emphasis placed by Jesus upon the spiritual nature of the kingdom? The answer is that the physical evils which the kingdom-power removes have a moral and spiritual background. Satan reigns not merely in the body, nor merely in the mind pathologically considered, but also in the heart and will of man as the instigator of sin and the source of moral evil. Hence Jesus made his miracles the occasion for suggesting and working the profounder change by which the bonds of sin were loosed and the rule of God set up anew in the entire inner life of men. Because this real connection exists, the physical process can become symbolical of the spiritual. *KGC*, 55.

Our Lord repeatedly speaks of the kingdom as a state of things lying altogether above the sphere of earthly and natural life, being so different from the natural conditions that it could not be evolved from the latter by any gradual process. KOG/*SW*, 307.

Kingship

Kingship means the performance of great acts of salvation for a people in which a relation of leadership is established. *BT*, 373.

Kingship in Israel

Our modern usage, as it makes us think of the king almost exclusively under the aspect of a constitutional ruler and executive of the law, more or less obscures the fact that to Israel the kingship was "a source of happiness, a fountain of blessing, a retreat for salvation." The kingship was a democratic institution. The king naturally took the part of the poor and oppressed, not of the powerful and violent; the king existed for the sake of Israel, not the reverse. *DAU*, 129.

176

Knowledge

The presupposition of all knowledge of God is man's having been created in the image of God. *BT*, 19.

The knowledge of God communicated by [revelation] is nowhere for a purely intellectual purpose. From beginning to end it is a knowledge intended to enter into the actual life of man, to be worked out by him in all its practical bearings. IBT/*SW*, 10

The Shemitic, and in particular the biblical, conception of knowledge is distinguished from the Greek, more intellectualistic idea, by the prominence of this practical element. To know, in the Shemitic sense, is to have the consciousness of the reality and the properties of something interwoven with one's life through the closest intercourse and communion attainable. IBT/*SW*, 10.

Paul evidently looked upon the knowing of God as in itself a religious ideal. This may best be seen from the fact that he conceives of the blessedness of the heavenly state as centered in that knowledge of God face to face which will take the place of the vision in the glass darkly (1 Cor. 13:12). TP/*SW*, 358.

The meaning of the word ["to know"] goes far beyond the intellectual sphere; to know is not a mere act or process of becoming informed, but an act of sympathetic absorption in the other's character. It describes Jehovah's original choice of Israel as a most affectionate determination of what Israel was to be, and the attitude of the people as a passionate searching after the perfections of the divine nature. It is that self-projection of the lover into the beloved which is more than knowledge through the understanding. . . . This is to such an extent the heart and soul of the marriage, that the one great adultery consists in this: that Israel does not know, and does not care to know Jehovah. WT/*GG*, 23.

[commenting upon John 17:3] The knowledge of God here spoken of is, of course, something which in principle is already imparted in the present, although its consummate possession still lies in the future. It is a knowledge which is far more than mere intellectual cognition: it includes that practical acquaintance, that affectionate apprehension, which arise from congeniality of nature and the highest spiritual love. *KGC*, 75.

Kosmos, Renewal of

The specific manner in which God realizes the renewal of this sinful kosmos [is] that of creating within the organism of the present world the center of the world of redemption, and then organically building up the new order of things around this center. Hence from the beginning all redeeming acts of God aim at the creation and introduction of this new organic principle, which is none other than Christ. IBT/*SW*, 12.

Lamb of God

[commenting upon Isa. 53:6–7] Its primary use is to depict the innocence, meekness, and willingness to render vicarious service for the people through suffering and death. The features of innocence and meekness are inherent in the character of the lamb generically, but they are with special emphasis suggested here, because, the people having been described as a wayward, wandering flock, the very quality of a lamb sets the servant in contrast with this sinful condition. *BT*, 324–25.

[commenting upon Isa. 53 and John 1] The phrase "Lamb of God" is the exact duplicate of the phrase "Servant of Jehovah." It means the lamb performing the task of sin-bearing as belonging to and in the service of Jehovah. *BT*, 325–26.

Last Days

Believers live in the "last days," upon them "the ends of the ages are come," but "the last day," "the consummation of the age," still lies in the future. ENT/*SW*, 26.

Law

The law was given after the redemption from Egypt had been accomplished, and the people had already entered upon the enjoyment of many of the blessings of the *berith*. Particularly their taking possession of the promised land could not have been made dependent on previous observance of the law, for during their journey in the wilderness many of its prescripts could not be observed. It is plain, then, that law-keeping did not figure at that juncture as the meritorious ground of life-inheritance. The latter is based on grace alone. *BT*, 127.

What God desires in the law is not to afflict man, but to benefit him—a principle most strikingly affirmed in the statement that the Sabbath was made for man, not man for the Sabbath. EC/*GG*, 190.

To fulfill the law becomes but another form of the imperative, to be like God. It is God's inalienable right as God to impress his character upon us, to make and keep us reflectors of his infinite glory. HTR/*GG*, 34.

The law in itself has no religious defect; it is neither weaker nor stronger than by reason of its nature one could expect it to be; within the category of law it is perfectly normal, spiritual and good (Rom. 7:12, 14); only, it addresses itself to a mind which is sinful and cannot react upon its stimulus, so that the result is "weakness," in the sense of inefficacy. The same is implied where Paul speaks of the law as bringing man under the curse. This again is an effect due entirely to the collision of the law and sin. AL/*SW*, 389.

It is a striking fact that the Torah, as little as the other parts of the Old Testament, contains the proposition, God is love; whereas it does contain the statement that he is a consuming fire (Deut. 4:24). The vocation of the law to perform a ministry of condemnation may explain this. SDL/*SW*, 434.

[commenting upon John 1:17] The ordinary meaning of "false" can certainly not be applied to the law with which the grace and truth come by Christ are contrasted. For it is said of this law that it was given "through Moses." The use of "through" instead of "by" presupposes that Moses was only the instrument in giving the law, and this again has for its supposition that the actual lawgiver was none other than God (John 1:17). TT/*SW*, 348–49.

The utmost charge that the New Testament (Paul, Hebrews, John) brings against the law relates to its inefficacy; hence in that passage just quoted from Hebrews the author adds "can never . . . make perfect" [7:19]. TT/*SW*, 348–49.

Law and Jesus

The law in the hands of Jesus becomes alive with God's own personality. Majestic and authoritative, he is present in every commandment, so absolute in his demands, so observant of our conduct, so intent upon the outcome, that the thought of giving to him less than heart and soul and mind and strength in the product of our moral life ceases to be tolerable to ourselves. HTR/*GG*, 33.

[Jesus] alone of all mankind fulfilled the law in its deepest purport and widest extent. His keeping of it proceeded from that sanctuary of his inner life where he and the Father always beheld each other's face. He made it his meat and drink to do the will of God. HTR/*GG*, 42.

[Jesus] once more made the voice of the law the voice of the living God, who is present in every commandment, so absolute in his demands, so personally interested in man's conduct, so all-observant, that the thought of yielding to him less than the whole inner life, the heart, the soul, the mind, the strength, can no longer be tolerated. *KGC*, 61.

That propitiatory rite and that propitiatory place in which all Old Testament sacrificial functions culminated find their higher, their ideal counterpart in the crucified Savior. In this respect also he is the end of the law, not because he does away with the idea of sacrifice as something antiquated and imperfect, but because he embodies this idea in its highest conceivable, its absolute form in himself, and thus, while rendering all previous forms superfluous, secures to it in his own person everlasting reality. SIP/*SW*, 376.

▨ The limitless perspective, all that makes for the eternal seriousness and solemnity of the values of righteousness and sin, are forgotten. "To be righteous" acquires the restricted meaning of being law-like, instead of God-like. Sin also loses its absolute character of disharmony with the divine nature. It appears a mere shortness in one's account, easily rectifiable by future extra-payments. To all this delusion Jesus puts an end by the simple word: "Ye shall be perfect as your Father in heaven is perfect," and: "Thus shall ye pray: Thy will be done, as in heaven so on earth." HTR/*GG*, 34.

Law and Priesthood

▨ [commenting upon the Epistle to the Hebrews] The author is so thoroughly convinced of the central place of the priesthood in both dispensations that in [Heb. 7:11] he even represents the Levitical priesthood as the higher category under which the whole law is subsumed: "Under it the people received the law." The entire legislation was grouped around it. The same thought finds formal expression a little later (v. 12) in the statement: "Where there is a change of priesthood there is made of necessity a change also of the law." The reason is not, as some think, that the law regulates the priesthood, and that consequently a change in the latter proves the former to have become invalidated. The author means it in the opposite sense: the priesthood, being changed, becomes a center from which the transformation of the religious system radiates in every direction. HED/*SW*, 221.

Law, Automaton of

▨ Although the religious atmosphere in [Jesus'] day was surcharged with the notions of law-keeping and merit and retribution, there was lacking the vivid consciousness of God as a perpetual witness and interested participant in every moral transaction. The automaton of the law had taken the place of the living God. HTR/*GG*, 32.

Leadership

Even when the plain people of God seem most destitute of leadership, the greatest leader is always there; not for a moment does he leave the helm or abandon either a single believer or the church as a whole to the waves of the world. TEC/*GG*, 203.

Legalism

There are still abroad forms of a Christless gospel. There prevails still a subtle form of legalism which would rob the Savior of his crown of glory, earned by the cross, and would make of him a second Moses, offering us the stones of the law instead of the life-bread of the gospel. MEM/*GG*, 102.

Legalism is a peculiar kind of submission to law, something that no longer feels the personal divine touch in the rule it submits to. *SDJ*, 17.

A consciousness of strict accountability in view of God's sovereign rights over man has always characterized the Reformed religion, even to such an extent as to invite the charge that its puritanic practice savors of a spirit of legalism more at home in the Old Testament than in the New. But legalism has nothing to do with this; it is . . . simply the correlate in life of the vivid impression of the majesty of God in belief. Legalism lacks the supreme sense of worship. It obeys but it does not adore. HED/*SW*, 231.

Liberalism

[Liberalism] often cherishes a most doctrinaire and tenacious belief in the inherent and endless perfectibility of human nature, a humanistic optimism which manages to thrive, no one knows how, in the face of the most discouraging circumstances. It is a faith and has some of the noble characteristics of faith, its imperviousness to discouragement, its sovereign indifference to obstacles, its resiliency under apparent defeat, but it is after all a faith in man rather than in God, and since faith in its last analysis can be glorified only through its object, it lacks the supreme glory of the faith of Christianity. It

182

cannot overcome the world, because it has its resources in the world itself. EP, 360.

Life

As [life] is strongly bound to God in its production, so it has a telic character directing it to God as its solitary goal. *PE*, 309.

No less than in the sphere of justification, the instinct of life tends to concentrate all its forces and aspirations upon God, and this law of existence is observable in the eschatological prolongation and consummation of the life of the world to come. *PE*, 309.

According to Scripture, life is an attribute of God. He alone has true life in and of himself. SR/*GG*, 216.

[Jesus'] classical definition of life is found in the so-called high-priestly prayer: to know the only true God, and him whom he did send, even Jesus Christ (John 17:3). *KGC*, 75.

In the biblical development of the idea two aspects of life may be distinguished, an objective and a subjective one. The former is the older of these. It denotes the sphere or realm of blessedness in which, under the favor of God, the pious live, whereas the other (the subjective aspect) denotes the inward potency of life as a spiritual possession. The latter was in course of time born out of the spiritualizing and internalizing of the former. *SDJ*, 266.

Life, and Communion with God

In its ultimate analysis the Pauline conception of "life," as well as that of Jesus, is that of something dependent on communion with God. ENT/*SW*, 55.

[commenting upon the tree of life in the garden] The truth is thus clearly set forth that life comes from God, that for man it consists in nearness to God, that it is the central concern of God's fellowship with man to impart this. *BT*, 28.

Life is to Paul by no means an exclusively physical conception, as Romans 7:8–11 and Ephesians 4:18 will show. The apostle even approaches the conception that it springs from communion with God (Rom. 8:7; Eph. 4:18), and explicitly defines its goal as lying in God (Rom. 6:10–11; Gal. 2:19). EAP/*SW*, 111–12.

Life, Roots of the Christian's

The roots of the Christian's life are fed from those rich and perennial springs that lie deep in the recesses of converse with God, where prayers ascend and divine graces descend. HM/*GG*, 115.

Logos

The furnishing of life and light to the world belongs to the very essence of the Logos-task. RLT/*SW*, 63.

Logos means both reason and word, owing to the fine Hellenic perception that the two processes of thinking and speaking are intimately related, thinking being a sort of inward speech, speaking a sort of outward thought. The *Logos* is, therefore, the outward Revealer of the inward mind of God. *BT*, 345.

It is through the Logos that all things were made; it is also through the Logos, become flesh, that all things in redemption were accomplished. RLT/*SW*, 63.

[commenting upon John 1] The first characteristic Logos-product is life, not light. This is all the more significant, since the sequence of the creative acts of God in the Genesis-account places the production of light before that of life, so that the reversed sequence in the prologue: "In him was life, and the life (that was in him) was the light of men," obtains a pointed significance. Here it plainly appears already that the equation Logos = Revealer fails to do justice to the pregnancy of the title as employed by the Evangelist. RLT/*SW*, 65–66.

The statement "the Logos became flesh" to our view absolutely requires the assumption that he of whom it was made was the Logos previously to his becoming flesh. Either in his previous mode of existence or in his previous mode of activity there must have been something that entitled him to this designation. RLT/*SW*, 60.

Lord

▨ [Lord] is a name expressive of the messianic sovereignty upon which our Lord entered to a new degree when he was raised from the dead, and to which he himself refers immediately before his ascension in the words, "All authority was given unto me in heaven and on earth" (Matt. 28:18). *SDJ*, 118.

▨ The Evangelists evidently agree with Peter and Paul in attaching a higher and richer significance to the name *Kyrios* beginning with the resurrection. They indicate this position by their occasional employment of the name soon after that point. They do so negatively by refraining, almost entirely, from its use during the earlier period. *SDJ*, 121.

Lord of the Sabbath

▨ [Lord of the Sabbath] means, of course, nothing less than the authoritative disposer of that institution. *SDJ*, 123.

Lord's Supper

▨ The Lord's Supper found and finds its analogy in the Old Testament sacrificial meal. Paul represents it from this point of view in 1 Corinthians 10:16–21. More particularly, it is associated with the Passover, which was a sacrificial meal joined as a second part to the first act of slaying the sacrifice and manipulating the blood. Paul speaks of the cup in the Supper as "the cup of blessing," a technical designation of one of the cups in the Passover celebration. *SDJ*, 289.

▨ [Paul] bears witness to [the] conception of the Supper as a sacrificial meal by calling it "the table of the Lord," for this name is meant in strict analogy to the communion of Israel after the flesh with the altar. *SDJ*, 290.

THE ANTHOLOGY

When Paul enjoins his readers to proclaim the Lord's death "until he shall come," this certainly is not intended as a mere chronological remark concerning the perpetual validity of the observance of the Supper in the church. It suggests rather the idea that when the Lord shall have come the necessity for further observance of the sacrament will no longer exist, and this in turn gives rise to the thought that in the present observance of it there is an anticipation of what the eschatological state has in store for the believer. *SDJ*, 294.

[The Lord] has made gracious provision in the institution of the Supper for recalling us again to a sense of what is the center and core of our relation to him, in order that we might not lose our contact with the heart of the gospel in which lie the issues of all true Christian life and activity. GP/*GG*, 235.

What the feasts were to Israel the sacraments are to us and the Lord's Supper especially ought to be to us. Our Passover also has been sacrificed, and each time that we repeat its observance, the Lord himself invites us to call our thoughts home to the contemplation of that one thing on which our very life as believers depends, his atoning death. GP/*GG*, 235.

[The Lord's Supper] places before our minds in condensed form the whole compass of what we have and are in Christ, the entire range of the salvation he has purchased for us, in its length and breadth and depth and height. GP/*GG*, 235.

[In the Lord's Supper] there is the eloquent reminder that there can be no true participation in the merits which flow from Christ's atoning death except through such a faith as effects a personal union with him; a faith consisting not merely in the mental acceptance of his sacrifice as a historic fact, but a faith which mystically feeds upon him, the living sacrifice as he now exists in heaven. GP/*GG*, 240.

If we were to hold up Christ as a mere example to be followed by us in our own strength to the exclusion of the supernatural work of the Holy Spirit in the heart, would we not be silently corrected by our Lord's own voice speaking to us at his table: "Except ye eat the flesh and drink the blood of the Son of man, ye have no life in your-selves"? GP/*GG*, 240.

Lord's Supper and the Word

The word and the sacrament as means of grace belong together: they are two sides of the same divinely instituted instrumentality. While addressing themselves to different organs of perception, they are intended to bear the identical message of the grace of God—to interpret and mutually enforce one another. . . . Let us therefore be careful to key our preaching to such a note that when we stand as ministrants behind the table of our Lord to distribute the bread of life, our congregation shall feel that what we are doing then is only the sum and culmination of what we have been doing every Sabbath from the pulpit. GP/*GG*, 239.

Lost

"To be lost" in its simple, primary sense, which it scarcely needs knowledge of the original to understand, is "to be missing," to have passed out of the active possession and use of one's owner. . . . It is not the vague general notion of forsakenness and misery Jesus has in mind when using it, but very particularly the fact of the sinner's being missing to God, that is, missing to the normal relations man sustains to God. SSL/*GG*, 57.

"To be lost" is more than to be missing to God. It has also the passive, even more terrible sense of "being ruined," "given up to destruction." The former sense remains within the sphere of the negative; it describes what is absent from the sinner's state; this other sense is positive, denoting the presence of something dread-ful there. SSL/*GG*, 59–60.

Love

Love is to [Jeremiah] the highest form of the spiritual embrace of person by person. To ascribe it to God in connection with a crea-ture is at the farthest remove from being a figure of speech. It means that in the most literal sense he concentrates all the light and warmth of his affection, all the prodigious wealth of its resources, his endless capacity of delight, upon the heart-to-heart union between the pious and himself. And what God for his part brings into this union has a generosity, a sublime abandon, an absoluteness, that, measured by human analogies, we can only designate as the highest and purest type of devotion. It is named love for this very reason, that God puts into it his heart and soul and mind and strength, and gathers all his concerns with his people into the focus of this one desire. JP/*SW*, 296.

The best proof that he will never cease to love us lies in that he never began. What we are for him and what he is for us belongs to the realm of eternal values. Without this we are nothing; in it we have all. JP/*SW*, 298.

This is the great mystery that no man can solve—how God could love sinners, without there being anything in them worthy of his love. Mysterious, eternal love of God, you are beyond comprehension! SR/*GG*, 213.

God's being consists of love, and therefore when it is said that he loved those who were his in Christ Jesus, that means that his whole being expressed itself in that love and carried over to its objects. SR/*GG*, 214.

The motives determining Jehovah's love for Israel are sought in himself alone. SDL/*SW*, 432.

In his general goodness God bestows various gifts upon the creature; in his love he gives himself and holds nothing back. Consequently it was felt that wherever such absolute, unreserved covenant self-communication was lacking, the term love could not properly apply. SDL/*SW*, 440.

The love of God is never allowed to swallow up the attribute of his justice, as if justice were a mere instrument in the hands of love for the pursuit of its own ends. Even in Hosea and Jeremiah, who both view the approaching judgment as a discipline of love designed for the people's conversion, this mode of viewing it is by no means the only one employed. The judgment has at one and the same time a double meaning: it is referred to love and justice as coexistent divine modes of dealing. In fact, the perception begins to dawn that in reality there are wrapped up in the one national organism two Israels—that of the reprobate mass, for which destruction is determined, and that of the elect remnant, to which the love and the promises belong. SDL/*SW*, 436–37.

The Scriptures do not leave room for the opinion that at any point, either in the eternal decree or in its historical unfolding, God's love for those intended to become his people has been undifferentiated from his love for wider groups of humanity. Every formula which would efface or even tend to obscure this fundamental distinction ought to be at the outset rejected as unbiblical. SDL/*SW*, 456.

Lovingkindness

[Lovingkindness is] mercy intensified a thousand times by the tenderness of an antecedent love. WT/*GG*, 13.

Chesed . . . is best rendered by "lovingkindness." It expresses the warm, affectionate feeling that should exist between persons bound together in a previous bond of love. It presupposes love. *BT*, 256.

Lutheranism

According to the Lutherans man had already reached his destination in that God had placed him in a state of uprightness. Eternal life was already in his possession. In his situation [in the garden] the highest ideal was realized. . . . Mankind's destination had already been reached before the fall in Adam. DCRT/*SW*, 242.

Magic

Magic is that paganistic reversal of the process of religion, in which man, instead of letting himself be used by God for the divine purpose, drags down his god to the level of a tool, which he uses for his own selfish purpose. Magic is full of superstition, and, after a fashion, full of the quasi-supernatural, but it is void of true religion. Because it lacks the element of objective divine self-communication from above, it must needs create for itself material means of compulsion that will bring the deity to do its bidding. *BT*, 137.

Magnificat

Faith will sing its supreme song when face to face, either in anticipation or reality, with the supreme act of God. Let Mary's case be witness from whose heart the great annunciation of messianic fulfillment drew that psalm of all psalms, the *Magnificat*. EP, 324.

The Magnificat is full of reminiscences from the Psalms, and from its Old Testament prototype, the prayer-song of Hannah [1 Sam. 2:1–10]. *BT*, 306.

Man, Greatness of

[commenting upon Isaiah's view of] The true greatness of man consists in the service of Jehovah; this being abandoned for idolatry, a universal abasement takes place. *BT*, 279–80.

Man, Psychic and Sarkic

It is worth observation that the distinction between the two strands that enter into the Pauline doctrine of the work of the Spirit is clearly marked by the twofold antithesis σαρκικός—πνευματικός and ψυχικός—πνευματικός. The psychic man is the natural man as such. The sarkic man is the sinful natural man. It is certainly significant that in 1 Corinthians 15:45–50, where Paul puts over against each other the creation state and the eschatological state of pneumatic life, he does not characterize the former as sarkic but as psychic. *KC/SW*, 541–42.

Man, Religious Nature of

Man's nature is so built that he must be religious either in a good or in a bad sense. Ill-religious he may be, but simply non-religious he cannot be. What he fails to bring into the temple of God, he is sure to set up on the outside, and not seldom at the very gate, as a rival object of worship. And often the more ostensibly spiritual and refined these things are, the more potent and treacherous their lure. The modern man who seeks to save and perfect himself has a whole pantheon of ideals, each of them a veritable god sapping the vitals of his religion. WT/*GG*, 15–16.

Man of Sin

The Man-of-Sin is bent upon and driven by Satan into reproducing and exploiting for his wicked ends certain grandiose concomitants of the Christ-epiphany, but is unable to sum these up under the supreme category of messiahship, for the simple reason that such would defeat his innermost, and public, aim of absolute emancipation from all that is divine or quasi-divine. *PE*, 118.

The Man-of-Sin is the irreligious and anti-religious and antimessianic subject *par excellence*. *PE*, 118.

[commenting upon 2 Thess. 2:3–4] The blasphemy against God constitutes to the apostle the supreme wickedness. The self-deification, so elaborately set forth in verse 4, is felt as the inmost sinfulness in the sin of the Man-of-Sin. The transition from verse 3 to verse 4, by means of the mere article strikingly brings out the nexus of thought: precisely because he goes to the *non plus ultra of sin*, he deserves fully the name "Man-of-Sin," and the doom announced by "Son-of-Perdition." Among the terrible things reserved for the proximity of the end, the most terrible to Paul's mind is this negation of God in his very existence, this willful insult to the divine majesty. In it the very foundations of religion are shaken. The "sitting in the temple of God" only sums up in one terse image that unholiest offense offered to the holiest of beings. Nor is this self-deification conceived as a purely passive attitude; it energetically asserts itself against all deity as such, pretended or true. *PE*, 124.

Marriage and the Covenant

▮ [commenting upon marriage and the covenant] Israel entered into . . . special union with Jehovah at the time of the exodus [Hos. 13:4; see also 11:1 and Amos 2:10]. . . . It was not a blind transaction, but one full of intelligence. The idea of marriage was eminently fitted to emphasize the historical birth of the union, better than that of fatherhood and sonship. Father and son never exist apart from each other. Husband and wife do so exist at first, and then are brought together at a definite point of time. *BT*, 260.

▮ Hosea uses the figure of the marriage union, based on mutual love, in order to contrast most vividly the physical nature of the Baal cult and the spiritual nature of the relation between Jehovah and Israel. The former constitutes a necessary bond to which the deity and its worshippers both find themselves subject by the very law of their existence. The latter, on the contrary, springs from free choice of love, and therefore dates from a definite point in history, previous to which both Jehovah and Israel existed without such mutual relationship. It is obvious that for bringing out this important idea the analogue of conjugal love was better adapted than that of paternal love. The relation between father and son is in its origin a necessary one, whereas that between husband and wife rests on the free consent of both, and insofar more faithfully reflects the historical and spiritual nature of the covenant. SDL/*SW*, 437.

Meal

▮ [commenting upon Ex. 24] The meal upon the mountain represents the goal and consummation of the *berith*. *BT*, 123.

Mediator

▮ The μεσίτης is one who stands between parties, especially parties in discord, to bring about a union. But sometimes the word has a more specific sense, in which it approaches ἔγγυος and signifies the one who obligates himself to render the mediation effective. PC/*SW*, 136.

The μεσίτης is he who guarantees for God the sure accomplishment of what has been stated or promised in the διαθήκη. HED/*SW*, 185.

Melchizedek

While Melchizedek was a historical person and not eternal, still as a scriptural figure he was regarded as eternal, being without recorded father or mother or genealogy, and having no recorded beginning of days nor end of life. In these respects he is like unto the Son of God, that is, stripped of all earthly attachments. As such, then, he is also a type of Christ. Thus *as he appears in Scriptures* he may be regarded as enveloped in an atmosphere of eternity. *TEH*, 106.

In the historical sequence of things Christ is said to be a priest after the order of Melchizedek. Here we have the ordinary correspondence between type and antitype, the former pertaining to the old, the latter to the new covenant. To Melchizedek belongs the first, to Christ the later appearance on the scene of history. But in the third verse of the seventh chapter [of Hebrews] the author reverses this relation, representing it in this way, not that Christ was made like unto Melchizedek, but, on the contrary, Melchizedek was made like unto the Son of God. The introduction of the name "Son of God" here is highly significant. It describes Christ in his divine, eternal nature. From this eternal life that places the Son of God above all time and history, the eternity-character enveloping Melchizedek in the record of Genesis was copied, that thus delineated he might again in the time-perspective of history prefigure the historic Christ. HED/*SW*, 202.

Mercy

The mercy that [Jehovah] shows [Israel] in their distress is at bottom something far deeper, finer and more spiritualized than the generic sense of pity. It is *chesed*, lovingkindness, that is, mercy intensified a thousand times by the tenderness of an antecedent love. WT/*GG*, 13.

Mercy Seat

It [the mercy seat] was the place where the application of blood in the most solemn exercise of the ritual of atonement took place; it was likewise the place where the divine glory manifested itself. SIP/*SW*, 375–76.

The Old Testament mercy seat was sprinkled with foreign blood; in Christ's case the blood was that of the living mercy seat himself. The thought that Christ was victim and mercy seat in one has nothing strange in it. SIP/*SW*, 376.

Messiah

Messiah stands for salvation; indeed, "Savior" is the most popular name by which the Christ has come to be known among his followers. *SDJ*, 25.

The Messiah is the introducer and beginner of the eschatological world. *PE*, 289.

So long as the Messiah's task is conceived as lying in the sphere of external, national, earthly kingship and salvation, it remains possible to regard him as the representative of God without investing him with divine attributes. But when his function comes to lie in the sphere of spiritual relationship to God, in those high regions where God touches the soul and the soul touches God, then his calling immediately places him in the center of the field where the forces of religion play. *SDJ*, 29.

A Messiah without an eschatological people of God is indeed inconceivable. *SDJ*, 60.

A Messiah who means to be no more than a teacher of ethics and religion is a mere philosophic abstraction, not a historically conceivable reality. OLDR/*SW*, 318.

The Messiah [is] the great representative figure of the coming aeon. EAP/*SW*, 92.

Messiahship

The deepest motivation of the messianic conception lies in the absolute, concrete, palpable assurance it affords of Jehovah's permanent presence among his people as the supreme bliss of the future. He is sacramental in the profoundest sense of the word. EP, 355.

To cast fire, to save, to fulfill—these acts are just as much the result of a messianic appearance as are the stupendous eschatological events that will result from [Christ's] future coming with the clouds of heaven. Although the messianic glory may be outwardly absent, the internal essence of the messiahship, consisting in the exercise of authority and power for establishing the kingdom of God around the nucleus of a new Israel, is there from the beginning. *SDJ*, 86.

Through the whole history our Lord seems to feel that the dignity is his, yet he refrains from stressing it. Both in the beginning and at the end, as well as in the period between, he appears to have looked upon his messianic honor and glory as something which it was not proper for himself to seek and to disclose, but for the Father to seek and to bring to light. *SDJ*, 92.

To him [the messiahship] was something for which nothing else could be substituted, something by which he felt absolutely bound in his conscience, something that he could not and would not surrender even to escape the loss of his life. The messiahship was a vital concern between God and himself: he clung to it with the utmost religious energy, and carried it through without swerving or wavering to the bitter end. *SDJ*, 100.

While our Lord, looking back (we speak after the manner of man) from the standpoint of his earthly life upon his pre-mundane, eternal abode with the Father, could regard all this temporal messianic task and experience as a fleeting episode, yet, relating himself to the plan and history of redemption, he could not but regard this same messiahship as a cardinal fact, transcending all other historical facts in its intrinsic importance. *SDJ*, 103.

Messiahship and Eschatology

▓ The eschatology of Jesus is nothing more nor less than the necessary correlate of the messianic role, which, according to the same record, he claims for himself. OLDR/*SW*, 318.

▓ The Messiah's entire significance is derived from the final things to follow; his activity belongs to the sphere of the eschatological as the vestibule belongs to the house. *SDJ*, 20.

▓ The conception of the messiahship is the most pronouncedly supernaturalistic conception in the whole range of biblical religion. Its eschatological parentage implies that it does not and cannot mean the gradual evolving of higher conditions out of previously existing potentialities. On the contrary, the conception of the messiahship implies the creation of a new system of things. *SDJ*, 22.

Messiahship and Jesus

▓ Jesus appears in the Gospels not merely as occasionally bearing witness to his messianic dignity, but as throughout silently presupposing it and making it the self-understood basis of the peculiar attitude he assumes toward his environment. UMG/*SW*, 338.

▓ To Jesus the messiahship was a matter of the will, a matter of obedience to God, and to put into it anything less than his whole heart and soul and mind and strength would have been, in his view, not merely to falsify the idea, but actually to prostitute the office. *SDJ*, 99.

▓ In many instances, [Jesus] reveals a consciousness of unique greatness, unique authority, and unique importance, for which nothing short of the messianic category of self-classification can adequately account. He is more than Solomon, than Jonah, than John the Baptist himself, the greatest born of women. He assumes a sovereign attitude toward the Old Testament institutions in the face of the strictest belief in the inspiration of the Scriptures, not hesitating to set aside what God has instituted. He is conscious of bringing something absolutely new, the new cloth, the new wine, of having come to cast a fire upon the earth, to kindle, as it were, the great conflagration that will introduce a new world. He sees himself stand-ing at the goal of history, where all the lines of the Old Testament revelation converge; the work of God for Israel, and through Israel for the world, is focused in his person. He claims to be the supreme factor in deciding the fate of Israel as well as of individuals, so that his time is the critical time for all who come in contact with him; acceptance of him means acceptance of all, rejection of him rejec-tion of all. He has the right to ask men to follow him even at the sac-rifice of all other things. He relates the deeds of men to himself, so that what is done to the poor, the sick, the prisoners, is done to him. And all this without finding it necessary to say a word explicitly about the messianic office. This silence is more eloquent than any outspoken affirmation could possibly be. And it constitutes that ele-ment in the messianic texture of the Gospels which criticism can-not disturb without unraveling the entire fabric and making it fall to pieces. UMG/*SW*, 338–39.

It should be noticed that Jesus by no means discards the imagery and vocabulary of conquest in connection with the messianic pro-gram. He only lifts it to a higher plane: the powers to be conquered are not political; they belong to the world of spirits. In connection with Satan and the demons the consciousness of bringing deliver-ance is retained without the least impairment. *SDJ*, 26–27.

Our Lord can refer to nothing else than the new exalted, heavenly state upon which his person and work would enter through his death and resurrection and seating at the right hand of God. In order to understand this we must remember that Jesus, while in one sense conscious of having messianic authority and doing messianic work already here on earth, yet in another sense regarded the exercise of his messianic function as beginning with his state of glory. *KGC*, 79.

Messiahship and Supernaturalism

To de-supernaturalize the consciousness of messiahship in Jesus means to unfit him for being the recipient of any truly religious approach on the part of man. *SDJ*, 24.

Messiahship and the Christian Religion

What the cross was in the days of the apostle, the messiahship is to the modern advanced "Christian" mind, the great rock of offense. But it is a rock not easy to remove, and moreover one from which there is no further retreat backward except into plain liberal Judaism. The attitude toward it determines in the profoundest way the character of the subjective piety that would feed upon the New Testament. Let no one delude himself with the soothing comfort that the controversy is all about scraps of external belief and does not touch the core of practical devotion. With its decision the Christian religion stands or falls. *SDJ*, preface.

Messiahship and the Spirit

The Spirit is brought into the eschatological era itself as forming the official equipment of the Messiah. *EAP/SW*, 96.

Messiahship, God-Centered

The dominating characteristic of Jesus' messiahship in the Gospels consists in its being absolutely God-centered. The office exists primarily for the sake of God. *SDJ*, 59.

Messiahship, Judaistic Conception of

Not God but Israel was in it the chief figure of the world to come, and the Messiah appeared as the agent who would raise Israel to this greatness. Jesus resolutely turned his back upon this irreligious perversion of the idea, and set his face toward the fulfillment of that God-centered form of it, which he recognized as already outlined in the Isaianic Servant of Jehovah. *SDJ*, 59.

Messiahship, Old Testament Conception of

The Old Testament takes the messiahship as an eschatological unit, and overleaps, as a rule, the preliminary relative states so familiar to us. Accordingly Jesus, approaching the idea from the Old Testament point of view, could let his eye rest on the glorious consummate state, and after the ancient fashion call this the messiahship;

indeed, he could even speak of its future arrival as *the coming, the appearing*, of the Messiah. *SDJ*, 82.

Metaphor, Biblical Use of

[Another way] our Lord's kingdom-message differs from the Jewish expectation consists in the absence of the sensualistic element so prominent in the latter. True, in connection with the kingdom he speaks of eating, drinking, reclining at table, inheriting the earth, etc., and it is said we have no right to spiritualize all this. But the Old Testament already used such forms of speech with the clear consciousness of their metaphorical character. *KGC*, 43.

Ministry

[For Isaiah] there [was] no recoiling when the disclosure followed that [his] ministry would be one of hardening and judgment. Isaiah knew that even when God does his strange work his purposes are accomplished and his honor vindicated; and that the ultimate significance of service in his kingdom is to be measured by this highest standard alone. And thus believing he spoke: "I will wait for Jehovah that hideth his face from the house of Jacob, and I will look for him!" (8:17). It is not likely that any of us will be called to a ministry offering so little prospect of what the world calls success. But even if some of us were, if Isaiah's vision is ours, if like him we walk face to face with the glory of Jehovah, there need be no disappointment or discouragement. OHGG/*GG*, 275–76.

[commenting upon Paul's view of his own ministry] His entire task, both on its communicative and on its receptive side, can be summed up in his reflecting back the Christ-glory, caught by himself unto others. To behold Christ and to make others behold him is the substance of his ministry. MEM/*GG*, 94.

After all it is not so much by what the minister contributes of himself to the cause of Christ, but rather by what he is enabled to draw out and utilize from the divine resources, that his office and work will be tested. It is not chiefly the question whether we are strong in the cause, but whether the cause is strong in and through us. MEM/*GG*, 85.

The servants of the new covenant are internally and permanently transformed by beholding the image of the Lord, and . . . they effect a similar transformation in others to whom through their ministry the knowledge of the glorified Savior comes. MEM/*GG*, 97.

It is absolutely essential for us that we should not only have our seasons of communion with God, but that all the time we should carry with us into our outward and public work in some degree a living sense of our nearness to God and of his nearness to us, because in this way alone can we make our service in the Lord's kingdom truly fruitful and spiritual. If the savor of this is wanting in our work, if we do not bring to the world when we come to it the unction and peace acquired in prayer, we cannot hope to impart any permanent blessing or to achieve any lasting results. SFS/*GG*, 180.

Ministry, Christ's

[commenting upon Mark 10:45] When it is said that the Son of man came to minister, this form of statement makes the purpose of ministering cover his entire earthly life. Our Lord's incarnate life not merely had this purpose among others, it had this purpose exclusively. It consisted in this—was exhausted by this. There was never in human history such an absolute concentration of life upon the single specific task as our Lord here and elsewhere ascribes to himself. Everything else for him was swallowed up in the one great intent to accomplish this ministry. All the forces of life flowed into this. CDW/*GG*, 248.

[Jesus] gave his life as a ransom in exchange for other lives. He died not merely for their benefit, but died in their place. This was a transaction which, strictly speaking, was possible to him alone. Others might minister unto death, or minister by their death, but no one else can minister through the payment of his death as a ransom in the literal, vicarious sense. CDW/*GG*, 248.

His ministry had for its supreme end the procuring of freedom for those for whom he gave his life. It was a ministry with that specific thing in view. It was not to help them generally but to set them free. This is clearly given with the contrast between what he does and what the rulers of the Gentiles do (Mark 10:42). They lord it over them and exercise authority. That is to say: their striving is to make their subjects minister to them and increasingly reduce them to a state of bondage. Jesus' purpose is the opposite. He came to minister to men so as to place them in a state of freedom. CDW/*GG*, 250.

Miracles

What is unique to the miracle is the assertion of absolutely divine supernatural power. The efficient cause of the miracle is something that man can contribute nothing to, because it is wholly dependent on the putting forth of the direct supernatural energy of God. *BT*, 388.

The miracles of our Lord are only very partially and superficially interpreted when regarded as primarily philanthropic acts. They belong rather to the great redemptive movement involved in the coming of the kingdom—in fact, they are "signs of the times," for not discerning which our Lord reproaches his opponents (Matt. 16:3). *SDJ*, 259–60.

In the Synoptists, where the teaching of Jesus is centered in the kingdom-idea, the miracles [appear as] signs of the actual arrival of the kingdom, because they show that the royal power of God is already in motion. *KGC*, 54.

[The miracles] are the appropriate supernatural concomitants of the supernatural Christ; they are signs of the times he is introducing, and prophecies of the more radical, comprehensive change still to follow. *SDJ*, 23.

Now the miracles [in the Synoptics] almost without exception have two features in common. In the first place, they are transactions where the result absolutely and exclusively depends on the forth-putting of the divine supernatural power, where no human effort could possibly contribute anything toward its accomplishment.

And secondly, the miracles are, as we have seen, healing miracles in which the gracious love of God offers itself to man for his salvation. *KGC*, 95.

Mission of Jesus

[commenting on Luke 4:43] In the last-mentioned passage [Jesus] even declares that the main purpose of his mission consists in the preaching of the good tidings of the kingdom of God. *KGC*, 9.

Missionary Activity

When we profess to missionarize, not in the last analysis, to improve the world, but to glorify God in the eternal salvation of sinners, this expresses not merely a theological conviction, but it is also eminently true to the principle inherent in the birth of the missionary idea itself. For this the missionary idea was born and for this cause came it into the world, that it should contribute to the glory of God. EP, 348.

For the Reformed believer Christianity, by virtue of its covenantal character, is a restless, re-creating principle which never withdraws itself from the world, but seeks to conquer it for Christ. Only out of this consciousness of the covenant comes a true zeal for missions, for in missions the body of Christ is striving toward its own completion, which it cannot reach as long as all its members have not been added. Wherever this thought is lacking, zeal for missions is exclusively fed by philanthropic motives which, by the nature of the case, are less enduring and powerful. DCRT/*SW*, 261.

Modern Liberal Christianity, against Its Reduction of the Attributes of God to Love

The love of God occupies a more prominent place than any other divine attribute in present-day Christian consciousness. . . . Not for the sake of its theological significance as a constituent factor in the divine character, but for the sake of its bearing upon human conduct and destiny has the love of God been exalted to this position of supremacy among its sister attributes. SDL/*SW*, 425.

So long as the intellect retained its legitimate place among the functions of the religious subject, so long as to know God was felt to be an essential part of glorifying God, the natural tendency was to make this knowledge as comprehensive and as many-sided as possible—to have it mirror the full content of the divine nature, and not merely a single one of its perfections. . . . The music of that theology may not always please modern ears, because it seems lacking in sweetness; but it ranged over a wider scale and made better harmonies than the popular strains of today. SDL/*SW*, 425.

It is plain that where the religious interest is exclusively concentrated upon the will and entirely exhausts itself in attempts at solving the concrete, practical problems of life, no strong incentive will exist for reflecting upon any other aspect of the nature of God than his love, because all that is required of God is that he shall serve as the norm and warrant for Christian philanthropic effort. It is a well-known fact that all heresy begins with a partial truth. So it is in the present case. SDL/*SW*, 425–26.

The very fact that it is not so much the grace but rather the love of God which is pitted against his righteousness betrays the true motive of the antagonism [of liberalism]. This fact means, first of all, that there is a weakening of the sense of sin. The modern religious subject thirsts for love as such, not in the first place for forgiving, justifying grace. [All this is symptomatic] of the general abandonment of the theocentric attitude in the present-day religious consciousness. Love is magnified because at bottom God is conceived of as existing for the sake of man. AL/*SW*, 399.

Modern Liberal Christianity, and Pelagianism

These conceptions of the function of Christianity, the intellectualistic as well as the moralizing, are tenable only from the standpoint of Pelagianism with its defective sense of sin. CFTBH/*SW*, 466.

■ [The] old solid idea of salvation, the basis of all evangelical religion, has become an offense to the modern mind in many quarters. While the terms "Savior" and "salvation" are not discarded, the substance of the transaction which they stand for is entirely abandoned. In every possible way it is attempted to free the Jesus of the Gospels from this antiquated, "magical" idea of salvation, and to make him the exponent of the new Pelagian evangel of "uplift." There is but one radical way of doing this, and that is by stripping Jesus of his messianic character. The moment this falls off from him, the distasteful soteric notions of atonement, regeneration, and whatever else belongs to this circle of ideas, one and all disappear with it. . . . It is nothing else but the Pelagian view of religion seeking to dislodge the Augustinian view from its double stronghold in prophecy and Gospel. *SDJ*, 27–28.

Modern Liberal Christianity, Failure of

■ This is where the old apostolic gospel of Paul and the modern moralizing interpretations of Christianity part ways. Because the modern world has ceased to take sin seriously, it has lost its sense for the necessity of the supernatural in the work of salvation; and to such a state of the mind the message of the resurrection of Christ no longer appeals. JRL/*GG*, 163.

■ [The] modern naturalistic spirit finds it easy to clothe itself in the old Christian forms and to retain the old Christian ways of speaking. But it will immediately rise up in protest when confronted with an intrusion of the supernatural in the external, physical sphere, such as the resurrection of the body. Need we wonder then that where Christians have begun to give ear to this seductive spirit, the doctrine of the resurrection should gradually have come to be regarded as a source of weakness rather than of strength? The conviction seems to be gaining ground that all practical ends of religion will be equally well served and a possible cause of offense removed by exchanging this doctrine for a simple belief in the immortality of the soul with reference both to Christ and believers. We may learn from Paul that skepticism on this concrete point is symptomatic of infection with the poison of naturalism in the very heart of the Christian faith. JRL/*GG*, 164–65.

■ [commenting upon Eph. 4:17–20] Perhaps no more incisive criticism of the false modern slogan "religion is not doctrine but life" than these few verses from Ephesians can be conceived. What Paul says is not that perverted ideas concerning religion and Christ are unimportant and their correction negligible; what he maintains is that they are subversive of the true Christian religion, and ought to be resisted to the utmost. *PE*, 311.

■ The modern, humanistic movement prefers to cultivate the secular and earthly in part because it has come to doubt the heavenly and eternal; its zeal for the improvement of the world often springs not from faith, but from skepticism. The church by compromising and affiliating with this would sign her own death-warrant as a distinct institution. When religion submerges itself in the concerns of time and becomes a mere servant of these, it thereby renders itself subject to the inexorable flux of time. Kronos has eaten all his children, and he will not spare even this noblest of his offspring, once it passes wholly into his realm and closes behind itself the doors of eternity. EP, 365.

■ [Liberal Christianity] often cherishes a most doctrinaire and tenacious belief in the inherent and endless perfectibility of human nature, a humanistic optimism which manages to thrive, no one knows how, in the face of the most discouraging circumstances. It is a faith and has some of the noble characteristics of faith, its imperviousness to discouragement, its sovereign indifference to obstacles, its resiliency under apparent defeat, but it is after all a faith in man rather than in God, and since faith in the last analysis can be glorified only through its object, it lacks the supreme glory of the faith of Christianity. It cannot overcome the world, because it has its resources in the world itself. EP, 360.

■ The modern mind has grown weary of all the toning down of the superhuman elements in the gospel-story, of all the laborious desupernaturalizing, which the "liberal" school has so long been practicing. The union in wedlock of extreme skepticism with regard to history and of the modern desire for realism with regard to exegesis has given birth to the new method, against which all the "liberals" are now up in arms not knowing that they are fighting their own offspring. There is no escape from this fatal law which the liberal theology carries in its members in virtue of which it is bound to produce what it would not. *DGJ*, 490.

[Modernists] deny the messiahship because they wish to substitute something lower and less difficult to believe. We are not asked to cease calling him the Christ because after calling him Lord and God we could not possibly do more. On the contrary, we are asked to drop the name Christ, because Jesus shall suffice us as an example, a teacher, a leader, a point of departure in religion. And, because it is awkward to receive him at this lower value with the historical fact staring us in the face that he himself thought it necessary to offer himself at an infinitely higher value, therefore it is held to be inconceivable that the messianic consciousness should be allowed to retain its place in Jesus' life without molestation. *SDJ*, 30.

How halting and inwardly disrupted a religious approach to Jesus must be which feels bound to stop short of accepting and receiving him at the face value of his own central self-estimate! *SDJ*, 16.

[Modern liberal Christianity prefers] to take its departure from Christ in addressing itself to the world, rather than a movement seeking the person of Christ in order to occupy itself with him. A religion intended to be first of all centripetal has become alarmingly centrifugal. *SDJ*, 37.

Modern Liberal Christianity, the Jesus of

The Jesus in whom liberal Protestantism finds its supreme ideal is the Jesus of the Sermon on the Mount, the sublime self-forgetful altruist, the man of delicate tender sensibilities, who puts all the intensity of his interest in the problems of the subjective spiritual life of man, and treats all matters lying outside of this one thing needful with neglect or disdain. *SDJ*, 42.

▓ This Jesus who is too high-minded or too idealistic to have anything in common with the messianic hope has no existence in the Gospels, but is entirely a product of the "liberal theology." From the outset his figure has to such an extent been made to serve a partisan purpose in the propaganda and defense of "liberal" ideas that its devotees finally became unable to see in this Jesus anything other than the reflection of their own cherished opinions. *SDJ*, 61.

▓ The modernizing of the character of Jesus has seized upon the *Sōtēr* idea with a certain eagerness, because it seems to offer a point of contact with the favorite liberal conception of him as a humanitarian idealist. The title "Savior" seems best adapted to mark him as the Uplifter and Benefactor, bent mainly upon relieving all manner of distress and abnormality among men. Unfortunately, revealed in their true historic sense, the title and function of *Sōtēr* prove themselves ill-fitted for incorporation into this philosophy of the life of Jesus. It is becoming increasingly clear that the "saving" of the New Testament is at bottom, not only something far deeper and more comprehensive, but also something differently oriented, than this modernized version of the vocation of Jesus which is read into the Gospels. In this respect the half century of toil of the "liberal" theology, instead of rehabilitating the historical Jesus, has only resulted in the construction of a far different figure—a figure which is now being felt to be unhistorical after all. And at no other point, perhaps, has the disillusionment attending this result proved so poignant as here. *SDJ*, 271–72.

▓ By its construction and exegesis of the words, the liberal theology made Jesus' consciousness about himself identical with the "liberal" view in regard to him, as to all intents not God but a man who, though unique as compared with others in his knowledge of God, yet had to acquire this knowledge after a truly empirical fashion, in a historical process. *SDJ*, 152.

THE ANTHOLOGY

Morning

From Isaiah we are familiar with the figure of the watchman peering into the darkness of the world-night, to whom the prophet addressed the question, "Watchman, what of the night?" and from whom he received the answer, "The morning cometh, and also the night." In the Psalter we find again this idea of "the morning" signifying the dawn of the new great day of Jehovah, and hence symbolic of all hope and deliverance: "God is in the midst of her; she shall not be moved, God will hear her and that in the morning." EP, 336.

Mosaic Law Code and the Roman Law Code

It would be historically wrong to institute a comparison between the Mosaic codes and the Roman body of law. The Romans were the people of law *par excellence*; in Israel the law was a subordinate means to a higher and spiritual end, subservient and adapted to the peculiar position which the nation occupied, and to its unique calling in the history of God's church. *MOP*, 52.

Moses

[Moses] is the prophet *par excellence*, the legislator to whose work the later prophets appealed, in whose institutions they lived and moved and had their being. *MOP*, 229.

Prospectively considered, Moses also occupies a dominant place in the religious development of the Old Testament. He is placed not merely at the head of the succession of prophets, but placed over them in advance. His authority extends over subsequent ages. *BT*, 103.

The prophets themselves are clearly conscious of the unique position of Moses. They put his work not so much on a line with their own, as with the stupendous eschatological work of Jehovah for his people expected in the latter days. *BT*, 103–4.

[Moses] may be fitly called *the redeemer* of the Old Testament. *BT*, 104.

208

There was in [Moses'] work such a close connection between revealing words and redeeming acts as can be paralleled only from the life of Christ. And the acts of Moses were to a high degree supernatural, miraculous acts. This typical relation of Moses to Christ can easily be traced in each of the three offices we are accustomed to distinguish in the soteric work of Christ. The "prophet" of Deuteronomy 18:15, reaching his culmination in the Messiah, is "like unto" Moses. Moses fulfilled priestly functions at the inauguration of the old *berith*, before the Aaronic priesthood was instituted (Ex. 24:4–8). *BT*, 104.

A royal figure, of course, Moses could not at that time be called, for Jehovah alone is King of Israel. None the less, through his legislative function Moses typified the royal office of Christ. *BT*, 104.

There was no prophet who was honored with the direct and continuous access to Jehovah that Moses enjoyed. In this respect also Moses seems to have prefigured Christ. As Christ reveals the Father in virtue of a most direct and an uninterrupted vision of him, and not as a result of isolated communications, so Moses, though to a lower degree, stands nearer to God, and is more, in all that he speaks and does, the mouthpiece of God than any subsequent prophet. *BT*, 105.

Than Moses no greater name was known in the annals of Old Testament redemption. Prophet, priest, lawgiver in one, he towers high above all the others. MEM/*GG*, 88.

[commenting upon 2 Cor. 3] Moses ministered with [covered face so that] the children of Israel should not perceive the passing away of the glory underneath the veil. Not that Moses acted as a deceiver of his people. Paul means to say, that in receiving the glory, and losing it, and hiding its loss, he served the symbolic function of illustrating, in the first place, the glory of the old covenant, in the second place its transitoriness, and in the third place the ignorance of Israel in regard to what was taking place. MEM/*GG*, 91.

When Moses in his own strength sought to deliver the people, the result was a failure. When, after an interval of forty years and actually commissioned by Jehovah to guide and effect the redemption, he assumes the task in the totally opposite spirit of absolute dependence upon God, thoroughly recognizing his own unfitness, God promises that he will smite Egypt with all his wonders (Ex. 3:20). *BT*, 113.

Motivation

Our very position as dependent creatures and God's very character as the source of all blessings render it absolutely of the essence of all religious approach to him that it should be accompanied and colored by the consciousness of our need. But from this it by no means follows that the desire to obtain something from God distinct from himself can rightly be the only or the supreme motive impelling us to seek his face. This is the attitude of the unregenerate man; the form which true religious instinct takes under the influence of his selfish isolation from God. But when the Spirit of God moves the center of our life, transferring it from self to God, there immediately awakes a longing to come in touch with God and possess him and enjoy him for his own sake. SFS/*GG*, 177–78.

Here it is impossible for us to tell how truly and to what extent our relation to God is a relation of pure, disinterested love in which we seek him for his own sake. There [in heaven], when all want and sin-frailty shall have slipped away from us, we shall be able to tell. HM/*GG*, 123.

Mysticism

Mystical revelation claimed by many in the interim as a personal privilege is out of keeping with the genius of biblical religion. Mysticism in this detached form is not specifically Christian. It occurs in all types of religion, better or worse. At best it is a manifestation of the religion of nature, subject to all the defects and faults of the latter. As to its content and inherent value it is unverifiable, except on the principle of submitting it to the test of harmony with Scripture. And submitting it to this it ceases to be a separate source of revelation concerning God. *BT*, 304.

Names

The biblical usage in regard to the word "name" differs considerably from ours. In the Bible the name is always more than a conventional sign. It expresses character or history. Hence a change in either respect frequently gives rise to a change of name. *BT*, 64.

In the Hebrew mind, there was a very intimate connection between the name and the nature of a thing; the name is never accidental or arbitrary, but the expression of the nature. *MOP*, 16.

"Names" (Poem)

Names are but tags through which we try
Un-ordered things to classify;
Trite formulas of cold address,
Conventional and colorless,
Futile to curse by or to bless,
With no life-pulses in them.

It was not so in days of old,
When God with man would converse hold,
And to hard-praying wrestlers came,
In earthquake, thunder, sheets of flame;
Then, trembling, would they ask his name,
A pledge of help and favor.

Because it was a sacrament,
No creature could such name invent;
It seemed a veritable part
Of God's own Self, his inmost heart,
A radiant Double which no art
Endeavor durst creating.

Those who received it dared and fought,
And through it saving victories wrought,
It was a buckler and a shield,
A weapon for attack to wield,
A tower uplifted in the field
Of the fierce-raging battle.

The prophets knew its mystery well,
Being sensitive to miracle;
There was in the revealing word,
Though through out-crowding voices heard,
A timbre that their heart-chords stirred,
The "name" in it was potent.

That Moses might his task fulfill,
Jehovah's name worked as one will,
Condensing all God's might and power;
Long-pent-up forces in one hour
Slew all the youthful manhood's flower
Of Egypt in one slaying.

And for Isaiah, stranger yet,
The name did for itself beget
Concreteness; it became a word
That could be seen, not merely heard,
It lighted, as swoops down a bird;
He was a man of vision.

Then in Habakkuk much the same
Image is visioned of the name;
He was a man of smaller mold,
Yet what he spake was finest gold;
As a loud storm-bell through it tolled:
"The Lord has come from Paran."

Habakkuk shows how prophecy
Evokes sublimest psalmody;
The God who wrought sun, moon and stars,
And all the farther still "afars,"
Controls the inter-stellar wars,
Made hymnodists of prophets.

The Psalter's own most glorious themes
Describe how God his saints redeems
By putting in each fighter's hand

His name through which the weakest band
Can, overwhelmed, maintain its stand,
And cut the foe to pieces.

There was in this no magic spell
To conjure aught from heaven or hell;
E'en from Sheol he suffered not
To having dim muttering voices brought
For learning chance or fixing lot,
Where he himself had spoken.

For he had woven round the core
Of what seemed but blind sound before
An aura of bright luminous rays,
That made it a transparent face
In pitch-dark nights, sun-flooded days,
Pregnant with revelation.

And when at last the ripened age
Brought with itself the final stage,
Then, with God's work's maturity,
Appeared the Name's epiphany,
And in a great synonymy
Christ's Name and Face were blended.

Yet there are some of Christian kind,
Who, to this marriage-union blind,
Make a new idol of the name
Of Christ or Jesus which they claim
Must work within some magic frame,
Detached from every doctrine.

Thus is our holiest mystery
Turned back to ancient sorcery;
From the Christ-name its face they wipe;
In vaunted wisdom over-ripe,
They have reverted to the type
Of old barbaric custom. *CEV*, 14–17.

THE ANTHOLOGY

"Nativity" (Poem)

"Elizabeth, Elizabeth"!
The Gospel saith,
A kinswoman with that good name
Greeted the Virgin as she came:
"Mother of her Lord Savior."

None bears in Scripture-registry
That name but she,
Though many, doubtless, bore it well
Of handmaidens in Israel,
Ere it was linked with Mary's.

And Mary, who the babe conceived,
Humbly believed,
Fore-feeling the exultant cry:
"Henceforth shall me beatify
All future generations."

O soul, rise early on this morn
A world is born;
Be present on such dawn as this,
Lest thou the jubilance shouldst miss
Of morning-stars and angels.

We, too, are of thy company,
Nativity!
With kings that, guided by their star,
Brought gold and incense from afar,
With shepherds from their pastures.

How strange, while worshipping we kneel,
I seem to feel,
Midst all the marvels of the place,
Only the marvel on thy face,
Forgetful of the others.

The kings, leaving their gifts, withdrew;
The shepherds, too.

214

Wilt thou not stay with me a while?
I love to see thine eyes the smile
Reflecting of the mother's. *CEV*, 1–2.

Natural Theology

[In the] world of redemption the substance of things is absolutely new. It is inaccessible to the natural mind as such. To be sure, God does not create the world of redemption without regard to the antecedent world of nature, nor does he begin his redemptive revelation *de novo*, as though nothing had preceded. The knowledge from nature, even though corrupted, is presupposed. Only, this does not involve that there is a natural transition from the state of nature to the state of redemption. Nature cannot unlock the door of redemption. *BT*, 21.

Salvation requires at all times more than God's general providence exerted in our behalf. It implies supernaturalism, not as a curious, marvelous self-demonstration of God, but as the very core of true religiousness. On the basis of this part, as well as of other parts of Scripture in general, it is quite proper to maintain that a belief entertained and a life conducted on the basis of a relation to God through nature alone do not yield the biblical religion at all. It is not merely a partial, it is a *different* thing. *BT*, 85.

Nature and Grace

[It cannot] be claimed that the Pauline soteriology breaks the continuity between nature and grace, for Christ restores precisely what the entrance of the σάρξ destroyed. Of course, it is quite true that the apostle's doctrine of salvation contains side by side with this another strand. It represents the *pneuma* as doing more than neutralizing the influence of sin. It lifts man to the higher stage of the supernatural life, which the first Adam even before he sinned did not possess. Insofar there is a *novum*, something superimposed in the Christian state. *KC/SW*, 541.

Neutrality, Myth of

▨ Where the love of God is absent, there an idolatrous love of the world and of self enters, and a positively offensive and hostile attitude toward God results. . . . Man is so necessarily bound to God in his inmost consciousness, that absolute indifference and neutrality are excluded. *KGC*, 93.

New Creation

▨ In Christ's case [the] exchange of one world for another possessed before aught else eschatological features and proportions. It made him not so much a "new creature," as the veritable beginner of a "new creation." *PE*, 49.

▨ [commenting upon 2 Cor. 5] The one in Christ is καινὴ κτίσις. In him the old things have passed away, all things from that point on become new. *PE*, 150.

▨ [commenting upon 2 Cor. 5] It is usually taken for granted, not merely in homiletical usage, but likewise in commentary-exposition, that καινὴ κτίσις describes the renovation in the subjective condition of the believer, if not entirely so, at least chiefly. The rendering "new creature" has promoted this partial misunderstanding. But κτίσις signifies "creation" no less commonly than "creature." The context shows that Paul's real point of view is better rendered by "a new creation." Through the redemptive provision afforded by God in Christ, and specifically by one's εἶναι ἐν Χριστῷ, the Christian has been transferred into a new world, a world which differs *toto genere* in all its characters, its whole environment, and (this could hardly remain unexpressed in such a sweeping statement) differs likewise principally as to the basis of objective righteousness on which the new man stands, from the present world. *PE*, 150.

▨ [commenting upon 2 Cor. 5] For the one who has undergone this experience of having become "in Christ," not merely individual subjective conditions have been changed, but "the old things are passed away, new things have come into being." There has been created a totally new environment, or, more accurately speaking, a totally new world, in which the person spoken of is an inhabitant and participator. It is not in the first place the interiority of the subject that has undergone the change, although that, of course, is not to be excluded. The whole surrounding world has assumed a new aspect and complexion.... The whole argument of the passage revolves around the substitution of one objective status and environment for another. *PE*, 46–47.

Jesus viewed his work as in the most direct manner interlinked with the life to come, to all intents the beginning of a new creation. EAP/*SW*, 92.

The καινὴ κτίσις spoken of in 2 Corinthians 5:17 means the beginning of that world-renewal in which all eschatology culminates. EAP/*SW*, 93–94.

New Heaven and New Earth

It must be remembered that the OT has no single word for "universe," and that the phrase "heaven and earth" serves to supply the deficiency. The promise of a new heavens and a new earth is therefore equivalent to a promise of world renewal. HN/*ISBE*, 1353.

Scripture does not look forward to a repetition of the same process, but to a restoration of a primeval harmony on a higher plane such as precludes all further disturbance. HN/*ISBE*, 1353.

In Matthew 19:28, the term *palingenesia* marks the world-renewing as the renewal of an abnormal state of things. The Scripture teaching therefore is that around the center of God's heaven, which is not subject to deterioration or renewal, a new cosmical heaven and a new earth will be established to be the dwelling-place of the eschatological humanity. The light in which the promise thus appears reminds us that the renewed kosmos, earth as well as cosmical heavens, is destined to play a permanent . . . part in the future life of the people of God. This is in entire harmony with the prevailing biblical representation, not only in the OT but likewise in the NT (see Matt. 5:5; Heb. 2:5), although in the Fourth Gospel and in the Pauline Epistles the emphasis is to such an extent thrown on the heaven-centered character of the future life that the role to be played in it by the renewed earth recedes into the background. Revelation on the other hand, recognizes this element in its imagery of "the new Jerusalem" coming down from God out of heaven upon earth. HN/*ISBE*, 1354.

New Israel

The truth is that to [Jesus] the entire relation hitherto supposed to exist between the Messiah and the people had been reversed. The principle was no longer to be that he who belongs to Israel will participate in the fruits of the messiahship; henceforth the principle will be that he who participates in the Messiah will thereby be assured of his place in the new Israel. It is not a case of Israel joining itself to the Christ; on the contrary, it is a case of the Christ creating his Israel. *SDJ*, 60.

New Testament

The New Testament [is] that period of the covenant of grace which has followed [Christ's] appearance and under which we still live. *BT*, 23.

The "New Testament" in the soteric, periodical sense of the word goes beyond the time of the life of Christ and the apostolic age; it not only includes us, but extends into and covers the eschatological, eternal state. *BT*, 26.

The New Testament documents from the least to the most christological among them are at one in this, that they make the religion of the believer terminate in Christ. He is the object of faith and trust throughout in such a high sense that no distinction is drawn between God and him. This attitude is inherent in Christianity from the first. A different kind of Christianity has never existed. *JG/SW*, 511.

Obedience of Christ

In one sense the Sermon on the Mount was a sermon preached out of his own personal experience. The righteousness he described

218

was not a distant ideal, it was an incarnate reality in himself. He alone of all mankind fulfilled the law in its deepest purport and widest extent. His keeping of it proceeded from that sanctuary of his inner life where he and the Father always beheld each other's face. He made it his meat and drink to do the will of God. HTR/*GG*, 42.

Office

After all it is not so much by what the minister contributes of himself to the cause of Christ, but rather by what he is enabled to draw out and utilize from the divine resources, that his office and work will be tested. It is not chiefly the question of whether we are strong in the cause, but whether the cause is strong in and through us. MEM/*GG*, 85.

Old Covenant

It should be noted that, when the Bible speaks of a twofold *berith*, a twofold *diathēkē*, it means by the "old" covenant not the entire period from the fall of man to Christ, but the period from Moses to Christ. Nevertheless, what precedes the Mosaic period in the description of Genesis may be appropriately subsumed under the "old covenant." It is meant in the Pentateuch as a preface to the account of the Mosaic institutions, and the preface belongs within the cover of the book. *BT*, 26.

The epistle [to the Hebrews] places the things of the old covenant as on the one hand looking upward to the world of heaven, on the other hand looking forward to the new covenant. HED/*SW*, 202.

[commenting upon the Epistle to the Hebrews] The old covenant, through the very externality and visibleness and earthliness and temporalness of its institutions, furnished an admirable foil to exhibit the glories of the spiritual, invisible, heavenly, eternal aspect of the work of Christ. PC/*SW*, 131.

Old Covenant and New Covenant

▓ [commenting upon the Epistle to the Hebrews] The concrete purpose for which the epistle was written gave occasion for placing great emphasis on the superiority of the new covenant to the old. HED/*SW*, 203.

▓ The dividing point between the old *diathēkē* and the new is the death of Christ. The end of the old covenant and the beginning of the new covenant lie in the death, or perhaps it would be more correct to say in the ascension, of Christ (Heb. 7:11). *TEH*, 49–50.

▓ The peculiarity of the old *diathēkē* is that it pertains to this present world, whereas the new *diathēkē* is that of the future eschatological world. *TEH*, 50.

▓ [commenting upon 2 Cor. 3:18] Paul affirms that the glory of the old covenant had to pass away, whereas that of the new covenant must remain. . . . What Moses stood for was glorious but lacked permanence. The day was bound to come when its splendor would vanish. On the other hand the new covenant is final and abiding. The times cannot outgrow, the developments of history cannot age it, it carries within itself the pledge of eternity. Not only did such a difference actually exist—but both Moses and Paul were aware of the state of things in each case. Moses was aware of it, for we are told that he put the veil on his face for the purpose of hiding the disappearance of the glory. And Paul was, since in pointed contrast to this procedure, he professes to minister with open face: "Not as Moses, who put a veil over his face" [v. 13]. MEM/*GG*, 88–89.

▓ The new covenant in its preexistent, heavenly state reaches back and stretches its eternal wings over the old, and the Old Testament people of God were one with us in religious dignity and privilege; they were, to speak in a Pauline figure, sons of the Jerusalem above, which is the mother of all. HED/*SW*, 199.

Old Testament

The Old Testament dispensation is a forward-stretching and forward-looking dispensation. Owing to the factual character of biblical religion its face is necessarily set toward new things. Prophecy is the best indicator of this . . . but more particularly eschatological and messianic prophecy are pointed toward the future, and not merely toward the future as a relatively higher state, but as an absolutely perfect and enduring state to be contrasted with the present and its succession of developments. *BT*, 299.

In a broad sense the Old Testament was the economy of conviction of sin. The law revealed the moral helplessness of man, placed him under a curse, worked death. There was, of course, gospel under and in the old covenant, but it was for its expression largely dependent on the silent symbolic language of altar and sacrifice and lustration. MEM/*GG*, 96.

The Old Testament is that period of the covenant of grace which precedes the coming of the Messiah. *BT*, 23.

Jesus [does not] criticize the Old Testament mode of life as though having been wrong for its own time, but only supersedes it as unsuitable for the incoming era. *BT*, 361.

Old Testament and Eschatology

The OT from the beginning has an eschatology and puts the eschatological promise on the broadest racial basis (Gen. 3). HN/*ISBE*, 1353.

Old Testament teaching concerning the end . . . lies in the realm of history, in the past creative and redemptive activity of God, ultimately in the theistic conception of the character of Jehovah himself, as an intelligent, planning, building God, whose delight is ever in the product of his freely shaping hands. And consequently, what Israel expects is not a quasi-consummation, which would bear on its face the Sisyphus-expression of endless toil; it is an absolute goal, consisting in an age of more than gold, made of a finer metal beyond all rust and deterioration. EP, 334.

The eschatological element in the religion of the Old Testament is but the supreme expression of its character as a religion of God's free historical self-assertion, a religion, not of nature-processes, but of redemption and revelation. EAP/*SW*, 95.

Old Testament and the Covenant of Works

The pre-redemptive special revelation is commonly given the name of "the covenant of works." Care should be taken not to identify the latter with the "the Old Testament." The Old Testament belongs after the fall. *BT*, 23.

Old Testament and the Heavenly

The Old Testament avails itself of earthly and eternal forms to convey heavenly and spiritual things. SC/*SW*, 417.

Old Testament as Prospective Period

The Old Testament was pre-eminently a prospective period, a period of anticipation, a period in which the believer was reminded at every step of something higher and better yet to appear. Enoch, Moses, Abraham and all the prophets bore witness by their whole manner of life that they appreciated this, that the present was to them something provisional. RR/*GG*, 130–31.

Old Testament Converges and Terminates in Jesus Christ

Indeed in appropriating for himself the function of bringing the kingdom, in laying claim to the messianic dignity, Jesus seized upon that in the Old Testament which enabled him at one stroke to make its whole historic movement converge upon and terminate in himself. *KGC*, 14.

Jesus regarded the whole Old Testament movement as a divinely directed and inspired movement, as having arrived at its goal in himself, so that he himself in his historic appearance and work being taken away, the Old Testament would lose its purpose and significance. *BT*, 358.

▮ Hence from the beginning all redeeming acts of God aim at the creation and introduction of this new organic principle, which is none other than Christ. All Old Testament redemption is but the saving activity of God working toward the realization of this goal, the great supernatural prelude to the incarnation and the atonement. IBT/*SW*, 12.

Old Testament, Jesus' Attitude toward the Scriptures of

▮ In His treatment of the Bible Jesus was the most orthodox of the orthodox. *BT*, 358.

▮ Jesus treats the Scriptures as a "rule of faith and practice." His gravest charge against the Pharisaic tradition-mongering is that for the sake of tradition it neglects the commandment of God. To the Sadducees he declares that their denial of the resurrection springs from not knowing the Scriptures. *BT*, 359.

▮ The underlying supposition of all arguing from Scripture as . . . our Lord practiced it, consists in this, that the Word of God has received from him the quality of unbreakableness: not to believe involves an attempt to break something that God has declared sure. *BT*, 360.

Old Testament, Relationship to New Testament

▮ We must note the continuity of the Old Testament with the New. In [Heb.] 3:1–6 Moses is compared with Christ. There we read that Moses was *in* the house, whereas Christ is *over* the house. The implication is that the same house is meant in both cases, namely, God's house. (Compare Num. 12:7.) In this house Moses is a servant, while Christ is a Son. The superiority of Christ to Moses is further brought out by the consideration that the builder of the house (Christ) is greater than the house and its contents (including Moses). Again the implication plainly is that the same house is meant, namely the house of which Moses was an inmate and in which he was a servant. *TEH*, 67.

[commenting upon the Epistle to the Hebrews] Again, when the writer draws a comparison between the Old Testament and the New Testament, he never turns it to account to warn the readers *away* from the Old Testament. He uses it only to show the *superiority* of the New Testament; for example, in 2:2–3 the angels and Christ are contrasted. The angels are the highest conceivable created beings, yet Christ stood out as superior to them. The Old Testament economy was superintended by angels. The writer does not say that it is folly to fall back into that system, but he does urge the need of a greater heed now, because of the higher object. *TEH*, 18–19.

Our whole New Testament life and heritage was, from the Old Testament point of view, an eschatological thing. Here, therefore, we find ourselves and them occupied with identical fact; what they eschatologically contemplated we retrospectively enjoy, and the religious apprehension of it, while formally different, is in essence the same. EP, 333.

The same purpose and method of God run through both [the Old and New Testaments]. The substance upon which the impression was made under the Old Testament may have been earthly clay; none the less the matrix that stamped it bore the lineaments of eternal law and truth. *BT*, 109.

The revealed religion of the Old Testament . . . resembles a tree whose root system and whose crown spread out widely, while the trunk of the tree confines the sap for a certain distance within a narrow channel. The patriarchal period corresponds to the root growth; the freely expanding crown to the revelation of the New Testament; and the relatively constricted form of the trunk to the period from Moses to Christ. *BT*, 79.

Old Testament Sacrificial System

All Old Testament sacrificial functions culminated find their higher, their ideal counterpart in the crucified Savior. In this respect also he is the end of the law, not because he does away with the idea of sacrifice as something antiquated and imperfect, but because he embodies this idea in its highest conceivable, its absolute form in himself, and thus, while rendering all previous forms superfluous, secures to it in his own person everlasting reality. SIP/*SW*, 376.

Omnipotence

[commenting upon John 1] That God acts in general, and in particular creates by his word, is a common Old Testament expression for describing the omnipotent mode of his activity. This was the case in the first creation of all things, when God spoke and by his mere speaking the effect was accomplished. Now if the Evangelist identifies the preexistent Christ with this omnipotent creative word, his first thought will have been that through Christ the divine omnipotence asserted itself, that Christ entered into the creation as the Logos of God because God made him the Mediator of his almighty power. RLT/*SW*, 65.

Before God there exists no "if thou canst." *BT*, 388.

According to Numbers 20:12, Moses and Aaron are rebuked for not having "sanctified" Jehovah (that is to say, for not having recognized and proclaimed him as "holy"), when they failed to ascribe to him the omnipotence that could make water flow from the rock at a simple word of command. *BT*, 247.

[commenting upon Isaiah] Jehovah works by a word, and this is but a way of saying that he works supernaturally. He sustains to the creature the relation of a potter to the clay, a great figure expressive of omnipotence as well as of sovereignty. *BT*, 239.

Both in nature and history, in creation and in redemption, [the divine power] produces and controls and directs everything that comes to pass. Nothing in the realm of actual or conceivable things is withdrawn from it (Amos 9:2–3; Dan. 4:35); even to the minutest and most recondite sequences of cause and effect it extends and masters all details of reality (Matt. 10:30; Luke 12:7). There is no accident (1 Sam. 6:9; cf. v. 12; Prov. 16:33). It need not operate through second causes; it itself underlies all second causes and makes them what they are. OM/*ISBE*, 2189.

Even more than the sphere of nature and history, that of redemption reveals the divine omnipotence, from the point of view of the supernatural and miraculous. Thus Exodus 15 celebrates the power of Jehovah in the wonders of the exodus. It is God's exclusive prerogative to do wonders (Job 5:9; 9:10; Ps. 72:18); he alone can make a "new thing" (Num. 16:30; Isa. 43:19; Jer. 31:22). In the NT the great embodiment of this redemptive omnipotence is the resurrection of believers (Matt. 22:29; Mark 12:24) and specifically the resurrection of Christ (Rom. 4:17, 21, 24; Eph. 1:19–20); but it is evidenced in the whole process of redemption (Matt. 19:26; Mark 10:27; Rom. 8:31; Eph. 3:7, 20; 1 Peter 1:5; Rev. 11:17). OM/*ISBE*, 2189.

The beauty of Jesus' teaching on the nature of God consists in this, that he keeps the exaltation of God above every creature and his loving condescension toward the creature in perfect equilibrium and makes them mutually fructified by each other. Religion is more than the inclusion of God in the general altruistic movement of the human mind; it is a devotion at every point colored by the consciousness of that divine uniqueness in which God's omnipotence occupies a foremost place. OM/*ISBE*, 2190.

A word for the conception of omnipotence the Old Testament does not possess. But Amos in a figurative, descriptive way succeeds in vividly conveying the impression of what it consists in. Jehovah forms the mountains, creates the wind, makes the Pleiades and Orion. He calls for the waters of the sea, and pours them out upon the face of the earth. The change from day into night and from night into day obeys his will. As a conqueror controls the land through occupying the high places, so he treads upon the high places of the earth. He sends fire, famine, pestilence, and all plagues and evil, all this again as instrumental in the execution of his judgment (2:5; 3:6; 4:6, 9, 10, 13; 5:8; 7:4). *BT*, 238–39.

Omnipotence in God is that to which human faith addresses itself. In it lies the ground for assurance that he is able to save, as in his love that he is willing to save (Pss. 65:5–6; 72:18; 118:14–16; Eph. 3:20). OM/*ISBE*, 2189.

Omnipresence

[Omnipresence] is but the correlate of the monotheistic conception of God as the infinite Creator, Preserver and Governor of the universe, immanent in his works as well as transcendent above them. OMP/*ISBE*, 2190–91.

Both from a generally religious and from a specifically soteriological point of view the omnipresence of God is of great practical importance for the religious life. In the former respect it contains the guaranty that the actual nearness of God and a real communion with him may be enjoyed everywhere, even apart from the places hallowed for such purpose by a specific gracious self-manifestation (Ps. 139:5–10). In the other respect the divine omnipresence assures the believer that God is at hand to save in every place where from any danger or foe his people need salvation (Isa. 43:2). OMP/*ISBE*, 2191.

Omniscience

It is in vain to seek to hide one's counsel from Jehovah, as the politicians try to do, who work in the dark and say: Who sees us, and who knows us? This is in vain, because Jehovah is, in reference to all plotting of man, as the potter is to the clay: he fashions the very mind that conceives the thought of hiding from him. *BT*, 245.

Omniscience is the omnipresence of cognition (Jer. 23:23–24). It is also closely related to God's eternity, for the latter makes him in his knowledge independent of the limitations of time (Isa. 43:8–12). God's creative relation to all that exists is represented as underlying his omniscience (Ps. 33:15; 97:9; 139:13; Isa. 29:15). His all-comprehensive purpose forms the basis of his knowledge of all events and developments (Isa. 41:22–27; Amos 3:7). OMS/*ISBE*, 2191.

The divine omniscience is most important for the religious life. The very essence of religion as communion with God depends on his all-comprehensive cognizance of the life of man at every moment. OMS/*ISBE*, 2192.

Ordo Salutis

From the eternal foreknowledge of God, i.e., from his sovereign love, follows the whole *ordo salutis* on its subjective side not only, but also the whole objective work of redemption (see Rom. 8:28–34). TP/*SW*, 360.

Original State of Man

Man's original state was a state of indefinite probation: he remained in possession of what he had, so long as he did not commit sin, but it was not a state in which the continuance of his religious and moral status could be guaranteed him. *BT*, 22.

Other-Worldliness

Herein also lies the defense against the charge that other-worldliness is a sickly strain in the religious consciousness, because inspired by selfish, eudaemonistic motives and because apt to hinder the development of a wholesome interest in and faithful performance of the duties of the present life. This would be so if it were anything else but God-centered. The root of all that is ugly and injurious in extreme eschatological preoccupation can always be traced back to this, that it is insufficiently religious, that people seek something else in the other world than the perfect union with and service of God. HED/*SW*, 229.

[The NT revelation] shows such a tremendous disproportion between what religion can mean and bring to us here, and what it will mean and bring to us hereafter, that merely to believe it is bound to make other-worldliness the dominating attitude of the Christian mind. EP, 362–63.

■ [Other-worldliness] is not essentially negative but positive in character. The core lies not in what it relinquishes but in what it seeks. Escape from the world here below and avoidance of the evil in the world do not furnish its primary motive. That is true only of the abnormal, morbid type of other-worldliness, that connected with pessimism and monastic seclusion. HM/*GG*, 112.

■ The desirability of heaven should never possess exclusively or mainly negative significance. It is not something first brought into the religious mind through sin. The lineage and birthright of other-worldliness are of the oldest and noblest. By God himself this traveler's unrest was implanted in the soul. Ever since the goal set by the covenant of works came within his ken, man carries with him in all his converse with this world the sense of belonging to another. HM/*GG*, 113.

■ From the highest religious viewpoint the coming world, the state of eternity, meant for [Jesus] the only possible religious consummation. His other-worldliness was a God-centered other-worldliness. *SDJ*, 65.

■ Without a certain detachment from this world, other-worldliness is not possible. Hope cannot flourish where the heart is in the present life. Two things, however, ought to be remembered here in order not to misunderstand this teaching. (i) This detachment from the world is not and ought not to be an external matter, but an internal disposition. The question is not whether someone should deny himself all earthly, temporal possessions. He might do that and yet in his heart be far from a pilgrim, a sojourner. And on the other hand, he might not do this and yet inwardly obey the exhortation of the apostle because he had succeeded in disengaging his heart. (ii) Such an inward attitude toward the world cannot be assumed and maintained artificially by merely compelling ourselves not to love the present life. If this is to be a natural, healthy state of mind it must be the result of a greater, supreme interest in the life to come. The negative must be the effect of the positive. The love of heaven must drive out the inordinate love of what is earthly. CH/*GG*, 146–47.

Precisely because the Christian other-worldliness is inspired by the thought of God and not of self, it involves no danger of monastic withdrawal from or indifference to the present world. The same thirst for the divine glory which is the root of all heavenly-mindedness, also compels the consecration of all earthly existence to the promotion of God's kingdom. EP, 364.

The structure of the two strata placed one above the other, with the higher stratum made regulative for the lower one in its laws and ideals . . . is the basis of what in devotional language we call other-worldliness. *PE*, 297.

Paganism

Precisely of pagan eschatologies it is characteristic to look for increasingly recurring cycles after the world-year shall have been ended. The reason is that in paganism the concept of eschatology is a piece of naturalism, sprung from astral, zodiacal observation of circuits among the heavenly bodies. When the longest circuit has been completed and brought back to its point of departure, it inevitably proceeds to repeat itself along the immemorial same self courses. The "year of gold" has "come round" again. The future age of God, though made of the finest gold, does not "come round"; it simply comes and then abides. *PE*, 316.

How desperate is the plight of those Canaanites, modern no less than ancient, who must look for the satisfaction of their hunger to the dead wood of the Asherah of nature, because they have no faith in the perpetual miracle of the fruit-bearing fir-tree of redemption. WT/*GG*, 8–9.

Pantheism

The pantheistic philosophy confounds mystery and contradiction. Pantheism first imports into the conceptions of infinitude, omnipotence, absoluteness, eternity, its own idea of God as the sum of all being, and then, on the basis of this, declares these attributes inconsistent with theism. *GD2/SW*, 486.

▓ Pantheism is fatal to the development of individual character. In the sphere of religion it is inconsistent with the supernatural claims of Christianity. Christianity is in itself a protest against all naturalism and evolution. Christ is *the* miracle. "Bethlehem makes a break in the genealogy of humanity." Hence, the attempt of pantheism to silence this protest by divesting Christianity of its supernatural elements. *DV*, 331.

Parousia

▓ In its secular as well as in its religious-eschatological use the word expresses the two closely connected ideas of arrival and presence. Parousia signifies "becoming present" and "being present" for a longer or shorter period. *PE*, 75.

▓ The noun means "arrival," not "return." It cannot correctly be rendered by "*second coming*." When the Christians spoke of the parousia of their Lord, they were, of course, aware and mindful that the event spoken of was in point of fact a second arrival, duplicating in a certain respect that of the incarnation. Still there did not develop out of this consciousness the phrase "second parousia." *PE*, 75.

▓ The word denotes "coming," "arrival." It is never applied to the incarnation of Christ, and could be applied to his second coming only, partly because it had already become a fixed messianic term, partly because there was a point of view from which the future appearance of Jesus appeared the sole adequate expression of his messianic dignity and glory. ENT/*SW*, 30.

▓ The parousia taken as an event is with Paul catastrophic. It is a point of eventuation, not a series of successive events. . . . It designates *the momentous event*, and consequently that which it opens up must needs carry a supreme, absolute weight to the religious consciousness. *PE*, 76.

Participation, in Heaven Presently

Heaven is present to the believer's experience in no less a real sense than Canaan with its fair hills and valleys lay close to the vision of Abraham. HM/*GG*, 115.

[The Christian] is given to taste the powers of the world to come, as Abraham breathed the air of Canaan, and was refreshed by the dews descending on its fields. HM/*GG*, 115.

Participation, in the Text

Still, we know full well that we ourselves live just as much in the New Testament as did Peter and Paul and John. *BT*, 303.

In the most immediate sense [the readers of Hebrews are] made recipients of the divine word spoken by Christ and through that word brought into no less direct communion with the supernatural world than were the contemporaries of the earthly life of Jesus. God spake unto the fathers in the prophets; he spake in a Son unto *us*. And through this speech they have come unto Mount Zion, and unto the city of the living God, nay unto God and Jesus the mediator of a fresh covenant himself; and, as we have seen, the danger incurred by disregarding this speech of God in Christ is for them not less but greater than it was for those who refused a hearing to the terrible voice of the Sinaitic legislation. HED/*SW*, 191–92.

It is true, these days of our Lord's flesh which he lived among his countrymen, acting and acted upon, were a real concrete piece of life interwoven with the life of Israel. They belong to that age and generation as truly as any section of human history can be said to belong to the times in which it happened. But it is also true that this is not common history, but sacred, redemptive history, which means that there runs through it, from beginning to end, a special design, ordering its course, shaping its frame, and fixing its issues, so as to make of it a proper stage for the enactment of the great mystery of redemption, whose spectators and participants were not merely the Jews of that age but the inhabitants of all subsequent ages. . . . And because this is so, you and I can come to the story of two thousand years ago and find a present salvation there, an ever open door to the house of peace and hope. SSL/*GG*, 44–45.

Passover, Feast of

Passover was pre-eminently a historical feast. It pointed back to the deliverance of the people from Egypt, a deliverance through sacrifice, a deliverance from the slaying angel, a deliverance in which manifestly the grace of God alone had made a distinction between them and their persecutors. Each time this feast was celebrated in the families of Israel, it proclaimed anew that redemption through blood, and by grace and sovereign choice was the great fact which lay at the basis of their historic existence; the source from which everything that Israel was and had or could ever hope to be and have ultimately flowed. GP/*GG*, 234.

Patience

The Christian virtue of patience is something that can spring only from true, vital connection with the spiritual, heavenly world. It is something entirely different from stoical apathy or resignation. If the Christian patiently endures, it is because he sees the invisible; because there is a counter-power, a counter-principle at work in his life which more than offsets, by the joy it creates, the pain of tribulation. This is nothing else but the power of the spiritual, heavenly world itself to which through faith he has access. RR/*GG*, 136–37.

The Christian race must be run with patience. Patience in this connection means more than perseverance or persistence; it describes the endurance of what is hard and painful. RR/*GG*, 134.

Patience is a term characteristic of the Stoic philosophy, but in Stoicism patience is sheer will power to hold out. . . . But Christian patience is not a suppressing of any powers; rather, it is a balancing of powers. There is another power which enters into the believer's life to offset the power of persecution. This new power comes to him through faith. *TEH*, 23.

In the Christian pursuit of the kingdom of God, suffering and trials are the inevitable concomitants; and far from hindering him in his progress, they must become the means of helping him onward through the development in him of patience. RR/*GG*, 134–35.

In point of fact, patience—negative as the conception may superficially appear to us—is in its Christian sense a most positive thing; at least it is the manifestation of a more positive thing, the manifestation of the supernatural energy that works in faith itself. RR/*GG*, 137.

Patriarchs

It was because God discerned in the souls of the patriarchs, underneath all else, this personal love, this homesickness for himself, that he caused to be recorded about them the greatest thing that can be spoken of any man: that God is not ashamed to be called their God, and that he has prepared for them the city of their desire. HM/*GG*, 123.

The first outstanding principle of divine procedure with the patriarchs is the principle of election. . . . Here one family is taken out of the number of existing Shemitic families, and with it, within it, the redemptive, revelatory work of God is carried forward. This is the tremendous significance of the call of Abraham. *BT*, 76.

Faith in its last analysis was to the patriarchs the apprehension, the possession, the enjoyment of God himself. HED/*SW*, 229.

Patriarchs, Other-Worldliness of

As Paul found in the patriarchal period the preformation of the religion of grace and of universalism which the law coming in after could only obscure but not abrogate, so the author of Hebrews finds in it an earlier stage of that thorough spiritual-mindedness and of that profound other-worldliness of Christianity which it was his specific task to set forth. HED/*SW*, 229.

The other-worldliness of the patriarchs showed itself in this, that they confessed to be strangers and pilgrims on the earth. It found its visible expression in their dwelling in tents. Not strangers and pilgrims outside of Canaan, but strangers and pilgrims in the earth. . . . They pursued their tent-life in the very land of promise, which was their own, as in a land not their own. HM/*GG*, 108–9.

⬛ The patriarchs had their vision of the heavenly country, a vision in the light of which the excellence or desirableness of every earthly home and country paled. HM/*GG*, 111.

⬛ [commenting upon the Epistle to the Hebrews] The author represents [the] ascent of the patriarchs' faith to the heavenly world as in no way mediated by the typical fulfillment of the promise that was to intervene between them and its final New Testament realization. The ascent to the heavenly country did not use as a stepping-stone the thought of the earthly Canaan; it was made directly from the vantage ground of the promises of God. It greeted from afar the Christ and drew near to the heavenly country above; in sublime sacrifice it surrendered whatever of earthly developments lay between. HED/*SW*, 228–29.

⬛ If even in Canaan [the patriarchs] carried within themselves the consciousness of pilgrimage then it becomes strikingly evident that it was a question of fundamental, comprehensive choice between earth and heaven. The adherence to the tent-life in the sight and amidst the scenes of the promised land fixes the aspiration of the patriarchs as aiming at the highest conceivable heavenly goal. HM/*GG*, 109.

⬛ [In Heb. 11] it is pictured how the patriarchs were contented to dwell in tents, and did not regret the non-possession of the promised land, and the reason for this frame of mind is carefully added; it was not that through faith they looked forward in the vista of time to a more solid and comprehensive possession of Canaan than was possible in their own days; the real reason was that from the earthly, possessed or not-yet-possessed, they had learned to look upward to a form of possession of the promise identifying it more closely with God himself: "They looked for the city that has the foundations, whose builder and maker is God" (i.e., because its builder and maker is God) (Heb. 11:10). *BT*, 87.

Paul and Theology

While belonging to the history of revelation, [Paul's] teaching at the same time marks the beginning of the history of theology. TP/*SW*, 355.

The flights of [Paul's] theological genius were for him veritable flights into heaven. TP/*SW*, 358.

Paul's theological vision spans the entire sweep of man's spiritual history and places it in its entirety under the point of view of an unfolding of the eternal purpose of God. TP/*SW*, 359.

Paul's religion was from the very outset of his Christian life "theocentric," and it could never have become so "Christocentric" as it actually is, had not the rich, religious occupation with the Savior secured for the latter the indisputable place wherein he appears in the closest unity with the Father. *PE*, 303.

[Paul's] religious consciousness differed from the modern one in that it revolved around the center, not of man, but of God. AL/*SW*, 399.

The most consistently Pauline theology is that which . . . seeks supremely the divine glory and thus teaches men to thirst alike for the divine righteousness and the divine love. AL/*SW*, 399.

All Paul's labor was a most strenuous endeavor to bring the restlessly-temporal to where it would lose itself in the forever-undisturbable *aiōnion*. *PE*, 316.

Pauline Eschatology

Paul had been the first to grasp with his master-mind the single items of eschatological belief scattered through Scripture, and to weave them into a compact, well-rounded system, so coherent, that, speaking after the manner of man, it became next to impossible for any of the precious texture henceforth to be lost. He it was who made the single items of hope find themselves and group themselves into crystal formations with symmetrical shapes. Truly for this, not his smallest gift, he may justly be called the father of Christian eschatology. *PE*, preface.

Pauline Eschatology, Distinct from Greek Belief

Against the Stoic humanitarian doctrine that all men are children of God Paul places the soteric sonship of believers. Paul had a profound conviction of sin, paganism had not. This makes all the difference in the complexion of eschatological ideas. Those of Paul are God-centered, profoundly religious, cultivated for the sake of God and with a thirst after God; those of the Greco-Roman world lack this character entirely. *HEL*, 149.

And, most of all, the eschatology of Paul has a historical, dramatic, redemptive background, an element which was utterly lacking in the Greek belief. *HEL*, 149.

Pauline Soteriology

It is quite true that the formulas of the imputation of our sin to Christ and of the imputation of Christ's righteousness to us are lacking in Paul, but the reason for this is not to be sought in the apostle's ignorance of or aversion to the conception itself. The reason simply is that Paul prefers to put the matter on the broader basis of the identification of the person of Christ with us. The Pauline formula is: Christ was made unto us or for us sin or righteousness. *LT*, 129.

Peace Offering

The idea prominent in every peace-offering was that of *berith*-fellowship with God. The meal was an exponent of the state of peace and blessedness enjoyed. *BT*, 120.

"Peace" is in Scripture a far more positive conception than it is with us. The peace-offering accordingly symbolizes the state of positive favor and blessedness enjoyed in the religion of Jehovah, which at all times includes more than the sacrificial relief obtained from sin. *BT*, 170.

Pelagianism

According to the Pelagian, it is precisely the lack of [built-in holiness or depravity] that gives man dignity: he is a free being who has to work himself up out of his moral neutrality and has to attain to holiness by a sort of ethical creative power. He, therefore, already was what he has to be because his destiny is the same as undetermined freedom of choice. DCRT/*SW*, 243.

Perfecting of Christ

[commenting upon Heb. 7:28] The participle perfect, τετελειωμένον, undoubtedly implies that a perfecting took place with Christ during his earthly life, that there was a time when he did not yet possess this τελείωσις. [The verse's] probable meaning may be best paraphrased as follows: "The law appoints as high priests men having infirmity; the word of the oath swearing appoints a Son (who not only has no infirmity, but) who has been made a perfect high priest forevermore, by the practice of perfect obedience on earth and by translation into the heavenly world from which all infirmity is excluded." PC/*SW*, 148–49.

The "perfecting" of the Savior . . . has two sides: it is perfecting in the sphere of sympathy with exposure to temptation and perfecting in the sphere of appreciation of obedience which overcomes temptation. PC/*SW*, 150.

Perseverance

He who is united to Christ and lives within the circle of his love, to him the eternal retention of the supreme eschatological life is absolutely secure. *PE*, 312.

The whole intimate life-union existing between the believer and Christ vouches for the certainty of the eternal persistence of this bond. *PE*, 312–13.

■ The Christian's hope is positive. His youth is like that of the heir who knows precisely what awaits him. No, more than this, the Christian has the assurance which no heir in temporal things can ever have. He knows with absolute certainty that the inheritance will not merely be kept for him, but that he will be kept for it. CH/*GG*, 143.

Pharaoh

■ [Pharaoh's] obduracy was to reveal the true inward nature of that of which he was a figure. Of course, this hardening was by no means an arbitrary divine act; it was a judicial process: the king first hardened himself, and then, in punishment for this, he was further hardened by God. *BT*, 110.

■ [The] kingdom of evil headed up in Pharaoh embraces first of all the human elements of paganism. *BT*, 111.

Pharisees

■ The Pharisees interpreted and observed the law from a meritoriously ascetic principle. They prided themselves on the profitableness of their fasting, of their punctilious abstention from all pleasure on the Sabbath, of their wearisome observance of all the rites of purification. Jesus squarely took issue with this standpoint, not merely because it is impossible to earn anything with God, but also because, if anything were to be earned, even then the self-mortification, the suffering of man as such could have no value in the sight of God. What God desires in the law is not to afflict man, but to benefit him—a principle most strikingly affirmed in the statement that the Sabbath was made for man, not man for the Sabbath. EC/*GG*, 190.

■ What Jesus condemned in the Pharisees was not externalism or hypocrisy alone, but also the seeking of righteousness for man's sake rather than for God's. Indeed, the latter was, in his view, the fundamental fault in the Pharisaic character. AL/*SW*, 396.

Piety

▨ [commenting upon Büchsel's *Der Begriff*] It is interesting to observe how the author explains the emphasis placed on truth and knowledge from the peculiar fundamental character of the piety portrayed in the Johannine writings. The idea that to be put in possession of the truth about God, to know God, is in itself productive and constitutive of religion, rests on the absolutely God-centered and self-forgetting character of the religious consciousness in John. The mind is to such an extent focused in God and absorbed by God as to cease altogether reflecting on itself and its own need. The majesty of God and of Christ overpowers it. *DBDW*, 671.

▨ In the ideal covenant-fellowship . . . the divine factor is the all-controlling one. Man appears as admitted into, adjusted to, subordinated to, the life of God. Biblical piety is God-centered. *BT*, 154.

▨ Undoubtedly utterances like that in the seventy-third Psalm, "Whom have I in heaven but thee? and there is none upon the earth that I desire beside thee," or that in the forty-second, "As the hart panteth after the water brooks, so panteth my soul after thee, O God. My soul thirsteth for God, for the living God," mark not only the highest point to which the aspiration of the pious heart has attained under the Old Testament, but, we may safely affirm, the highest point to which it can ever attain in the form of pure, disinterested spiritual love. These are voices coming, as it were, from the world of ideal religion, in which the soul is lifted for a moment above the consciousness even of her own soteriological needs and tastes the enjoyment of God as such. SDL/*SW*, 438.

Pilgrim Nature of Christianity

▨ The Christian is a sojourner here and must live in the future because he knows full well that under the present conditions he can never attain to that full possession of God and his Savior for which in his best moments his heart and flesh cry out. CH/*GG*, 154.

240

■ Like Abraham we must resolutely confess that we are strangers and pilgrims in a land of time, and that the best this land can offer us is but a caravanserai to tarry in for a day and a night. HM/*GG*, 117.

■ [Christians are pilgrims] with heaven's door wide open in our sight. HM/*GG*, 111.

■ The necessary consequence of this life of the Christian in hope is that he learns to consider the present earthly life as a journey, a pilgrimage, something necessary for the sake of the end but which does not have any independent value or attraction in itself. CH/*GG*, 146.

Platonism and Biblical Eschatology

■ In the abstract [Paul] practices no cult of the invisible as partaking *per se* of a superior complexion; that would be a Hellenic thought, but he has learned to recognize in the things unseen to the present aeon the enduring things of the world to come, a world already in principle present, the contemplation of which can consequently render solace and support in the affliction of the moment. *PE*, 292.

■ The difference between the higher things and the lower things is not Platonically conceived, as though there were more reality of being in the former than in the latter. Both are equally real. The difference comes in through an appraisal of quality. The technical term in John to mark the contrast is that of *alētheia*, "truth." *BT*, 355–56.

■ Notwithstanding a certain formal resemblance in the two-sidedness of the Christian life, it stands at a far remove from Greek philosophical dualism. Its very genesis forbids identification with this even to the slightest degree. Its mother-soil lies in eschatological revelation, not in metaphysical speculation. For this reason it is important to be able to show that the horizontal historical line of perspective is the older one, out of which only through an eminently-historical event the parallel structure of the two spheres was begotten. The historical was first, then the theological. And because the latter came from the former every possibility of conflict was from the outset excluded; neither of the two could interfere with the other. *PE*, 41.

Post-millennialism

The idea of the Antichrist in general and that of the apostasy in particular reminds us that we may not expect an uninterrupted progress of the Christianization of the world until the parousia. As the reign of truth will be extended, so the forces of evil will gather strength, especially toward the end. ENT/*SW*, 41.

It is well to remember for this reason that, however high the Scriptures encourage us to set our hopes with reference to the future of the kingdom of God in this world, there are certain inherent limitations upon every such outlook, which the Bible itself never fails to remind us of, lest our hope should outrun the methods of God and expect from this world what only the world to come is able to bring. All the nations must be evangelized, the fulness of the Gentiles go in and all Israel be saved, the kingdom of heaven must grow to a great tree, and the leaven permeate the entire lump. But all this certainly does not mean, not even to the mind of the most pronounced pre- or post-millenarian, that there will be a period before the end of the world when the power of sin and evil will be entirely eliminated. The same kingdom parables which seem to set no limit upon the progressive extension of the kingdom also teach us that the wheat and the tares, the good and the bad fish remain together until the judgment day. The same Paul who outlines for us in Romans a program of uninterrupted progress of the kingdom of God and points as its goal to the Christianization of all the nations and the salvation of all Israel, likewise teaches us that toward the end the power of evil will gather its greatest strength and find its supreme product and leader in the man of sin, the lawless one, usually called the Antichrist. SC/*SW*, 419–20.

The extension of Christianity on the periphery to the ends of the earth does not preclude a progressive apostasy within the bosom of Christianity itself. Historically considered, the judgment day will surely mean what its name implies it to be—a two-sided divine interposition in the state of the then existing world, where both its good and its evil as still active forces will be reckoned with. SC/*SW*, 420.

THE ANTHOLOGY

242

"Power of Praying" (Poem)

At dusk, before thee kneeling,
Could I confess it all,
In one complete revealing,
The things both great and small,
Were room left for confiding,
With deep humility,
That, in great love abiding,
Thy heart would pardon me?

Words written may bring censure,
Estranging miles between,
But speech will win its venture,
Let eye to eye be seen.
Prayer overclimbs the mountains,
Till it has found the place
Where spring the mystic fountains
Of woman's sovereign grace.

Faith will, to force repairing,
God no release accord,
As showed with dauntless daring
Jacob at Jabbok's ford.
Firm hold on Him retaining,
It fights while sinews last;
What cords endure such straining,
These hold forever fast. *CEV*, 40.

Prayer

It was a correct instinct that led to naming the prayer of Jesus in John 17 the *high priestly* prayer, for this outpouring of soul expresses the high mood of One who goes before and draws his own upward with himself out of this world into the light above. To speak with Hebrews, Jesus is the "Forerunner." His supreme desire is that where he is his disciples shall be also (John 14:3; 17:24). He "sanctifies" himself for them, that they also may be "sanctified." *SDJ*, 301.

Praise and prayer are inseparable, because God's very divinity is in his saving habit. EP, 340.

Preaching

Jesus never spoke without a clear sense of the consequence with which his words were fraught. And blessed is the preacher of whom it can be truly said that ministering the Word of God is to him a holy task. HTR/*GG*, 25.

Faith presupposes knowledge, because it needs a mental complex, person or thing, to be occupied about. Therefore, the whole modern idea of preaching Jesus, but preaching him without a creed, is not only theologically, not merely scripturally, but psychologically impossible in itself. *BT*, 389.

To preach a risen Christ means to preach a gospel which claims to come with the demonstration of the Spirit and with power. It means to assume that this world is dead in trespasses and sins; and that no word of persuasion, no force of example, no release from the body, in fact nothing short of a new creation can give it life. This is where the old apostolic gospel of Paul and the modern moralizing interpretations of Christianity part ways. JRL/*GG*, 163.

[Paul] was aware that to his preaching of the gospel there belonged an invisible background, that at every step his presentation of the truth was accompanied by a ministry from heaven conducted by the Christ of glory. His work was for him imbued with divine power; the life-blood of the supernatural pulsed through it. MEM/*GG*, 99–100.

There is nothing to withhold, nothing to conceal: the entire plan of redemption has been unfolded, the mystery hidden through the ages has been revealed, and there is committed to every ambassador of Christ an absolute message, no longer subject to change. Not the delicate procedure of the diplomat, who hides his aim, but the stately stepping forward of the herald who renders an authoritative pronouncement characterizes his task. MEM/*GG*, 92–93.

244

■ There is a straightforwardness, a simplicity in preaching, which is proportionate to the preacher's own faith in the absoluteness, and inherent truthfulness of his message. MEM/*GG*, 93.

■ All the distinctive elements of Paul's preaching relate to Christ, and bear upon their face his image and superscription. God is the Father of our Lord Jesus Christ. The Spirit is the Spirit of Christ. In the procuring of righteousness Christ is the one efficient cause. In Christ believers were chosen, called, justified, and will be glorified. To be converted is to die with Christ and to rise with him. The entire Christian life, root and stem and branch and blossom, is one continuous fellowship with Christ. MEM/*GG*, 94–95.

■ Peace of conscience, renewal of life, assurance of heaven: what more than this could we endeavor to bring to our fellow men? What less than this could we dare to offer them under the name of the gospel? As preachers of Christ and the resurrection, let us always remember to give due prominence to these three great things. Is there not a special satisfaction in being able to proclaim a gospel which so completely covers the needs of a sinful world? JRL/*GG*, 167.

■ There can be a betrayal of the gospel of grace by silence. There can be disloyalty to Christ by omission as well as by positive offense against the message that he has entrusted to our keeping. It is possible, Sabbath after Sabbath and year after year, to preach things of which none can say that they are untrue and none can deny that in their proper place and time they may be important, and yet to forgo telling people plainly and to forgo giving them the distinct impression that they need forgiveness and salvation from sin through the cross of Christ. GP/*GG*, 238.

■ I sometimes feel as if what we need most is a sense of proportion in our presentation of the truth; a new sense of where the center of gravity in the gospel lies; a return to the ideal of Paul who determined not to know anything among the Corinthians save Jesus Christ and him crucified. GP/*GG*, 238.

Whatever topic you preach on and whatever text you choose, there ought not to be in your whole repertoire a single sermon in which from beginning to end you do not convey to your hearers the impression that it is impossible for you to impart to them what you want other than as a correlate and consequence of the eternal salvation of their souls through the blood of Christ, because in your own conviction that alone is the remedy which you can honestly offer to a sinful world. GP/*GG*, 238.

And, oh the pity and shame of it, the Jesus that is being preached but too often is a Christ after the flesh, a religious genius, the product of evolution, powerless to save! MEM/*GG*, 102.

Predestination

Nor does the Bible leave us in doubt as to why such great practical importance for our instruction is attached by God to the discriminating element in predestination. The motive is none other than to impress most profoundly upon the mind of believers the conviction of the absolutely gracious character of their redemption. No stronger way of bringing this out is conceivable than by showing in actual experience that under entirely equal conditions, as viewed from the human standpoint, one man is saved, another is left unsaved in his sin. To use the classical statement of the apostle Paul on this very same problem (Rom. 9:11–12): "For the children being not yet born, neither having done anything good or bad, that the elective purpose of God might stand, not of works, but of him that calleth, it was said unto her, the elder shall serve the younger." BIP/*SW*, 414.

Predestination, and the Active Obedience of Christ

There is an equally intimate connection between predestination and the doctrine of the merits of Christ. Here again a denial of election means a change in the doctrine of Christ's merits. The answer to the question, What did Christ merit for us? must be (1) the satisfaction of guilt and punishment (*strafschuld*) by means of his active obedience. Since Scripture teaches that eternal life includes the whole application of the merits of the Mediator, it must include the

Holy Spirit, who works regeneration, faith, and conversion. But if man makes his decision to believe or not to believe independently, then faith is man's work, and it is no longer the fruit of Christ's merits. That which we give to ourselves Christ cannot have merited for us. And the same thing applies not only to faith but to all other parts of the application of salvation. Denial of predestination implies therefore a denial of the merits of the active obedience of Christ. NST, 145–46.

Pre-millenarianism

Pre-millenarian is an adjective before the implied noun parousia, expressing the assumption that the return of Christ will take place before the millennium. *PE*, 228.

Pre-millenarianism is only a species of eschatological construction, and not the genus. *BT*, 380.

If certain types of post-millennialism leave too little room for eschatology, pre-millenarian schemes bring in too much. *BT*, 380.

Pre-redemptive Special Revelation

We understand by [pre-redemptive special revelation] the disclosure of the principles of a process of probation by which man was to be raised to a state of religion and goodness, higher, by reason of its unchangeableness, than what he already possessed. *BT*, 27.

Preterition

The absoluteness with which the Bible subsumes all events under the sovereign decree of God extends to sinful developments as well as to the morally good activities of men. Consequently, the human unbelief of the gospel which prevents the salvation of many is as truly subject to a divine decree as the faith by which others are saved. No matter whether we call this decree an act of preterition, or give it some other name, the general Bible doctrine on the all-comprehensiveness of the divine decree forces us to recognize it as a reality. BIP/*SW*, 413.

The Bible . . . teaches the principle of preterition, by way of implication, as a corollary of certain other fundamental doctrines. No more is necessary than to combine the two single truths, that all saving grace, inclusive of faith, is the supernatural gift of God, and that not all men are made recipients of this gift, to perceive immediately that the ultimate reason why some are saved and others passed by can lie in God alone. Insofar every confession which adheres to these two primary facts—and no Calvinistic confession could for a moment hesitate to do so—is also bound to imply the doctrine of preterition. BIP/*SW*, 412–13.

It is an utterly futile endeavor to attempt to construe a formula which shall adequately reproduce the scriptural doctrine of election, and yet leave unexpressed the correlated doctrine of preterition . . . for . . . the Bible thinks it necessary to teach us not merely that Christians are predestined by free grace into eternal salvation, but also thinks it necessary persistently to remind us how this appointment of some into life took place from among a number of others who were sovereignly passed by; then this can only mean that in the view of God the principle of preterition is essential to the expression of the most important aspect of the decree of salvation. BIP/*SW*, 414.

There may be many other motives, all equally wise and holy, entering into [God's] choice and which it has not pleased him to reveal to our finite understanding. But this one motive he has made known to us, and thereby also indirectly taught us, that whatever other reasons for his sovereign decree may exist, they can have nothing to do with anything meritorious possessed by one man above another. Thus the sole purport of the doctrine of preterition as presented to our faith in the Scriptures is the exaltation of the grace of God. BIP/*SW*, 414.

Can a church which professes preeminently to uphold the gospel of free grace refuse to echo this part of God's revelation in her confession? And can it be safe for any church to erase from her creed a mode of expressing the divine grace, which God himself has used to instruct us, on the plea that she deems its use unpopular and inexpedient? Shall man be wiser than God? BIP/*SW*, 414.

THE ANTHOLOGY

Pride

▨ Pride is in its essence a form of self-deification. *BT*, 281.

▨ Pride is . . . self-deification, and such self-deifying pride being the controlling principle of diabolical sin, it was not unnatural to find in the king of Babel here described the type of Satan (cf. Luke 10:18; Rev. 9:1). SDFI/*SW*, 283.

Priest, High

▨ [In the] ministry of the day of atonement, prefiguring to an exceptional degree of exactness the high priestly ministry of Christ, the center plainly lay in the high priest's appearance before the face of Jehovah in the most holy place. This and no other act differentiated the task of the high priest from that of every other servant of the tabernacle. He and he alone could thus come near to God and representatively bring the people near. HED/*SW*, 219.

▨ The place of his priesthood was emphatically the holy of holies, not the first tabernacle, far less the court. It might have been truly said that he officiated and could officiate nowhere else than there, and that if he had had to minister in the other compartments of the tabernacle, he would not have been a high priest at all, since ordinary priests and Levites performed this service, leaving nothing distinctive that he could have claimed as his own. HED/*SW*, 219–20.

▨ Now it is altogether probable that the author of Hebrews looked upon the sacrifice of Christ on the cross as exactly corresponding to this act which by the hand of the high priest on the day of atonement took place in the court before the altar of burnt-offering. And since this single act of the high priest in the court does not prevent the Old Testament from assigning him to the holy of holies as the one true scene of his ministry, where alone this can develop its consummate function, so the single act of self-offering by Christ on the earthly mountain does not prevent the author from affirming that his priesthood belongs to heaven as the only sphere where it can truly accomplish its highest purpose, the bringing of the sacrifice and those for whom it is offered near to God. HED/*SW*, 220.

Priest, Office of

A priest is one who stands at the head of others and thus mediates their approach unto God. PC/*SW*, 133.

What is the essence of the office of priest? A priest is one who brings near to God. His function differs from that of a prophet in that the prophet moves from God toward man, whereas the priest moves from man toward God. This idea is found in [Heb. 5:1], where the author gives a quasi-definition of a priest: "For every high priest, being taken from among men, is appointed for men in things pertaining to God, that he may offer both gifts and sacrifices for sins." Thus a priest is one who brings men near to God, who leads them into the presence of God. *TEH*, 94.

The priest himself must approach God first. Therefore the representative element must be included in the conception; the priest brings men to God representatively, through himself. Secondly, in the priest, the nearness to God is not merely *counted* as having taken place for the believers, as a mere imputation. Rather, so close is the connection between the priest and the believers that a contact with God on his part at once involves also a contact with God for them. The contact with God is passed on to them as an electric current through a wire. Thirdly, a priest does not content himself with establishing contact only at one point; he draws the believers after himself, so that they come where he is. *TEH*, 94–95.

The movement of the priestly function is in a direction opposite to that of the prophetic function. The prophet officiates from God to man, represents God with man; the priest officiates from man to God, represents man with God. PC/*SW*, 133.

In [Heb. 5:1] we are given a statement of what a priest does: he acts for man in things pertaining to God, and he brings both gifts and sacrifices for sins. *TEH*, 99.

The priesthood . . . is viewed as embodying in itself the result of all instrumental processes, the attainment of the goal of all religion. Through the priest the people enter representatively into the sanctuary of perfect communion with God. Thus the priest not merely works in their interest, but also receives and enjoys in their behalf the fruit of his own labors. He dwells with God as the first heir of the blessedness to which his ministry has opened the way. PC/*SW*, 137–38.

The priest takes care for man of the things pertaining to God. HED/*SW*, 205.

Gideon and Manoah offered, because Jehovah, in approaching them visibly, sanctioned an immediate exercise of that priestly right, which, belonging to all Israel, was representatively vested only in the Levitical priests. Wherever the LORD appears, there is his altar. To whomsoever he draws near, he gives the right to come near, which is the essence of the priesthood. *MOP*, 219.

Priesthood of Believers

In placing the covenant before Israel Jehovah promised them that under it they would be a kingdom of priests, a holy nation; in other words, that in their collective capacity they would sustain to him the same relation that a priest sustains to the deity in whose temple he ministers (Ex. 19:6). Peter transfers this to the New Testament congregation, addressing his readers as "a holy priesthood, to offer up spiritual sacrifices through Jesus Christ" (1 Peter 2:5). And the seer of the Apocalypse bases a doxology upon the fact that Christ has made believers joint-kings and priests with himself and God, or priests of God and of Christ (Rev. 1:6; 5:10; 20:6). HED/*SW*, 223.

Priesthood of Christ

In the priesthood, the emphasis is on [Christ's] human nature. If he had been an angel, he could not have been a priest. *TEH*, 95.

[The priesthood of Christ means] that Christ's work has a Godward reference, that he sustains a representative relation to believers, that in his lot both in the state of humiliation and in the state of glory he is closely identified with his people, that through the voluntary sacrifice of himself in death he has wrought expiation, that as the first heir and participant of the eschatological state he leads us in the attainment unto glory. HED/*SW*, 214.

His priestly ministry performed on earth certainly partook of the characteristics of the Melchizedek-order. It was eternal in its absoluteness, in its spiritual nature, in its reference to the heavenly world. In all these respects it was the very opposite of the Levitical ministry after the order of Aaron, so that it certainly could in no wise be identified with the latter. Nor is it possible to separate between the high-priestly ministry connected with the death and that performed in heaven, because the latter is but the carrying out of the former, the two constituting one continuous service, inasmuch as Jesus presented before God in heaven the offering brought on earth. PC/*SW*, 157.

The principle to be strenuously maintained is that the priestly activity of Christ in heaven rests on the preceding sacrifice [on earth] and therefore derives from the latter a strictly propitiatory character. PC/*SW*, 154.

It has been observed that the slaying of the sacrifice was not under the Old Testament law the work of the priest, but of the offerer. Jesus might therefore be conceived as first acting in the double capacity of offerer and victim, and then acting, in his exalted state, in the capacity of priest on the basis of the preceding sacrifice. PC/*SW*, 154.

The whole discussion of the priesthood [in Hebrews] serves primarily the end of justifying the necessity of Christ's heavenly state of existence and heavenly mode of ministry. It is intended to bring out the superiority of the spiritual, invisible, as over against the sensual, and visible. PC/*SW*, 131.

The main act of Christ's high-priestly work was the entering in, once for all, into the heavenly holy place, and by this he obtained eternal redemption (Heb. 9:12). The purpose of his priesthood is to cleanse the heavenly things by sacrifice (Heb. 9:23). And all that is said in [Heb. 9–10] about the sacrificial work of Christ presupposes that it has reference to sin. PC/*SW*, 139.

◼ This is the meaning of Christ's being ἀρχηγός and πρόδρομος. As he fulfills the destiny of the race in his lordship over the world to come, so he fulfills its destiny in entering upon the closest contact with God. He is within the veil. If we draw nigh to God it is through the fresh and living way he himself has dedicated. Hence also it is not human nature in the abstract that is demanded for Jesus, but human nature placed in that specific spiritual relation to God which is expressed by the ideas of sonship and faith. PC/*SW*, 141.

◼ [commenting upon Heb. 7:28] The Savior's entire separateness from sin and sinners is emphasized as essential to his priesthood. The comparison is between Christ and the Old Testament high priests, and the former is here described not as he was in his earthly life but as he now is in his exalted state. PC/*SW*, 148.

◼ [Christ] is not merely priest and victim in one, but also plays the part of the Old Testament giver; through him the people of God bring to the altar the required gift that is to make covering for their sin. He represents us both in dying and in offering himself to die. HED/*SW*, 208.

Priesthood of Christ and the Day of Atonement

◼ [commenting on the Epistle to the Hebrews] The author does not so much compare the ministry of Christ to the work of the Old Testament priests in general, but rather to the ministry performed by the high priest on the day of atonement. Now in the law for the day of atonement it is expressly prescribed that the high priest must with his own hand slay the sacrificial animal (Lev. 16:15). . . . [This act was] in the strictest sense of the word an official, high-priestly act. In analogy with this the author may have looked upon the self-surrender of Christ to death as an act of priestly nature. But the slaying of the animal by the high priest took place outside of the tabernacle, and the analogy would require that Jesus' self-sacrifice also should occur outside the heavenly tabernacle, i.e., on earth. Still, from this single act of the high priest outside of the tabernacle it did not follow that . . . his ministry as a whole pertained to the court, and as little does it follow that, because Jesus offered himself up on earth, his ministry as a whole cannot pertain to heaven. PC/*SW*, 159–60.

The ministry of the high priest under the old covenant belonged to the holy of holies, where he alone could officiate, and so the ministry of Christ belongs to heaven, where he alone can be a priest. PC/*SW*, 160.

[commenting upon the Epistle to the Hebrews] The one transaction in the Old Testament ritual on which the epistle dwells more than on any other feature and the act to which it makes the central act of Christ's priestly ministry correspond, is the entrance of the high priest into the holy of holies on the day of atonement. The Savior is a high priest because in the discharge of his ministry he enters into heaven. This is of the very essence of his priestly work. PC/*SW*, 132.

Priesthood of Christ, Locality of

It is throughout [in the Epistle to the Hebrews] represented as a priesthood exercised in heaven. The days of our Lord's flesh were the days of his perfecting, that is, of his equipment for the office, and this equipment included the event of his death, so that the actual entrance upon the function lies beyond his earthly life and coincides with his entrance into heaven (Heb. 2:17). He becomes a high priest forever after the order of Melchizedek when he enters within the veil as our forerunner (Heb. 6:20). In accordance with this he is called a minister of the sanctuary and of the true tabernacle which the Lord pitched, not man, so that, it would seem, his priesthood could have begun only when he entered that heavenly sanctuary (Heb. 8:2). HED/*SW*, 218.

[commenting upon the Epistle to the Hebrews] The author determines the sphere to which Christ's priesthood belongs according to his view concerning the location of its center of gravity. Since this center of gravity lies in the act of bringing near to God, and not in the preparatory operations which were necessary for its accomplishment, the priesthood must have its true home where the approach to God is effected. And this is nowhere else than in the heavenly sanctuary. HED/*SW*, 219.

[Christ] created his own environment. It was within the boundaries of his own personality that the sacrifice was made. Through the eternal Spirit he offered himself up to God, and therefore the acts of his priesthood, though spatially taking place on earth, really belonged to the sphere of the αἰώνιον. Its ideal reference was not to any earthly order of priesthood but in the ministry in heaven, for which it proved the necessary basis. HED/*SW*, 220.

Probation

Man's original state was a state of indefinite probation: he remained in possession of what he had, so long as he did not commit sin, but it was not a state in which the continuance of his religious and moral status could be guaranteed him. In order to assure this for him, he had to be subjected to an intensified, concentrated probation, in which, if he remained standing, the status of probation would be forever left behind. The provision of this new, higher prospect for man was an act of condescension and high favor. *BT*, 22.

Man was to attain something he had not attained before. He was to learn the good in its clear opposition to the evil, and the evil in its clear opposition to the good. Thus it will become plain how he could attain to this by taking either fork of the probation-choice. Had he stood, then the contrast between good and evil would have been vividly present to his mind. . . . The perception of difference in which the maturity consisted related to the one pivotal point, whether man would make his choice for the sake of God and of God alone. *BT*, 31–32.

It was precisely the purpose of the probation to raise man for a moment from the influence of his own ethical inclination to the point of a choosing for the sake of personal attachment to God alone. *BT*, 32.

Promise and Fulfillment

Jesus occupies historic ground from the outset. It is *the* kingdom, the well-known kingdom, with which he presupposes familiarity, not merely on his own part but also on the part of his hearers. Our Lord did not come to found a new religion, but simply to usher in the fulfillment of something promised long beforehand. KOG/*SW*, 304.

Promises of God

[commenting upon the patriarchs] Abraham learned to possess the promises of God, in the promising God alone. The promises had no chance of becoming materialized through detachment from their center in God. They could be had and enjoyed only as a part and potential outflow of the divine heart itself. For the promises are like an ethereal garment, more precious than the body of the promised thing over which it is thrown. Had the promises been quickly fulfilled, then the danger would have immediately arisen of their acquiring importance and value apart from God. *BT*, 87.

Prophecy

Prophecy is objective, being the address of Jehovah to Israel in word and act. EP, 324.

There is no more characteristic trait in prophecy than that it never makes the crisis of judgment a road to mere restoration of what existed before, but the occasion for the bringing in of something wholly new and unexperienced in the past, so that Jehovah comes out of the conflict, not as one who has barely snatched his work from destruction, but as the great Victor who has made the forces of sin and evil his servants for the accomplishment of a higher and wider purpose. WT/*GG*, 7.

[commenting upon the phrase, "spoken by God through the prophet"] If the one from whom the prophetic word proceeded is God, then it will follow that the word ceases to be a dead utterance shut up in itself; it becomes invested with the divine power of projecting itself across the ages and omnipotently creating its own counterpart of fulfillment. This thought has found pointed expression in the statement that God's word cannot return to him void, but must prove able to accomplish that which he pleases and to prosper in the thing whereto he sent it. For this reason it is compared to the rain and the snow which water the earth and make it bring forth and bud, to give both seed and bread (Isa. 55:10–11). In other words, the "dabar Jahweh" is never in its entire course separated from God who spake it; it possesses and retains a divine efficacy that cannot fail to precipitate itself into a new reality. IFP/*SW*, 353.

▋ The prophets did not create facts, they upheld principles; and whatever future facts they spoke of were placed by them in the pure light of prediction. Through prophecy biblical religion has first come to be, to the extent it is, the religion of truth, of faith, of Scripture. In this respect the prophets were the precursors of Protestantism, at least from a formal point of view. More than ever before, the religious consciousness of Israel felt itself bound up with the cardinal fact of revelation. Jehovah's approach to Israel is eminently the approach of speech; God gives himself in the word of his mouth. *BT*, 187.

▋ It goes without saying that the prophetic orientation is God-centered. This is but another way of saying that it is religious, for without that, no religion deserving that name can exist. The prophets feel this so instinctively that they have no need nor occasion for reflecting upon or expressing it. It is only when reaching its highest point, and becoming a veritable passion for Jehovah, that it sets its crown upon itself by reflecting upon its own nature and delighting in its own expression. For in religion everywhere, not the instinctive, unreflected, but the clearly-recognized, the thoroughly illuminated, constitutes the finest product of the process. *BT*, 234.

Prophet(s)

▋ Every bearer of the Spirit forms a link of connection between man and the higher world. In the ecstatic state the Spirit lifts the prophet into the supernatural sphere, which is peculiarly its own. Even in his ordinary life the prophet is, on account of his pneumatic character, as it were, concentrated upon a higher world; "he sits alone because of Jehovah's hand" (Jer. 15:17). EAP/*SW*, 97.

The prophets affirm and imply everywhere a real communication from Jehovah to themselves. They believe themselves recipients of revelation in the solid, unmodernized, unsubjectivized, original sense of the word. *BT*, 212.

The prophets were guardians of the unfolding theocracy, and the guardianship was exercised at its center, the kingdom. The purpose was to keep it a true representation of the kingdom of Jehovah. *BT*, 186.

In a sense which made them true types of Christ the prophets bore the unfaithfulness of the people on their hearts. As Jesus had a sorrowful acquaintance with the spirit no less than the body of the cross, so they were led to explore the deeper meaning of the judgment, to enter recesses of its pain undreamt of by the sinners in Israel themselves. JP/*SW*, 288.

The prophet was not placed as a stranger in the midst of a mass of unassimilated material, but made at home in a world of truth where he would discover on all sides the correlates and implications of the supreme thought that filled his soul. Such a supreme thought is, for example, in Amos the absolute energy of the divine justice, and in Hosea the tenderness of Jehovah's covenant-love for Israel notwithstanding her sin. SDFI/*SW*, 272.

For it is true of the past as well as of the future, that the prophet's eye takes in more than a single day: it covers periods, and sees them in the light of their most significant features. Hence the prophet Moses, looking back upon the last forty years, could even in the fields of Moab, at the dawn of a new period, truthfully say, "Not as we are *now* accustomed to do." *MOP*, 93.

In the repertoire of the prophets the choicest always belongs to the farthest. When their eye rests on the world to come, a miracle is wrought in their speech, so that, in accord with the things described, it borrows from the melodies of the other world. WT/*GG*, 2.

■ It is not to be expected of any prophet that he shall put into his prophecies relating to the end indiscriminately of his treasure, but chiefly what is to him its most precious part, that which the Spirit of revelation had led him, and him above others, to apprehend and appreciate. WT/*GG*, 2.

■ As the second Adam is greater than the first, and the paradise of the future fairer than that of the past, so the newborn Israel to the prophet's vision is a nobler figure and exists under far more favorable conditions than the empirical Israel of before. WT/*GG*, 7.

Prophet(s), and the Law

■ Prophecy presupposes the law, roots itself in it, and grows out of it. The legal and formal is before the spiritual and ideal, not in the mind of God, but in its historical realization. *MOP*, 172.

■ So far as we know, the mission of all prophets was to enforce and vindicate the law. They never pretend to introduce a new religion, never require of the people that it shall commit itself to unreasonable authority. All their appeals are addressed to the conscience, the moral or national consciousness of Israel, both of which presuppose the law as their root and norm. *MOP*, 230.

Prophet(s), Office of

■ [A priest's] function differs from that of a prophet in that the prophet moves from God toward man, whereas the priest moves from man toward God. *TEH*, 94.

■ The prophet officiates from God to man, represents God with man. PC/*SW*, 133.

■ The Son's unique greatness, his difference from, his exaltation above man constitutes his chief qualification for the revealership. As a revealer he represents not man but God; therefore the nearer he stands to God the better he is qualified. PC/*SW*, 134.

Jehovah does not endeavor to teach Moses what a prophet is. He takes for granted that Moses knows this, and on that supposition constructs the analogy wherein Moses figures as a god and Aaron as a prophet. Whatever the etymology of the name in its origin, to the Old Testament mind the prophet stood from beginning to end as the authoritative speaker for Jehovah [and this] marks the religion of the Old Testament as a religion of conscious intercourse between Jehovah and Israel, a religion of revelation, of authority, a religion in which God dominates, and in which man is put into the listening, submissive attitude. *BT*, 193.

Prophetism

Prophetism at its rise marks an epoch in sacred history. The modern hypothesis, however, having reduced everything in the oldest period to a naturalistic level, is bound to make this epoch a creative one; to it the prophets are the originators of the unique ethical and religious teaching Israel has given to the world, whereas according to the traditional view the prophets simply enforced and applied and developed what was already contained, germinally at least, in the Mosaic revelation. RCEP, 215.

Providence of God

Providence is the execution of the decree. God's providence includes not one point that does not also occur in the decree, and nothing of that over which God's providence extends can be eliminated from the decree. NST, 133.

The decree is providence in outline, but that outline is an approved outline and it bears in itself the mark of the possibility of realization. He who might be of the opinion that God decreed certain things without decreeing the means only needs to be pointed to providence, where means and ends are constantly related to each other. NST, 133.

Psalter

The Psalter is of all books of the Bible that book which gives expression to the experimental side of religion. In the law and the prophetic writings, it is God who speaks to his people; but in the Psalter we listen to the saints speaking to God. SFS/*GG*, 169.

Some of the Psalms . . . reach the . . . high altitude, where the soul rises above every thought of self, even above the consciousness of its own need of salvation, and desires and receives God for his own sake. HED/*SW*, 186.

Our Lord himself, who had a perfect religious experience and lived and walked with God in absolute adjustment of his thoughts and desires to the Father's mind and will, our Lord himself found his inner life portrayed in the Psalter and in some of the highest moments of his ministry borrowed from it the language in which his soul spoke to God, thus recognizing that a more perfect language for communion with God cannot be framed. SFS/*GG*, 169–70.

In the Psalter it is the individual soul which comes face to face with God. SFS/*GG*, 170–71.

The deeper fundamental character of the Psalter consists in this that it voices the subjective response to the objective doings of God for and among his people. EP, 324.

Christ was in the Psalms and back of their writers; Christ and his mystical body are one; consequently the church spake in the Psalter. EP, 330.

We have here a great province of objectivity translated into terms of living religion, and that religion at the very acme of its functioning. The Psalter teaches us before all else what the proper, ideal attitude of the religious mind ought to be with reference to its vision of the absolute future. EP, 332.

If one will only read and sing with the understanding, he shall perceive that the psalmists pray and sing out of a rich knowledge of

God. It is not for nothing that they have "meditated" upon him and his works. EP, 333.

Psalter and Eschatology

It is Jehovah's rest which the psalmist desires Israel to enter; the city of his vision is the city of God. EP, 350.

If the great change, the reversal of destiny, the deliverance, the victory so often spoken of in the Psalms, concern not individuals, but Israel, or even the pious nucleus of Israel, is it not plain that this whole complex of ideas moves on eschatological ground? What else could such a crisis, such a marvelous turn for the better, nay for the best, when predicated of Israel, mean but the eschatological transformation? EP, 331.

[A] striking feature of the eschatology of the Psalter consists in the central, dominating position it assigns to Jehovah in all that pertains to the coming change. The prospect of the future is God-centered in the highest degree. EP, 338.

When the psalmists make eschatology the anchor of salvation, this is not done in a self-centered spirit. [The psalmist] is able to forget [his own woes] for the overwhelming thought of the glory of Jehovah. The *gloria in excelsis* which the Psalter sings arises not seldom from a veritable *de profundis* and, leaving behind the storm-clouds of distress, mounts before Jehovah in the serenity of a perfect praise. EP, 339.

Rabbi

[*Rabbi* was used in Gospel times] in a great variety of applications, in all of which the ideas of obedience and submission stood in the foreground to a far greater extent than in the average relation between a modern pupil and teacher. *SDJ*, 133.

Rainbow, Sign of

The representation with regard to the sign of the rainbow is anthropomorphic, but for that very reason more impressive than it could possibly be otherwise. The idea is not, as usually assumed, that by the bow man will be reminded of the divine promise, but that God himself, were it possible for him to forget, will by the sign himself be reminded of his oath: "When I bring a cloud over the earth, it shall come to pass that the bow shall be seen in the cloud, and I will remember my *berith*." *BT*, 55.

Ransom

A ransom is something which buys the freedom of a person. CDW/*GG*, 250.

The ransom is nothing else but the price paid to God the Judge in the last day for the deliverance of a soul from eternal retribution. CDW/*GG*, 252.

What [Jesus] did was to give [his] life as a ransom. That is to say he deliberately took his life and put it into the bondage of guilt and shame and death in which our lives were held by the divine justice. To become a ransom means to take the place of the other and accept all the consequences. And this Jesus did. CDW/*GG*, 254.

Underneath the service rendered by Jesus to men lay a service rendered to God. He gave his life *for* men, but he gave it *to* God. The ransom which effected our freedom was paid to the divine justice, paid to satisfy God. CDW/*GG*, 255.

Rationalism

Rationalism is from its cradle devoid of historic sense. It despises tradition; the past it ignores and the future it barely tolerates with a supercilious conceit of self. Moreover rationalism is bent upon and enamored of the inward. To it the essence and value of all religion lie in purely-subjective ethico-religious experiences. *PE*, preface.

[Rationalism] is defective, ethically considered, in that it shows a tendency toward glorification of its own present (that is, at bottom, *of itself*) over against the future no less than the past. *BT*, 10.

Recapitulation Theory of the Book of Revelation

▩ The principle of "recapitulation," i.e., of contemporaneousness of things successively depicted, seems to underlie the visions, and numbers are elsewhere in the book meant symbolically. ENT/*SW*, 44.

Reconciliation

▩ [commenting upon 2 Cor. 5] Because God has brought about the reconciliation in Christ, Christ himself is supremely interested in the attainment of the end for which it was designed. This being so, the appeal [for reconciliation] made by Paul is in reality an appeal made on behalf of, for the sake of, in the interest of, Christ. TPCR/*SW*, 363.

Redemption

▩ First of all, redemption is . . . portrayed as, before everything else, a deliverance from an objective realm of sin and evil. *BT*, 110.

▩ In redemption God opens up himself to us and surrenders his inner life to our possession in a wholly unprecedented manner of which the religion of nature can have neither dream nor anticipation. WT/*GG*, 6.

▩ Herein lies one of the chief glories of the work of redemption, that it produces in the heart and mind of the sinner such a profound, ineffaceable impression of the realities in God. HTR/*GG*, 37.

▩ [Paul ascribes] to God in the process of redemption [a] threefold relationship. . . . He bought us for himself with reference to his love; he bought us through himself, viz., in Christ; he bought us from himself with reference to his justice or wrath. PCR/*SW*, 371.

Reformed Theology

▩ A consciousness of strict accountability in view of God's sovereign rights over man has always characterized the Reformed religion, even to such an extent as to invite the charge that its puritanic practice savors of a spirit of legalism more at home in the Old Testament than in the New. But legalism has nothing to do with this; it is here . . . simply the correlate in life of the vivid impression of the majesty of God in belief. Legalism lacks the supreme sense of worship. It obeys but it does not adore. And no deeper notes of adoration have ever been struck than those inspired by the Reformed faith; no finer fruit of the lips making confession to God's name has ever been placed upon the Christian altar. HED/*SW*, 231–32.

Had there been no sin in the world, even then [Paul] would not have been able to conceive of an ideal religious relation between God and man, without a solid substructure of a forensic nature rendering the whole religious process subordinate to the revealed moral excellence of God. It is to the credit of Reformed theology that it has appreciated this deeper motive of the Pauline doctrine and has given it formal recognition in its conception of the covenant of works. It was enabled to do this because it took its stand theocentrically in the supremacy of the glory of God. AL/*SW*, 397–98.

Whatever has grown in synergistic soil cannot bear any healthy Reformed fruits. DCRT/*SW*, 235.

[commenting upon the original state of man] The Reformed view fixes its gaze on something higher. It sees man not as being placed in eternal bliss from the beginning, but as being placed in such a way that he might attain to eternal bliss. There still hovers above him the possibility of sin and death which is given with his mutable freedom. He is free to do the good out of his good nature, but he has not yet attained the highest freedom which can do good only. The latter is placed before him as an ideal. DCRT/*SW*, 243.

We have [in Reformed theology] the strongest recognition of the antecedent work of God. Man cannot create the good for himself, but he has to develop the divinely given good that lies within him. DCRT/*SW*, 244.

[The Reformed felt the necessity] to leave the waves of Rome's salvation by works . . . but beside and behind this necessity there lay a deeper longing: a thirst for the glory of God that did not primarily meditate on its own peace. When the Reformed takes the obtaining of salvation completely out of man's hands, he does this so that the glory which God gets from it might be uncurtailed. What is important for him is the realization that God glorifies himself in the salvation of sinners. DCRT/*SW*, 247.

Reformed theology ascribes to the Christian life a unique degree of devotion to the interests and the glory of God. The believer does not merely desire to have intercourse with God, but specifically to make this intercourse subservient to glorifying God. Hence on the one hand the high place which the direct worship of God holds in the exercise of the religious function, on the other hand the consistent effort to organize the whole of life on the principle of a comprehensive service of God, the religious impulse imparting to every human activity and achievement that spirit by which they are made to redound to the honoring of God's name. No brighter examples of absolute devotion and self-surrender to God in unstinted covenant service can be found anywhere than in the annals of the Reformed faith. HED/*SW*, 232.

The root idea which served as the key [for Reformed theology] to unlock the rich treasuries of the Scriptures was the preeminence of God's glory in the consideration of all that has been created. DCRT/*SW*, 241–42.

Reformed Theology and Lutheran Theology

Reformed theology has this in common with Rome over against the Lutherans that it distinguishes between the original state of man in which he was placed by creation and the ideal destiny he was yet to obtain through obedience. From the Reformed standpoint this is expressed in the conception of the *foedus operum*. GD2/*SW*, 492.

All other explanations of the difference between the Lutheran and the Reformed traditions in the end come down to this, that the former begins with man and the later with God. God does not exist because of man, but man because of God. This is what is written at the entrance of the temple of Reformed theology. DCRT/*SW*, 242.

Reformed Theology and the Epistle to the Hebrews

▨ In no other theology have the principles that shape the epistle [to the Hebrews] been so fully and faithfully incorporated as in that produced by the Reformed churches. . . . It may be briefly pointed out how in the Reformed theology the same great perceptions lie embedded that we have found shaping the doctrine of the epistle. The first place should be given to the recognition of the majesty and sovereignty of God in the whole process of religion and redemption. It is all embraced in a διαθήκη, a comprehensive system, and in this system all things are of God. His is the originality in conceiving, his the initiative in inaugurating, his the monergism in carrying out. There is no room for any fortuitousness of chance, any uncertainty of issue, no point anywhere where the hand of God is not in absolute control. It is a system that has an oath of God and a sponsorship of Christ back of all its provisions. HED/*SW*, 231.

Regeneration

▨ The term "to be begotten again" or "to be born again" does not always have the same meaning in Scripture. Sometimes it stands for that fundamental act whereby God implants a new spiritual life in us deep beneath our consciousness and beneath all our experience in the center of our nature. In that case regeneration is confined, as it were, to a single point and from this point the implanted life expands and unfolds itself. But there is also in the New Testament a wider conception of regeneration, according to which it describes the change in us as it presents itself to our own conscious experience and therefore the change not of a single point within us but the change as reflected in the entire compass of our consciousness. It is the coming in of the new life as a complex, rich world of new relations, new realities and new reactions. In this sense Paul says that when anybody is in Christ, he is a new creation (2 Cor. 5:17); not merely a new creature, but a new creation—behold the old things have passed away, all around him has become new. CH/*GG*, 148–49.

Religion

Religion is love of God or a sense of dependence upon God but not entirely after the same manner as we cherish love for our fellow creatures or feel dependent on them in certain relations. Religion begins when we realize our dependence on the absolute, infinite being, the eternal, omnipresent, omnipotent, omniscient God. OHGG/*GG*, 268.

If not the essence, creaturely dependence is certainly the foundation of all religion. The seat of religion lies not in the intellect, nor in the will, nor in the feelings exclusively, but in the center of man's life. *GD1/SW*, 479.

The directness and immediacy pertaining to every true exercise of religion in the ethereal Christian sense render it imperative that [the Messiah] shall himself belong to the category of the divine. Otherwise our communion with God would be intercepted and diverted by him to the impairment or nullification of it as a religious act. *SDJ*, 29.

So far from being a matter of gloom and depression, religion in its true concept is an exultant state, the supreme feast and sabbath of the soul. WT/*GG*, 5.

[commenting upon the temptation of Christ] [Satan] appeals to Jesus' deep-seated instinct for obedience and service. . . . This seems an attempt to betray him into that form of religious subjectiveness, wherein it makes no longer much difference who or what the object of service is, provided there be scope for the unfettered assertion of the religious instinct. This, of course, gives rise to a pseudo-religion, in which the processes are governed by man and not by God. Religion is not worship or service in the abstract; it is worship and service of the true God, and according to his revelation specifically. *BT*, 339.

Here lies the infallible test of what is truly religious in our so-called religion. Everything that lacks the unique reference to God, as its supreme owner and end, is automatically ruled out from that sphere. Anything that is cherished and cultivated apart from God (in such a sense that we cannot carry it with us in the Godward movement of our life) becomes necessarily a hindrance, a profanation, and at last a source of idolatry. WT/*GG*, 15.

▮ The beauty of Jesus' teaching on the nature of God consists in this, that he keeps the exaltation of God above every creature and his loving condescension toward the creature in perfect equilibrium and makes them mutually fructified by each other. Religion is more than the inclusion of God in the general altruistic movement of the human mind; it is a devotion at every point colored by the consciousness of that divine uniqueness in which God's omnipotence occupies a foremost place. OM/*ISBE*, 2190.

▮ Religion, which by its very nature seeks to eternalize its possession of God, feels the need of doing so not merely with reference to the future, but also with reference to the past. In his consciousness of election the believer carries within himself the sublime assurance that in the eternal life of God himself there has never been a moment in which even the idea of his personality was indifferent to God. SDL/*SW*, 455.

Religion and Communion with God

▮ Religion means personal intercourse between God and man. Hence it might be *a priori* expected that God would not be satisfied, and would not allow man to be satisfied with an acquaintance based on indirection, but would crown the process of religion with the establishment of face-to-face communion, as friend holds fellowship with friend. *BT*, 22.

▮ The Scriptures teach that [God] is all-sufficient unto himself and forever blessed in himself. Nevertheless having created man, it is natural in God to receive man as an inmate of his house and companion of his own blessed life. God himself takes pleasure in the immediate personal fellowship with us to which he invites us. There is that in him which corresponds to the highest in our religion. SFS/*GG*, 176.

■ What must ever be the essence of religion, a true communion between God and man. *KGC*, 25.

■ [commenting upon Ps. 25:14] The covenant being conceived [here] not as a formal contract . . . but as a communion in which life touches life and intertwines with life so that the two become mutually assimilated. Evidently the psalmists recognize in this private intercourse with God the highest function of religion—the only thing that will completely satisfy the child of God. SFS/*GG*, 173.

■ [commenting upon Ps. 25:14] What the psalmist strives after is nothing more nor less than that mutual revelation of person to person, that grasping of God himself in the various forms of his approach unto us which is the culminating act of all religion. It is safe to say that both in the guarding of this idea from every kind of mystical excess and perversion, and in the thoroughness on the other hand of its application within the proper limits imposed by the personality of God, the biblical religion stands unique among the religions of the world. You may find enough elsewhere of absorption into the deity, just as you may find plenty in other quarters of co-ordination between the gods and men as if the two had separated spheres of life. But you will find nowhere such a clear grasp upon the principle that from the very nature of religion man is designed to hold converse with God and to become practically acquainted with him. SFS/*GG*, 175–76.

Religion and Eschatology

■ When we say that the biblical religion is an eschatological religion, we mean that it ascribes to the world-process a definite goal such as cannot be attained by it in the natural course of events, but will be brought about catastrophically through a divine interposition, and which, when once attained, bears the stamp of eternity. In the center of this eschatology-complex stands the Messiah. *SDJ*, 19.

Religion and Redemption

We all know that religion is older than redemption. At the same time the experience of redemption is the summit of religion. HM/*GG*, 121.

Religion and the Covenant

[commenting upon the Epistle to the Hebrews] Religion is to his view so essentially and so inevitably a matter of mutual union and fellowship in the conscious sphere, that its manner of appearance and mode of exercise cannot help suggesting the thought of the covenant even where there is no conscious desire on the writer's part to obtrude it upon our attention. HED/*SW*, 227.

[commenting upon the Epistle to the Hebrews] [The covenant] appears as constituting in itself the ideal of religion realized, the perfect covenant being the consummate approach and nearness to God. As such it is the highest category of religion itself. PC/*SW*, 137.

Religion and the World to Come

Did you ever observe what is the thought that seems to have most acutely distressed and perplexed the writers of some of the Psalms when they tried in vain to pierce [the] veil of mystery enveloping to them the future world? It was the fear that in these strange regions there might be no remembrance of God, no knowledge of his goodness, no praise of his glory. We may be assured that when a religious want is projected into the world to come in this way, so that the fear of its not being satisfied proves stronger than the fear of death in itself, we may be sure that there it has been recognized as the supreme, the essential thing in religion. SFS/*GG*, 179.

Jesus was not a person the center of whose thought lay in the natural relation of man to God, with a little fringe remaining upon him from the outworn garment of apocalyptic. He lived and moved and had his being in the world of the supernatural. The thought of the world to come was to him the life-breath of religion. *SDJ*, 24–25.

Ours is a religion whose center of gravity lies beyond the grave in the world to come. . . . Christianity does many things for the present life, but if we wish to apprehend how much it can do, we must direct our gaze to the life beyond. JRL/*GG*, 165.

The vanishing of the belief in the transcendent importance of the world to come would most surely spell the death of the Christian religion itself. Whatever may have been possible under Old Testament conditions, in the beginnings of revelation, it is absolutely impossible now with the New Testament behind us to construe a religious relationship between God and man on the basis of and within the limits of the present life alone. A religion which touched only the little span of consciousness between birth and death would be a pseudo-religion and its God a pseudo-God. EP, 364.

[commenting upon 1 Cor. 15:19] What else does this mean other than that the Christian's main thinking, feeling and striving revolve around the future state; and that, if this goal should prove to have no objective reality, the absoluteness with which the believer has staked everything in its attainment must make him appear in his delusion the most pitiable of all creatures? What a gulf then lies between this statement of the apostle and the sentiment we sometimes meet with—that Christianity had better disencumber itself of all idle speculation about an uncertain future state and concentrate its energies upon the improvement of the present world. Paul could not have entertained such a sentiment for a moment because the thirst for the world to come was of the very substance of the religion of his heart. JRL/*GG*, 165–66.

Religion, Necessity of Doctrine and Life in

When thus the soul inwardly delights in the infinite perfections of Jehovah, then and not until then is fear changed into reverence; or, as the prophet [Isaiah] calls it, humility of spirit. But it is impossible to cultivate such worship (the highest flower of religion) where the perception of God's transcendent glory has been obscured. Religion may not be metaphysics, but there is a theology of the heart, the banishment of which means blight and starvation for all vital piety. OHGG/*GG*, 268.

There is no better means of silencing the supercilious cant that right believing is of small importance in the matter of religion, than by showing what infinite care our Father in heaven has taken to reveal unto us, in the utmost perfection, the *knowledge* of what he is and does for our salvation. IBT/*SW*, 24.

Religious Life

[commenting upon Hosea 14:8] This prophetic utterance represents one of the two inseparable sides in the make-up of religion. If we say that religion consists of what God is for man, and of what man is for God, then our text in the divine statement, "From me is thy fruit found," stands for the former. To balance it with the other side some such word as that of Isaiah might be taken, "The vineyard of Jehovah of hosts is the house of Israel." . . . Until we learn to unite the Isaiah type of piety with that of Hosea, we shall not attain a full and harmonious development of our religious life. WT/*GG*, 1.

I need not tell you that there is a tendency at the present day to make the religious life seek the surface, the periphery; to detach it more or less from its center which lies in the direct face-to-face communion of the soul with God. SFS/*GG*, 179.

Repentance

The specific character of biblical repentance, as distinguished from experiences so named in paganism, lies first of all in the comprehensiveness of the turn of mind. It is "after-sorrow," or reversal of consciousness, or redirection of the life upon an opposite goal, with regard to the whole content of the ethico-religious life. *BT*, 397.

In the crisis of repentance the offense against God and the need of God are that upon which the repenting consciousness is focused. The sorrow of true repentance is one which arises from conviction of sin. It is also a sorrow after God, such as proceeds from a sense of spiritual destitution. *KGC*, 93.

■ True repentance strips sin of all that is accidental. It resembles an inner chamber where no one and nothing else is admitted except God and the sinner and his sin. HTR/*GG*, 37.

■ A repentant sinner acquits God and condemns himself. HTR/*GG*, 37.

■ God is the central object on whom the repenting consciousness is focused; it is the offense offered to him that stands in the foreground of the sorrow experienced. *BT*, 398.

■ The new direction of life which the repentance brings about finds its explanation in the absolute and exclusive subjection of the whole life with all its desires and purposes to God. *BT*, 398.

■ Of the three words that are used in the Greek Gospels to describe the process, one emphasizes the emotional element of regret, sorrow over the past evil course of life, *metamelomai* (Matt. 21:29–32); a second expresses reversal of the entire mental attitude, *metanoeō*, (Matt. 12:41; Luke 11:32; 15:7, 10); the third denotes a change in the direction of life, one goal being substituted for another, *epistrephomai* (Matt. 13:15 and parallels; Luke 17:4; 22:32). *KGC*, 92.

■ Repentance is not limited to any single faculty of the mind: it engages the entire man, intellect, will and affections. Nor is it confined to the moral sphere of life in the narrower sense: it covers man's entire religious as well as his moral relation to God. *KGC*, 92.

■ [commenting upon the parable of the prodigal son] Jesus [here] has so marvelously described the psychological process of repentance. The prodigal "comes to himself." Previously he had been out of himself, had not known and felt himself in the simple truth of his fundamental relation to God. He realizes that he perishes with hunger, whilst in his Father's house there is bread enough and to spare. *KGC*, 93.

274

Again, in the new life which follows repentance the absolute supremacy of God is the controlling principle. He who repents turns away from the service of mammon and self to the service of God. Our Lord is emphatic in insisting upon this absolute, undivided surrender of the soul to God as the goal of all true repentance. *KGC*, 93.

Repentance, Relationship to the Kingdom of God

[commenting upon Luke 14:16–24] It is plain from the nature of the invitation, that what this wedding garment stands for is not to be regarded as in any way entitling the bearer to a place at the feast. Those who come are taken from the highways and hedges, from the streets and lanes of the city and compelled to enter. They are received, therefore, without merit on their part, on the principle of free grace. Nevertheless, when once within, it is indispensable that they should wear the garment appropriate to the occasion. Thus repentance and righteousness, while they do not in any meritorious sense earn the benefits of the kingdom, are yet indispensable concomitants of the state in which alone these benefits can be received. *KGC*, 92.

Repristination

Repristination [to restore to an original state or condition] may sometimes be necessary, but even at its best, even when it is repristination of that which is good and of permanent value, it is little conducive toward a healthy spiritual growth and development, least of all so when it aims at the revival of something that has served its purpose and is close to vanishing. RR/*GG*, 126.

Rest

The rest of the land of Canaan given to Israel of old was a type of the supreme rest opened up by Jesus in the new covenant. But this rest of Canaan was by no means the first or original embodiment of the religious idea of rest. Back of it and above it lay in the heavenly world the "sabbatismos" of God spoken of in the account of creation, and which is identical with the Christian rest, since believers are received by God into the rest that is his own. HED/*SW*, 202.

[commenting upon the fourth commandment] In connection with God, "rest" cannot, of course, mean mere cessation from labor, far less recovery from fatigue. Such a meaning is by no means required by the Old Testament usage of the word. "Rest" resembles the word "peace" in this respect, that it has in Scripture, in fact to the Shemitic mind generally, a positive rather than a negative import. It stands for consummation of a work accomplished and the joy and satisfaction attendant upon this. Such was its prototype in God. Mankind must copy this, and that not only in the sequences of daily existence as regards individuals; but in its collective capacity through a large historic movement. For mankind, too, a great task waits to be accomplished, and at its close beckons a rest of joy and satisfaction that shall copy the rest of God. *BT*, 139–40.

Inasmuch as the old covenant was still looking forward to the performance of the messianic work, naturally the days of labor to it come first, the day of rest falls at the end of the week. We, under the new covenant, look back upon the accomplished work of Christ. We, therefore, first celebrate the rest in principle procured by Christ, although the Sabbath also still remains a sign looking forward to the final eschatological rest. The Old Testament people of God had to typify in their life the future developments of redemption. *BT*, 141.

Resurrection

By raising Christ from death, God as the supreme Judge set his seal to the absolute perfection and completeness of his atoning work. The resurrection is a public announcement to the world that the penalty of death has been borne by Christ to its bitter end and that in consequence the dominion of guilt has been broken, the curse annihilated forevermore. JRL/*GG*, 161.

The resurrection . . . serves for restoring what has become the prey of decadence and death. *PE*, 72.

For Paul, the resurrection stands in the center of the gospel as a gospel of justification—of deliverance from the guilt of sin. To him, the one religious question which overshadows in importance all others is the question: "How shall a sinful man become righteous in the sight of God?" Now if the resurrection of Christ had nothing to contribute towards the solution of this one stupendous problem, then (whatever significance in other connections might belong to it) it could scarcely be said to be of the heart of the gospel. JRL/*GG*, 157.

The crucifixion and the resurrection of Christ were acts not exclusively intended to reveal something to man, but primarily intended to serve some definite purpose in reference to God. IBT/*SW*, 9.

The NT confines the event of the resurrection to a single epoch, and nowhere teaches, as chiliasm assumes, a resurrection in two stages, one, at the parousia, of saints or martyrs, and a second one at the close of the millennium. ENT/*SW*, 43.

[Jesus] regards doubt concerning the resurrection as doubt concerning the supernatural exercise of the power of God. *SDJ*, 23.

Heaven and earth were concerned in this event; it was the turning-point of the ages. Nor was this merely objectively so: Jesus felt himself the central figure in this new-born universe; he tasted the exquisite joy of one who had just entered upon an endless life in the possession of new powers and faculties such as human nature had never known before. R/*GG*, 75–76.

[commenting upon 1 Cor. 15:55–57] [Resurrection] is pictured as the swallowing up of death in victory, and death is here pointedly named as the penalty for sin imposed by the law, so that the resurrection is the final removal of the condemnation of sin. *PE*, 152–53.

That the resurrection is made prominent by Paul as a saving factor can never be made to prove that the atoning death had not the emphasis to Paul's mind traditionally ascribed to it. As a matter of fact the resurrection has its dynamic not only side by side with the effect of the death, but even in virtue of the latter. *PDR*, 139.

It would be unworthy of God to take into the fellowship of his own perfect life a being which he did not intend to raise to the full fruition of communion with himself of which its nature is capable. He is not a God of the dead but of the living, and life in this pregnant sense postulates the resurrection of the body. OLDR/*SW*, 320.

The truth about God and the reality of the resurrection for [Jesus] stand and fall together (Matt. 22:32). OLDR/*SW*, 320.

The resurrection of Jesus anticipates and secures the general resurrection. EAP/*SW*, 93.

Peter looked upon the risen Christ as the beginning, the firstfruits of that new world of God in which the believer's hope is anchored. Jesus did not rise as he had been before, but transformed, glorified, eternalized, the possessor and author of a transcendent heavenly life at one and the same time, the revealer, the sample and the pledge of the future realization of the true kingdom of God. CH/*GG*, 150.

Resurrection and Assurance

It is just as impossible that any one for whom Christ rose from the dead should fail to receive the righteousness of God as it is that God should undo the resurrection of Christ itself. Consequently, knowing ourselves one with Christ, we find in the resurrection the strongest possible assurance of pardon and peace. When Christ rose on Easter morning he left behind him in the depths of the grave every one of our sins; there they remain buried from the sight of God so completely that even in the day of judgment they will not be able to rise up against us any more. JRL/*GG*, 161–62.

Resurrection and Christianity

The great question for us all is not whether we shall believe or disbelieve the resurrection as a single historic event, but whether we shall maintain or surrender the character of Christianity as a resurrection-religion—a religion able to bring life out of death, both here and hereafter. Can the choice be difficult for any of us? JRL/*GG*, 165.

[commenting upon 1 Cor. 15] We may say Paul here exhibits the resurrection as that toward which everything in Christianity tends;

the goal in which all thinking and striving and hoping of believers find perfect rest and triumphant solution. JRL/*GG*, 156.

[The resurrection] is, next to the cross, the outstanding event of redemptive history. But Paul has first made it a focus of *fundamental* Christian teaching and built around it the entire conception of the faith advocated and propagated by him. *PE*, 147–48.

Resurrection and Judgment

The two overtowering final events in the drama of eschatology are the resurrection and the judgment. As we shall presently see they are the points where the rivers of history issue into the ocean. *PE*, 72.

Resurrection and Justification

In the justification of Christ lie the certainty and the root of the Christian's resurrection. For the supreme fruit of Christ's justification, on the basis of passive and active obedience, is nothing else but the Spirit, and in turn the Spirit bears in himself the efficacious principle of all transformation to come, the resurrection with its entire compass included. Resurrection thus comes out of justification, and justification comes, after a manner most carefully to be defined, out of the resurrection; not, be it noted, out of the spiritual resurrection of the believer himself, but out of the resurrection of Christ. On the basis of merit this is so. Christ's resurrection was the *de facto* declaration of God in regard to his being just. *PE*, 151.

Resurrection and Last Things

The general resurrection of the saints being an eschatological event, indeed constituting together with the judgment the main content of the eschatological program, it follows that to Paul in this one point at least the eschatological course of events had already been set in motion; an integral piece of "the last things" has become an accomplished fact. EAP/*SW*, 92–93.

Resurrection and New Creation

We do not sufficiently realize the profound sense the early church had of the epoch-making significance of the appearance, and especially of the resurrection of the Messiah. The latter was to them nothing less than the bringing in of a new, the second, creation. And they felt that this ought to find expression in the placing of the Sabbath with reference to the other days of the week. Believers knew themselves in a measure partakers of the Sabbath-fulfillment. *BT*, 142.

[commenting upon Rom. 1:3–4] [Paul] wished to contrast the resurrection-process in a broad generic way with the processes of this natural life; the resurrection is characteristic of the beginning of a new order of things, as sarkic birth is characteristic of an older order of things. What stands before the apostle's mind is the contrast between the two aeons, for it was a familiar thought to the Jewish theology that the future aeon has its characteristic beginning in the great resurrection-act. EAP/*SW*, 105.

Resurrection and Sonship

[commenting upon Rom. 1:3–4] The reference is not to two coexisting states in the make-up of the Savior but to two successive-stages in his life. . . . By the twofold κατά the manner of each state of existence is contrasted, by the twofold ἐκ the sphere of origin of each. As to the one, he was "from the seed of David"; as to the other, he was "out of resurrection from the dead." The resurrection (both of Jesus and of believers) is therefore according to Paul the entering upon a new phase of sonship characterized by the possession and exercise of unique supernatural power. *PE*, 155–56.

[commenting upon Rom. 1:3–4] The resurrection is to Paul the beginning of a new status of sonship; hence, as Jesus derived his sonship, κατὰ σάρκα, from the seed of David, he can be said to have derived his divine-sonship-in-power from the resurrection. EAP/*SW*, 104.

The resurrection constitutes, as it were, the womb of the new aeon, out of which believers issue as, in a new, altogether unprece-

280

dented, sense, sons of God: "They are sons of God, being sons of the resurrection." *PE*, 156.

[commenting upon Rom. 1:3–4] From resurrection-beginnings, from an eschatological genesis dates the pneumatic state of Christ's glory which is described as a sonship of God ἐν δυνάμει. EAP/*SW*, 105.

Resurrection and the Spirit

We are taught by the apostle that the resurrection of Christ, besides being the divine acknowledgment of his perfect righteousness, is also the fountain-head of all the renewing and quickening influences that descend from him to us. To preach a risen Christ means to preach a gospel which claims to come with the demonstration of the Spirit and with power. JRL/*GG*, 163.

Resurrection and the Transition of the Ages

Through the appearance or resurrection of Christ the eschatological process has been set in motion. As soon as the direction of the actual spiritual life-contact becomes involved, the horizontal movement of thought on the time-plane must give way immediately to a vertical projection of the eschatological interest into the supernal region, because there, even more than in the historical development below, the center of all religious values and forces has come to lie. The other, the higher world is in existence there, and there is no escape for the Christian from its supreme dominion over his life. Thus the other world, hitherto future, has become present. *PE*, 37–38.

If we may judge the resurrection of believers *mutatis mutandis* after the analogy of that of Christ, we shall have to believe that the event will mark the entrance upon a new world constructed upon a new superabundantly dynamic plane. It is for the body, no less than for the soul a new birth. *PE*, 156.

Resurrection of Christ and of Believers

[Paul] views the resurrection of Christ as the beginning of the general resurrection of the saints. EAP/*SW*, 92.

That a change will take place inherent in the resurrection-act for believers that are raised follows not only from explicit or more or less implicit statements, but rests besides on the stronger ground of the analogy between the resurrection of Jesus and that of believers which Paul throughout presupposes. *PE*, 209.

Nowhere is it said of Jesus that he contributed toward his own resurrection, far less that he raised himself. His role is throughout that of the terminus upon whom God's resurrective action works, in order that through him it may work upon others. *PE*, 147.

[commenting upon Rom. 8:11] It should be noticed how significantly Paul varies in this connection the name of Christ. First he speaks of the raising of *Jesus* from the dead. Here the Savior comes under consideration as to himself, his own human nature. Then he speaks of the raising of *Christ Jesus* from the dead. Here the Savior comes under consideration as the Messiah in his representative capacity, which furnishes a guarantee that his resurrection must repeat itself in that of the others. *PE*, 163.

Resurrection Body

Our Lord's doctrine of the final kingdom is so dominated by the principle of the celestial character of the life in this kingdom, that he cannot have conceived of the body otherwise than as fully adjusted to the conditions of such a life and to the entire supernatural environment in which it will have to move. OLDR/*SW*, 323.

John 5:28–29 and Luke 14:14; 20:35–36 make it probable that the body of glory will be the immediate product of the resurrection, and not the result of a subsequent transformation of the body first risen from the grave in its previous natural condition. OLDR/*SW*, 323.

The kingdom of God and the salvation it brings cannot stop short of the complete reclaiming of men, *body as well as soul*, from death, nor of their complete equipment for the consummate fellowship with God in heaven. OLDR/*SW*, 320.

THE ANTHOLOGY

The two classical contexts 1 Corinthians 15 and 2 Corinthians 5 are explainable only from the standpoint of one to whom a bodiless existence in the world to come would have fallen short of the ideal of supreme blessedness. *PE*, 70.

The raising of the body marks, as it were, the final admission of the completely restored man into the enjoyment of the fatherly love of God. OLDR/*SW*, 320.

The resurrection-body is from heaven because it is in a special supernatural sense from God. Heaven is the seat and source of the Pneuma by which the resurrection-body is formed. *PE*, 189.

In [the] Hellenizing writings the body is felt to be a burden and a detraction to the state of future blessedness, whereas Paul considers the body absolutely essential to the consummate eschatological life. *AUP*, 668.

All that is related in the messianic prophecies concerning the enjoyments of the future age is inseparable from the existence and functioning of the body. It is not otherwise with Jesus, who likewise associated with the resurrection the reendowment of the heirs of the age to come with a true body. *PE*, 69.

Revelation

Revelation is not an isolated act of God. It constitutes a part of the formation of the new world of redemption, and this new world does not come into being suddenly and all at once, but is realized in a long historical process. This could not be otherwise, since at every point its formation proceeds on the basis of, and in contact with, the natural development of this world in the form of history. It is simply owing to our habit of unduly separating revelation from this comprehensive background of the total redeeming work of God that we fail to appreciate its historic, progressive nature. NABT, 5.

Revelation is designed to prepare, to accompany, and to interpret the great objective redemptive acts of God, such as the incarnation, the atonement, the resurrection. It is not intended to follow the subjective appropriation of redemption in its further course. To expect revelations after the close of the apostolic age would be as unreasonable as to think that the great saving facts of that period can be increased or repeated. NABT, 5.

All revelation from a scriptural point of view ultimately has God for its object. *BT*, 363.

The Scriptures of the Old Testament and the word spoken in Christ are as personal an address from God to the later generations as they were to those who first heard the divine voice proclaim them. HED/*SW*, 190.

God's word, even when written, has this peculiarity that it retains the character of inspired, vitalized speech, opening up the depths of the divine mind and addressing itself in the most direct face-to-face way to the inner personality of the hearer. HED/*SW*, 190.

Revelation . . . serves the purpose of establishing as from God to man that train of personal communication in which the end of religion consists. HED/*SW*, 187.

God reveals himself because in his love for his own and interest in them it is natural for him to open up and communicate himself. Revelation in a sense is the highest that God has to give because in it he gives himself. HED/*SW*, 187.

Revelation as an act of God, theistically conceived of, can in no wise be associated with anything imperfect or impure or below the standard of absolute truth. IBT/*SW*, 16.

[God] has caused his revelation to take place in the milieu of the historical life of a people. The circle of revelation is not a school, but a "covenant." To speak of revelation as an "education" of humanity is a rationalistic and utterly unscriptural way of speaking. All that God disclosed of himself has come in response to the practical religious needs of his people as these emerged in the course of history. *BT*, 8–9.

THE ANTHOLOGY

■ [Revelation] is actually coextensive with the whole course of sacred history, if only revelation be taken not in the abstract theological sense of a communication of truth, but in the practical sense of a self-manifestation of God for the purpose of establishing and cultivating the true religion. *TOT*, 116.

■ Revelation is not an isolated act of God, existing without connection with all the other divine acts of supernatural character. It constitutes a part of that great process of the new creation through which the present universe as an organic whole shall be redeemed from the consequences of sin and restored to its ideal state, which it had originally in the intention of God. IBT/*SW*, 8.

Revelation, against Continuing

■ The revelation of God being not subjective and individual in its nature, but objective and addressed to the human race as a whole, it is but natural that this revelation should be embedded in the channels of the great objective history of redemption and extend no further than this. IBT/*SW*, 8.

■ It is as unreasonable to expect revelations after the close of the apostolic age as it would be to think that the great saving facts of that period can be indefinitely increased and repeated. IBT/*SW*, 9.

■ Unless we adopt the mystical standpoint, which cuts loose the subjective from the objective, the only proper answer to this question is, that new revelation can be added only in case new objective events of a supernatural character take place, needing for their understanding a new body of interpretation supplied by God. *BT*, 304.

Revelation, against Liberal View of

■ [commenting upon H. Wheeler Robinson's view] The main fault we have to find with the book is that it entirely subjectivizes the process of revelation: all truth is the result of historical experience, collective or individual. It is not the object of communication on the part of God, but the precipitate of faith and vision on the part of man. *RIOT*, 110.

If revelation is in its whole compass subjective, and at the same time through its subjective emergence acquires the character of relativity and fallibleness, no objective norm remains by which its actual provenience from the mind of God and its degree of authoritativeness can be tested. To say that all truth inherently commends itself is no solution for a mind conscious of its own spiritual inadequacy through sin in the noetic sphere. *RIOT*, 110.

Revelation and Christ

To take Christ at all he must be taken as the center of a movement of revelation organized around him, and winding up the whole process of revelation. When cut loose from what went before and came after, Jesus not only becomes uninterpretable, but owing to the meteoric character of his appearance, remains scarcely sufficient for bearing by himself alone the tremendous weight of a supernaturalistic world-view. *BT*, 302.

As a matter of fact, Jesus does not represent himself anywhere as being by his human earthly activity the exhaustive expounder of truth. Much rather he is the great fact to be expounded. And he has nowhere isolated himself from his interpreters, but on the contrary identified them with himself, both as to absoluteness of authority and adequacy of knowledge imparted (Luke 24:44; John 16:12–15). *BT*, 302.

Revelation and Human Instrumentality

For, God having chosen to reveal the truth through human instruments, it follows that these instruments must be both numerous and of varied adaptation to the common end. Individual coloring, therefore, and a peculiar manner of representation are not only not detrimental to a full statement of the truth, but directly subservient to it. God's method of revelation includes the very shaping and chiseling of individualities for his own objective ends. IBT/*SW*, 14.

To put it concretely: we must not conceive of it as if God found Paul "ready-made," as it were, and in using Paul as an organ of revelation, had to put up with the fact that the dialectic mind of Paul reflected the truth in a dialectic, dogmatic form to the detriment of the truth. The facts are these: the truth having inherently, besides other aspects, a dialectic and dogmatic side, God, intending to give this side full expression, chose Paul from the womb, molded his character, and gave him such a training that the truth revealed through him necessarily bore the dogmatic and dialectic impress of His mind. The divine objectivity and the human individuality here do not collide, nor exclude each other, because the man Paul, with his whole character, his gifts, and his training, is subsumed under the divine plan. IBT/*SW*, 14.

The human is but the glass through which the divine light is reflected, and all the sides and angles into which the glass has been cut serve no other purpose than to distribute to us the truth in all the riches of its prismatic colors. IBT/*SW*, 14.

Revelation and Redemption

Special, supernatural revelation is necessary for a soteriological reason, because man in his sinful, lost, helpless condition is dependent on the sovereign, gracious approach of God in word and act to recover his normal religious state. As such, revelation bears an instrumental saving character. HED/*SW*, 187.

Redemption and revelation, in order to be intelligible and credible, require a degree of continuity. A system of supernatural interpositions which suddenly emerges from the midst of an immemorial evolutionary past satisfies neither our intellect nor our heart. CFTBH/*SW*, 469.

In redemption and revelation naturally not the human, subjective side, not the religious views and sentiments of men, stand in the foreground, but the great objective acts and interpositions of God, the history as it is in itself, not as it reflected itself in the mind of man. Facts, rather than the spirit of times or the consciousness of periods, should be here the primary object of investigation. CFTBH/*SW*, 460.

[Revelation] has not completed itself in one exhaustive act, but unfolded itself in a long series of successive acts. In the abstract, it might conceivably have been otherwise. But as a matter of fact this could not be, because revelation does not stand alone by itself, but is (so far as special revelation is concerned) inseparably attached to another activity of God, which we call *redemption*. Now redemption could not be otherwise than historically successive, because it addresses itself to the generations of mankind coming into existence in the course of history. Revelation is the interpretation of redemption; it must, therefore, unfold itself in installments as redemption does. And yet it is also obvious that the two processes are not entirely co-extensive, for revelation comes to a close at a point where redemption still continues. *BT*, 5–6.

As soon as we realize that revelation is at almost every point interwoven with and conditioned by the redeeming activity of God in its wider sense . . . its historic character becomes perfectly intelligible and ceases to cause surprise. IBT/*SW*, 8.

Revelation is so interwoven with redemption that, unless allowed to consider the latter, it would be suspended in the air. *BT*, 15.

Revelation, Natural

[John 1:4–5 and 10] taken together are preeminently the *sedes* for the church-doctrine of natural revelation in its relation to God's redemptive disclosure in Christ. While it is plainly taught that mankind subjectively fails to appropriate this revelation of nature, it is likewise implied that it nevertheless remains objectively valid. RLT/*SW*, 90.

Revelation, Organic Nature of

[The organic unity of Scripture convinces] the student that what the Bible places before him is not the chance product of the several human minds that have been engaged in its composition, but the workmanship of none other than God himself. IBT/*SW*, 22.

288

Jesus never loses sight of the continuity that ought to exist in revelation. The old is not ruthlessly sacrificed to the new, purely on account of the latter's newness. The idea is always that the old had the seeds of the new in itself. For this reason also a revolutionary discarding of the Old Testament is out of the question. *BT*, 362.

Since on our behalf and for our salvation [God] has condescended to work and speak in the form of time, and thus to make his works and his speech partake of that peculiar glory that attaches to all organic growth, let us also seek to know him as the One *that is, that was, and that is to come*, in order that no note may be lacking in that psalm of praise to be sung by the church into which all our theology must issue. IBT/*SW*, 24.

God has not communicated to us the knowledge of the truth as it appears in the calm light of eternity to his own timeless vision. . . . The self-revelation of God is a work covering ages, proceeding in a sequence of revealing words and acts, appearing in a long perspective of time. The truth comes in the form of growing truth, not truth at rest. IBT/*SW*, 7.

The truth of revelation, if it is to retain its divine and absolute character at all, must be perfect from the beginning. Biblical theology deals with it as a product of a supernatural divine activity, and is therefore bound by its own principle to maintain the perfection of revealed truth in all its stages. When, nevertheless, biblical theology also undertakes to show how the truth has been gradually set forth in greater fulness and clearness, these two facts can be reconciled in no other way than by assuming that the advance in revelation resembles the organic process, through which out of the perfect germ the perfect plant and flower and fruit are successively produced. IBT/*SW*, 10–11.

All salvation, all truth in regard to man, has its eternal foundation in the Triune God himself. It is this Triune God who here reveals himself as the everlasting reality, from whom all truth proceeds, whom all truth reflects, be it the little streamlet of Paradise or the broad river of the New Testament losing itself again in the ocean of eternity. After this nothing higher can come. All the separate lines along which through the ages revelation was carried, have converged and met at a single point. The seed of the woman and the angel of Jehovah are become one in the Incarnate Word. And as Christ is glorified once for all, so from the crowning glory and perfection of his revelation in the New Testament nothing can be taken away; nor can anything be added thereunto. IBT/*SW*, 13.

Biblical theology exhibits to the student of the Word the organic structure of the truth therein contained, and its organic growth as the result of revelation. It shows to him that in the Bible there is an organization finer, more complicated, more exquisite than even the texture of muscles and nerves and brain in the human body; that its various parts are interwoven and correlated in the most subtle manner, each sensitive to the impressions received from all the others, perfect in itself, and yet dependent upon the rest, while in them and through them all throbs as a unifying principle the Spirit of God's living truth. IBT/*SW*, 21–22.

Romans 1:18–20 shows that all "truth" is ultimately truth concerning God. To find God everywhere of necessity leads to conceiving of all religious knowledge as organically one. TP/*SW*, 357.

In the history of redemption there are critical stages in which the great acts of God as it were accumulate, so we find that at such junctures the process of revelation is correspondingly accelerated, and that a few years show, perhaps, more rapid growth and greater expansion than centuries that lie between. For, although the development of the root may be slow and the stem and leaves may grow almost imperceptibly, there comes a time when the bud emerges in a day and the flower expands in an hour to our wondering sight. IBT/*SW*, 12.

Revelation, Special and Natural

[commenting upon Bavinck's view of revelation] Revelation in its most general sense, as the correlate of all religion, is every activity proceeding from God intended to place and keep man in that specific relation to himself which is called religion. It is to be regretted, we think, that the author has let this general definition influence his idea of supernatural revelation in the Christian sense to such an extent as to subsume under the latter all redemptive acts, thus making it virtually synonymous with redemption. "Revelation," he says, "coincides with all works in nature and in grace. It embraces the whole of creation and redemption." This seems to us to obliterate the distinction between creative and redemptive acts of God insofar as they address themselves to the consciousness of man, and insofar as they concern his subconscious being. *GD1/SW*, 479.

General revelation is also called natural revelation, and special revelation called supernatural revelation. These names explain themselves. General revelation comes to all for the reason that it comes through nature. Special revelation comes to a limited circle for the reason that it springs from the sphere of the supernatural through a specific self-disclosure of God. *BT*, 19.

Reward

We must . . . disabuse ourselves of the modern idea, as though every thought of reward in ethical relations were unworthy of the sacredness of ethics. This is an opinion ultimately based on the philosophy of the autonomy or deification of ethics, and behind that on the principle of unmotivated free will. Man is not such an autonomous being that he can afford to scorn a reward from God, provided the idea of meritoriousness be kept absent from it. *BT*, 394–95.

Judaism put the doctrine of reward on a commercial (and therefore self-righteous) basis. It was a matter of man paying so much and getting back a proper equivalent. This principle of *quid pro quo* is destructive of the religious relation. *BT*, 395.

Righteousness

According to Scripture "righteousness" is that which agrees with and pleases God, and exists for his sake, and can be adjudicated only by him. *BT*, 392.

Ethically considered, [righteousness] covers all converse with God; to be righteous acquires the meaning of possessing and practicing the true religion. *BT*, 392–93.

Righteousness is from God as its source, it exists for God as its end, and it is subject to God as the ultimate Justifier. *BT*, 393.

Righteousness is in Scripture an idea saturated with the thought of God. Throughout the Old Testament this is so. It is a commonplace of its teaching, especially in the prophets, that there can be no true obedience of heart and life without the constant presence to the mind of man of the thought of Jehovah. HTR/*GG*, 31.

Righteousness is to the apostle that ideal sublimate of human conduct through which it serves its highest purpose of revealing the glory of the ethical character of God. AL/*SW*, 397.

Righteousness is the opposite of sin, and as the reference to God is inseparable from the conception of sin, so the reference to God is in precisely the same manner inherent in the idea of righteousness. HTR/*GG*, 31.

The tree of righteousness is planted in us by God for his own sake, and consequently he delights in its blossoms and desires to eat of its fruit. HTR/*GG*, 35.

Righteousness and Christ

In the same real sense in which on earth Christ was identified with our sin, he is now in his resurrection-life identified with our state of pardon and acceptance. According to the profound words of the apostle, we have become the righteousness of God in him (2 Cor. 5:21) because he has become the righteousness of God for us. JRL/*GG*, 162.

The two things . . . on which righteousness depends are the descent of Christ from heaven to bear our sins and the resurrection. JRL/*GG*, 159.

Righteousness is always taken by Jesus in a specific sense which it obtains from the reference to God as Lawgiver and Judge. *KGC*, 59.

To Jesus righteousness . . . meant such moral conduct and such a moral state as are right when measured by the supreme norm of the nature and will of God, so that they form a reproduction of the latter, a revelation, as it were, of the moral glory of God. *KGC*, 60.

It should be remembered that the glory possessed by Christ in heaven is, to Paul, the emphatic, never-silent declaration of his absolute righteousness acquired during the state of humiliation. It sprang from his obedience and suffering and self-sacrifice in our stead. It is righteousness translated into the language of effect, the crown set upon his work of satisfaction. MEM/*GG*, 96.

Righteousness of God

[Righteousness of God denotes] the objective righteousness imputed by God consisting in the merit of Christ. SIP/*SW*, 378.

Midway between the transcendental and the communicative attributes stands the righteousness of Jehovah. *BT*, 250.

First of all it ought to be observed that when righteousness is predicated of Jehovah, the analogy is not the duty of fair dealing between man and man, but always the procedure according to strict justice on the part of a judge. *BT*, 250.

Righteousness, Standard of

The standard, the norm of righteousness, in the kingdom of God lies in God himself, [and not] any lower rule abstracted from purely human relations, but the holy nature, the supreme perfection of the Father in heaven is the pattern to which all must conform. KOG/*SW*, 313–14.

[commenting upon Amos's view of righteousness] Righteousness and God are identical; to seek the one is to the seek the other (5:4, 6, 14). To such an extent does the prophet feel righteousness to be the inward governing principle of world-control, that it appears to him as the normal, the departure from which is monstrous and absurd (5:7; 6:12). God stands beside every wall of conduct, a plumbline in his hand (7:8). *BT*, 251.

[commenting upon Matt. 5:48] [These sayings affirm] not merely that the norm of righteousness is to be found in God, they likewise imply that the aim of righteousness, the final cause of obedience, lies in God. Righteousness is to be sought from the pure desire of satisfying him, who is the supreme end of all moral existence. *KGC*, 60.

Righteousness, Striving after

The striving after righteousness is made the absolutely supreme concern of the disciple. He must hunger and thirst after it, endure persecution for its sake, sacrifice for it all other things. It is plain that only one thing can in this absolute sense be the supreme object of human striving, and, if the place here assigned to righteousness is elsewhere given to the kingdom, it follows that the two must be identical. This is confirmed by Matthew 6:33, "Seek ye first his kingdom, and his righteousness, and all these things shall be added unto you." Here righteousness is introduced not so much as a second object to be sought by the disciples in addition to the kingdom, but rather as a more precise specification of what the kingdom consists in. KOG/*SW*, 313.

[Righteousness] is the highest concern of the disciple. He must hunger and thirst after it, treat it as the very sustenance of his life, the only thing that will satisfy his most instinctive desires. He must submit to persecution for its sake. *KGC*, 63–64.

Ritschl, Albrecht

Ritschl himself errs when he finds the whole content of the conception of God in love, whereas in Scripture God appears throughout in the fullness of his attributes. *GD2/SW*, 488.

We are accustomed to say, and understand the Bible as saying, that forgiveness is the source from which fellowship flows. Ritschl would turn this around, making fellowship the source from which forgiveness proceeds. *BT*, 168.

Ritschlians

The truth is simply this, that when Ritschlians speak of the revelation of God in the historic Christ, they do not mean the same thing by the use of these words as we would mean in employing them. To us the history of Christ, and therefore the historical Christ, means the entire life of the Savior with all its eternal issues included, replete with supernatural elements, involving the incarnation, the miracles, the resurrection; in other words, we find nothing in the two conceptions of the supernatural and historical which would be mutually exclusive. A thing is no less historical because it is supernatural; the supernatural is the highest history. Not so the Ritschlians. To them the historic Christ who reveals is not the Christ in the totality of his life, but a distinction is made between revealing and nonrevealing elements in the history of Jesus. And if we inquire more closely we find that the revealing elements consist in this, that in Christ there was presented to mankind a piece of perfect moral and religious consciousness and mediately through this, an indication of what God is for man. The much-used phrase, "the historical Christ," therefore means the empirical, phenomenal Christ and that subjectively considered. CFTBH/*SW*, 464.

The desire [of Ritschlianism] is not to know the higher world, but, to use Ritschl's own definition, "with the help of the spiritual power which man adores, to solve the contradiction in which man finds himself as a part of the natural world, and as a spiritual personality." And, if we are not mistaken, precisely here lies the strength of the appeal which this theology makes to the consciousness of our age. It offers a deliverance from the troublesome and compromising supernatural facts which is not seized upon, as it were, under the stress and compulsion of the onslaught of criticism, but which seems to rest on a respectable philosophical and theological foundation. People no longer have to say: Christianity must be possible without belief in the facts, for the facts have become uncertain and religion is a necessity. They are now able to say: Christianity from its very essence, as we construe it, can dispense with the facts, and, if history fails to authenticate them, this makes us neither cold nor warm, because our faith is superior to such considerations. CFTBH/*SW*, 463–64.

In the Ritschlian theology . . . the primacy of the love of God and the restriction of religion to the sphere of the will have ceased to be abnormalities of an unevenly distributed development. They have become the supreme maxims, clearly realized and systematically upheld, to whose sway the religious consciousness in its whole extent is made absolutely subject. SDL/*SW*, 426.

Ritschlianism is the application of the principle of empiricism to the sphere of theological knowledge, and that in its extreme positivistic form. Not what God has objectively and supernaturally revealed to us concerning himself, but only that which can enter into our subjective religious experience, forms the proper content of theology. Under the reproach of being metaphysical, all that the church has hitherto believed concerning the triune existence of God, concerning his transcendental attributes, concerning the preexistence and incarnation of Christ, and many other vital facts, is ruled out of her creed. SDL/*SW*, 426–27.

The philosophical positivism to which the school of Ritschl and other allied movements owe their origin, seeks on principle to restrict all that is religiously knowable and valuable to the surface processes of conscious experience, and thus the deeper-going, creative acts of divine power, which affect the subconscious reality of things, in part even the physical world, and which occupy so large a place in the eschatological drama, are easily dismissed as unessential and indifferent from a moral and religious point of view. OLDR/*SW*, 317.

In the Ritschlian system the old names for the attributes [of God] are, to be sure, retained, but the reality designated by these names is in each case reduced to terms of love. SDL/*SW*, 427.

296

The Ritschlian school has made of the kingdom almost exclusively an association of man interacting on the principle of love. This is not wrong in itself, but as a definition of the kingdom it is utterly misleading, because it virtually dereligionizes the idea, and moreover shifts the realization of the kingdom almost entirely from the work of God to the activity of man. Man brings in the kingdom according to this view. According to Jesus' conception the opposite is true. *BT*, 384.

Roman Catholicism

[commenting on monasticism] The Church of Rome has taught men to look down upon ordinary life as something comparatively worthless, inferior in dignity to an artificially produced and artificially maintained state of renunciation. [This theory is] irreconcilable with the teaching of Jesus. EC/*GG*, 189.

How easy, how natural, how seemingly innocent, how tempting it is for you to suppose that, after your guilt is atoned for in Christ, you then have life of yourself; that, where your Surety has accomplished the first half by bearing your affliction, you can achieve the second half in your own power by earning eternal life for yourself. . . . This, in fact, is what Rome teaches us, and with such teaching it wrests the crown from God's work of grace. SR/*GG*, 228.

[It is] possible to commit [the error of] perpetuating the Old Testament typical form of religion through importing it into the New Testament. This the Romish Church does on a large scale. And in doing so, instead of lifting the substance of the types to a higher plane, it simply reproduces and repeats. This is destructive of the whole typical relation. *BT*, 148.

Sabbath

The Sabbath is not only the most venerable, it is likewise the most living of all the sacramental realities of our religion. It has faithfully accompanied the people of God on their march through the ages. *BT*, 139.

The principle underlying the Sabbath is formulated in the Decalogue itself. It consists in this, that man must copy God in his course of life. The divine creative work completed itself in six days, whereupon the seventh followed as a day of rest for God. In connection with God, "rest" cannot, of course, mean mere cessation from labor, far less recovery from fatigue. Such a meaning is by no means required by the Old Testament usage of the word. "Rest" resembles the word "peace" in this respect, that it has in Scripture, in fact to the Shemitic mind generally, a positive rather than a negative import. It stands for consummation of a work accomplished and the joy and satisfaction attendant upon this. Such was its prototype in God. *BT*, 139–40.

Sabbath and Eschatology

Before all other important things . . . the Sabbath is an expression of the eschatological principle on which the life of humanity has been constructed. There is to be to the world-process a finale, as there was an overture, and these two belong inseparably together. To give up the one means to give up the other, and to give up either means to abandon the fundamental scheme of biblical history. *BT*, 140.

The Sabbath brings [the] principle of the eschatological structure of history to bear upon the mind of man after a symbolical and a typical fashion. It teaches its lesson through the rhythmical succession of six days of labor and one ensuing day of rest in each successive week. Man is reminded in this way that life is not an aimless existence, that a goal lies beyond. This was true before, and apart from, redemption. The eschatological is an older strand in revelation than the soteric. The so-called "covenant of works" was nothing but an embodiment of the sabbatical principle. *BT*, 140.

The Sabbath is not in the first place a means of advancing religion. It has its main significance apart from that, in pointing forward to the eternal issues of life and history . . . a day devoted to the remembrance of man's eternal destiny. *BT*, 141.

Sabbath and the Tabernacle

[commenting upon Ex. 31:12–17] The Sabbath as a covenant-sign between Israel and the Lord . . . is subjoined [here] to that other visible bond of fellowship, the tabernacle. As in the latter, God by his glorious presence signified his gracious attitude toward Israel, so Israel by the observance of this day of rest would show its faithful adherence to Jehovah's covenant. *MOP*, 63.

Sabbath, Lord of the

"Lord of the Sabbath" means, of course, nothing less than the authoritative disposer of that institution. *SDJ*, 123.

Sacrifice

[commenting upon Heb. 9] All through the ninth chapter the worshipper is represented as one who serves. This service is organized on the same principle as the Old Testament service. It is a service in a sanctuary, with priest, altar and sacrifice. The idea of sacrifice is wider, therefore, than that of atonement. Its essence is proper worship of God in his presence. *TEH*, 43.

All biblical sacrifice rests on the idea that the gift of life to God, either in consecration or in expiation, is necessary to the action or the restoration of religion. *BT*, 92–93.

It is not merely necessary that a sacrifice be slain; it is equally necessary that the sacrifice be brought into the immediate presence of God as he dwells in the heavenly tabernacle. The sacrifice is not completed until this is done. *PC/SW*, 142.

Sacrifice was to [Paul] the very essence of the redemptive transaction, the very basis of redemption as an accomplished result. *SIP/SW*, 375.

The Old Testament nowhere presents us with what could be fairly called a theory of sacrifice. It describes the sacrificial system, here and there hints at its leading principles, but in the main leaves it to the New Testament to illumine the facts by means of what can be properly called a doctrine of sacrifice. This the New Testament does both by the ideal exhibition of the principle of sacrifice in the work of Christ and by the interpretation given thereof in the teachings of our Lord and of the apostolic writers. SIP/*SW*, 374.

Sacrifice of Christ

[commenting upon Rom. 3:25–26] Paul bases the necessity of the propitiatory exhibition of Christ on the principle of the divine righteousness. God set him forth as a ἱλαστήριον "to show his righteousness." This manifestation of divine righteousness was rendered necessary "because of the passing over of the sins done aforetime," and this "passing over" had been possible only because it was done "with a view to the showing of his righteousness at this present season." Obviously then, there is in the sacrifice of Christ, before all other things, an exercise of the righteousness of God. SIP/*SW*, 377.

[commenting upon 1 Cor. 5:7] [Paul] compares the death of Christ to . . . another form of Old Testament sacrifice, the Passover. Paul here represents the Christian state as the ethical counterpart to what the feast of unleavened bread was symbolically. But this Old Testament feast was introduced by the feast of Passover. Thus the thought emerges that the new state of ethical purity in which the Christian lives was also introduced by a Passover sacrifice, and this Paul finds in the death of Christ. Obviously the connection between Christ's death and the Christian life of purity is not conceived of as merely chronological; it must be causal: in Christ's sacrifice lies the ground or reason why the Christian should be pure. SIP/*SW*, 381.

Sadducees

In Jesus' argument with the Sadducees certain points are brought out which go to show that such is really the underlying principle of the entire doctrine [of resurrection]. . . . It would be unworthy of God to take into fellowship of his own perfect life a being which he did not intend to raise to the full fruition of communion with himself of which its nature is capable. He is not a God of the dead but of the living, and life in this pregnant sense postulates the resurrection of the body. OLDR/*SW*, 320.

■ The nerve of our Lord's argument with the Sadducees does not require that the patriarchs were at the time of Moses in possession of *the resurrection body*, but only that they were in possession of *the covenant life*, which would inevitably issue in due time into the raising of their bodies; John 11:25, where the resurrection and the spiritual life are identified, is another passage appealed to in this connection. OLDR/*SW*, 321.

Salvation

■ So far as Paul is concerned . . . (a) the *sōtēria* is past to the believer: "by grace have ye been saved" (Eph. 2:5); (b) nevertheless it can be represented as still in process of realization: "the word of the cross is to them that *are perishing* foolishness, but unto us who *are being saved* it is the power of God" (1 Cor. 1:18); (c) there is a certain part of the act still outstanding: "much more then, being now justified by his blood, *shall we be saved* from (the eschatological) wrath through him" (Rom. 5:9). *SDJ*, 269.

■ Even the idea of σωτηρία "salvation," which is to us predominantly suggestive of our Christian state and experience in this life, is shown to have been with Paul in its original signification an eschatological idea denoting deliverance from the wrath to come, salvation in the judgment, and from this it is believed to have been carried back into the present life, first of all to express the thought, that even now the believer through Christ possesses immunity from the condemnation of the last day. EAP/*SW*, 93.

■ With Christ it is therefore possible for God to raise us up also. He took upon himself the curse and the demands of the law; we reap the fruits together with him. In his resurrection from the dead ours is given in fact and guaranteed by right. That new life, which he received as the reward for his obedience, passes over from him by the working of his Spirit to all that belong to him, so that they, awakened from the sleep of sin, let Christ shine on them, say "Amen" with a living faith to all God's words of life, hunger and thirst after the righteousness of life, and end by praising God's rich mercy which, because of his great love, even when they were dead in their transgressions, made them alive with Christ the Lord. SR/*GG*, 227.

According to the uniform usage of the New Testament—the Gospels no less than the Epistles—"to save" means, when applied in a spiritual sense, to rescue from the judgment and to introduce into the blessedness of the world to come. *SDJ*, 27.

To taste and feel the riches of his Godhead, as freely given unto us, one must have passed not only through the abjectness and poverty and despair of sin but through the overwhelming experience of salvation. WT/*GG*, 6.

We speak of our saving men, but this, while conveying a legitimate idea, is a metaphor. At bottom it signifies no more than that through the means of grace we arrange and prepare the situation in which it pleases God to perform the unique saving act. It is ours to let in the light and lay ready the garments which afterwards Lazarus will need, but we cannot wake the sleeper under the stone. SSL/*GG*, 54.

[commenting on Luke 19:10] How many of us would have been saved, if the Lord had waited till we sought him out? Thanks be to God, he is a Savior who seeks the lost, who with eyes supernaturally far-sighted discerns us a long way off, and draws our interest to himself by the sweet constraint of his grace, till we are face to face with him and our soul is saved. As once, in the incarnation, [Jesus] came down from heaven to seek mankind, so he still comes down silently from heaven in the case of each sinner, and pursues his search for that individual soul, following it through all the mazes of its waywardness and the devious paths of its folly, sometimes unto the very brink of destruction, till at last his grace overtakes it and says, "I must lodge at thy house." SSL/*GG*, 52–53.

Seeking and saving meant for [Jesus], before anything else, seeking and saving for God. It had no humanitarian or world-improving purpose apart from this. It began with the thought of God and ended there. For that he came. And at that we should aim. SSL/*GG*, 64–65.

Salvation and the Glory of God

▮ Salvation with all it contains flows from the nature and subserves the glory of God, and we can clearly perceive that Jesus was accustomed consciously to refer it to this divine source and to subordinate it to this God-centered purpose (see John 17:4). *KGC*, 11.

▮ In the phrase "for thy name's sake" the recognition is expressed that the ultimate purpose of salvation lies in the glory of God. EP, 340.

Salvation and the World to Come

▮ It is . . . of the very essence of salvation that it correlates the Christian's state with the great issues of the last day and the world to come. *PE*, 236.

▮ On our interpretation the messianic provisional kingdom and the present σωτηρία are identical and coextensive, so that what the Christian now possesses and enjoys is the firstfruits and pledge of the life eternal. *PE*, 259.

Salvation, Centrality of Jesus Christ in

▮ Jesus does not as an outside person procure salvation for the race; by breaking his own way to the goal he has carried the others in his wake. And again, Jesus has not produced faith in us while himself living above the plane and beyond the need of faith; it is through his own perfect exercise of faith that he helps believers to follow in his footsteps. HED/*SW*, 213.

▮ In Acts (3:15; 5:31) [Peter] calls Jesus "the ἀρχηγός of life" and "an ἀρχηγός and σωτήρ." . . . He as a beginner took this life to himself, and then opened it to others. In "Prince and Savior" the two elements are distributed. Jesus is first of all the leader in salvation, then the giver of salvation. HED/*SW*, 213.

But most clearly of all the theological genius of Paul can be seen at work in the manner in which he subsumes the entire saving work of God under his conception of the person of Christ. TP/*SW*, 360.

From the beginning to the end man's salvation appears to Paul not merely associated with Christ, but capable of description in terms of Christ. We are chosen in him in the premundane eternity and shall share his glory in the eternity of the world to come. And in all that lies between, the figure of Christ accompanies that of the believer through every stage of its progress in the grace of God. The determination with which the apostle has carried through this principle appears from the fact that even such subjective experiences as conversion and regeneration are described by him in christological terms, viz., as a dying and rising with Christ, as steps in the reproduction of the life of Christ in us. TP/*SW*, 360.

[Paul viewed] everything from the standpoint of the living, glorified Christ, who sums up and carries in himself all the saving energies and gifts acquired during his life in the flesh, so that the whole work of salvation has an eternally fixed personal center of unity in the exalted Lord. In this soteriological reduction of everything to terms of Christ, as well as in the reduction of everything to terms of God in the broader theological sense, we feel how perfectly the head and heart of Paul interacted and responded to each other. TP/*SW*, 360.

To be found by Jesus is to be saved for the simple reason that in his person God himself restores the lost contact, gathers up the cords of life into his own bosom, and throws about us the circle of his divine beatitude, so that our soul, like a star in its native course, once more moves around him, and knows no other law or center. . . . Consequently it is true . . . that where Jesus is, there is salvation, and away from him there is none. SSL/*GG*, 58–59.

Salvation, Gift of God

The unavoidable conclusion is that this life was in Christ before it came to us, that, consequently, it was not earned by us but acquired by him. He possessed it, long before we had performed any works;

it was not manifested in us until we, by faith, came into contact with him, the living Christ. Thus our faith becomes an unimpeachable witness which, with every drink we take from the cup of God's redemption, cries out: "By grace you have been saved!" So it becomes an everflowing stream, whose incessantly rushing waters do not cease mentioning: "Not of yourselves, it is God's gift!" SR/*GG*, 229.

The most absurd conclusion that can ever be drawn from this truth is that it gives you the right to sit still. The opposite is true. In its deepest grounding this truth comes down to the fact that you are completely powerless, that you are wholly dependent upon God, that in yourself you are irretrievably lost. To what must such an awesome thought now lead you? To continue sleeping calmly upon the dregs of idleness? Or, with holy trembling, to call upon that God from whom alone your help can come? SR/*GG*, 231.

The consciousness of having nothing, absolutely nothing, is the certain pledge of untold enrichment. So much is salvation a matter of giving on God's part that its best subjects are those in whom his grace of giving can have its perfect work. HTR/*GG*, 29.

After the fall man will never again be able to work in a manner pleasing to God except a completed work of God be performed on his behalf. Earning eternal life has forever been taken out of man's hands. Everything that subjectively happens within him can only be a principle and phenomenon of eternal life itself and in no way a prerequisite for eternal life. The obtaining of eternal life thus comes to lie in God, as a work that is his alone, in which his glory shines and of which nothing, without detracting from that glory, can be attributed to the creature. On this point the entire Reformation, both Lutheran and Calvinist, took exception to Rome, which failed to appreciate this fundamental truth. DCRT/*SW*, 246.

Sanctification

Sanctification ought to be to every child of God not a desultory matter, but an intelligent systematic pursuit. RR/*GG*, 134.

The conception of "sanctification" ... has for its irremovable core the idea of consecration to God and consequent appurtenance to him. It cannot be too much emphasized that "holiness" is in the Pauline vocabulary never ethical perfection as such and without regard to its terminus in God. *PE*, 309–10.

The whole Christian life, the whole process of sanctification is one continuous exercise of self-denial. EC/*GG*, 195.

There can be no standing still in the spiritual life; for precisely because it is life—a growing, developing thing—progress is of its very essence. The suspension of progress means that there is something wrong, that a decline has set in which, if not arrested, must lead to a fatal issue. Such a thing as a stationary Christian in reality does not exist. TEC/*GG*, 201.

Through sanctification his holy character is impressed upon our souls, so that, notwithstanding our imperfections, God takes a true delight in us, seeing that the inner man is changed from day to day after the likeness of Christ. HTR/*GG*, 43.

The true disciple does not seek to be made better for his own glory but in the interest and for the glory of God. He feels with Paul that he must apprehend, because he was apprehended for that very purpose. . . . The believer, therefore, sanctifies himself, that God's purpose may not be frustrated in him, but find glorious fruition. HTR/*GG*, 39.

Sanctification and Justification

Justification and sanctification are not the same, and an endless amount of harm has been done by the short-sighted attempt to identify them. But neither are these two independent one of the other; the one sets the goal and fixes the direction, the other follows. *PE*, 149.

Sanctification and the Spirit

Πνεύματι περιπατεῖν is a comprehensive phrase for the God-pleasing walk of the Christian (Gal. 5:16); *κατὰ πνεῦμα* designates the standard of ethical normality, both as to being and striving (Rom. 8:5). The contrast between σάρξ and πνεῦμα is an ethical contrast (Gal. 5:17). Paul represents the Christian virtues and graces as fruits and gifts of the Spirit (Gal. 5:22; Rom. 12:6–13). Particular love, which the apostle regards as the essence of fulfillment of the law, is derived from the Spirit (Rom. 15:30; Col. 1:8). The whole range of sanctification belongs to the province of the Spirit, whence it is called ἁγιασμὸς πνεύματος (2 Thess. 2:13), and likewise, of course, the "renewal" at the beginning (Titus 3:5). EAP/*SW*, 111.

Satan

Satan is called in 2 Corinthians 4:4, ὁ θεὸς τοῦ αἰῶνος τούτου, and the very point of this bold comparison seems to lie in this that, as the true God by his Spirit illumines the minds of believers, enabling them to behold the glory of Christ in the gospel, so the false god of the present age has a counter-spirit at work (or is a counter-spirit), which blinds the minds of the unbelieving that the light of the gospel of the glory of Christ should not dawn upon them. EAP/*SW*, 120.

Saving

All our seeking and saving, that is, all our religious endeavor, ought to carry the image and superscription of Christ. SSL/*GG*, 64.

The purpose, the goal of seeking and saving were for our Lord pronouncedly religious. Seeking and saving meant for him, before anything else, seeking and saving for God. It had no humanitarian or world-improving purpose apart from this. It began with the thought of God and ended there. For that he came. And at that we should aim. SSL/*GG*, 64–65.

Savior

According to Ephesians 5:23 Christ is the Savior of the body, that is, of the church, in like manner as the man is the head of the woman, that is, through providing for the sustenance of her life. What is expected from the *Sōtēr*, whom the Christians are looking for from heaven, is that he shall change the body of their humiliation and make it like unto his own glorious body (Phil. 3:21). *SDJ*, 266.

The "lost" are such as require a "Seeker" and "Savior"; when tempted to dilute or tone down the meaning of this word, it should suffice to remember, that in the same proportion as this is done we also detract from the Savior-title of our Lord a substantial part of its significance. And conversely, if we allow ourselves to lose sight of even the smallest part of what the words "to save" and "Savior" connote, it necessarily modifies the sound which the word "lost" carries to our ear. There is no escape from this; it is the inherent logic of the structure of the gospel. To refuse to be bound by it puts one beyond the pale of consistent Christianity. SSL/*GG*, 56.

Schleiermacher, Friedrich

Schleiermacher committed the twofold error of making this sense of dependence terminate upon the universe, and of limiting it to feeling. *GD1/SW*, 479.

Scripture

The simple truth is that the Bible itself shows us God condescending to clothe his Word and make it as it were incarnate in the peculiarities of human nature. But the organic view should never be held to the detriment of the divine authorship of the Scriptures. As Christ, notwithstanding his incarnation and weakness and contumely inseparable from it, nevertheless remained free from sin, so Scripture is *sine labe concepta. GD1/SW*, 480.

It is an unchristian and an unbiblical procedure to make development superior to revelation instead of revelation superior to development, to accept belief and tendencies as true because they represent the spirit of the time and in a superficial optimism may be regarded as making for progress. Christian cognition is not an evolution of truth, but a fallible apprehension of truth which must at each point be tested by an accessible absolute norm of truth. To take one's stand upon the infallibility of Scripture is an eminently religious act; it honors the supremacy of God in the sphere of truth. HED/*SW*, 233.

■ All our investigations as to the origin of the Scriptures, their collection into a canon, their original text, as well as the exegetical researches by which the contents of the biblical writings are inductively ascertained, ultimately serve the one purpose of teaching us what God has revealed concerning himself. IBT/*SW*, 6.

Scripture and Criticism

■ Whether we like it or not, criticism can touch the essence of our religion, because religion has become incarnate, and for our sakes had to become incarnate and make itself vulnerable in historic form. As the Son of God while on earth had to expose himself to the unbelief and scorn of men, so the word of the gospel could not be what it is for us unless it were subject to the same humiliation. CFTBH/*SW*, 467.

■ Once the sense of allegiance to the Word of God as the only authoritative rule of faith has become weakened, or, while still recognized in theory has ceased to be a living force in the mind of believers, then the hope of return to the truth once forsaken is reduced to a minimum. BIP/*SW*, 412.

Scripture, Inspiration of

■ The conception of partial inspiration is a modern figment having no support in what the Bible teaches about its own makeup. Whenever the New Testament speaks about the inspiration of the Old, it is always in the most absolute, comprehensive terms. Consulting the consciousness of the Scriptures themselves in this matter, we soon learn that it is either "plenary inspiration" or nothing at all. *BT*, 13.

■ [commenting upon Briggs's view of inspiration] We are constrained to ask whether inspiration with no higher results than to make a writing generally appropriate and sufficiently accurate for its purpose can retain anything of the unique, supernatural character hitherto ascribed to it. There are numerous writings not inspired of which the same attributes may be predicated. We do not mean to say that historical accuracy is the only or even the chief interest guarded by inspiration. There may be other and higher qualities of Scripture equally dependent on it. But the historic credibility of the Bible appears to be one of the few points on which our belief in the divine origin of its contents can be subjected to the concrete test of an apparent conflict with lesser authorities. It represents the point where the struggle inherent in all faith becomes acute. To withdraw here and then to maintain the fact of inspiration in regard to other aspects of Scripture, which by their very nature lie outside the range of such acute conflict, may indeed render our faith invulnerable to the assaults of criticism, but in the same proportion that it does so, will detract from the heroism which is the highest glory of faith, and will create misgivings as to the substantial character of the restricted, intangible, and as it were sublimated inspiration that is left on this view. *MGMA*, 720.

Self-Denial

Denial of self, a course of action as if self did not exist, certainly does not seem a pleasant procedure. But remember that it is not the true, it is only the sinful self that we are called upon to abrogate. EC/*GG*, 196.

[There is] a self-denial which the disciple is required to practice for the sake of God and the kingdom of God. God claims our supreme affection. He asks that we love him with all the mind, all the soul, all the heart, all the strength; that there be no division of allegiance; that nothing else shall be interposed between ourselves and him as the great end for whom we exist; that we shall worship no other gods beside him. EC/*GG*, 191–92.

The demand for sacrifice always presupposes that what is to be renounced forms an obstacle to that absolute devotion which the kingdom of God requires (Mark 9:43). That not the external possession but the internal entanglement of the heart with temporal goods is condemned, Jesus strikingly indicates by the demand "to hate"

310

one's father and mother and wife and children and brethren and sisters, yea and one's own life also. *KGC*, 94.

Self-Disclosure of God

Owing to [the] permanent identification of God with his word, the lapse of time is not able to detract aught from the freshness and force that belonged to the self-disclosure of God at its first historic occurrence. It is not necessary to project one's self backward through the interval of the ages in order to feel near to the source of the revelation. The fountain of the living water flows close to every believer. HED/*SW*, 191.

No redemptive religion, however conceived, covenantal or otherwise, can dispense with the basis of divine, supernatural self-disclosure. HED/*SW*, 186.

The inward hidden content of God's mind can become the possession of man only through a voluntary disclosure on God's part. God must come to us before we can go to him. *BT*, 3–4.

If God be personal and conscious, then the inference is inevitable that in every mode of self-disclosure he will make a faultless expression of his nature and purpose. He will communicate his thought to the world with the stamp of divinity on it. *BT*, 11.

Seraphim

[commenting upon Isa. 6] In Jehovah's temple everything is expressive of his holiness, pervaded by the atmosphere of the divine; here everything created covers and humbles and effaces itself. Most strikingly this idea is symbolized by the seraphim, who, though themselves the highest representatives of a higher world, yet in the presence of God are made to feel their own insignificance as profoundly as the earth-born prophet. SDFI/*SW*, 274–75.

Servant of the Lord

The suffering Servant of Jehovah was portrayed under the figure of a lamb, to indicate that, while in one sense identical with the wayward flock, he was yet in another respect different from them, because innocent himself and willing to bear in patience the punishment the others had deserved. JB/*SW*, 302.

Service

■ [commenting upon Mark 10:43–45] The pagan princes exploit their subjects for their own selfish ends. But in the kingdom of God the opposite principle is to prevail: "Whosoever would become great among you shall be your minister, and whosoever would be first among you shall be servant of all." Then Jesus represents himself as the ideal example of such conduct, and for this purpose points to his own death as the consistent carrying out of the principle of self-sacrifice in the service of others. His death is the culminating act in his life of service. *SDJ*, 281.

■ [In Hebrews] the Christian life is called a λατρεία, a "service." As the word in the original shows, we must keep away from this conception all the modern associations of altruistic endeavor in the cause of God; it stands strictly for the service of worship which directly terminates upon God. It too has been taken from the ritual vocabulary of the Old Testament. Of the priests it is said that they "serve" in the tabernacle. "They that draw near" and "they that serve" are used in entirely the same connections to describe believers in their central religious occupation (Heb. 9:9; 10:1). The purifying of Christ's blood is for this purpose, that believers may be enabled by it "to serve the living God." HED/*SW*, 223.

■ We in our own way should also see to it that we do not foolishly squander our efforts at serving men in a thousand various directions when they will touch only the periphery of the evil of this world and can hardly expect to make a transitory ripple on the great sea of its sorrow. Rather let us concentrate our energies where alone they can permanently tell for the true betterment of things not for time merely but for eternity. Let us work for the salvation of souls from the judgment of God. If this is attained, then by the grace of God all the other

312

regenerative, cleansing and uplifting effects are bound to follow in the wake of our service. CDW/*GG*, 256.

The grand teaching of the epistle [to the Hebrews] that through Christ and the new covenant the heavenly projects into the earthly, as the headlands of a continent project into the ocean, should be made fruitful for the whole tone and temper of our Christian service. Every task should be at the same time a means of grace from and an incentive to work for heaven. HM/*GG*, 119.

Jesus . . . placed his whole life in the most absolute sense in the service of God. *SDJ*, 99.

Service, Motivation for

The question . . . is an extremely simple one: Do we love God for his own sake, and find in this love the inspiration of service, or do we patronize him as an influential partner under whose auspices we can better conduct our manifold activities in the service of the world? WT/*GG*, 17.

There is so much talk of service at the present day and it is so often deplorably noticeable that the idea people connect with this word is purely that of benevolence and helpfulness to man. If that is the meaning then the word is not fit to be the synonym of religion. The only true religious service is the one that puts foremost and guards foremost the supreme interest of God. That and nothing else is a true copy of the ministry of Jesus. CDW/*GG*, 255.

Shadow

[commenting upon Paul's usage in Col. 1:17] Paul in thus for-mulating it thinks along the horizontal line of historic development: the shadow is the obscure outline which the reality approaching through time casts before itself. Hence the correlative to the shadow is the body. HED/*SW*, 200.

The author of Hebrews . . . lets his thought move along the per-pendicular line that runs from heaven to earth: the shadow is a shadow not of something that comes after, but of something that lies above; it is not cast before, but reflected down; hence its correlate is not the body, but the εἰκών, the image, by which is meant the celestial prototype. According to [Heb. 10:1] the law has the shadow of the good things of the world to come, not the image itself. That image the new covenant possesses; but it existed in the presence of God in heaven when he gave the law to Israel, and from it the shadow came forth which the law presents. HED/*SW*, 200.

Sin

The source of sin according to the apostle does not lie in the flesh as a product of creation, but in the act of the first Adam imputed to all. *PE*, 299.

The slighting of the thought of God has for its inevitable correlate the weakening and ultimate loss of the specific consciousness of sin. EP, 361.

Sin is nothing other than renouncing, abandoning God's fellowship, turning away from him and choosing one's own way. SR/*GG*, 217.

[Sin] interposes a barrier between us and the goal of our Christian striving . . . it obscures the vision of the heavenly state; it weakens the desire for its enjoyment; it breaks the energy of the will in pursuing it. RR/*GG*, 133.

It is for sin an easy thing to approach us; we always carry it with us; it runs, as it were, the race with us; it is at the same time the most dangerous and the most ubiquitous of our spiritual foes. RR/*GG*, 134.

Every sin which we allow to stay with us may at any moment cause us to fall. RR/*GG*, 134.

There is no state of privilege, no degree of sanctification, that can render us absolutely secure to the allurements of sin. It is only the continuous supply of the grace of God in answer to our prayer and our faith that can shield us. EC/*GG*, 184.

314

Outside the sphere of Christianity all sin is interpreted as virtually a matter of ignorance. CFTBH/*SW*, 467.

[commenting upon the liberal notion of sin] Its essence is not opposition to God, but the failure to recognize the true attitude of God toward man as love. The most pronounced form of sin is unbelief with reference to the love of God in Christ. That with such a view of sin, and from a standpoint which makes love the only knowable attribute of God, the church doctrine of satisfaction has no ground left to stand on is plain. CFTBH/*SW*, 467–68.

Paul looks upon sin as transgression, unrighteousness, entailing the curse of the law, and therefore as requiring penal suffering of a vicarious nature in order to expiation. HED/*SW*, 215.

The author of Hebrews looks upon sin as defilement, entailing exclusion from the presence of God and therefore as requiring lustration, cleansing. HED/*SW*, 215.

Sin appears to [Isaiah] first of all, an infringement upon the honor of God. The idolatrous practices of the people are denounced for this reason. *BT*, 279.

Sinner

[The sinner] does not seek God, and when God comes to seek him, he does not answer, gives no signs of life, and remains insensible. SR/*GG*, 219.

Sitting

The sitting posture, with the hearers standing around, was characteristic of the relation between teacher and pupils, in distinction from the standing position, marking the prophet or gospel herald. HTR/*GG*, 26.

Skandalon

The *skandalon* is the chip of wood that holds the bait in a trap and causes the animal to be caught. *BT*, 389.

Social Gospel

A great difference [exists] between the social message of the prophets, and much that passes as social preaching nowadays. To the prophet it is the sinfulness of the wrong social conduct, to the modern social preacher it is too often the injuriousness to the social organism, that stands in the foreground. The prophets view the facts in their relation to God, as measured by the standards of absolute ethics and religion; the modern sociological enthusiast views them mainly, if not exclusively, in their bearing upon the welfare of man. What the prophets feature is the religious in the social; what many at the present time proclaim is the social devoid of or indifferent to the religious. *BT*, 276.

Socinians

The Socinians were bent upon showing that the death of Christ was not in any true sense an atoning sacrifice. PC/*SW*, 154.

For the Socinians the heavenly priesthood came to mean no more than a general position of influence with God. The error of this teaching lay not so much in denying that with reference to his death Jesus acted as a priest at the moment of its occurrence, but rather in severing the death from the priesthood generally. The principle to be strenuously maintained is that the priestly activity of Christ in heaven rests on the preceding sacrifice and therefore derives from the latter a strictly propitiatory character. PC/*SW*, 154.

Son

The messiahship appears in the reception on Jesus' part of the commission to *reveal* all things. But the sonship underlies this as the only basis on which it could take place, and the only basis on which it can be understood. And the sonship of this messianic person altogether transcends his historic appearance. It exists, as it were, in a timeless present, where he knows the Father and the Father knows him. Just as little as "the Father" and "Lord of heaven and earth" are titles derived from the historic situation or soteric undertaking, even

316

so little is "the Son" a designation of Jesus ultimately derived from such. He is called "the Son" not simply because of his being the Messiah, but because his messiahship is determined by an anterior sonship lying back of it. *SDJ*, 151.

▨ [commenting upon the parable of the wicked husbandmen] The Lord of the vineyard sends servant after servant, and when the mission of all these has proved fruitless, he sends his son (Matt.) or his one beloved son (Mark) or his beloved son (Luke). Here it is clear that sonship involves a higher dignity and a closer relation to God than the highest and closest official status known in the Old Testament theocracy. More is expected from the mission of the Son, precisely because he is the Son. And the parable further implies that the Son is the last, the final, ambassador, after the sending of whom nothing more can be done. The Lord of the vineyard has no further resources; the Son is the highest messenger of God conceivable. Hence absolute destruction befalls the husbandmen as the penalty for rejecting the Son; no sooner is the Son introduced and cast out than the whole process of God's dealing with the theocracy reaches its termination. *SDJ*, 161.

Son of God

▨ In regard to the title Son of God . . . we consider here primarily the relation of God to the Messiah, and of the Messiah to God. . . . Here we see the messiahship, though existing in time, yet solidly resting upon the eternal things of the Godhead. Here the profoundest Christology of the New Testament shows its ultimate roots. *SDJ*, 141.

▨ The names "Son of God" and "Son of man" cannot be thus simply distributed over the two natures of Christ as descriptive of the divine and the human respectively. Nor do the facts of the usage bear out such an impression. The mention of the resurrection jointly with the passion and death in some of the sayings shows that the conception of "Son of man" does not exclusively go with the thought of debasement and shame. The name as easily enters into the prospect beyond the passion, opened up by the transfiguration, as does the name "Son of God" (Mark 9:7, 9). *SDJ*, 236–37.

It is the name Son of God which holds [the] two aspects in [Jesus'] life, the eternal aspect and the temporal aspect, together in a common designation. *SDJ*, 187.

Son of Man

The special disgrace associated with the delivery of the Son of man to the Gentiles (Mark 10:33) points rather to a designation of high inherent dignity than to the opposite. The betrayal of the Son of man is an extreme crime, not merely, it seems, because committed upon the Messiah in general, but particularly because it is inflicted upon that high, majestic type of a Messiah which the name Son of man connotes (Mark 14:21). *SDJ*, 237.

The Son of man is the One greater than Jonah and Solomon, who is not appreciated in his greatness by his own generation (Luke 11:30–32). In all these instances the note of dignity and majesty is more or less clearly perceptible. *SDJ*, 237.

Even the transcendent glory which belongs of right to the Son of man Messiah as portrayed in Daniel cannot in the least dispense him from the experience of humiliation and death. Indeed, we may go even one step further and find it intimated that, notwithstanding the paradox involved, the glorious Son of man can come to complete revelation only after the impending disgrace and death shall have been suffered and surmounted. *SDJ*, 238.

In the Fourth Gospel the title Son of man connotes the heavenly, superhuman side of Jesus' mysterious existence; consequently it becomes the classical expression of what is called his pre-existence. *SDJ*, 239.

By calling himself the Son of man Jesus imparted to the messiahship his own heaven-centered spirit. And the height to which he thus lifted his person and his work may well have had something to do with the hesitancy of his early followers to name him with this greatest and most celestial of all titles. As a matter of fact, we can still test this by ourselves. Neither in the language of private piety, nor in that of common worship, hymnodic or otherwise, has the title Son of man ever become thoroughly domesticated. And it is perhaps good that this should be so. *SDJ*, 254.

■ The thought of humiliation and death is not analytically obtained from the name Son of man. Rather, it is joined to it on the principle of contrast. The conjunction to insert for paraphrasing is not "because" but "although." It is not that he must undergo humiliation, suffering and death *because* he is the Son of man, but that *although* he is the Son of man such a destiny is, paradoxically, in store for him. *SDJ*, 236.

■ In the saying that contrasts the shelterless Son of man with the foxes and birds the contrast loses its point if Jesus is set over against these animals merely as a man, generically, and even more so if he is set over against them as a weak, humiliated subject *per se*. The very point of the saying obviously is that the highest of the high, according to the name borne by him, should nevertheless have to do without such common creature comforts as even foxes and birds enjoy. *SDJ*, 237.

■ This is the favorite self-designation of Jesus; indeed, the Gospel writers never represent others as having so designated Jesus. *SDJ*, 39.

■ [When Jesus] uses the term Son of man, he speaks prospectively of his person . . . as the One who comes to judge, with the glory of his Father, and attended by the holy angels. *SDJ*, 84.

■ This name [Son of man] points back to the glorious, heavenly figure that appeared in Daniel's vision (Dan. 7:13–14); the one to whom the earth and its fulness belonged; for whom the service of all nations was destined as his rightful inheritance; this Son of man came to submit to and seek the very opposite—service, obedience, death. So the title Son of man brings before us as nothing else could do the unspeakable grace of our Lord, who being rich as God alone can be rich yet for our sakes became poor as only a dying creature can be poor that by his poverty we might be made rich. CDW/*GG*, 247–48.

Sonship

Of trinitarian sonship alone can it be said that it is anterior to messianic sonship, and at the same time possesses not a poorer but a richer content than the Old Testament idea of sonship. *MGMA*, 721.

Our Lord's eternal sonship qualifies him for filling the office of Messiah. This office is such, and implies such a relation of close affiliation with God, such an acting as the absolute representative of God, such a profound communion of life and purpose with God, that only a Son in the highest sense can adequately fill the office. Thus the office of messiahship calls for *a Son*. *SDJ*, 190.

[Jesus] did not become the Son through receiving the Spirit; on the contrary, he was baptized with the Spirit because he was already the Son. *SDJ*, 202.

The messianic sonship is simply the eternal sonship carried into a definite historical situation. *SDJ*, 190.

Sonship is from the nature of the case unmeritorious. *BT*, 114.

Matthew 11:27 (Luke 10:22) is by far the most important seat of the testimony which Jesus bears to his sonship. In fact, it marks the culminating point of our Lord's self-disclosure in the Synoptics. The Christology is so high as to call forth the comment that the words have a pronounced Johannine sound. *SDJ*, 143–44.

The kingdom neutralizes the effects of sin, but it does far more than this. It carries man to the highest limit of knowledge and love and service and enjoyment of God of which he is capable, and nothing less than the attainment of this our Lord associates with the term "sonship." *KGC*, 73–74.

The words recorded in Luke 20:36, "They are equal unto the angels; and are sons of God, being sons of the resurrection," suffice to show that sonship to God appeared to him as the acme rather than as the common level of religious privilege (see also Matt. 5:9). *KGC*, 74.

The most perfect mutual knowledge, the most direct communion of life, the most absolute unity of purpose, the joint possession of consummate blessedness and peace between God and man, all this forms part of the sonship in which the kingdom consists. *KGC*, 74.

The state of sonship, insofar as it involves communion with God, forms to Paul the religious aspect of life; justification lies at the basis of this sonship-life. *DB*, 317.

Religious sonship begins with justification, for justification is in its very conception an adoptive act. SDL/*SW*, 453.

[commenting upon Heb. 3:6] The superiority of Christ is again connected with his being *Son*. Moses was faithful as a servant, but Christ was faithful as a Son. Further, Moses was faithful *in* the house, because he was a servant; but Christ was faithful *over* the house, because he was a Son. . . . This is explained from the messianic conception of sonship. Christ had perfect supervision over the house. The thought, it should be carefully noted, is not that Moses was over the Old Testament house and Christ is over the New Testament house, but rather that Christ is a Son over *the same* house in which Moses was a servant. Christ was also the messianic Son, and therefore, in the time of Moses, it was Christ that built the house. Hence his messianic sonship goes back of his incarnation and reaches back into the historical pre-existence. *TEH*, 76–77.

Sonship and Priesthood

In [Heb. 1:3] the priestly office . . . stands under the ontological sonship. . . . In [Heb. 3:6] we read of Christ being set over the whole house of God, as a Son. Because he was a Son, he was also set over the priestly functions of the house of God. In [Heb. 4:14] he is called *a great high priest* because he is *Jesus the Son of God*. In [Heb. 5:5] we read, "Christ also glorified not himself to be made a high priest, but he that spake unto him, Thou art my Son, this day I have begotten thee." No one may usurp the office of high priest, which includes a great honor. Even Christ did not take this honor himself; it was given to him by God, who said to him, *Thou art my Son.* Thus the priestly honor is the outcome of the higher honor of the divine sonship. *TEH*, 105.

Now, if the greatness and eternity of the person of the Son of God determined the greatness and eternity-appearance of the figure of Melchizedek, and in consequence also determined the character of Melchizedek's priesthood, and if further the priesthood of Christ was, historically speaking, copied after the order of Melchizedek, then it follows that it is ultimately nothing else but the divine eternal nature of the Son of God by which his priesthood is shaped and from which it derives its unique character. His sonship makes his priesthood what it is in distinction from every other kind of priesthood. PC/*SW*, 153.

Sorrow

There is as much reason to pity the man to whom religion has brought no sorrow as the one to whom it has brought no joy. The bitter herbs may not be omitted from the paschal feast of deliverance. WT/*GG*, 6.

Sovereignty of God

Sovereignty denotes a relation existing by right, even where it is not actually enforced. *KGC*, 23.

In the case of Esau and Jacob everything is carefully arranged so as to eliminate from the outset all factors tending to obscure the moral issue of the absolute sovereignty of God. The two children are born of the same mother, and moreover at the same birth; and to exclude every thought of natural preference, the younger is preferred to the elder. No conceivable way remained of accounting for this differentiation except to attribute it to the sovereign choice of God. *BT*, 95.

One who makes a decree concerning a matter is above that matter; it is subject to his authority; he may do with it as he pleases. Thus

God's sovereignty is above all possible things; whether they will receive being and how they will be depends entirely upon his eternal purpose. NST, 18.

Space, God's Relation to

[commenting upon the Old Testament prophetic books] In regard to God's presence in space two representations occur. He abides in Zion, whence he roars (Amos 1:2), and where he has his royal throne (Isa. 2:3; 8:18). Hosea calls Canaan Jehovah's land (9:3). These statements do not involve any earthly limitation of God's presence. They are not remnants of a crude theology. These writers elsewhere represent God as dwelling in heaven (Hos. 5:15, of a return to heaven; Isa. 18:4; 33:5; Mic. 1:2–3). In Zion there is a presence of gracious revelation. Of course, the same is true with reference to heaven, for heaven, no more than any locality on earth, can circumscribe or bind God. The heaven is his throne, and the earth his footstool. *BT*, 243.

According to Amos 9:2, the reach of Jehovah's power is absolutely unlimited by space. True, this is expressed in anthropomorphic popular language. There is no hint of the idea that God is above all space, and strange to it in his own inner life. He, of course, recognizes space as an objective reality in the existence of the creature, but his own divine mode of existence it does not affect. *BT*, 243.

Special Revelation

It is a mistake to think that the sole result of the fall was the introduction of a supernatural revelation. As we shall presently see, supernaturalism in revelation, though its need was greatly accentuated by sin, did not first originate from the fact of sin. But, sin entering in, the structure of natural revelation itself is disturbed and put in need of correction. Nature from within no longer functions normally in sinful man. *BT*, 20.

The most important function of special revelation, however, under the regime of sin, does not lie in the correction and renewal of the faculty of perception of natural verities; it consists in the introduction of an altogether new world of truth, that relating to the redemption of man. *BT*, 20.

Spirit, against Platonic Conception of

Here lies the point in which the Pauline doctrine of the Spirit and the Hellenic or Hellenistic conception of the pneuma are sharply differentiated, striking though their similarity in other respects may be. The Greek philosophical pneuma, whether in its dualistic Platonic or neo-Platonic form, or in its hylozoistic Stoic form, lacks every historic significance; it is, even where it appears in contrast to an opposing element, the result of a bisection of nature, not the product of a supernatural divine activity. With Paul, both in regard to the σάρξ and the πνεῦμα, the historical factor remains the controlling one. If the sphere of the σάρξ is evil, this is not due to its natural constitution, because it is material or sensual, but because it has historically become evil through the entrance of sin. And when Paul views the pneumatic world as the consummated world, this also is not due simply to its natural constitution as the ideal nonsensual world, but because through the Messiah it has become the finished product of God's designs for man. EAP/*SW*, 116.

Spirit and Christ

Possession of the Spirit was that which marked [Christ's] entire life, with all its activities, to himself and to others, as belonging to the sphere of the supernatural. *SDJ*, 112.

The Spirit is to Jesus . . . above all else the author of God's wonderworld in general. *SDJ*, 112.

Now since the Spirit [Christ] dispenses is not only his own as an external possession, but has become through the resurrection thoroughly incorporated into his exalted nature, he gives, when he gives it, of his own, and the union effected between him and the Spirit and through the Spirit and believers, acquires the character of an organic mystical union, so that to be in the Spirit is to be in Christ. *BT*, 387.

Our Lord needed the Spirit as a real equipment of his human nature for the execution of his Messianic task. Jesus ascribed all his power and grace, the gracious words, the saving acts, to the possession of the Spirit (Matt. 12:28; Luke 4:18; Acts 10:36–38). And, through qualifying him in this manner for achieving his messianic task, the Spirit laid the foundation for the great pentecostal bestowal of the Spirit afterwards, for this gift was dependent on the finished work. *BT*, 321.

The apostle clearly teaches that Christ as God-man—as Mediator—in his exalted state has in a special, unique sense the disposal of the Spirit; inasmuch as the Spirit dwells in his own human nature and invests it with transcendent power and glory. Christ is the Lord of the Spirit; no, in even stronger language we say with Paul, Christ is the Spirit (1 Cor. 15:45; 2 Cor. 3:17). JRL/*GG*, 162–63.

[The] unique and close relationship between the Spirit and Christ dates from the moment of the resurrection. By the resurrection of the dead he was effectually decreed to be the Son of God in power (Rom. 1:4). At the resurrection he became the last Adam who is a life-giving Spirit (1 Cor. 15:45). In still another form the same thought is expressed when Paul represents the glory of Christ as the source from which supernatural power is brought to bear upon the believer (2 Cor. 3:18). This glory of Christ again is none other than his resurrection-glory. JRL/*GG*, 162–63.

Now everywhere in the Pauline teaching the Spirit is the mediating factor, whereby the reproduction of the experience of Christ in believers takes place. *PE*, 176–77.

Spirit and Eschatology

The Spirit is from the beginning to Paul the element of the eschatological, heavenly world. *SPC*, 485.

Because of [the] close association with the higher world the Spirit appears in closest conjunction with God, who is the center of that sphere. Every bearer of the Spirit forms a link of connection between man and the higher world. EAP/*SW*, 97.

The Spirit's proper sphere is the future aeon; from thence he projects himself into the present, and becomes a prophecy of himself in his eschatological operations. *PE*, 165.

The eschatological state [is] the state in which the Spirit is the pervasive element and characteristic force. *BT*, 387.

For Paul, the Spirit was regularly associated with the world to come, and from the Spirit thus conceived in all his supernatural and redemptive potency the Christian life receives throughout its specific character. EAP/*SW*, 125.

It is the Spirit of God who gives form and character to the eschatological life in the broadest and most pervasive sense, that the coming age is the age of the Spirit *par excellence*, so that all that enters into it, forms part of it, or takes place in it, must necessarily be baptized into the Pneuma as into an omnipresent element and thus itself become "spiritual" in its mode of existence and quality. EAP/*SW*, 122.

The Spirit "guides into all the truth," and hence is called "the Spirit of truth" (John 15:26; 16:13), and this must be taken in connection with the peculiar Johannine objective conception of "truth" as designating the transcendental realities of the heavenly world, that truth of which Jesus is the center and incarnation, whence also the Spirit in supplying it takes of Jesus' own (16:14–15). EAP/*SW*, 95.

Indeed, so absolutely does the Spirit belong to the other world, that the kosmos is simply declared incapable of receiving, beholding, and knowing him (John 14:17). EAP/*SW*, 95.

The Spirit has his proper sphere and a dominating part in the eschatological world. EAP/*SW*, 95.

[commenting upon the Spirit and the Old Testament] The Spirit appears as the source of the future new life of Israel, especially of the ethico-religious renewal, also as the pledge of divine favor for the new Israel, and as the author of a radical transformation of physical conditions in the eschatological era, and thus becomes characteristic of the eschatological state itself. EAP/*SW*, 96.

█ The Spirit [is] representative of the supernatural, heavenly world in [John] 3:3, 5, 6, 8. EAP/*SW*, 100.

█ It is still our conviction that the wide range of the Spirit's influence which forms so striking a feature of Paul's teaching, has its ultimate source in the apostle's eschatological conception of the pneuma. Because the Spirit is the bearer of the whole future life, and because the future life already projects into the present Christian state, therefore, and not for any reason connected with the cultus, the Spirit becomes a pervasive dominating force at every point in the believer's life. *KC/SW*, 540.

█ The connection of the Spirit with eschatology reaches back far into the Old Testament. The fundamental sense of [Spirit] is in the Hebrew, and other Semitic languages, that of air in motion, whilst with the Greek *pneuma* the notion of air at rest seems to have been chiefly associated. This rendered the Hebrew term fitted for describing the Spirit on his energizing, active side, which further falls in with his ultimate eschatological function of producing supernatural effects on the highest plane. Thus, the Spirit comes to be linked together with eschatology. *PE*, 160.

█ The actual elements into which the eternal and heavenly unfold themselves are chiefly four: the Spirit, life, glory, the kingdom of God. The first of these four underlies and produces the second and the third, so that the whole might be reduced to the Spirit and the kingdom of God. The Spirit is the fundamental creative factor as regards life and glory in the saints. *PE*, 298.

█ The present enjoyment of the Spirit's gifts is an anticipation of the world to come. EAP/*SW*, 100.

█ [commenting upon 2 Cor. 5:5 and Rom. 8:23] The Spirit is viewed as pertaining specifically to the future life, nay as constituting the substantial make-up of this life, and the present possession of the Spirit by the believer is regarded in the light of an anticipation. The Spirit's proper sphere is according to this the world to come; from there he projects himself into the present, and becomes a prophecy of himself in his eschatological operation. EAP/*SW*, 103.

Spirit and Ethics

The Spirit is the source of the moral and religious renewal of man, the author and bearer of the entire Christian life with all its graces and virtues. *KGC*, 57.

The Spirit cannot deny himself in whatever sphere his energy is introduced, least of all where he works in the consummate state, where all God's works and ways run together to produce a perfect issue. *PE*, 308.

The glory and the Spirit to [Paul] are identical. As we have seen the glory means the equipment, with supernatural power and splendor, of the exalted Christ. And this equipment, described from the point of view of its energizing source, consists of the Holy Spirit. MEM/*GG*, 98.

Spirit and Righteousness

The possession of the Spirit is for Paul the natural correlate, the crown and insofar the infallible exponent of the state of δικαιοσύνη. . . . The life and glory of the exalted Savior are the product and seal and exponent of his status of righteousness. Speaking in our own terms, and yet faithfully rendering the Pauline conception, we may say that in his resurrection-state Christ is righteousness incarnate. EAP/*SW*, 109.

It must be remarked that the resurrection-state which is thus exponential of righteousness is entirely based on the Spirit (cf. 1 Tim. 3:16, ἐδικαιώθη ἐν πνεύματι). By becoming Pneuma Christ has become the living witness of the eternal presence of righteousness for us in the sight of God. EAP/*SW*, 109.

For in Christ [the] Spirit which is the seal and fruit of righteousness is none other than the Spirit of the consummate life and the
consummate glory, the circumambient element of the eschatological state in general. The conclusion, therefore, is fully warranted that
the Spirit as a living attestation of the state of righteousness in the
believer has this significance, because he is in principle the fountain
of the blessedness of the world to come. EAP/SW, 110.

[commenting upon Gal. 5:5] Here the righteousness of the world
to come, which is to be bestowed in the last judgment, is represented
as a thing which the Christian still waits for. This waiting, however,
is determined by two coordinated factors: on the one hand it takes
place ἐκ πίστεως, on the other hand πνεύματι, and these two designate the subjective and the objective ground respectively on which
the confident expectation is based. In the Spirit, not in the σάρξ, in
faith, not in ἔργα νόμου, has the Christian assurance that the full
eschatological righteousness will become his (see also Titus 3:7).
EAP/SW, 110–11.

Spirit and the Kingdom of God

Where the Spirit of God operates, there the kingdom of God
comes. KGC, 56.

The Baptist makes the Holy Spirit the element wherein Jesus will
baptize, and thus the distinctive element of the coming kingdom.
EAP/SW, 99.

Spirit and the Old Testament

In the Old Testament the Spirit is the Spirit of the theocratic
charismata, who qualifies prophets, priests and kings for their office,
but is not communicable from one to the other. Of this charismatic
Spirit Jesus has received the fulness, and, having the fulness, dispenses of it to his followers, first partially and by means of promise,
then in greater fulness by way of fulfillment at Pentecost. BT, 387.

329

In the Old Testament the emphasis still rests on the charismatic character of the Spirit's work as qualifying the office-bearers of the theocracy for their task. *KGC*, 58.

The connection of the Spirit with eschatology reaches back into the Old Testament. The fundamental sense of רוּחַ is, in the Old Testament, that of air in motion, whilst that of air at rest seems to have been chiefly associated with the Greek πνεῦμα. This rendered the word fit to describe the Spirit on his energizing, active side and falls in with his ultimate eschatological function. *EAP/SW*, 95.

In the Old Testament Spirit appears as the comprehensive formula for the transcendental, the supernatural. *EAP/SW*, 97.

Spirit and the Resurrection

The Spirit and the resurrection belong together, and that in a twofold sense. On the one hand the resurrection as an act is derived from the Spirit, on the other hand the resurrection-state is represented as in permanent dependence on the Spirit, as a pneumatic state. *EAP/SW*, 101.

The Spirit is not only the author of the resurrection-act, but likewise the permanent substratum of the resurrection-life, to which he supplies the inner, basic element and the outer atmosphere. *PE*, 165.

[commenting upon 1 Cor. 15:42–49] The whole tenor of the argument . . . compels us to think of the resurrection as the moment at which τὸ Πνευματικόν entered. Christ appeared then and there in the form of a Πνευματικός and as such inaugurated the eschatological era. *PE*, 168.

Both the origin of the resurrection life and the continuance of the resurrection state are dependent on the Spirit (Rom. 8:10–11; 1 Cor. 15:45–49; Gal. 6:8). *ENT/SW*, 45.

On the one hand the Spirit is the resurrection-source, on the other he appears as the substratum of the resurrection-life, the element, as it were, in which, as in its circumambient atmosphere the life of the coming aeon shall be lived. He produces the event and in continuance underlies the state which is the result of it. He is Creator and Sustainer at once, the *Creator Spiritus* and the Sustainer of the supernatural state of the future life in one. *PE*, 163.

[commenting upon Rom. 8:11] In verse 11 there is substituted for the simple *pneuma* the full definition "the Spirit of him that raised Jesus from the dead." In this designation of God resides the force of the argument: what God did for Jesus he will do for the believer likewise. It is presupposed by the apostle, though not expressed in so many words, that God raised Jesus through the Spirit. *PE*, 163.

If the Spirit of God who raised Jesus dwells in you, then God will make the indwelling Spirit accomplish for you what he accomplished for Jesus in the latter's resurrection. The idea of the "indwelling" of the Spirit in believers, occurring as it does in a train of thought prospective to the resurrection, can hardly help suggesting a process of preparation carried on with a view to that supreme eventual crisis. The Spirit is there as indwelling certainly not only for *assuring* the Christian of his ultimate attainment to the resurrection. The indwelling must attest itself by activity also. *PE*, 164.

Paul means to characterize the resurrection-state as the state in which the *Pneuma* rules. *PE*, 167.

Spirit and the Resurrection Body

First Corinthians 15:42–49 contrasts the two bodies that belong to the preeschatological and the eschatological states successively. The former is characterized as ψυχικόν the latter as πνευματικόν. This adjective *pneumatikon* expresses the quality of the body in the eschatological state. Every thought of immaterialness or etherealness or absence of physical density ought to be kept carefully removed from the term. *PE*, 166.

[commenting upon 1 Cor. 15:42–49] The passage is unique . . . in that it contrasts not the body affected by sin, not the body as it came to exist as a result of entrance of evil into the world, with the future body, but the primordial body of Adam ("the first Adam") and the body of the consummation. *PE*, 167.

Spirit and the Supernatural

Jesus performs all his work, even that pertaining to the immanent kingdom, in the Spirit, and the Spirit stands for the supernatural. *KGC*, 44–45.

The Spirit is pre-eminently . . . the source of the supernatural. *SDJ*, 22.

Spirit versus the Letter

The Spirit stands for the living, energizing, creative grace of God, the letter for the inability of the law as such to translate itself into action. MEM/*GG*, 98.

Spirituality

Devotion, worship, the giving answer to God, cannot but spiritualize. It is, as it were, the projection into the objective sphere of the intrinsically translucent essence of the religious soul itself. And it is called to enter into the direct presence of and lay hold upon Jehovah himself, in doing which it grasps the root of all spirituality. EP, 350–51.

State

According to our modern conception, especially in its republican form, the institution of the state with its magistrate exists for the sake of the subjects; even the king, at least in a constitutional monarchy, may be considered as a means to an end. In the ancient state this is different. Here the individual exists for the state, and in the Oriental monarchy the state is centralized and summed up in the person of the ruler. *KGC*, 50.

Subjective Element of Christianity

In the biblical religion the subjective element is nowhere lacking; on the contrary, it enters into the fabric of practical Christianity with exceptional richness such as no pagan form of piety can rival. But it always keeps in the closest touch with what God has done in the objective sphere, outside the subjectivity of the believer. *SDJ*, 21.

Suffering

[commenting upon 1 Peter] The suffering of which the epistle speaks so much was not suffering in general, but suffering of a specific kind—that brought upon believers by the enmity of the world; whence also it was prefigured by the suffering of Christ. And the world makes the Christian suffer because it instinctively recognizes that the latter belongs to a different, to an opposite order of things than itself. The malice of the world springs from reservations that the believer should refuse to identify himself with the world. CH/*GG*, 147.

Just as our Lord Jesus did not merely bear his cross, but entered into its spirit, approved of it and made it by his obedience and submission effective for atonement, so we must take upon ourselves (or receive, as another passage says) the chastisement of the Lord. We must search ourselves to discover the purpose God has in sending it to us and then deliberately set ourselves to give effect to it. EC/*GG*, 195.

What is more natural than that God should in his grace reward with the heavenly life those who thus suffer for him, so that patience and glory appear in relation to one another as the race does to the crown? God cannot but honor this loyalty to himself evinced in suffering; of such patient runners he is not ashamed to be called their God and he has prepared for them a city. RR/*GG*, 136.

In the Christian's pursuit of the kingdom of God, suffering and trials are the inevitable concomitants; and far from hindering him in his progress, they must become the means of helping him onward through the development in him of patience. RR/*GG*, 134–35.

Peter's rebuke of Jesus involved a temptation. Satan had his hand in it. Peter had disapproved of the program of suffering and death announced by Jesus. There is here, then, apprehension of the *fact*, even though it be without apprehension of the *purpose* of the fact. *SDJ*, 77.

[commenting upon Heb. 2:17–18] Because Christ's sufferings were not sufferings in general, but specifically temptation-sufferings, sufferings which became for him a source of temptation, therefore he can succor those who are in an analogous situation, i.e., tempted to sin by their sufferings. The aorist participle πειρασθείς has causal force and assigns the temptation-aspect of his sufferings as the ground for his ability to succor. It is not the memory of suffering in general that evokes his sympathy; the thought is much more concrete and specific: the sufferings which he has behind him and carries with him as a past experience (notice the perfect tense πέπον-θεν) enable him to know what force of temptation suffering exerts to make the sinner fall. PC/*SW*, 145.

Supernatural

The supernatural is the *liebstes Kind* [beloved child] of eschatology. *SDJ*, 23.

[commenting on the relationship between the supernatural and historical] The historical can be supernatural, the supernatural can enter history, and so become a piece of the historical in its highest form. There is no mutual exclusiveness. It is pure prejudice, when historians lay down the principle that they are allowed to reckon with the natural only. *BT*, 305.

Supernaturalism and Christ

In [Christ's] mind were perfectly united the two hemispheres of supernaturalism, that of the source of power behind, and that of the eternal goal of life beyond every work. HM/*GG*, 119.

Supernaturalism and Historic Christianity

It is safe to say that a Christianity which plants itself squarely upon the foundation of the supernatural history will always be a doctrinal Christianity and vice versa. CFTBH/*SW*, 462.

334

We find nothing in the two conceptions of the supernatural and historical which would be mutually exclusive. A thing is no less historical because it is supernatural; the supernatural is the highest history. CFTBH/*SW*, 464.

[commenting upon the modern hypothesis and the Book of Isaiah] The *truth* of salvation preached by an accredited prophet in close connection with supernatural facts—this is what the healthy realism of the church has always believed in and judged essential to its faith; to cease insisting upon this and deem the *bare idea* of salvation, as developed in the fancy of some postexilic writer, and lacking all adequate historical basis, sufficient, is nothing else than rationalism and Pelagianism in principle. RCEP, 617.

It is in the bold realism of the biblical doctrine of the last things that the fundamental supernaturalism of the Bible most emphatically asserts itself. OLDR/*SW*, 317.

Surety

[commenting upon Heb. 7] It becomes very clear from this passage that in virtue of his priesthood Jesus is the ἔγγυος, "surety," of the new covenant. "Surety" means here the one who guarantees that the covenant shall accomplish what it is designed to accomplish. The idea stands in contrast to the inefficacy of the old covenant, which possessed no such guarantor. What the writer means is that Jesus by his supernatural personality, by his whole character, affords the assurance that the covenant administered by him will be efficacious. PC/*SW*, 136.

Symbol

A symbol is in its religious significance something that profoundly portrays a certain fact or principle or relationship of a spiritual nature in a visible form. The things it pictures are of present existence and present application. They are in force at the time in which the symbol operates. *BT*, 144.

Symbol and Type

▨ [commenting on the relationship between symbol and type] The main problem to understand is, how the same system of portrayals can have served at one and the same time in a symbolical and a typical capacity. . . . The solution of the problem lies in this, that the things symbolized and the things typified are not different sets of things. They are in reality the same things, only different in this respect that they come first on a lower stage of development in redemption, and then again, in a later period, on a higher stage. Thus what is symbolical with regard to the already existing edition of the fact or truth becomes typical, prophetic, of the later, final edition of that same fact or truth. From this it will be perceived that a type can never be a type independently of its being first a symbol. The gateway to the house of typology is at the farther end of the house of symbolism. *BT*, 145.

Tabernacle

▨ It is the place where the people offer their worship to God. It is the palace of the King in which the people render him homage. *BT*, 151.

▨ The tabernacle represented absolute unity of worship. *MOP*, 92.

▨ The tabernacle affords a clear instance of the coexistence of the symbolical and the typical in one of the principal institutions of the Old Testament religion. It embodies the eminently religious idea of the dwelling of God with his people. This it expresses symbolically so far as the Old Testament state of religion is concerned, and typically as regards the final embodiment of salvation in the Christian state. The tabernacle is, as it were, a concentrated theocracy. That its main purpose is to realize the indwelling of Jehovah is affirmed in so many words (Ex. 25:8; 29:44– 45). It derives its most general name from this, namely, *mishkan*, "dwelling-place." *BT*, 148.

Tabernacle and Heaven

▨ If the tabernacle symbolized the heavenly habitation of God, and the ideal destiny of God's people has always been to be received of

336

him to the most consummate fellowship there, then there must have been at least an ideal reflex and foreshadowing of this in the tabernacle. *BT*, 154.

In [Heb. 9:24] the author speaks of the earthly tabernacle as the *antitype* of the true tabernacle (*antitupa tōn alēthinōn*). This manner of speaking differs from our own, and also from that of Paul and Peter. The latter uniformly regard the Old Testament as the type of which the New Testament is the antitype; this is the common New Testament usage. But the author of Hebrews, on the contrary, speaks of the Old Testament as the *antitype*. An antitype, of course, always has a type lying back of it as its model. To find the original *type*, of which the Old Testament is the antitype, then, we must go back of the Old Testament to heaven. This heavenly type was shown to Moses on Mount Sinai. *TEH*, 58.

Tabernacle, Fulfilled in Jesus Christ

We must ask: where do [the] religious principles and realities, which the tabernacle served to teach and communicate, reappear in the subsequent history of redemption, lifted to their consummate stage? First we discover them in the glorified Christ. Of this speaks the Evangelist (John 1:14). The Word become flesh is the One in whom God came to tabernacle among men, in order to reveal to them his grace and glory. In John 2:19–22 Jesus himself predicts that the Old Testament temple, which his enemies by their attitude toward him are virtually destroying, he will build up again in three days, i.e., through the resurrection. This affirms the continuity between the Old Testament sanctuary and his glorified person. In him will be for ever perpetuated all that tabernacle and temple stood for. *BT*, 154–55.

Temple

Isaiah in his temple vision sees Jehovah himself. And he sees Jehovah in his temple, that is to say, in the place where everything is subordinated to God, and God sets the stamp of his presence upon everything, the place of worship. *BT*, 235.

A temple is not intended to contain God in the sense of a human habitation; it is intended to be filled with the glorious presence of God. The ideal temple in all its parts, in its ritual of sacrifice and service, with its music and incense, in its very construction is nothing but the receptacle and the reflector of the glory of him who inhabits it. OHGG/*GG*, 263.

Temple, Building of

There is the building of the house of God by the son of David who is honored with the title "son of God." It will be noticed that in this revelation David is not called the "son of God," but only his successor, Solomon, is so designated. The proximate reason for this is that David was a man of war and blood, whereas the house of Jehovah should be built by a man of peace—and for the reason that the final kingdom must be characterized by peace and not war. But there shines through still another reason for this arrangement, viz., that the one who is to build the house of God cannot proceed of himself. He is not allowed to undertake this function unless previously he will have appeared in his own person as the product of the building activity of God. *ESOT*, 125.

Neither David nor any other mere man can construct the house of God. God must build first; then, on the basis of this, the successor of David, i.e., Solomon, can proceed with the building of the temple. This is so arranged to uphold within the frame of the prophecy the principle of the precedence of God's work before and above every human work in the realization of the consummate theocracy. *ESOT*, 126.

Temptation, Satan's

The plan of temptation followed by Satan evinces, though not equal subtlety in all its parts, nevertheless a certain profundity of insight into the issues at stake, and a certain strategic eagerness to conquer Jesus, not at some subordinate point, but at the central, pivotal position, on which the successful outcome of the plan of redemption depended. Satan knew very well that this pivotal point lay in Jesus' absolute and resolute adherence to the principle of humiliation and suffering as the only road to victory and glory. It gave him, no doubt, a sinister satisfaction to attempt to overthrow the work of God and Christ at its very center. Any kind of sin would have disqualified Jesus for his messianic task, but the sin suggested here would have been a sin against the very heart and essence of the task. *BT*, 342.

[commenting upon Israel in the wilderness and the second temptation of the Lord by Satan] To tempt Jehovah has the meaning of "proving God," that is, of seeking to ascertain by experiment whether his power to lead them to Canaan could be relied upon. It was a proving springing from doubt or outright unbelief. What happened at Massah figured in later times as the typical example of the sin of unbelief (Ps. 95:8; Heb. 3–4). Our Lord plainly implies that casting himself down from the height of the temple, trusting that angels would intercept his fall, would not in principle differ from the conduct of these murmuring Hebrews in the wilderness. *BT*, 338.

It must be acknowledged that the third temptation was a more fundamental one in that it uncovered the ultimate issue around which things had been revolving from the outset. The question at stake was, whether God should be God, or Satan should be God, and correspondingly, whether the Messiah should be God's or Satan's Messiah. For this is the deeper background which Satan's conditional "if" and his consequent promise about the gift of the glory of the kingdoms reveal to us. The two acts would not have been single, isolated acts of sin. They would have involved a transfer of allegiance on Jesus' part from God to Satan. *BT*, 339.

[Satan's] only hope lay in making Jesus fall out of [the] role of self-sacrifice and humiliation. Satan grasped better than some human theologians have done in what lay the inner principle, the true essence of our Lord's redeeming work. However evil his intentions, he was sound in his doctrinal views on the atonement. EC/*GG*, 183.

In our case temptation chiefly raises the question of how we shall pass through it and issue from it without loss. In Jesus' case, while this consideration was not, of course, absent, the higher concern was not avoidance of loss, but the procuring of positive gain. *BT*, 333.

▨ [Jesus] existed as Messiah in a state of humiliation. After that had been passed through, a state of exaltation would follow, in which these various things now offered to him as temptations would become perfectly normal and allowable. What was not inherently sinful became so in his case, because of the law of humiliation and service under which his life had for the present been put. The animus of the temptation, from Satan's point of view, consisted in the attempt to move Jesus out of this spirit and attitude of service and humiliation, so as to yield to the natural desire for his messianic glory without an interval of suffering. *BT*, 335.

▨ It is highly significant in this connection, that the words wherewith Jesus repels the tempter are taken from the Torah, the Book of the Law (Deuteronomy), as though by thus placing himself under the law Jesus wished to remind Satan of the real matter at issue, the question of humiliation versus the assertion of the prerogatives belonging to a state of glory. *BT*, 335.

Theocracy

▨ [commenting on the parable of the wicked husbandmen] The Lord of the vineyard has no further resources; the Son is the highest messenger of God conceivable. Hence absolute destruction befalls the husbandmen as the penalty for rejecting the Son; no sooner is the Son introduced and cast out than the whole process of God's dealing with the theocracy reaches its termination. Herein lies the reason why Jesus rectifies the answer given by the rulers to his question: "What will the Lord of the vineyard do to those husbandmen?" They had answered: "He will miserably destroy those miserable men, and will let out the vineyard unto other husbandmen, who shall render him the fruits in their season." This answer assumed that nothing more radical would follow than a change of administration; that Caiaphas and his fellows, the Sanhedrists, would be destroyed, and other rulers put in their places, after which the theocracy might go on as before. Jesus corrects this facile assumption; to his mind this answer was utterly inadequate. They had not appreciated the full gravity of the rejection of the Son of God as entailing the complete overthrow of the theocracy, and the rearing from the foundation up of a new structure in which the Son, thus rejected, would receive full vindication and supreme honor: "Did ye never read in the Scriptures, the stone which the builders rejected, the same was made the head of the corner; this was from the Lord, and it is marvellous in our eyes? Therefore I say unto you, the kingdom of God shall be taken away from you, and it shall be given to a nation bringing forth the fruits thereof." *SDJ*, 161–62.

[The] theocratic organization of Israel had something ideal about it from the beginning. It could not be attained. It hovered over the life of the people. *ESOT*, 118.

Toward the close of his ministry our Lord opened up the prospect of a new form of development upon which in result of his death and glorification the spiritual kingdom would enter. This is the church (Matt. 16:18–19). The connection in which this announcement occurs is highly significant. It is immediately followed by the announcement of our Lord's sufferings and death and resurrection. Obviously the church here appears as that which is to take the place of the Old Testament theocracy, which, by finally rejecting Jesus, has sealed its own fate of destruction. KOG/*SW*, 315.

In the theocracy the church had dominated the life of the people of God in all its extent. State and church were in it most intimately united. Jesus on more than one occasion gave to understand that in this respect at least the conditions of the old covenant were not to be perpetuated (see Matt. 22:21; John 18:36; 19:11). *KGC*, 88.

The great principles and realities of theocratic life were embodied in external form. This was the only way to clothe the essence of the theocracy in a way that the Israelites could grasp. In order to keep the future eschatological picture in touch with Israel's religion these forms had to be maintained. The prophets had to give the essence in particular forms. Eschatological revelation is presented in the language of the Mosaic institutions. The New Testament first transposes it into a new key. Here in the New Testament it is spiritualized. In the Old Testament it is expressed in terms of perfection of the forms of Israel's theocracy. The holy city is center; offices, organization, peace, abundance, etc., are there, but this all is to be eternalized in the messianic era, and will be free of the vicissitudes of the present era. *ESOT*, 118.

Theocracy and Heaven

A missionary institution the theocracy never was intended to be in its Old Testament state. The significance of the unique organization of Israel can be rightly measured only by remembering that the theocracy typified nothing short of the perfected kingdom of God, the consummate state of heaven. In this ideal state there will be no longer any place for the distinction between church and state. The former will have absorbed the latter. *BT*, 125–26.

The primary purpose of Israel's theocratic constitution was not to teach the world the principles of civil government, though undoubtedly in this respect also valuable lessons can be learned from it, but to reflect the eternal laws of religious intercourse between God and man as they will exist in the consummate life at the end. *KGC*, 50.

The eschatological idea influencing the constitution of the theocracy becomes dependent on the interaction of the type and the antitype. The future state imposes its own stamp on the theocracy, an actual institution of Israel. The theocratic structure projects its own character into the picture of the future. Heaven reflected itself on Israel and Israel became part of the future. The type inevitably influences the conception of the antitype. The future is depicted in terms drawn from the present, earthly, material reality. There is somewhat of the shadowy, inadequate character of the prefiguration that passes over into the description of what the eschatological will be like when it comes. The antitype impresses its stamp upon the theocratic structure and imparts to it somewhat of its transcendent, absolute character. The theocracy has something ideal or unattainable about it. Its plan, as conceived by the law, hovers over the actual life of Israel. The theocracy in the idea transcends its embodiment in experience. *ESOT*, 117–18.

Theologian's Duty

[The Christian's] attitude from the outset must be a dependent and receptive one. To let the image of God's self-revelation in the Scriptures mirror itself as fully and clearly as possible in his mind, is the first and most important duty of every theologian. IBT/*SW*, 5.

Theology

Etymology, in many cases a safer guide than *a priori* constructions, tells us that theology is *knowledge concerning God*, and this primitive definition is fully supported by encyclopedic principles. IBT/*SW*, 4.

God, as distinct from the creature, is the only legitimate object of theology. IBT/*SW*, 4.

In theology the object, far from being passive, by the act of creation first posits the subject over against itself, and then as the living God proceeds to impart to this subject that to which of itself it would have no access. For "the things of God none knoweth, save the Spirit of God." Strictly speaking, therefore, we should say that not God in and for himself, but God insofar as he has revealed himself, is the object of theology. IBT/*SW*, 5.

Theophany

No theophany took place without a sacrifice, which shows how closely the ideas of a revelation made by God, and of a sacrifice made by man, were connected in the Israelitish mind. *MOP*, 218.

The theophanic form of appearance does not disclose what God is ontologically in himself, but merely how he condescends to appear and work for the redemption of his people. It establishes a redemptive and revelatory presence in definite localities, which does not, in the mind of the writer, detract from the divine omnipresence. OMP/*ISBE*, 2190.

It may seem at first a trite thought, that Jehovah must appear on the scene before he can interpose. But the theophany does not occur as the mere prerequisite or precursor of the divine action, it is the vehicle of the action itself. EP, 344.

Theophanies are personal representations of God in visible form. They go beyond the mere purpose of revelation; they express, in primitive form, God's approach to and communion with man. God does not merely speak in a theophany; he acts! *ESOT*, 85.

Thousand Years

[In the Book of Revelation] the principle of "recapitulation," i.e., of cotemporaneousness of things successively depicted, seems to underlie the visions, and numbers are elsewhere in the book meant symbolically. These facts leave open the possibility that the thousand years are synchronous with the earlier developments recorded, and symbolically describe the state of glorified life enjoyed with Christ in heaven by the martyrs during the intermediate period preceding the parousia. ENT/*SW*, 44–45.

The symbolism of the thousand years consists in this, that it contrasts the glorious state of the martyrs on the one hand with the brief season of tribulation passed here on earth, and on the other hand with the eternal life of the consummation. The binding of Satan for this period marks the first eschatological conquest of Christ over the powers of evil, as distinguished from the renewed activity to be displayed by Satan toward the end in bringing up against the church still other forces not hitherto introduced into the conflict. ENT/*SW*, 45.

344

Time

Eternity is not pregnant with other eternities. We do not hear of further sowings nor further reaping in the fields of the blessed. It is useless to carry the spirit of time into the heart of eternity. *PE*, 316.

The category of time is exchanged for that of space when the final state is located in or identified with heaven. *PE*, 297.

Like Abraham we must resolutely confess that we are strangers and pilgrims in a land of time, and that the best this land can offer us is but a caravanserai to tarry in for a day and a night. HM/*GG*, 117.

Time, especially time with the wasting power it acquires through sin, is the arch-enemy of all human achievement. It kills the root of joy which otherwise belongs to working and building. All things which the succeeding generations of mankind have wrought in the course of the ages succumb to its attacks. The tragic sense of this accompanies the race at every step in its march through history. It is like a pall cast over the face of the peoples. MEM/*GG*, 89.

Translation, as the Goal

The only reasonable interpretation of the Genesis-account (*e mente Pauli*) is this, that provision was made and probation was instituted for a still higher state, both ethico-religiously and physically complexioned, than was at that time in the possession of man. In other words the eschatological complex and prospect were there in the purpose of God from the beginning. *PE*, 304.

The divine method in general is not to bring out of the chaos and dissolution of sin the return simply of the former state of affairs but the attainment of a higher order of things. *BT*, 189.

For the eschatological process is intended not only to put man back at the point where he stood before the invasion of sin and death, but to carry him higher to a plane of life not attained before the probation, nor, so far as we can see, attainable without it. *PE*, 72.

■ The concrete purpose God had in view [was] the advance from [the state in which man was created] to a still higher estate. Man had been created perfectly good in a moral sense. And yet there was a sense in which he could be raised to a still higher level of perfection. On the surface this seems to involve a contradiction. It will be removed by closely marking the aspect in regard to which the advance was contemplated. The advance was meant to be from unconfirmed to confirmed goodness and blessedness; to the confirmed state in which these possessions could no longer be lost, a state in which man could no longer sin, and hence could no longer become subject to the consequences of sin. *BT*, 22.

■ Man's original state was a state of indefinite probation: he remained in possession of what he had, so long as he did not commit sin, but it was not a state in which the continuance of his religious and moral status could be guaranteed him. In order to assure this for him, he had to be subjected to an intensified, concentrated probation, in which, if he remained standing, the status of probation would be forever left behind. The provision of this new, higher prospect for man was an act of condescension and high favor. *BT*, 22.

■ To Paul the supernatural state stands at the end of the development, and therefore can, discounting the intervening reign of sin, be brought into connection with the first man only as a prospect or goal placed before him, not as a remedy to offset any inherent deficiencies of created human nature. *LT*, 127.

■ The Christian religion was born under the auspices of [the] primordial and irreducible contrast of the two worlds involving the trend of the pious from below to on high and their destiny to arrive at the goal of their deepest aspiration. *PE*, 298.

■ The apostle's doctrine of salvation . . . represents the pneuma as doing more than neutralizing the influence of sin. It lifts man to the higher stage of the supernatural life, which the first Adam even before he sinned did not possess. *KC*, 643; *KC/SW*, 541.

346

▓ Christ's work for us extends even farther than the restoration of what sin has destroyed. If Christ placed us back there where Adam stood in his rectitude, without sins and without death, this would be unspeakable grace indeed, more than enough to make the gospel a blessed word. But grace exceeds sin far more abundantly than all this: besides wiping out the last vestige of sin and its consequences, it opens up for us that higher world to whose threshold even the first Adam had not yet apprehended. And this is not a mere matter of degrees in blessedness, it is a difference between two modes of life; as heaven is high above the earth, by so much the conditions of our future state will transcend those of the paradise of old. JRL/*GG*, 166.

▓ The question why Paul, after having up to [1 Cor. 15:44a] . . . constructed his whole argument on the basis of a comparison between the body of sin and the body of the resurrection, substitutes from verse 44b on, for the body of sin, the body of creation, is both a difficult and interesting one. The answer cannot be found by ascribing to him the view that the creation-body and the body of sin are identical, in other words that the evil predicates of φθορά, ἀτιμία, ἀσθένεια enumerated in verses 42–43 belong to the body in virtue of creation. Paul teaches too plainly elsewhere that these things came into the world through sin. The proper solution seems to be to us the following: The apostle was intent upon showing that in the plan of God from the outset provision was made for a higher kind of body than that of our present experience. From the abnormal body of sin no inference can be drawn as to the existence of another kind of body. The abnormal and the eschatological are not so logically correlated that the one can be postulated from the other. But the world of creation and the world of eschatology are thus correlated, the one points forward to the other; on the principle of typology the first Adam prefigures the second Adam, the psychical body, the pneumatic body (see Rom. 5:14). EAP/*SW*, 106.

▓ The ideal destiny of God's people has always been to be received of him to the most consummate fellowship [in the heavenly habitation]. *BT*, 154.

THE ANTHOLOGY

Treasures, Earthly

Jesus requires of his disciples the renunciation of all earthly bonds and possessions which would dispute God his supreme sway over their life (Matt. 10:39; 16:25; Luke 14:25–35). The statements to this effect are not meant in the sense that external abandonment of these things is sufficient or even required. The idea is that the inward attachment of the soul to them as the highest good must be in principle destroyed, that God may take the place hitherto claimed by them. *KGC*, 94.

Treasures, Eternal

To be a child of God and a disciple of Jesus means to hold in one's hand the treasures of eternity. HTR/*GG*, 29.

Tree of Knowledge of Good and Evil

The tree is called the tree of "knowledge of good and evil," because it is the God-appointed instrument to lead man through probation to that state of religious and moral maturity wherewith his highest blessedness is connected. *BT*, 31.

Tree of Life

It appears from Genesis 3:22, that man before his fall had not eaten of it, while yet nothing is recorded concerning any prohibition which seems to point to the understanding that the use of the tree was reserved for the future, quite in agreement with the eschatological significance attributed to it later. The tree was associated with the higher, the unchangeable, the eternal life to be secured by obedience throughout his probation. *BT*, 28.

After man should have been made sure of the attainment of the highest life, the tree would appropriately have been the sacramental means for communicating the highest life. *BT*, 28.

The tree of life contains a prophetic element (see Gen. 3:22). The narrative plainly excludes the idea that man was without life—religious, physical, and ethical. The distinction is between a life in possession and one in prospect. It is eternal life in prospect. The essence of eschatology lies in this prospective element. *ESOT*, 75.

Tribulation, Overcoming

Let us thank God that, when we ourselves enter into the valley of the shadow of death, we have infinitely more than a promise to stay our hearts upon, that ours is the fulfillment of the promise, the fact of the resurrection, the risen Lord himself present with rod and staff beside us. R/*GG*, 68.

In . . . trials there can be no comfort for us so long as we stand outside weeping. If only we take the courage to fix our gaze deliberately upon the stern countenance of grief, and enter unafraid into the darkest recesses of our trouble, we shall find the terror gone, because the Lord has been there before us, and, coming out again, has left the place transfigured, making out of it by the grace of his resurrection a house of life, the very gate of heaven. R/*GG*, 72.

Triune God

All salvation, all truth in regard to man, has its eternal foundation in the Triune God himself. It is this Triune God who here reveals himself as the everlasting reality, from whom all truth proceeds, whom all truth reflects, be it the little streamlet of Paradise or the broad river of the New Testament losing itself again in the ocean of eternity. IBT/*SW*, 13.

The fact that redemption is God's work by which he wills to be glorified can in no wise be more strongly expressed than by thus exposing its emergence from out of the depths of the divine being himself. Here it is God who issues the requirement of redemption as God the Father. Again, it is God who for the fulfillment of that requirement becomes the guarantor as God the Son. Once again, it is God to whom belongs the application of redemption as God the Holy Spirit. In the clear light of eternity, where God alone dwells, the economy of salvation is drawn up for us with pure outlines and not darkened by the assistance of any human hand. It is a creation of the Triune One from whom, through whom, and to whom are all things. DCRT/*SW*, 247.

Trust

No one can take a Savior to his heart in that absolute, unqualified sense which constitutes the glory of religious trust, if there persists in the background of his mind the thought that this Savior failed to understand himself. *SDJ*, 16.

Truth

Not only must truth from the nature of the case be the prime mover in every religious activity of the soul and in all progress of piety, but also the more fundamental and ultimate the truth apprehended, the greater will prove the power stored up in it for fructifying and quickening spiritual life. OHGG/*GG*, 274.

Truth, Johannine Conception of

When Jesus is called "the true light" (John 1:9), or "the true bread" (6:32), this has nothing to do with his telling the truth, but may be approximately rendered "the veritable light," "the veritable bread." Veritable is that which answers to the highest conception or ideal of something. TT/*SW*, 344.

[Jesus] is specifically the truth, the veritable essence of that region to which he is going; and within that essence again he is the life characteristically belonging to it. TT/*SW*, 345.

[Jesus'] kingdom is not of this world (but of the heavenly world), and for this very reason he came from the higher into the lower world that he should bear witness unto "the truth," and that every one that is of "the truth" should hear his voice (John 18:37). TT/*SW*, 348.

The difference between "the true things" and "the not-true things" is not conceived after a Platonic or Philonic fashion. The world above is not called "true" as though it contained a higher reality of being in the substantial metaphysical sense. Both spheres are equally real.

The difference comes in through an appraisal of quality and importance. What is practically involved is the principle of ultimate spiritual value in regard to destiny. The practical name for this is the principle of "other-worldliness." TT/*SW*, 350.

The contrast [is] drawn in the prologue between the law given through Moses, and the grace and truth which came through Jesus Christ, for here, it will be observed, the Christian revelation is characterized as "truth" in distinction from the Mosaic law, to which [the] predicate does not belong. The meaning is not, of course, that the Mosaic law is untrue or false in the ordinary sense of the word; in fact, this misunderstanding is carefully guarded against by the form of statement employed: the law was given "through" Moses, which implies that Moses in the lawgiving was only the instrument of God, from whom nothing false or untrue can come. "Truth" here means what it means in Hebrews; it expresses the heavenly character of the Christian realities of revelation and redemption in which the higher world directly communicates itself, and the opposite of "the true" is the typical, wherein the connection with the heavenly world is present only in a mediated, shadowy form. And Jesus, because he is the center and exponent of this great projection of the supernatural into the lower world, is called "the Truth." HED/*SW*, 201.

Tübingen

The Tübingen school conceived of the early history of Christianity as essentially a process of evolution of ideas, in which the intellect was the prime moving force. TP/*SW*, 355.

Type and Antitype

We say, as a rule, that the old covenant has the type, the new covenant the antitype. And this is scriptural; for the apostle Peter so conceives of it when he represents the water of the deluge as the type, the water of baptism as the antitype (1 Peter 3:21). And yet the author of Hebrews distinctly tells us (9:24) that the Old Testament tabernacle was the antitype, not the type. The explanation is very simple. It lies in this, that antitype means copy, that which is fashioned after the type, and the Old Testament tabernacle was copied, fashioned after the tabernacle in heaven. Likewise the author also finds it significant that Moses was shown a type, a model of the sanctuary on the mount (8:5; cf. Ex. 25:40). And all the Old Testament things in general are in this sense called copies of the things in the heavens (9:23). HED/*SW*, 201.

To "type," the impression, corresponds "antitype," the counter-impression. Both Peter and the Epistle to the Hebrews employ it. It stands for the copy taken of the technical type. There is, however, a difference between these two writers. Peter finds the technical type in the history of the Old Testament. The water of baptism to him is the antitype of that of the deluge (1 Peter 3:21). The writer of Hebrews finds the type, the model, in the heavenly world. To him, therefore, the same Old Testament things that Peter would call types are already antitypes (Heb. 9:24). The former is a more theological, the latter a more purely historical view of the relationship. *BT*, 145.

The bond that holds type and antitype together must be a bond of vital continuity in the progress of redemption. Where this is ignored, and in the place of this bond are put accidental resemblances, void of inherent spiritual significance, all sorts of absurdities will result, such as must bring the whole subject of typology into disrepute. Examples of this are: the scarlet cord of Rahab prefigures the blood of Christ; the four lepers at Samaria, the four Evangelists. *BT*, 146.

The type inevitably influences the conception of the antitype. The future is depicted in terms drawn from the present, earthly, material reality. There is somewhat of the shadowy, inadequate character of the prefiguration that passes over into the description of what the eschatological will be like when it comes. *ESOT*, 117.

Typology

The mere fact that no writer in the New Testament refers to a certain trait as typical, affords no proof of its lacking typical significance. Types in this respect stand on a line with prophecies. The New

Testament in numerous cases calls our attention to the fulfillment of certain prophecies, sometimes of such a nature that perhaps we might not have discerned them to be prophecies. And yet we are not restrained by this from searching the field of prophecy and looking in the New Testament for other cases of fulfillment. *BT*, 146.

The instances of typology vouched for by the New Testament writers have nothing peculiar to themselves. To recognize only them would lead to serious incompleteness and incoherency in the result. *BT*, 146.

Union with Christ

The bond between the believer and Christ is so close that, from Paul's point of view, a detachment of the Christian's *interest* not only, but even a severance of his *actual life* from the celestial Christ-centered sphere is unthinkable. *PE*, 37.

Paul is persuaded that neither death nor life, nor any of the demonic principalities, nor any creature will be able to separate him from the love of God which is in Christ. He who is united to Christ and lives within the circle of his love, to him the eternal retention of the supreme eschatological life is absolutely secure. *PE*, 312.

The whole intimate life-union existing between the believer and Christ vouches for the certainty of the eternal persistence of this bond. *PE*, 312–13.

Nothing can be more personal than the intimate relation which the Christ (particularly the risen Christ) sustains to the believer. *PE*, 166.

It is not Pauline to conceive of believers who are in Christ as enveloped by him after a quietistic, unproductive fashion. *PE*, 158.

As long as a believer fastens his eyes of faith on Christ Jesus, as long as he holds fast to the Mediator, he can do nothing else but testify with Paul: "By grace I have been saved," and, "It was God's gift." By that faith life flows from Christ to the believer. He not only knows that but feels it. "Outside of Jesus there is no life," his soul says to him. Or it repeats after Paul: "I live, yet no longer I, but Christ lives in me, and the life which I now live in the flesh I live by faith in the Son of God, who loved me and gave himself for me." SR/*GG*, 229.

▨ And for you who perceive that life-giving power of Christ in your own soul, this truth must be a new stimulus to humility and meekness. Your life came from Christ, it continues to be hid with Christ in God. You must draw all your lifeblood from him, so that the excellence of the power may be from God and not from you. Do not look for it anywhere else but from him. Let Christ dwell in your hearts by faith, so that you may be rooted and grounded in love. The more that happens the less you will become and will sink away deeper in your insignificance. God, on the other hand, will become greater and more glorious, and the more the language of your life will become that beautiful word of the apostle, in which prayer and thanksgiving fuse together. SR/*GG*, 231–32.

▨ [commenting upon Paul's use of the title *Kyrios*] On the whole, where the redemptive basis of the believer's status and his mystical union with the Savior are spoken of, Paul by preference seems to employ "Jesus Christ" or "Christ Jesus," to which again "our Lord" easily attaches itself, indicating that the servantship and appurtenance are rooted in what Jesus has done and purchased for the believer. *SDJ*, 136.

▨ The pneumatic life of the Christian is a product and a reflex of the pneumatic life of the Christ. It is a life ἐν πνεύματι to the same extent as it is a life ἐν Χριστῷ. EAP/*SW*, 113.

▨ According to Paul Jesus at the resurrection receives the Spirit not merely as an objective gift, something that he can dispense; the Spirit becomes his own subjective possession, the Spirit dwelling in him, the source of his own glorified life, so that when he communicates the Spirit he communicates of his own, whence also the possession of the Spirit works in the believer a mystical, vital union with Christ. EAP/*SW*, 113.

Paul speaks of the process of renewal and sanctification in terms which are not merely derived from the death and resurrection of Christ, for this might be a purely figurative usage, but in terms which posit a real, vital connection between the two, so that what takes place in the believer is an actual self-reproduction of what was transacted in Christ. To be joined with the Lord is to be one Spirit with him (1 Cor. 6:17). EAP/*SW*, 114.

Universalism

[commenting upon the principle of election] Deists and all sort of rationalists frequently argued [that if] God had gone to the trouble of introducing such a process of supernaturalism, he would have certainly taken pains to make it universal. Looked at closely, this argument proves a reflex of the general spirit of cosmopolitanism abroad in those times, which is but one of the unhistorical conceptions of rationalism. Because the God of rationalism was at the bottom simply the God of nature, and nature is universal, therefore his self-disclosure must be as wide as nature. No account is had of the abnormal features of a state of sin, nor of the unique exigencies of a procedure of redemption. No distinction is felt between the beginning and early stages of the divine work and its later maturing. It should have been created all-finished, incapable of further progress from the outset. *BT*, 76.

Walk

To walk before God means so to walk as to have the thought of God's presence and supervision constantly in mind, and to shape one's conduct accordingly. HTR/*GG*, 32.

[commenting upon Gen. 5] In distinction from the pride and arrogance of Lamech, Enoch is related to have "walked with God." This means more than that he led a pious life, for the customary phrases for that are "to walk before God," and "to walk after God." "To walk with God" points to supernatural intercourse with God. *BT*, 47.

Weeks, Feast of

The feast of weeks, by requiring [the pious Israelites] to bring the first loaves of bread prepared from the new harvest to the sanctuary of Jehovah, reminded them that all the fruits of the land, all the blessings of their life, were on the one hand the free gift of God, on the other hand designed to be consecrated to God. GP/*GG*, 233.

Wellhausen Theory

[One's] interpretation put upon the alternative use of the divine names in Genesis will differ according as one enters upon its study with or without a firm belief in the fundamental fact of redemption and special revelation. This factor becomes much more influential in historic criticism. The critics from the Kuenen-Wellhausen school lay down the principle that in Israel's history all phenomena are to be explained according to the law of natural causation. On the other hand believing critics necessarily deal with the history of Israel and the origin of the Scriptures from the point of view of supernatural revelation, and will be led at each step by considerations ultimately rooted in this idea. Kuenen and Wellhausen candidly admit that there is an antithesis between naturalism and supernaturalism, not merely in the results, but likewise in the principle of investigation. *DMOV*, 107.

As the dying patriarchs saw and foretold the future fate of their descendants, and blessed their house in their last moments, so Moses, the greatest of all Old Testament saints, left to the whole house of Israel, as a dying father, the best of all blessings, a law adapted to all future conditions. His work was not for one generation: "mediator of the old covenant," he stands high above all other prophets and saints; already half glorified, no longer subject to the limitations of time, he surveys the Israel of all ages until the coming of Christ, and accordingly his work assumes a prospective and ideal character, so striking that unbelieving critics could not but mistake it as the evidence of a much later origin. *MOP*, 171.

[commenting upon the prejudice of the Wellhausen theorists] Is it unthinkable that one and the same person should combine in himself the qualifications of a legislator and a prophet? That the modern criticism has answered this question in the negative is enough to show how incapable it is of a deeper philosophical conception and appreciation of the Old Testament. *MOP*, 170.

[commenting upon Wellhausen's theory that the prophets preceded the law] The removal of the Pentateuch from its place before the prophets had created a clear field for that form of naturalistic theorizing to which hitherto the law with its sharply defined supernaturalistic signature had always formed an insuperable barrier; the question had now become open, What is it that lies back of prophecy, evolution or revelation, the physical or the ethical, the imperfect or the perfect? RCEP, 215.

Westminster Confession

The Westminster Confession is the first Reformed confession in which the doctrine of the covenant is not merely brought in from the side, but is placed in the foreground and has been able to permeate at almost every point. DCRT/*SW*, 239.

Wisdom

The counterpart of the OT idea of the law as an institution for the wise guidance of Israel is furnished by St. Paul, who represents the gospel as a teleological arrangement in which the highest wisdom is manifested and recognized by the believer (Rom. 11:33). FOOL/*DB*, 44.

Word

God acts in and through his word, and thus the word has the same power and effect that belong to God himself. Especially the figure of the sword searching the vitals and laying bare the inner attitude and disposition of man is very striking. Because the word of God confronts man with God personally, he cannot in the presence of it remain neutral and treat it after an indifferent, disinterested fashion; it is a challenge to his soul that must provoke reaction and incite to faith or unbelief according to the inner disposition of the heart with reference to God. HED/*SW*, 191.

▪ [commenting upon Isa. 6] Throughout, the prophet is keenly conscious of the divine character of the word of revelation and of the immediate contact into which it brings its recipient with the supernatural world. It is on account of the holiness inherent in the word that his lips are cleansed in the vision in order that God's message may pass over them. SDFI/*SW*, 280–81.

▪ The word remains what it was at the beginning when it fell fresh from the lips of Christ, a signal of the presence of God and a vehicle of approach for the world of the supernatural. HED/*SW*, 192.

▪ Because the divine word is not merely for instruction or salvation but brings God personally near to the believer, it becomes in itself an object of enjoyment; hence the epistle speaks of tasting the good word of God (Heb. 6:5). HED/*SW*, 187.

▪ The Gospel of John everywhere makes a point of it that in the soteriological process the light of revelation comes first in order, as supplied by Christ after an objective, supernatural fashion, and not as something that emerges out of the new life of man, and passes through his subjectivity. It is the word, the truth, that quickens and cleanses and sanctifies. In this sphere it could be more truthfully said that the light is the life of men, than conversely that the life is their light. RLT/*SW*, 76.

▪ In agreement with this conception of revelation as a process of fellowship between God and man, the writer conceives of God as speaking through the Scripture (Heb. 4:12–14). He conceives of this as a continuous or permanent speech; God is *in his Word*, and this consideration leads the writer of the epistle to personify the Word of God. He speaks of the Word judging, penetrating, etc. Such things could not be said of a word that stood by itself. After carrying out this personification, the author naturally returns to the idea of the speaking of God. Hence follows the identification of the Word with God. *TEH*, 69–70.

358

■ The word is like a two-edged sword. This is a figure of searching, which also contains the idea of judging. The revelation of God in Christ is both a searching and a judgment. It brings to light what is in a man. If unbelief is found in a man, he is searched and judged. *TEH*, 70.

Word and Acts of God

■ We must remember that the revealing acts of God never appear separated from his verbal communications of truth. Word and act always accompany each other, and in their interdependence strikingly illustrate . . . that revelation is organically connected with the introduction of a new order of things into this sinful world. Revelation is the light of this new world which God has called into being. IBT/*SW*, 9–10.

■ Divine acts are no doubt an integral part of revelation, but they derive their revealing power only from the *divine words* preceding, accompanying and following them, by which they are placed in their proper light. *PvBG*, 143–44.

Word and Sacrament

■ The word and the sacrament as means of grace belong together: they are two sides of the same divinely instituted instrumentality. While addressing themselves to different organs of perception, they are intended to bear the identical message of the grace of God—to interpret and mutually enforce one another. GP/*GG*, 239.

Works Righteousness

■ The idea, as though man could do anything whatsoever in order to effect a change in the disposition or attitude of God toward sin or the sinner, is utterly repugnant to the spirit of biblical religion. Between man and man that may be possible, but not between God and man. If the normal relation is to be restored, it is the prerogative of God to resolve this and to put his resolve into operation. *BT*, 167.

World, Renewal of

It had to be shown immediately, that the work inaugurated by Jesus aims at nothing less than a supernatural renewal of the world, whereby all evil will be overcome, a renewal of the physical as well as of the spiritual world (Matt. 19:28). *KGC*, 56.

An annihilation of the substance of the present world is not taught (see the comparison of the future world-conflagration with the deluge in 2 Peter 3:6). The central abode of the redeemed will be in heaven, although the renewed earth will remain accessible to them and a part of the inheritance (Matt. 5:5; John 14:2–3; Rom. 8:18–22). ENT/*SW*, 55.

World to Come, Present Participation in

The spiritual world is infinitely more real and infinitely more powerful than the things which our eyes can see. Hence the Christian, while not having seen it, loves it and rejoices in it greatly with joy unspeakable and full of glory. He fashions himself according to it. He purifies his soul in harmony with the purity that intrinsically belongs to that world. He abstains from fleshly lusts because they war against the spiritual nature of the soul by which he is related to that spiritual realm which is the object of his hope. He is of sound mind, sober unto prayer. In all these things he conforms himself and responds to the claims which his heavenly destiny has upon him. He lives in the presence of the world to come and allows it to be the ruling factor in all he thinks and does. CH/*GG*, 153.

Christians are really in vital connection with the heavenly world. . . . For example, in Philippians 3:20 Paul states, "We have our commonwealth in heaven." Christians therefore are colonists, living in the dispersion in this present world. The same idea is set forth still more strongly in Ephesians 2:6, "made us sit with him in the heavenly places," and also in Galatians 1:4, "that he might deliver us out of this present evil world." The Christian therefore is a peculiar chronological phenomenon. In Romans 12:2 the apostle Paul draws the practical inference from this fact: Christians should be fashioned according to the world to come. To Paul, the death and resurrection of Christ are the beginning of the world to come, and of the eschatological process. *TEH*, 51.

For [the Christian] not to have his face set forward and upward would be an anomaly, sickliness, decadence. To have it set upward and forward is life and health and strength. The air of the world to come is the vital atmosphere which he delights to breathe and outside of which he feels depressed and languid. CH/*GG*, 143.

How imperative becomes the duty of every true believer in the present age to cultivate the grace of hope; to make himself remember and to make others feel, not so much by direct affirmation but rather by the tone of life, that the future belongs to us and that we belong to the future; that we are children of the world to come and that even now we allow that world to mold and rule and transform us in our thoughts, desires and feelings. CH/*GG*, 145.

To the saints of the new covenant, life and immortality and all the powers of the world to come have been opened up by Christ. The Christian state is as truly part and foretaste of the things above as a portal forms part of the house. If not wholly within, we certainly are come to Mount Zion, the city of the living God. HM/*GG*, 111.

World to Come, Thirst for

The thirst for the world to come was of the very substance of the religion of [Paul's] heart. JRL/*GG*, 166.

Worldliness

If [Christians] at any time feel perfectly at home in the world, if our consciousness of its necessary antagonism to us is entirely in abeyance, then there is abundant reason for us to examine ourselves. And the probability is that we have been backward in cultivating our hope upon God and the world to come. CH/*GG*, 147.

If you have ever moved for a time in circles where the Christian faith has ceased to exist, where the belief in immortality has practically vanished, where people live consciously and professedly for this world only (and do not even attempt to break down the bars that shut them in), then you will have felt how sadly life was degraded, how pitifully brought down to the animal stage, even though it had all the advantages of worldly refinement and culture, simply because [the] element of [Christian] hope had been taken out of it. CH/*GG*, 144–45.

Worlds, Two

There are two worlds, the lower and the higher, and it is affirmed of the believer that he belongs to the latter and no longer to the former reality. Each has its own σχῆμα, but the σχῆμα after which the Christian patterns himself is that of the other world, not that of this world (Rom. 12:2). EAP/*SW*, 115.

If the second world has received its actual beginning through Christ, and if nevertheless, as cannot be denied, the first world, this present world, is still continuing in its course, then it is clear that both now exist contemporaneously. From thinking of the eschatological state as future, the Christian mind is led to conceive of it as actually present but situated in a higher sphere. The horizontal, dramatic way of thinking gives place in part to a process of thought moving in a perpendicular direction and distinguishing not so much between before and after, but rather between higher and lower. HED/*SW*, 197–98.

Worship

In [John] 4:23 the worship of the Father "in Spirit and truth" bears no immediate reference to the sincerity pertaining to worship, for Jesus would probably not have denied that to the Jewish or the Samaritan worship. It relates to the worship no longer bound by typical forms as to place and time and ceremony. In the place of these will come a worship directly corresponding in an unshadowy form to the heavenly original of God, who is Spirit. *BT*, 357.

[There is that note heard] of joyful self-surrender, wherein Isaiah, at first overwhelmed by the revelation of the divine majesty, regains his mental poise and comes to rest in the worship of Jehovah as the only satisfying purpose of all created existence. SDFI/*SW*, 276.

The psalmists sometimes succeed in transporting themselves into the midst of the joy and blessedness wherewith Jehovah himself contemplates the consummate perfection of his work. This faculty for entering into the inner spirit of God's own share in the religious process represents the highest and finest in worship; it closes the ring of religion. EP, 341.

Even in giving himself God remains God and requires from Israel the acknowledgment of this. The gift is divine and desires for itself a temple where no other presence shall be tolerated. If we feel God to be ours, then we also feel that no one but God can ever be ours in the same exclusive ineffable sense and that every similar absorption by any purely human relationship would partake of the idolatrous. The only thing that can give a faint suggestion of the engrossing character of the divine hold upon his people is the first awakening of what we call romantic love in the youthful heart with its concentration of all the intensified impulses and forces and desires upon one object and its utter obliviousness to all other interests. This actually in some measure resembles the single-minded, world-forgetful affection we owe to God, and for that very reason is called worship. WT/*GG*, 14–15.

[commenting upon Isa. 57:15] We find then in our text indirectly expressed if not explicitly formulated what must always be the governing principle of the highest worship of Jehovah. The relation here defined between Jehovah's exalted being and the humble spirits of his acceptable servants is typical of every God-centered attitude that may be properly called religious. Were we to seek an abstract name for this, we might say that it consists in the full adjustment of man's conscious life to the nature, the claims, the purposes of God; the joyful subordination of the creature to the Creator and his glorious kingdom. OHGG/*GG*, 264.

[When] the soul inwardly delights in the infinite perfections of Jehovah, then and not until then is fear changed into reverence; or, as the prophet calls it, humility of spirit. But it is impossible to cultivate such worship (the highest flower of religion) where the perception of God's transcendent glory has been obscured. Religion may not be metaphysics, but there is a theology of the heart, the banishment of which means blight and starvation for all vital piety. OHGG/*GG*, 268.

[commenting upon OT worship] Unity of worship stood and fell with pure Jahveism, of which the central idea is the recognition of one personal God, to whom belongs the initiative in all that pertains to his service. *MOP*, 93.

Zurich Theologians and Covenant Theology

The theologians of Zurich . . . are to be regarded as the forerunners of federal theology in the narrower sense insofar as the covenant for them becomes the dominant idea for the practice of the Christian life. DCRT/*SW*, 236.

Works Cited

Books

Biblical Theology: Old and New Testaments. Edited by Johannes G. Vos. Grand Rapids: Eerdmans, 1985.

The Eschatology of the Old Testament. Edited by James T. Dennison Jr. Phillipsburg, N.J.: P&R Publishing, 2001.

The Mosaic Origin of the Pentateuchal Codes. With an introduction by Professor William Henry Green. New York: A. C. Armstrong & Son, 1886.

The Pauline Eschatology. With an appendix entitled "Eschatology of the Psalter." Grand Rapids: Eerdmans, 1986.

The Self-Disclosure of Jesus: The Modern Debate about the Messianic Consciousness. Phillipsburg, N.J.: P&R Publishing, 2002.

The Teaching of Jesus Concerning the Kingdom of God and the Church. Nutley, N.J.: Presbyterian and Reformed, 1972.

The Teaching of the Epistle to the Hebrews. Edited and rewritten by Johannes G. Vos. Nutley, N.J.: Presbyterian and Reformed, 1974.

Poetry

Charis, English Verses. Princeton, N.J.: Princeton University Press, 1931.

Sermons

Grace and Glory: Sermons Preached in the Chapel of Princeton Theological Seminary. Edinburgh: Banner of Truth, 1994.

"The Christian's Hope"
"Christ's Deliberate Work"
"The Essence of Christianity"

"The Eternal Christ"
"The Gracious Provision"
"Heavenly-Mindedness"
"Hungering and Thirsting after Righteousness"
"The Joy of Resurrection Life"
"The More Excellent Ministry"
"Our Holy and Gracious God"
"Rabboni"
"Running the Race"
"Seeking and Saving the Lost"
"Songs from the Soul"
"The Spiritual Resurrection of Believers"
"The Wonderful Tree"

Articles and Book Reviews in *Shorter Writings*

Redemptive History and Biblical Interpretation: The Shorter Writings of Geerhardus Vos. Edited by Richard B. Gaffin Jr. Phillipsburg, N.J.: P&R Publishing, 2001.

Major Biblical and Theological Studies
"The Doctrine of the Covenant in Reformed Theology"
"The Eschatological Aspect of the Pauline Conception of the Spirit"
"Eschatology of the New Testament"
"Hebrews, the Epistle of the *Diathēkē*"
"The Idea of Biblical Theology as a Science and as a Theological Discipline"
"The Priesthood of Christ in the Epistle to the Hebrews"
"The Range of the Logos Title in the Prologue to the Fourth Gospel"

Shorter Biblical Studies
"The Alleged Legalism in Paul's Doctrine of Justification"
"The Biblical Importance of the Doctrine of Preterition"
" 'Covenant' or 'Testament'?"
"The Idea of 'Fulfillment' of Prophecy in the Gospels"

WORKS CITED

"Jeremiah's Plaint and Its Answer"
"The Kingdom of God"
"The Ministry of John the Baptist"
"Modern Dislike of the Messianic Consciousness in Jesus"
"Our Lord's Doctrine of the Resurrection"
"The Pauline Conception of Reconciliation"
"The Pauline Conception of Redemption"
"The Sacrificial Idea in Paul's Doctrine of the Atonement"
"The Second Coming of Our Lord and the Millennium"
"Some Doctrinal Features of the Early Prophecies of Isaiah"
"The Theology of Paul"
" 'True' and 'Truth' in the Johannine Writings"
"The Ubiquity of the Messiahship in the Gospels"

Addresses
"Christian Faith and the Truthfulness of Bible History"
"The Scriptural Doctrine of the Love of God"

Book Reviews
Review of *Die Erwählung Israels nach der Heilsverkündigung des Apostels Paulus*, by J. Dalmer
Review of *Gereformeerde Dogmatiek*, vol. 1, by H. Bavinck
Review of *Gereformeerde Dogmatiek*, vol. 2, by H. Bavinck
Review of *Jesus and the Gospel: Christianity Justified in the Mind of Christ*, by J. Denney
Review of *Kyrios Christos: Geschichte des Christusglaubens von den Anfängen des Christenthums bis Irenaeus*, by W. Bousset
Review of *The Quest for the Historical Jesus: A Critical Study of Its Progress from Reimarus to Wrede*, by A. Schweitzer

Articles outside *The Shorter Writings*

"Fool." In *A Dictionary of the Bible*, 2:43–44. Edited by James Hastings. New York: Charles Scribner's Sons, 1990.

"Heavens, New (and Earth, New)." In *International Standard Bible Encyclopedia*, 2:1353–54. Edited by James Orr. Grand Rapids: Eerdmans, 1939.

"Jerusalem, New." In *International Standard Bible Encyclopedia*, 3:1622. Edited by James Orr. Grand Rapids: Eerdmans, 1939.

"The Modern Hypothesis and Recent Criticism of the Early Prophets." *Presbyterian and Reformed Review* 9 (1898): 214–38 (Amos and Hosea), 411–37 (Isaiah), 610–36 (Isaiah).

"The Modern Hypothesis and Recent Criticism of the Early Prophets." *Presbyterian and Reformed Review* 10 (1899): 70–97 (Isaiah), 285–317 (Micah).

"The Nature and Aims of Biblical Theology." *Kerux* 14.1 (May 1999): 3–8.

"Notes on Systematic Theology." Translated by Marten Woudstra, *Reformed Review* 1 (1952): 18, 19, 37, 38, 58, 59, 76, 77, 93, 94, 98, 113–16, 133–36, 144–46, 155.

"Omnipotence." In *International Standard Bible Encyclopedia*, 4:2188–90. Edited by James Orr. Grand Rapids: Eerdmans, 1939.

"Omnipresence." In *International Standard Bible Encyclopedia*, 4:2190–91. Edited by James Orr. Grand Rapids: Eerdmans, 1939.

"Omniscience." In *International Standard Bible Encyclopedia*, 4:2191–92. Edited by James Orr. Grand Rapids: Eerdmans, 1939.

Book Reviews outside *The Shorter Writings*

Review of *Alexander Comrie*, by A. G. Honig. *Presbyterian and Reformed Review* 5 (1894): 331–34.

Review of *Der alttestamentliche Unterbau des Reiches Gottes*, by Julius Boehmer. *Princeton Theological Review* 1 (1903): 126–31.

Review of *Auferstehungshoffnung und Pneumagedanke bei Paulus*, by Kurt Diessner. *Princeton Theological Review* 11 (1913): 664–68.

Review of *Der Begriff der Wahrheit in dem Evangelium und den Briefen des Johannes*, by F. Büchsel. *Princeton Theological Review* 11 (1913): 668–72.

Review of *Der Begriff Diatheke im Neuen Testament*, by Johannes Behm. *Princeton Theological Review* 11 (1913): 513–18.

Review of *Die Begriffe Geist und Leben bei Paulus in ihren Beziehungen zu einander*, by Emil Sokolowski. *Princeton Theological Review* 3 (1905): 317–21.

Review of *The Christology of the Epistle to the Hebrews, Including Its Relation to the Developing Christology of the Primitive Church*, by Harris L. MacNeill. *Princeton Theological Review* 13 (1915): 490–91.

Review of *Het eeuwige leven bij Paulus*, by Johan T. Ubbink. *Princeton Theological Review* 17 (1919): 143–51.

Review of *Der Geschichtliche Jesus*, by Carl Clemen. *Princeton Theological Review* 10 (1912): 489–90.

Review of *Israel's Ideal or Studies in Old Testament Theology*, by John Adams. *Princeton Theological Review* 9 (1911): 482–83.

Review of *Joseph and Moses*, by Buchanan Blake. *Princeton Theological Review* 1 (1903): 470–72.

Review of *The Messiah of the Gospels* and *The Messiah of the Apostles*, by Charles Augustus Briggs. *Presbyterian and Reformed Review* 7 (1896): 718–24.

Review of *De Mozaische oorsprong van de wetten in de boeken Exodus, Leviticus en Numeri*, by Ph. J. Hoedemaker. *Presbyterian and Reformed Review* 8 (1897): 106–9.

Review of *Paul's Doctrine of Redemption*, by Henry B. Carre. *Princeton Theological Review* 14 (1916): 138–39.

Review of *Paulus en zijn brief aan de Romeinen*, by A. van Veldhuizen. *Princeton Theological Review* 15 (1917): 180–81.

Review of *Prolegomena van Bijbelsche Godgeleerdheid*, by E. H. van Leeuwen. *Presbyterian and Reformed Review* 4 (1893): 143–45.

Review of *Die Reichsgotteshoffnung in den ältesten christlichen Dokumenten und bei Jesus*, by Paul Wernle. *Princeton Theological Review* 1 (1903): 298–303.

Review of *The Religious Experience of Saint Paul*, by Percy Gardner. *Princeton Theological Review* 11 (1913): 316–20.

Review of *The Religious Ideas of the Old Testament*, by H. Wheeler Robinson. *Princeton Theological Review* 13 (1915): 109–11.

Review of *St. Paul's Conceptions of the Last Things*, by H. A. A. Kennedy. *Princeton Theological Review* 3 (1905): 483–87.

370

Review of *La Théologie de Saint Paul*, by F. Prat. *Princeton Theological Review* 11 (1913): 126–29.

Review of *De Theologie van Kronieken*, by Jelte Swart. *Princeton Theological Review* 10 (1912): 480–81.

Review of *The Theology of Christ's Teaching*, by John M. King. *Princeton Theological Review* 1 (1903): 653–54.

Review of *The Theology of the Gospels*, by James Moffatt. *Princeton Theological Review* 13 (1915): 111–14.

Review of *The Theology of the Old Testament*, by A. B. Davidson. *Princeton Theological Review* 4 (1906): 115–20.

Review of *De verflauwing der grenzen*, by Abraham Kuyper. *Presbyterian and Reformed Review* 4 (1893): 330–32.

Index of Scripture

Geerhardus Vos (1862–1949) has been called "the father of Reformed biblical theology." He was born in the Netherlands and emigrated to the United States in 1881. He earned degrees from Calvin Theological Seminary, Princeton Theological Seminary, and the University of Strasbourg (Ph.D. in Arabic). In 1894 he was ordained as a minister in the Presbyterian Church in the USA. Before beginning his 39-year tenure on Princeton's faculty, he was professor of systematic and exegetical theology at Calvin for five years.

Danny E. Olinger (M.A., Duquesne University; M.Div., Reformed Theological Presbyterian Seminary) is General Secretary of the Committee on Christian Education in the Orthodox Presbyterian Church and editor of *New Horizons*. He is co-editor of *History for a Pilgrim People* and has contributed articles to *Kerux*, a journal dedicated to Geerhardus Vos and biblical-theological exegesis.